Health and Wellness Tourism

ASPECTS OF TOURISM
Series Editors: Chris Cooper, *Nottingham University Business School, UK*, C. Michael Hall, *University of Canterbury, New Zealand* and Dallen J. Timothy, *Arizona State University, USA*

Aspects of Tourism is an innovative, multifaceted series, which comprises authoritative reference handbooks on global tourism regions, research volumes, texts and monographs. It is designed to provide readers with the latest thinking on tourism worldwide and push back the frontiers of tourism knowledge. The volumes are authoritative, readable and user-friendly, providing accessible sources for further research. Books in the series are commissioned to probe the relationship between tourism and cognate subject areas such as strategy, development, retailing, sport and environmental studies.

Full details of all the books in this series and of all our other publications can be found on http://www.channelviewpublications.com, or by writing to Channel View Publications, St Nicholas House, 31–34 High Street, Bristol BS1 2AW, UK.

ASPECTS OF TOURISM
Series Editors: Chris Cooper, C. Michael Hall
and Dallen J. Timothy

Health and Wellness Tourism

Spas and Hot Springs

Patricia Erfurt-Cooper
and Malcolm Cooper

CHANNEL VIEW PUBLICATIONS
Bristol • Buffalo • Toronto

Library of Congress Cataloging in Publication Data
A catalog record for this book is available from the Library of Congress.
Erfurt-Cooper, Patricia.
Health and Wellness Tourism: Spas and Hot Springs/Patricia Erfurt-Cooper and Malcolm Cooper.
Aspects of Tourism: 40
Includes bibliographical references and index.
1. Health resorts. I. Cooper, Malcolm, 1946– II. Title. III. Series.
RA794.E74 2009
613'.122–dc22 2009017291

British Library Cataloguing in Publication Data
A catalogue entry for this book is available from the British Library.

ISBN-13: 978-1-84541-112-1 (hbk)
ISBN-13: 978-1-84541-111-4 (pbk)

Channel View Publications
UK: St Nicholas House, 31–34 High Street, Bristol BS1 2AW, UK.
USA: UTP, 2250 Military Road, Tonawanda, NY 14150, USA.
Canada: UTP, 5201 Dufferin Street, North York, Ontario M3H 5T8, Canada.

The policy of Multilingual Matters/Channel View Publications is to use papers that are natural, renewable and recyclable products, made from wood grown in sustainable forests. In the manufacturing process of our books, and to further support our policy, preference is given to printers that have FSC and PEFC Chain of Custody certification. The FSC and/or PEFC logos will appear on those books where full certification has been granted to the printer concerned.

Typeset by Techset Composition Ltd., Salisbury, UK.
Printed and bound in Great Britain by Short Run Press Ltd.

Contents

Figures and Tables

Tables

Preface

I was honoured and delighted when Patricia and Malcolm visited Peninsula Hot Springs and asked me to write the preface to this wonderful book. In my 16 years of passionate research and work I am yet to come across a text as comprehensive in the field of hot springs. Patricia and Malcolm have managed to weave the many diverse elements of the industry into this book making it valuable and interesting reading for the hot spring enthusiast and operator alike.

Laying in our hot springs in Australia, easing back into the warmth of the natural healing waters, looking up at the trees and southern sky, my mind drifts back to where my connection to hot springs began. Sixteen years have passed since 1992 and first taking the waters in the snow covered hills in the central Japan town of Kusatsu. Still as fresh in my mind today is that original sensation of blissful, gentle connection, a weightless body, relaxed mind and of timelessness. From that day the goal of helping establish a culture and community of hot springs in Australia become a lifelong dream.

Five years on, in 1997, I learnt about the natural thermal waters deep underground on the Mornington Peninsula in Victoria, Australia. That discovery sparked off a lifelong search for the many ways people of the world use this natural resource. Over the years I have travelled to hot springs in Japan, Korea, China, Taiwan, Indonesia, Malaysia, Nepal, Russia, the Czech Republic, Greece, England, Yemen, Egypt, Australia, New Zealand, the United States (inc. Alaska) and Canada. Every country you can imagine has hot springs and to date I have not found a country without them. Hot springs are being utilised in many ways by people all over the word including heating greenhouses for horticulture production, heating fish ponds in aquaculture, in medically prescribed health and wellness practices, in the generation of electricity, as a source of heat for hydronic warming of buildings and the most popular use being the practice of recreational bathing.

On these travels I observed that the global bathing practices of hot springs and the spa world are divided into three broad and distinctive approaches. In Europe, the emphasis is on the medical and health benefits that can be gained from the use of the thermal waters. There doctors develop detailed health programs for patients who visit spa towns for periods of several weeks and even months in a row. In Asia, the emphasis is on a connection with nature and this is provided by the outdoor bathing experience. There the tourism and recreation industry plays the dominant role. In the United States, the industry is defined by the modern concept of spa where tactile therapies and bathing experiences are woven together with cosmetic brands and the possibility of taking the experience home in the form of a retail product. As globalisation of knowledge and cultures continues, there is a convergence of these practices blurring the distinctions.

The history of hot springs and spas is a living one with a potential of incredible longevity. In the Czech Republic, the famous spa town of Karlovy Vary (Karlsbad) was discovered by Holy Roman Emperor King Karl in 1370 when he tracked a wounded deer to where it was bathing itself in a hot spring deep in the forest. For over 600 years Karlovy Vary has been famous as a centre of natural health and well-being. In Sanah, the Capital of Yemen, Hammam Shuker is a bathhouse that had been operating for the past 2200 years. The current owners have been operating the centre for what they said was 'only the past 100 years'! In Japan, the Daimaru hot spring has been operated by the Sato family for the past 1500 years.

The dream of an Australian hot spring culture has grown to a dream of a global connection between hot springs. The connection with nature, the relaxation, the slowing down and the bringing together of a diversity of people from all over the globe provides a step in the direction towards harmony and sustainability. Hot springs have the potential to contribute to the societies in which they exist in many ways. Health and Wellness Spa Tourism opens our eyes to many of those ways. I look forward to the possibilities for the development it will create.

Charles Davidson
Director and Co-founder
Peninsula Hot Springs
Mornington Peninsula,
Victoria,
Australia
December 2008

Chapter 1

Introduction: Development of the Health and Wellness Spa Industry

PATRICIA ERFURT-COOPER and MALCOLM COOPER

> Spas have been a way of relieving stress and physical ailments for
> thousands of years and … sanus per aquam (health through water)
> originated around the practice of bathing in hot springs and thermal waters
> LaForest, 2004: 1

Introduction

The wellness concept originally based on the use of natural hot and mineral springs (thermalism, balneology) forms the foundation for the discussion of the development and growth of Health and Wellness Spa Tourism in this book. Wellness facilities and programmes became a worldwide tourist attraction during the last decade of the 20th century and this trend shows no sign of abating, with excellent prospects for continued growth in the future. However, both the term and concept of wellness have a complex history (EUPHA, 2005), and dating the exact onset of the trend towards wellness is not easy because opinions are divided, with several sources suggesting that spa and wellness holidays have been around for hundreds if not thousands of years (Foster & Keller, 2008; LaForest, 2004; Smith & Kelly, 2006).

The latter discussion does not refer to spa towns with thermal springs in particular but to all spa centres that existed in the past even without the added attraction of natural hot springs. In the Middle East tradition Pharaoh Cleopatra is said to have established one of the world's first spa resorts on the shores of the Dead Sea in about 25 BC (Svart, 2006), and the Romans of course left behind a long list of bathing facilities (bathhouses, thermae) that they built between 54 BC and 450 AD while they were occupying large parts of what has become Europe, the Middle East and North Africa. To heat their bathing facilities and their houses the Romans took advantage of natural geothermal resources wherever these were available locally.

The origin of the term *spa* that describes such facilities is usually linked to the town of Spa in Belgium, where from the 14th century AD local hot mineral springs have been frequented for their therapeutic benefits and which has subsequently developed into a health resort. The word spa has now become a household name and the common designation for health resorts around the world (Altman, 2000), whether based on natural hot springs or not.

In Japan, where the main attraction is the traditional *Onsen* (hot spring bathing facilities), the wellness tradition revolves around the use of hot springs by people who enjoy sharing a bath in the evening after work (a form of corporate stress relief) or as families and other groups of users. *Onsen*-type spas in Japan are, however, used differently from the spas of European tradition, where the emphasis is more on *health treatment* than the act of *bathing*; however, this is fast becoming popular in Japan too as the implicit health benefits of Japanese mineral springs are used more explicitly to attract customers. Nevertheless, given the approximately 26,000 natural geothermal springs in Japan and the Japanese preference for authentic hot water bathing as a social custom, European-style wellness centres that incorporate bathing with 'beauty therapy' are unlikely to be serious competition to the traditional *Onsen* in the immediate future (Hotta & Ishiguro, 1986).

In other parts of the world a blending of these two somewhat polar types (wellness treatment facilities vs. simple bathing) may be found, whose exact shape will be dependent on the status of the natural resource available and its cultural use that prevails in any particular location. This book provides case studies of the main forms of health and wellness spa tourism based on hot and mineral springs as well as a comprehensive discussion of their geological and historical antecedents, their nature, social and cultural usage, their technology and economics, and their management and marketing. While there are many coffee-table style books on spas and the health and wellness industry, to date there have been very few discussions of this form of tourism in the academic literature. This book is designed to redress this lack of attention and provide a framework for the expanded analysis and discussion of health and wellness spa tourism befitting its growing importance.

The Wellness Concept: An Important Resource for Tourism in the 21st Century

The wellness concept is a term subject to different interpretations (Cohen & Bodecker, 2008; Foster & Keller, 2008; Smith & Kelly, 2006), but almost invariably has its origins in a natural and holistic approach to health that includes the use of water and the minerals within it (derived from sources at different temperatures) to provide cures for various human ailments. While the European tradition can be traced back in historically attested sources to the Greek and Roman cultures (Hall, 2003), it is likely to be far older (see Chapter 3; Foster & Keller, 2008). In the Americas, and especially in the Asia Pacific region (Lund, 2005; Schafer, 1956), the use of thermal and mineral springs has a very long tradition attached to it, dating back thousands of years to the Native North and South Americans, the Indus Valley, China and Japan, and the Polynesian peoples in the Asia Pacific area and New Zealand (see Chapter 4). More recently, the revived wellness concept of the 19th to 21st centuries is aimed at the prevention of illness not just through the mineral content and use of thermal waters, but also through informed health promotion, education and encouragement of a holistic approach to nutrition, and achieving mental and spiritual balance (see Chapter 2). For many people a very personal decision involving a change in lifestyle and a desire to achieve balanced well-being that includes physical, mental and spiritual health has been made, and this very often includes attendance at spa and wellness facilities (Cohen & Bodecker, 2008; IUTO, 1973).

Impact of information

The recent growth of the health and wellness movement has also brought an increased availability of 'coffee-table' marketing information and other published literature relating to the hot and mineral springs spa experience in the form of books, magazines and DVDs (see Chapter 8). Use of the immediacy and visual nature of the internet has also triggered a heightened awareness of the long-term benefits of taking care of personal health. This increased information supply has also included non-scientific versions for laypeople of discussions on the results of clinical trials and studies of the effects of thermalism (balneology and hydrotherapy at thermal spas) on problems such as rheumatism, osteoarthritis and psoriasis (Chapters 2 and 3). Given the range of general information now available, almost every spa visitor or tourist has different expectations of the likely experience and/or outcome that they are seeking and/or will tolerate (Adams, 2003). The health and wellness spa industry has recognised this complexity and is endeavouring to cater for it. In fact different types of spas are directly linked to these customer expectations through media advertising and marketing (see Chapter 8; Cohen & Bodecker, 2008). Some of the more common threads are:

- taking time out in a peaceful and calming environment;
- relaxing and unwinding in comfort and quality;
- enjoying the benefits for personal health and well-being from 'taking the waters';
- feeling safe and well cared for;
- experiencing professionally trained and qualified staff; and
- receiving value for money.

Definitions of Health and Wellness Tourism

In order to establish some guidelines on how to define and classify health and wellness tourism based on the use of hot and mineral springs and spa and wellness centres, a segmented approach has been adopted for this book. Figure 1.1 outlines the conceptual model we use to relate health and wellness spas to hot springs spas. This model also suggests important definitional segmentations within our subject matter and these too are followed in this book. The following individual segments are discussed independently:

- health;
- wellness;
- tourism;
- health tourism;
- medical tourism;
- wellness tourism;
- hot and mineral springs; and
- mineral composition and geological background of the springs.

Health, according to the Merriam-Webster Dictionary (n.d.(a)), is defined as

(1) The condition of an organism or one of its parts in which it performs its vital functions normally or properly.
(2) The state of being sound in body or mind.
(3) Freedom from physical disease and pain.

There are many definitions along similar lines, but all these indicate the same condition of optimal well-being combined with vigour, vitality, strength, fitness and stamina. The most cited definition of health is that by the World Health Organization

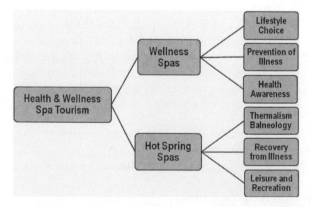

Figure 1.1 Health and Wellness Spa Tourism includes both wellness spas with hot springs and wellness spas without hot springs

(WHO), which can be found on the first page of that organisation's constitution (WHO, 2006). The original constitution came into force on 7 April 1948, with the following definition of health in its preamble:

> Health is a state of complete physical, mental and social well-being and not merely the absence of disease or infirmity.

This definition has not been changed or updated significantly in over 5 decades and in recent years there have been critics calling for its reconsideration. One of the most vocal has been Saracci (1997), who advocated a change of terminology in the original definition to:

> Health is a condition of well being free of disease or infirmity and a basic and universal human right.

His concern is that the original definition of 'a state of complete physical, mental and social well-being' in fact corresponds much more closely to happiness than to health and therefore poses conceptual problems when used as a basis for the study of wellness as a motivator for travel to destinations comprising hot or mineral springs. Because it also manifestly downgrades important mediating variables such as politics, economics and poverty, to mention but a very few, Awofeso (2005) argues 'that the WHO definition of health is utopian, inflexible, and unrealistic'. Following Awofeso we argue in this book that it is important to recognise that health is as much an *ideal* as an *actual* state of existence, and that this opens up the possibility of seeking a desired *future* state of health through conscious action to modify health patterns in the present. This wider definition of the nature of health allows consideration to be extended to states of health (in this case wellness), and it is this concept that underlies the health and wellness spa industry's claim to be of importance to the individual and group health of tourists.

Wellness is defined as:

(1) an approach to health care that emphasises preventing illness and prolonging life, as opposed to emphasising the treatment of diseases;
(2) the condition of good physical and mental health, especially when maintained by proper diet, exercise and habits (American Heritage® Dictionary of the English Language (n.d.));
(3) a healthy state of well-being free from disease (American Heritage® Stedman's Medical Dictionary (n.d.)); and
(4) the quality or state of being in good health especially as an actively sought goal, for example lifestyles that promote *wellness* (Merriam-Webster Medical Dictionary (n.d.(b)).

More dictionary-sourced definitions are not hard to find, but they all contain similar variables and their purpose and meaning do not vary widely (Cohen, 2008; Foster & Keller, 2008). Essentially, wellness is an *approach* to health care and lifestyle choice that is based on active prevention of illness and active promotion of a state of well-being. It is this sense of action that attracts many clients and ultimately supports the unique form of tourism known as Health and Wellness Spa

Tourism (Cohen, 2008; Hall, 2003). Adams (2003) refers to four main principles of wellness:

1. Wellness is multi-dimensional.
2. Wellness research and practice should be oriented towards identifying causes of wellness rather than causes of illness.
3. Wellness is about balance.
4. Wellness is relative, subjective or perceptual.

These will be elaborated below and in Chapter 2, but it is reasonably clear that wellness is as much a psychological as a physical state. Indeed, what little research there is in the tourism literature concerning wellness makes much of this distinction.

Tourism on the other hand has almost as many definitions as there are scholars and businesses that study or operate within it. It has been defined by the United Nations World Tourism Organization (UNWTO) as 'the activities of persons travelling to and staying in places outside their usual environment for not more than one consecutive year for leisure, business or other purposes' (TIAC, n.d.). Tourism is also defined as 'The entire world industry of travel, hotels, transportation and all other components, including promotion that serves the needs and wants of travellers' (Goeldner & Ritchie, 2003). Weaver and Lawton (2002) define tourism in their glossary as 'the sum of the phenomena and relationships arising from the interaction among tourists, business suppliers, host governments, origin governments, universities, community colleges and non-governmental organisations, in the process of attracting, transporting, hosting and managing these tourists and other visitors'.

One of the major motivations for the act of tourism is that of escape (Goeldner & Ritchie, 2003). Escape from an everyday personal or physical environment to one perceived to be likely to give to the traveller all the elements of 'life' he or she feels are missing from those everyday experiences. In addition, satisfaction of the desire for a healthy lifestyle, which as Hall (2003) notes is a significant intrinsic reward of much travel, has become a very important part of the range of new products available to tourists in recent years. This growing desire for the combination of escape with satisfaction of the need to maintain or recapture personal well-being has been recognised by the tourism industry through the promotion of health and wellness tourism.

Health tourism is defined by Ross (2001) and Tabacchi (2003) as 'any kind of travel to make yourself or a member of your family healthier'. Ross also refers to the concept of health tourism as 'as ancient as pre-history and as up-to-date as tomorrow', reinforcing the fact that we do not know exactly when health tourism first started because of the absence of written records. With reference to the healing benefits of hot springs Ross points out that in Europe post the Roman Empire these resources were used at least during the Middle Ages period (*c.* 900–1400 AD) and at that time were characterised by a firmly established belief in their curative powers (de la Barre *et al.*, 2005). In recent years health tourism has undergone significant renewal and expansion, and is now incorporating medical tourism (Hall, 2003). Hall also gives spa and health tourism a positive prognosis for the future, suggesting that this particular type of tourism could well be reclaiming its position after a time of dormancy during the past century.

In France and Germany, and in many of the countries of the former Soviet bloc, health tourism is 'emphatically medicalised' with spa therapy or *thermalisme*, as the French call it, still going strong. This is, according to Weisz (2001), due to the fact that 'thermalism found a place in the health care structure of those countries from which it cannot easily be dislodged'. Weisz gives valuable insight into the French hot and mineral spring spa system, which is rather unique by global standards. In France most medical spa treatments are covered by the national health system, which was and is partly true of several other European countries, especially Germany and the countries of the former Soviet Union.

The growth of *Medical Tourism* has been so rapid that there is as yet little scholarly work on it (Eades, 2010). Given this problem, the following definition has been derived from Wikipedia:

> Medical tourism (also called medical travel, health tourism or global health care) is a term initially coined by travel agencies and the mass media to describe the rapidly-growing practice of travelling across international borders to obtain health care. Such services typically include elective procedures as well as complex specialized surgeries such as joint replacement (knee/hip), cardiac surgery, dental surgery, and cosmetic surgeries. As a practical matter, providers and customers commonly use informal channels of communication-connection-contract, and in such cases this tends to mean less regulatory or legal oversight to assure quality and less formal recourse to reimbursement or redress, if needed. Leisure aspects typically associated with travel and tourism may be included on such medical travel trips. (http://en.wikipedia.org/wiki/Medical_tourism)

As this Wikipedia page acknowledges, this is a rapidly growing field of medicine that makes use of the differential prices of treatment in different countries. The range of services listed is also suggestive: first there are chronic conditions related to joints (especially hips and knees) and dentistry. These may be painful but are unlikely to be life threatening, at least in the short term. Second, there are more life-threatening conditions related to vital organs such as the heart, liver or kidneys, which if left untreated can soon prove fatal. Interventions may include complex surgery and/or transplantation, which, for one reason or another, may not be available in the patient's home area or may not be available at a price the patient can afford. Third, there are interventions such as cosmetic surgery, which from the point of view of life expectancy may not be necessary at all, but which may result in an improvement in the psychological state of the patient. Finally, there are a range of wellness therapies and interventions involving massage, aroma, diet and hot or cold water treatments that may have little medical effect at all but that undoubtedly make some clients feel good, at least temporarily.

The final point is that the medical treatment may be packaged along with more conventional tourism attractions, such as first-rate hotels, scenic attractions, pleasant climate, regional cuisine, recreational activities or local culture. Any such combination of course depends on the medical condition of the traveller, and there may be another continuum involved here. At one end are cases in which the *raison d'être* for the travel may be almost entirely medical. The average heart transplant or hip replacement patient is unlikely to be able to go swimming or playing golf very often during his or her treatment. A pleasant hotel bed with a nice view out of the window may be more appreciated than proximity to scenic hiking opportunities or tennis courts. On the other hand, the client in search of massage, yoga, aromatherapy, hot springs or mud bath beauty treatments might well value these kinds of amenities much more, and make more regular use of them. In other words, the clientele for medical tourism might range from the completely healthy on the one hand to the terminally ill on the other. This helps to explain the extraordinary number of products now available in the medical tourism sector and the large number of countries that appear to be jumping onto the bandwagon.

Wellness tourism, as defined by the Research Institute for Leisure and Tourism at the University of Berne, Switzerland is the 'sum of all the relationships and phenomena resulting from a journey and residence by people whose main motivation is to preserve or promote their health' (TIAC, n.d.). Specialised hotels or spas provide the appropriate professional know-how and individual care, usually delivered through a comprehensive service package comprising elements of physical fitness/beauty care, healthy nutrition/diet, relaxation/meditation and mental activity/education (TIAC, n.d.). Myers *et al.* (2005) on the other hand define wellness tourism as being 'a way of life oriented toward optimal health and well-being in which the body, mind, and spirit are integrated by the individual to live more fully within the human and natural community'. This definition accords with the approach taken in this book in assessing the importance of health and wellness spa tourism.

Role of Hot and Mineral Springs

Bathing in hot and mineral springs and drinking mineral spring water is part of this holistic approach to health and wellness, and the literature on this (Altman, 2000; Bullard, 2004; Cohen & Bodeker, 2008; Leavy & Bergel, 2003) thus complements and supports research into the human use of natural springs for health and wellness tourism. As a result of this trend a new kind of spa travel has emerged worldwide in recent years, where the curative properties of mineral waters are successfully combined with other wellness treatments and therapies (which has been done in European spa towns for centuries) – as well as with enjoyable holidays. This change of focus has led historic thermal spas to update their facilities, as well as encouraging established and new hotels to install these types of services where possible. The basic offerings of such health and beauty centres are wide-ranging and varied:

- thermal baths with an array of techniques and elements including balneotherapy and hydrotherapy;
- face and body beauty treatments;
- massages;

- alternative therapies for relaxation;
- specific cures, including slimming cures; and
- aromatherapy and other new treatments.

Health and wellness spa tourism also includes both the medical and the wellness side of treatments. Hot and mineral springs are an option for both these approaches in the creation of treatments; therefore segmentation into medical and wellness tourism does not necessarily reflect the traditional use or availability of such facilities. Thermal and mineral springs have a place in more than one treatment area, such as:

- traditional clinics to 'take the cure or the waters';
- hot spring spa resorts with medical as well as leisure and wellness facilities;
- modern aqua parks using mineral spring water to attract families as well as individuals, both locals and foreigners; and
- treatments for healthy and not so healthy visitors.

Although Weaver and Lawton (2002: 32) emphasise in their text on tourism management that 'health related travel is undertaken in order to receive medical treatment', it will be argued in this book that this is not always the case and there is in fact a lot of room for individual wellness preferences in health tourism which may or may not include medical treatment.

In this book hot and mineral springs are included in health and wellness spa tourism as both the location *and* a major form of treatment for visitors. However, although there are various definitions of health and wellness spa tourism by several authors, not many refer directly to the use of hot springs. There are some exceptions though as the following examples will demonstrate: the International Union of Tourist Organisations (IUTO, 1973: 7) interprets health tourism as the provision of health facilities utilising the natural resources of the country, in particular hot and mineral water and climate. It is evident that mineral springs and hot springs fall into the category of natural resources that are often favoured and given preference if available. Reference to the history of health tourism and mineral spring waters is also made by Jasen (1995: 107), who verifies that 'The therapeutic holiday...was nothing new, as the sea, the spa and foreign travel in general had long been favoured by doctors as treatments for well-to-do patients. Sea air or the taking of mineral waters restored the body...'. This is confirmed in the contemporary view of Hall (2003: 275) that 'Spa tourism is a component of health tourism that relates to the provision of specific health facilities and destinations which traditionally include the provision of mineral waters.' However, none of these examples acknowledges explicitly that mineral waters may in actual fact be derived from genuine hot springs or other geothermal resources, although it is common to describe hot springs as thermal springs, mineral springs or thermal waters, with the only significant differences between them often being the temperature and the mineral content.

From a *geological* point of view a hot or mineral spring is a naturally occurring water source that rises to the surface under pressure, usually along fault lines or in the vicinity of active volcanic environments. While circulating underground the water can undergo significant changes in its mineral composition through heat and pressure, which causes interaction with the surrounding rock. During this process minerals and trace metals are dissolved out of the parent rock into the hot water, which returns to the surface enriched with minerals and metallic trace elements often deemed beneficial for balneological treatment (Chapter 5).

Various definitions of hot springs can be found in the geological literature. A representative definition from Allaby and Allaby's (2003) *Earth Science Dictionary* describes hot springs as 'a continuous flow of hot water through a small opening on to the Earth's surface. The water is usually groundwater heated at depth by hot rocks and recycled to the surface by convection'. Several other definitions have been collected for this book and are included in Chapter 5, where the geology of hot and mineral springs will be examined and discussed in more detail. For now it should be noted that the term thermal water is also used by some spas where cold mineral water is artificially heated and then promoted as a hot spring or a thermal spring. In a paper researching the different definitions of hot, thermal and mineral springs, Pentecost *et al.* (2003) contribute a very interesting and valuable analysis as their findings recognise two major benchmarks for the use of such resources: human body temperature and the mean annual local air temperature. They take the position that while no scheme can claim to provide an objective and unbiased classification, waters emerging with a temperature in excess of the core human body temperature of 36.7°C should be defined as hot springs. The term 'thermal spring' is not recommended by Pentecost *et al.* (2003) as it cannot be defined satisfactorily for all springs. Neither do they consider the term 'warm spring' as being particularly useful.

Minerals are the most sought-after ingredients of hot or cold springs for spa resorts and thermal treatment facilities. In other words, the important feature of such destinations for tourists is not just a pleasant water temperature or a natural environment, but the health-related mineral composition of the water. The desired curative value is related to the various minerals and metallic trace elements, which are understood to have a beneficial effect on the human body, presumably assisting in the healing process of various ailments and diseases. Högl (1980), in his analysis of the thermal and mineral springs of Switzerland for healing purposes, classes water as an extraordinary substance without which life would not be possible. His book is a compilation of the chemical analyses of 66 of the most important natural mineral springs in Switzerland, both hot and cold, and their use. Other scientists worldwide, but especially in Europe, have researched the connection between minerals and potential health benefits of hot and mineral springs used in balneology and hydrotherapy.

Human beings have used mineral water since ancient times to cure such ailments as rheumatism, skin infections and poor digestion (Hall, 2003), and today the waters from countless springs are bottled and exported to many countries worldwide. Indeed, the sale of bottled water in many countries, including the export of brands such as *Perrier* and *Evian* from France, *San Pellegrino* from Italy and *Bad Pyrmonter* from Germany, is testimony to the continued belief in the healthy characteristics of mineral water. So widespread and important is this belief that it has led to many cities developing health spas and resorts around mineral and hot springs. Examples of such cities include Baden in Switzerland, Baden-Baden and Wiesbaden in Germany, Baden near Vienna in Austria, Budapest in Hungary, Rotorua in New Zealand, Beppu in Japan, Bath in England, Huaqing in China and El Dorado Springs, Missouri in North America to name a few examples (Bullard, 2004; Erfurt, 2006; Goodrich & Goodrich, 1987; Schafer, 1956).

In many hot spring destinations the type and amount of minerals is covered by individual government standards. In some countries the water must flow from the earth at a minimum temperature as well to achieve the classification of a hot or mineral spring. In Japan for example, a spring is considered therapeutic only if the spring waters arrive on the surface at a temperature of at least 25°C (77°F) and contain at least a minimum concentration of certain mineral components.

One of the primary goals of the majority of the literature on hot and mineral springs is to present evidence on the medical value of hot springs and mineral springs by revealing the various forms of scientific research into the value of balneology and balneotherapy. But it is also important to draw attention to the fact that such scientific studies are often not supported by the relevant government authorities (Altman, 2000). The reason for this is that it is difficult to evaluate medically the effectiveness of treatment with hot or cold mineral waters because these are often used as part of a *holistic* approach to medicine, which in some countries (e.g. the United States) falls outside the general medical profession's accepted worldview of healing, and thus their value for both consumer and provider alike is lessened.

The Health and Wellness Spa Industry

Having said that, rising customer expectations concerning health and wellness are the foundation on which the modern health and wellness spa industry is building an ever-increasing supply of facilities for the medical and general (wellness) visitor, to the extent that this form of tourism is now worth in excess of 250 billion US dollars per year and attracts some 150 million active *spa*-goers worldwide (ISPA, 2007). Caution is needed here though, because for example these figures are said to include 19.1 million Japanese spa-goers. Japanese data (Beppu International Tourist Office, 2007) suggest that there are over 150 million *Onsen* users alone in that country (Chapter 9). This discrepancy would appear to relate to the varying definitions of wellness and spa use that were discussed earlier, where the Japanese tradition is more about simply bathing in hot water than about the American tradition of beauty spa that underlies the research undertaken by the International Spa Association. As a result of this, many Japanese users may not be counted if the data are concentrating on analysing the spa experience rather than the totality of health and wellness tourism based on the use of hot and mineral springs.

The trend towards indulgence in a relaxing environment, which began after World War II (Foster & Keller, 2008), has thus turned into a global movement, but one that is a significant departure from the original concept of health spas that mainly specialised in rehabilitation or recovery from illness and/or injury. The new emphasis lies in prevention of disease and maintenance of good health more than cure, with high expectations regarding health improvements even if there are no particular health problems. Along with the body, mind and soul are also catered for in many spas in a holistic approach of creating harmony for those in need. This often includes new-age treatments as well as the more traditional water-based therapies.

The key element in all such facilities is water. Be it a part of the natural landscape surrounding a facility (ocean, rivers, lakes and waterfalls), decoration in the background (pools, fountains) or an active treatment component, water is a very important element in the world of spas and wellness. More and more spas without natural hot springs are investigating the possibility of tapping into mineral or geothermal water resources to enhance their business. The trend towards natural looking environments or settings is also evident in many spa hotels and resorts where swimming pools and thermal bathing facilities are designed and built to look as natural as possible, with rock pools the most typical and widespread design. The development of these spa and wellness water resources can be divided into two broad types:

(1) *Hot springs*: These are usually well known and generally appreciated for their curative value and their therapeutic benefits based on both water temperature and mineral content.
(2) *Mineral springs*: These can be cold or warm water from a natural spring, with curative value based on the type and concentration of minerals in the water. Often, the water can be taken internally too and is bottled and distributed.

Hot Springs and the Wellness Movement in the Literature

This book is based on the results of our ongoing research into the use of hot and mineral springs, their social and cultural backgrounds and their geology, as well as the associated facilities now being developed due to the growth of the Wellness Movement. In countries like Japan, Germany and New Zealand the health tourism industry has received a welcome boost through this new wellness and health awareness, although New Zealand seems never to have experienced a downturn in hot spring spa tourism. But for regions that had experienced a noticeable decline this has led to either a revival of many pre-existing hot spring resorts or the development of new facilities. However, while there is a great deal of general literature on spas and health tourism in a glossy magazine style context, there is little in-depth analysis relating to the physical origin of therapeutical waters, the environmental management of hot and mineral spring spa tourism, or regional development based on spa tourism (Cohen & Bodeker, 2008; Erfurt, 2006).

One of the few authors specifically dealing with the benefits of hot and mineral spring spas believes that water is a powerful healing tool that rejuvenates the body, mind and soul, while preventing a host of illnesses (Altman, 2000). Bathing in mineral springs and drinking their waters is presented as the most important part of a holistic approach to health and wellness, thus complementing and supporting research into the worldwide human use of hot springs. Altman reviews their healing modalities as part of a discussion of diseases and disorders, and follows this with a brief list of springs around the world where a particular disorder is treated. Additional inclusions contain a directory of several hundred hot springs world-wide, ranging from the best known to the most obscure, as well as the names and addresses of government tourist bureaus (if any) to contact for more detailed information about healing springs and related accommodation.

The other contributions to the small selection of academic literature on natural hot and mineral springs, thermalism and healing springs are mainly dedicated to individual areas. Bullard (2004) for example focuses exclusively on the American State of Missouri and its mineral springs and resorts, which in the past had played a vital role in the social and economic development of that state. A further limiting factor in Bullard's analysis is the timeframe: the period from 1800 to about the 1930s. However, during this period there were at least 80 operating sites that would now be described as hot spring spas or tourist resorts. Importantly, Bullard also traces the demise of Missouri's mineral water resorts and towns after modern medicine had taken hold in the 20th century, and American medical science and popular opinion discounted the immediate medical usefulness of mineral waters (unlike the contemporary support of the medical profession in Europe for such waters in medical treatments).

Leavy and Bergel's (2003) *Spa Encyclopaedia* is a useful compendium of the variations on the use of hot springs and other spa types worldwide and provides an informative overview of the current usages within the spa industry. The fact that few other therapeutic agents have been used continuously for thousands of years in virtually the same form with continuously increasing popularity is one of their major points. The book *Understanding the Global Spa Industry* by Marc Cohen and Gerard Bodeker (2008), published as this book was going to press, also assists in rectifying this lack of academic analysis, but again concentrates on the spa itself rather than on health and wellness tourism. Nevertheless it is a very welcome addition to our understanding of the spa industry from a management, design, marketing and product perspective.

Much of the remaining spa and wellness literature in the public domain is limited to descriptions of different locations, with many illustrations and little scientific or other contextual information. Over the last decade a considerable collection of coffee-table books has been published, mainly to interest potential travellers or spa clients in certain locations, spas and resorts and their picturesque settings. Typical examples are *Spa* by Arieff and Burkhart (2005), *Australia's Best Spas* by Clark (2005) and *Spa and Wellness Hotels* by Asensio (2002), which list and describe a select group of such destinations. The text of the latter is rendered simultaneously in English, French, German and Spanish and contains nothing more than brief descriptions of the spa facilities available in representative hotels from countries in those language groups.

The general pattern of such illustrative works on the health and wellness spa industry is that they lead off with the statement that water is the wellspring of life, the origin of creation and/or the source of purity and strength. For thousands of years humanity has considered it an element beyond modification – an element of vital importance that is impossible to do without. And generally again, they also make the point that while the idea of water as a curative and beneficial element is surging back into fashion, it is of course nothing new. In Asia, the Pacific and the Americas the association between hot and mineral springs water and wellness has been extremely important throughout all periods, and in countries like Japan where the use of hot springs is part of everyday life the bathing customs have not changed much at all over time.

However, it was not until the 18th and 19th centuries, with their reassertion of European Classical culture, that the Western world changed its habits with respect to hygiene and began once again to consider water as a beneficial element. During this period the custom of 'taking the waters' in medicinal springs and spas once more became popular (Asensio, 2002; Havins, 1976; Weaver & Lawton, 2002). As a result, there was an upsurge in spa use in Europe, with the existing facilities becoming the core of important centres for health and recreation.

With respect to the Asian tradition of the use of hot springs, Edward Schafer (1956), a pioneer in the study of medieval Chinese civilisation, wrote in 1956 a monograph on *The Development of Bathing Customs in Ancient and Medieval China* (Schafer, 1956). His paper referred to what is now known as the Huaqing Hot Spring Palace not far from the City of Xian in Western China. For the tourist this attraction is in convenient proximity to the Terracotta Warriors display and the Qin (First) Emperor's mausoleum. In his work Schafer also takes into account balneological highlights in Europe, India, Japan and some Islamic countries and mentions common bathing practices related to spiritual and physical cleansing purposes in many areas. He goes back in history as far as Mesopotamia and the Indus Valley, where bathing establishments, such as the great bath in Mohenjo Daro, were well-developed centres of these ancient civilisations. Schafer (1956) suggests that the influence of these early users of water as health therapy ultimately extended all over the world, with the spread of Roman bathing habits being only one example.

In his paper Schafer (1956) also mentions a Chinese book entitled *Shui-ching Chu*, which was a systematic record of all the ancient hot springs in China and their locations, including those visited by sufferers from various diseases. But not only sick people enjoyed the springs. The imperial rulers of China and their Ministers were great supporters and recreational users of such springs. They even built their palaces close to these natural resources to benefit from them year round, and one of the Emperors is said to have conducted imperial business from the bath, where he received his visitors (Schafer, 1956).

John W. Lund from the Geo-Heat Centre of Oregon's Institute of Technology has authored several research papers on the use of hot springs for wellness purposes. He sets the scene for his *Basic Principles of Balneology and Examples in the*

United States (Lund, 2005) by stating that the 'standard human use of geothermal and mineral waters for bathing and health has extended over several thousand years'. Like most authors Lund links the history of balneology back to Roman times and comments on this style of spa and wellness facility as still being common in Europe and Japan. While his deliberation makes balneology sound somewhat like an outdated practice, a relic from the past, Lund's work is a confirmation of the general history of natural hot spring use for health and wellness purposes, even though in the current situation in the United States beauty therapy-based spas are more common than in Europe. While people in the United States visit spas to improve their health, the emphasis is more on improvements in appearance, and stress relief and relaxation than on targeted treatment under strict professional medical supervision as in Europe. Nevertheless, Lund also describes an impressive number of spa and treatment facilities in Europe and Asia, as well as referring to two other sources: *A Guide to Japanese Hot Springs* by Hotta and Ishiguro (1986) and *Stories from a Heated Earth* by Cataldi *et al.* (1999) during this discussion. Some statistics given by Lund are mentioned here in order to demonstrate the current extent of the health spa industry:

Russia – 3500 spas and 5000 'reconditioning' centres run by the government.

Slovakia and the Czech Republic – 52 mineral water health spas and more than 1900 mineral springs, with approximately 220,000 people yearly receiving treatment that is fully covered by national health insurance.

Rotorua in New Zealand – the Queen Elizabeth Hospital has a long tradition in using hot springs and volcanic muds for health treatments, again covered by the national health insurance system.

Japan – over 20,000 *Onsen* and 150 million spa-goers per year.

In his main work Lund summarises the North American hot spring history of spa development as having gone through three stages:

(1) The Indians used hot springs as sacred locations.
(2) Early European settlers in America tried to copy the spas of Europe.
(3) Hot springs are now used as wellness spas in America rather than solely 'for taking the waters', following instead the trend 'back to nature'.

His differentiation between European and American spas concludes as follows: 'Unlike European spas, where medical cures of specific ailments are more important (and therefore have been covered by national health systems), US spas give more importance to personal exercise, reducing stress, lifting depression and losing weight' (Lund, 2005). This is quite a significant difference in approach, and Lund suggests that unless the American health insurance system considers the therapeutical use of hot springs worth subsidising, nothing will change and the beneficial use of thermal waters will be available only for those who can personally afford thermal treatments at hot spring spas.

Some additional historical background relating to the use of hot springs is presented by Cataldi *et al.* (1999). The historical and cultural use of hot springs in nearly 30 countries worldwide is covered here in an attempt to present a reference that clearly documents the early use of geothermal resources with a broader, more global coverage. Other similar material may be found in the German language academic literature, in numerous texts about balneology, hydrotherapy and medicinal climatology. These titles (some examples are listed below) are indisputably scientific and medical literature regarding natural hot springs and their practical applications and effect and are authored by highly qualified medical specialists; but they are not the more usual coffee-table style referred to by the travelling public for information about hot springs (Box 1.1):

Box 1.1 Scientific reading

Steinkopff, L. (1989) *Kompendium der Balneologie und Kurortmedizin*, Schmidt, Klaus (Hrsg.).

Pratzel, H.G. and Schnizer, W. (1991) *Handbuch der Medizinischen Bäder Indikationen – Anwendungen – Wirkungen*, Haug, K F.

Amelung, W. (n.d.), *Balneologie und medizinische Klimatologie* (In 3 Bänden), Hildebrandt (Hrsg.).

Springer, G. (n.d.), *Einführung in die Balneologie und medizinische Klimatologie*, Bln Nachfolgewerk der 1952 erschienenen 2. Aufl. Vogt/Amelung.

Limitations of the Previous Literature

It appears from this brief survey that natural hot and cold mineral springs used as spas have not received much attention from authors in the field of tourism (Cohen & Bodeker, 2008; Goodrich, 1994; Hall, 2003), nor has the correlation of thermalism with the physical environment (geology) been covered extensively in the literature.

Generally, a natural hot or mineral spring can be classified as 'therapeutic' if it contains a minimum amount of one or more minerals per litre of water: the type and amount of minerals is determined by specific government standards of individual countries. In some countries the water must flow from the earth at a minimum temperature as well (e.g. Japan). But in developing such definitions, past and currently available publications often reflect opinions from a North American point of view only (e.g. Lund, 2005). Regrettably this generally does not take into account 'the rest of the world', where the majority of hot springs are located. On the other hand, considering the vast amount of natural hot springs worldwide it is understandable that existing studies commonly focus on a specific area, which is usually made obvious in the introduction (e.g. Ross, 2001). However, some publications give the impression that apart from the United States and/or specific European countries there is not much else worth documenting. Some of this may be due to time constraints, word limits and other restrictions authors have to cope with; therefore this observation is not intended as criticism, merely as an attempt to point out the limitations of the existing literature.

A classic among the small number of texts on the use of spas that specifically mention tourism (Havins, 1976) refers to English spas, their history and use. Havins looks at a range of methods of hydrotherapy (the water cure) and the establishment of spas where the cure was taken, at times in a regime of bleak austerity. This book, while quite old now, remains an important source of information about the social and cultural origins of the English spa towns such as Bath, the only genuine hot spring in England.

The existing academic literature on the tourism industry does not include much comment on health and wellness spa tourism. Goeldner and Ritchie's (2003) text for example is aimed at hospitality and tourism students worldwide, but only briefly mentions spa tourism as an 'interesting aspect in the history of tourism' influenced by the Romans (no mention of the Asian or Pacific context), and merely acknowledges the most common 'facts' regarding the historical use and development of hot spring centres in England and on the European continent. In a similar fashion, *Tourism Management* by Weaver and Lawton (2002) presents two brief sections dealing with spa tourism and their often associated resorts, but these only include a short reference to the continuity aspects of hot spring use before or after the Romans. Most other books are remarkably silent on this key element of tourism, even in relation to Europe, where wellness therapies during the holiday experience have always formed an important sub-sector of tourism and do so increasingly in the rest of the world.

It should perhaps be mentioned here that the literature reviewed for this book focused mainly on publications available to the general public seeking information about hot spring use (past and present) and health and wellness spa tourism-related issues. It was not deemed necessary to analyse specific medical literature on such therapies in depth; nevertheless our research has shown that the medical professions of many countries consider thermalism based on the use of natural hot springs as a significant contribution to the improvement of health (Cohen & Bodeker, 2008; Fabiani *et al.*, 1996; Ghersetich & Lotti, 1996; Parish & Lotti, 1996).

The Rationale for this Book

The lack of description and analysis of hot and mineral springs and spa and wellness destinations in relation to tourism in the literature indicates that there is a considerable gap in the existing tourism literature that is in need of being supplemented with more comprehensive and updated research. It also became quite obvious during the process of reviewing essential literature that the same basic information regarding the history of health and wellness spa tourism is referenced or paraphrased time and time again. Virtually the same statements are repeated in a number of texts and websites and therefore do not add any new insights.

In order to more fully examine this point several of the more important English language journals specialising in tourism research, tourism management and international travel were reviewed (Box 1.2):

Box 1.2 Tourism journals reviewed

Annals of Tourism Research published by Elsevier.
Tourism Management published by Elsevier.
Journal of Travel Research published by Sage Publications.
Vacation Marketing published by Sage Publications.
Progress in Tourism and Hospitality Research published by Wiley-InterScience.
International Journal of Tourism published by Wiley-InterScience.
Tourism Recreation Research.

In each case, the individual journal databases were accessed and searched from the current (at the time of writing) edition back over a time span of up to seven years (this is the timeframe covering the concurrent availability/existence of many of the researched journals). As far as could be determined, only one special issue and a few general articles have been published, which directly relate to the key topics below:

- spa tourism;
- hot spring tourism;
- wellness tourism;
- health tourism;
- thermal tourism; and
- thermalism.

This situation implies that little active academic research seems to have been undertaken in these particular fields of tourism in recent years, or no findings and results have been published in the main tourism journals. Is this an indication of a general ignorance of health and wellness spa tourism, notwithstanding the enormous contribution this tourism sub-sector is making towards the industry as a whole, or is it that the current focus on general management issues, destination branding and competitiveness in tourism precludes attention on an intensely personal lifestyle sub-set? Whatever the reason, articles on 'wine tourism', 'shopping' and 'rural destinations' stand more of a chance of being found among articles in tourism journals. The journals *Annals of Tourism Research* and *Tourism Management* also both offer a list of their '25 Top Articles' as determined by citations and downloads; however, none of these have ever been remotely related to spa, wellness or health tourism.

The most recent journal-based review of wellness tourism is that by Smith and Kelly (2006) in a special issue of *Tourism Recreation Research*. This special issue is dedicated to understanding the concepts of wellness and wellness tourism, and provides some indication that research in this area is beginning to be published in the tourism literature. The individual papers provide an insight into the debate on the nature of wellness and wellness tourism that will be covered in Chapter 2 of this book, but come down heavily on the existential side of wellness rather than the physical side that seems to be a greater motivation for the spa and wellness tourist (Steiner & Reisinger, 2006). Nevertheless, as the editors of this collection note, if wellness tourism is merely about relaxation then it could be argued that the traditional beach holiday with its emphasis on sunbathing is its ultimate form. Alternatively, if wellness tourism is not passive then it is driven by the desire to actively seek enhanced wellness of some sort, be it physical or psychological (Smith & Kelly, 2006: 2).

The use of hot and mineral springs in spa and wellness facilities is in fact more likely to be discussed on a global academic level in earth science journals or in medical journals, as the examples given in Box 1.3 show (although see Cohen & Bodeker, 2008).

Box 1.3 Medical journals reviewed

Clinics in Dermatology published by Elsevier, Official Journal of the International Academy of Cosmetic Dermatology (IACD).

Deutsches Ärzteblatt published by Verlag Deutsches Ärzteblatt, Bundesärztekammer, Köln.

Anales de Hidrología Médica published by la Sociedad Española de la Hidrología Médica, Universidad Complutense: Servicio de Publicaciones, Madrid.

Archiv der Balneologie und Hydrotherapie published by Institut für Geschichte der Medizin – Universität Wien.

Balneologia Bohemica published by Institut für Umweltphysiologie – Universität Wien;

Physikalische Medizin – Rehabilitationsmedizin – Kurortmedizin published by Thieme-Verlag, Wien (Vienna).

Heilbad und Kurort published by Institut für Biometeorologie, Wien (Vienna);

Zeitschrift für Bäder – Klimaheilkunde published by Institut für Umweltphysiologie – Universität Wien.

Zeitschrift fuer Physikalische Medizin, Balneologie und Medizinische Klimatologie published by Institut für Umweltphysiologie – Universität Wien.

European countries, including some Middle East countries, with a long-standing medical acceptance of the curative effects of hot springs are Bulgaria, France, Germany, Greece, Hungary, Iceland, Israel, Italy, Jordan, Poland, Portugal, Spain and Turkey. In these countries there are many texts (including academic) available dealing with hot spring use or thermalism on a health and wellness basis, but again this literature, if available, is very difficult to obtain. Non-European countries with a history of hot spring use are Australia, China, Japan, Korea, New

Zealand, Russia and the Americas, but not all of these countries publish their research findings in English, which creates another obstacle for collecting data. However, relevant texts, journals and books in the Spanish, French, Portuguese, Italian, Icelandic, Japanese and German languages were accessed for this book.

On the whole, however, there are remarkably few academic works in English or any other language, and not just in the tourism literature, that recognise the significance of natural hot and mineral springs and their relation to health, wellness and leisure tourism. The existing information is scattered and there seem to be no major reference books that include a global overview of natural hot and mineral springs in general and health and wellness spa tourism in particular. The *Proceedings of the World Geothermal Congress* from the years 2000 and 2005 are a good source of international information regarding hot and mineral spring use on a global scale, but it is difficult to verify the significance of hot spring use in health and wellness tourism with data gained from cyberspace rather than from existing academic literature. The only reliable and credible sources are, as mentioned above, the medical journals and some earth science journals. However, these cannot be accessed by the general public with their full content via the standard journal databases and only very few articles can be viewed in full, unless at considerable cost. So, while there is a great deal of scientific research being conducted in relation to hot springs and their use in (medical) thermalism and for a variety of purely wellness-related purposes, the uses of hot and mineral springs in health and wellness spa tourism is underreported as yet, especially in the tourism literature. Nevertheless, the term 'wellness' is in fact widely used in European and other tourism industry circles when assessing a tourist's likely behaviour in a market (Foster & Keller, 2008; Mueller & Kaufmann, n.d.). The principal problems regarding wellness as a tourism industry resource and attractor for tourists in this situation of inadequate understanding concern the expanding supply of facilities in a situation of insufficiently researched demand for such facilities. This situation impacts on the quality dimension of wellness services, which has increasingly become the decisive competitive factor in the market. For this reason quality management is now seen as playing an important role. What market research there is shows that average three- to five-star hotels now are forced to provide fairly comprehensive wellness facilities (see Chapter 8; Cohen & Bodeker, 2008), where they specialise in health information, individual care and a wide range of cultural and relaxation programmes. However, although the same hotel can host health (cure) guests and wellness guests simultaneously, these two segments have to be considered separately when deciding on appropriate marketing strategies. It is therefore assumed in the industry that wellness is pursued solely by 'healthy' people, the primary aim being prevention rather than cure in comparison to health resort guests, who may seek rehabilitation and recovery from injury or illness or postoperative trauma. Nevertheless, some overlap cannot be excluded.

This form of analysis is supported by the work of Bennett *et al.* (2004), which provides a profile of the health resort sector in Australia. Their study was based on resort directories, an analysis of promotional materials produced by each of the resorts within the study group, and on discussions with representatives of

Australia's various state tourism organisations. Bennett *et al.* (2004) found that most properties in the health resort category in Australia may be described as being *mainstream wellness* facilities offering a health and wellness spa tourism focus not based on hot or cold mineral springs, of which there are very few in that country. The smallest number of properties in this category were found to be in the *alternative* and *medical treatment* focus areas (unlike in Europe), although these components of the health resort sector in Australia do appear to be dynamic and innovative. The development of a dynamic and innovative health resort sector in Australia has thus occurred in the absence of a strong local tradition of spa use or of hot springs (Bennett *et al.*, 2004).

Summary

While health and wellness tourism is not new according to historical accounts of travelling for health purposes, the recent wellness movement has resulted in changes in lifestyle choices for an increasing number of people, no matter whether this is actually based on natural hot springs or not. Several authors have given valuable insights into the natural hot and mineral spa system in a variety of countries, some of which are quite unique by global standards. Bathing in hot and mineral springs and drinking mineral water sourced from natural springs is part of the holistic approach to the multi-dimensional health and wellness concept. Wellness tourism includes both the medical and the wellness side of treatments. Hot and mineral springs are therefore included in health and wellness tourism as both the location *and* the form of treatment for visitors. Minerals are the most sought after ingredients of hot or cold springs for spa resorts and thermal treatment facilities, and in many countries natural hot spring destination use is covered by national health insurance. For this reason the International Union of Tourist Organisations (IUTO, 1973: 7) interprets health tourism as the provision of health facilities utilising the natural resources of the country, in particular hot and mineral water and climate.

Due to the popularity of natural hot springs and their attraction as health and wellness tourist destinations, more and more spas without natural hot springs are investigating the possibility of tapping into local geothermal water resources to enhance their business. Existing hot spring resorts have been granted a new lease of life that has consequentially resulted in a boom in spa hotels and resorts, and hot spring spas worldwide (Ryrie, 1999). Wellness, however, is more than hot springs, spas, sauna and fitness; it is a comprehensive lifestyle concept, which is attracting large numbers of people (Cohen & Bodeker, 2008). Bathing in mineral springs and drinking their waters is presented in the literature as the most important part of a holistic approach to health and wellness, thus complementing and supporting research into the worldwide human use of hot springs. However, the existing information is scattered and there appear to be no major reference books that include a global overview of natural hot and mineral springs and health and wellness spa tourism. In addition, some of the contributions to the small selection of academic literature about natural hot and mineral springs, thermalism and healing springs are mainly dedicated to individual areas or travel marketing (Williams, 1996) and not to the industry or its importance for tourism in general. Thus, while there is a great deal of scientific research being conducted in relation to hot springs and their commercial use in health and wellness spas, medical thermalism, and for a variety of purely wellness-related purposes, the field of hot spring and spa tourism is underreported as yet, especially in the tourism-related literature (see Smith & Puczko, 2008).

Outline of the book

This book provides an overview of the traditional and contemporary use of natural hot spring use for leisure, health and wellness activities from a non-Eurocentric viewpoint with the intention of closing gaps in the existing literature. One of its key objectives is to correct the common perception that wellness centres, including thermal spas, have their sole (or even major) origin in Europe, namely in imperial Rome and its immediate antecedents. While the Roman Empire certainly contributed to the development of recreational health and wellness facilities and thermal bathhouses (*thermae*) in its constituent countries, most of the sites they utilised near natural hot springs were already used from ancient times by local native inhabitants, and the rest of the world enjoyed just as many if not more sites across a similar or longer span of history. This book is intended to clarify the factual origins of hot spring use for health and wellness in all continents and thus present comprehensive support for the worldwide significance of natural hot springs for health and wellness spa tourism.

This introductory chapter has examined the background of the general aspects of the current trend in wellness spa visits, including giving a brief analysis of the wellness model, and has defined the general terminology of health and wellness spa tourism. A review of the existing literature related to the use of natural hot springs for leisure, health and wellness purposes indicates that there are significant gaps, some of which this book anticipates to close.

The second chapter examines in detail the health and wellness concept and its origins, with examples from a selection of countries. Growing awareness regarding health and wellness and the resulting consumer expectations is increasingly combined with environmental concerns on a personal level due to the 'back to nature' factor. This is reflected in the diversity of spa types and the reasons for visiting them. An extensive list of different spa types provides an overview of what is available in the health and wellness spa industry.

Chapter 3 investigates the history of health and wellness spa tourism based on the use of natural hot and mineral springs. A timeline reaching back as far as could possibly and reasonably be determined is supported either by officially documented written records of human use of these geothermal resources or by traditional accounts passed down over generations. The history of over 60 countries was researched to identify the first human interactions with geothermal phenomena such as natural hot springs and their resulting use for health and wellness purposes. This chapter shows that ancient health and wellness spas were linked inextricably to natural hot springs and the global belief in the curative value of natural hot spring water.

In Chapter 4 special consideration is given to the remarkable cultural importance of the use of water in human society, as expressed in religion and mythology. This chapter includes examples of the special cultural relationship different cultures and civilisations have had and still have with natural thermal springs. The various forms of their use for religious and cultural purposes provide an insight and understanding of the significance of health and wellness spa treatments in a variety of socio-cultural settings.

Chapter 5 outlines the key geological processes that lead to the existence of natural hot springs and their use in the health and wellness spa industry. The geological components as well as some noteworthy locations are described. The co-locations of other attractions based on the same geological processes such as geysers, mud pools, hot streams and lakes, which also provide destinations for geotourism, are briefly mentioned as hot spring tourism for health and wellness has a tendency to overlap into nature-based tourism or geotourism and is often successfully combined with this.

The spa industry and its environments are examined and analysed in Chapter 6, which includes fundamental resources in the form of natural settings and geothermal resources as well as social, psychological, behavioural and regulatory environments of the health and wellness spa tourism industry, individual tourists and their host communities. This chapter thus assesses the impact of the different environments of the health and wellness spa industry, which act as facilitators, moderators, barriers and regulatory frameworks to its existence and functioning.

Chapter 7 looks at the growth of the health and wellness spa industry from the point of view of its technology and economics. The discussion traces the recent huge expansion in the demand and supply of health and wellness products. New products are appearing in the traditional markets of thermal spa facilities. Aquatic entertainment centres based on the supply of natural geothermal water resources and Japanese *Onsen* style spas provide additional attractions for leisure, health and wellness tourists around the world. New technologies are also advancing health products within the tradition of thermalism.

Chapter 8 outlines how the health and wellness spa tourism industry has marketed itself to tourists using natural hot and mineral springs as a unique selling point (USP). The industry's management, human resource development and the impact of changes in the national health systems in selected countries on the growth of health and wellness spa tourism are discussed, as well as the local, national and global competition for health (including medical) and wellness tourists.

Chapter 9 takes a different approach to examples of the various types of spa and wellness facilities discussed in earlier chapters and provides small case studies based in a selection of countries in order to better represent international trends involving natural hot and mineral spring spas for health and wellness. The similarities and differences across countries, regions and localities are exposed and examined in this chapter.

The final chapter summarises the unprecedented growth of the health and wellness spa tourism industry in recent years. Natural hot and mineral springs are noted as a significant element of this type of tourism, serving both the medical and the wellness side with thermal treatment facilities as well as being used for bathing and thermal aqua parks. The chapter concludes with a discussion of emerging views on the likely future trends in health and wellness spa tourism.

Chapter 2

The Health and Wellness Concept: A Global Overview

PATRICIA ERFURT-COOPER

Introduction

During the late 20th century a new imperative regarding fitness and well-being emerged worldwide and was turned into an ideology for all age and income groups (Foster & Keller, 2008). This awareness of the importance of personal well-being was supported to a large degree by the 'baby boomers' becoming middle aged, which started to have impacts on the fitness industry over a relatively short time period during the 1980s and 1990s, and led to the development of a new *Wellness Movement* (Miller, 2005; Westgate, 1996). Growing concerns for their well-being in the face of ageing has caused many baby boomers to become more aware of their personal options for improving their health through lifestyle management and a choice of preventive therapies on a personal level (Brisbane Courier Mail, 2006). For many, this increased awareness encompasses preventative therapies based on travel to health resorts and spas. For the health tourism industry itself in countries such as Japan, Germany, Austria, the United States and New Zealand this increased motivation to seek out wellness benefits from natural hot and mineral spring waters could not have been more welcome, as it brought in the wake of the desire for wellness a much needed revival of many hot and mineral spring resorts.

Wellness in the Past

The modern spa holiday, having begun in the 18th century and developed into a tourist standard product in the 19th century, came of age in the 20th and 21st centuries. It … combines several requirements: along with the wish for health and well-being, from the very start factors such as entertainment, sociability and the prospect of making interesting contacts came into play. (Austria Info, n.d.: 1)

The spa and wellness concept has turned into a worldwide bestseller over the last decade with excellent prospects for the future (Chapter 1). However, both the term and the concept of wellness have a complex past (EUPHA, 2005; Foster & Keller, 2008). When it comes to dating the exact onset of the spa and wellness trend opinions are divided. The organisation *Austria Info* suggests that spa holidays have been around for centuries; however, this particular quotation does not refer to spa towns with thermal springs in particular, but to all spas that have a history of use even without the added attraction of hot springs (Austria Info, n.d.). In the Middle East Pharaoh Cleopatra is said to have established one of the world's first purpose-built spas on the shores of the Dead Sea in about 25 BC (Svart, 2006). However, the original term *spa* is generally traced back to a town in Belgium during the Renaissance Era (1450–1600 AD), where a mineral-rich hot spring was used by an ironmaster to cure his rheumatism (Altman, 2000). Subsequently this location developed into a health resort town called *Espa* and over time the word spa became the common designation for health resorts based on mineral waters. In the Europe of the 18th century spas were the places to go and be seen. Quite often they were used as 'meet markets' to assist in finding suitable partners for daughters and sons or single individuals looking for some amusement. 'Taking the waters' was deemed an acceptable excuse to behave in a way otherwise and elsewhere frowned upon; the spa scene made this possible.

In one of the major formative traditions for current patterns of health and wellness spa tourism worldwide, the Roman Empire left behind a long list of spas (*thermae*) all over Europe, which they built while they were occupying new territories. With the demise of the Western Roman Empire in 450 AD, so too came the demise of the Roman bath tradition in Europe, although Spain, North Africa and the Middle East maintained a highly developed bathing culture. This was a result of the influence of the Byzantine or Eastern Roman Empire and the subsequent Arab conquests and maintained the influence of the Roman bathing tradition in those countries (The Spa Association, 2005).

The City of Bath in England provides an example of the fusion of Roman history with later trends in spa and wellness demand and supply in Europe (White, 2000). After the springs had been abandoned as a bathing resource in 1978 (although not touristically or in respect of their mineral waters), the *Bath Spa Project* was launched by the City Council in 1997 in order to restore Bath to the leading spa town of England, with the expectation that the project would stimulate the revival of spa culture in the UK. The new spa facilities in Bath are just a short distance from the original Roman Bath site and they use natural hot spring water drawn from the same springs that have served visitors for at least the last two thousand years. The new facilities are designed to offer relaxing and extended therapeutic treatments. Although they will not act as a cure for serious illness they will act as a cure for the human spirit, as outlined in reference to the conservation statement for the adjacent Roman Baths (Clews, 2000).

In countries such as Hungary the change from centuries of thermal bathing culture to modern wellness facilities has been slower than in countries without a history of hot or mineral springs. In Budapest the increased use of day spas builds on the ancient way of relieving stress and physical ailments through hot water treatments, and day spas and wellness facilities are now being established in a society that is becoming more conscious of the importance of a healthy lifestyle (LaForest, 2004). In Budapest the locals congregate in public thermal baths such as the *Szechenyi* to relax, swim and take many of the cures and treatments on offer. They are also known for taking the national pastime of playing chess into the thermal pools (The Age, 2005). And further to the east in Russia during the Soviet era thermal baths were an integral part of the national health system.

In Europe Austria was one of the first countries to adopt the more recent concept of wellness and to act upon it quickly. The country effectively appeals to key tourist target groups by positioning itself to offer wellness treatments that unite the body, spirit, personal desires, culture and natural resource embodied by the spring (Nahrstedt, 2002). Austria has an unmatched infrastructure when it comes to wellness holidays and health-related tourism, and was ranked number one in the world for quality of life and its healthcare services in the early 2000s (Garelli, 2002). According to Nahrstedt (2002) Austria boasts an intact natural environment in conjunction with its wellness spas, an association that is also very popular in the Japanese tourist market. In Japan itself though, with literally thousands of geothermal springs and the Japanese preference for authentic and unadulterated hot spring water, wellness centres are not yet developed to quite the same extent, leaving the European style wellness facility as a potential favourite for the Japanese while on holiday.

In Japan, some traditional hot springs have been developed into day spas known as *kuahausu* (derived from the German word *Kurhaus*), providing separate bathing areas for men and women with thermal mineral pools at different temperatures, a cold pool area with fountains and waterslides, bowling alleys, gyms, saunas and steam rooms, massage services, restaurants and bars, relaxation rooms, music rooms and video games (Altman, 2000: 17). But the main bathing attractions are the traditional hot springs called *Onsen*. Often used by groups of people who enjoy sharing a bath after leaving the world of corporate work behind, as well as families and couples, a trip to an *Onsen* is classed as the ultimate bonding experience because all are equal once they shed their designer clothes and other status symbols.

The capital of Iceland, Reykjavik, has been designated an official 'spa city' by the European Spa Association (Iceland Express, 2006). This seems well deserved and quite logical, because the Icelanders have many facilities where they can take care of their health, well-being and leisure. Several active volcanoes and high-temperature geothermal fields provide natural hot springs all over Iceland and most towns have at least one public geothermal swimming pool. The *Blue Lagoon* (see Figure 2.1) south of Reykjavik is a geothermal spa that coexists with

Figure 2.1 The Blue Lagoon south of Reykjavik. In the background is the Svartsengi geothermal power station
Source: Photograph courtesy of P. Erfurt-Cooper.

a geothermal power station surrounded by nothing but hardened lava flows which are totally devoid of vegetation. These lava flows, which cover most of this seismic-active island in the North Atlantic, together with the white steam clouds from the power station, give the area around the lagoon a very distinct atmosphere and make the Icelandic spa culture an experience worth travelling around the world for.

The Blue Lagoon also has its own skin care products and treatment clinics, with special focus on the treatment of psoriasis. Similar in style to the Blue Lagoon, and also in its proximity to a high-temperature geothermal field and power station, is a relatively new development near *Lake Mývatn* in Iceland's north – the Mývatn Nature Baths (opened on June 30, 2004). This facility is not as yet overrun by international tourists, but with the increasing popularity of Iceland as a tourist destination it is only a matter of time before the 'Blue Lagoon of the North' attracts as many visitors as its counterpart in the south of Iceland.

Another Icelandic example of unusual spa design and technology in relation to wellness and fitness is the *Laugar Spa* in Reykjavik (Nguyen, 2006). This facility also opened in 2004 and admits visitors (after payment) through the use of a retinal scan, which allows a day of 'free' use of any facility, including seven saunas with different themes and various degrees of humidity and temperature. Sauna themes include a cave with stalactites, a room with moving constellations of stars in the ceiling and another room in which jungle noises can be heard. The health and spa resort also features botanical gardens, a family zoo and an activity park as well as an 18,000-m² health and swimming area with a full-sized outdoor pool and an

Olympic-sized indoor pool, seven Jacuzzis and a big thermal pool for family fun (Laugar Spa, n.d.). Other facilities at Laugar include a gym, a spa, a beauty and massage salon, a restaurant, a hairdressing salon and a sports shop.

Hawaii is another location with volcanic activity and is one of the most popular spa destinations in the Pacific, along with the west coast of North America including Mexico and California. All these regions have vast amounts of geothermal energy at their disposal; however, Hawaii seems to be successful in the spa and wellness world without using its thermal waters. A few studies over the past decades have looked at utilising hot springs for spa treatments, but so far nothing has eventuated (Woodruff, 1987; Woodruff & Takahashi, 1993). However, for anything else that is desired in ultimate spa luxury, Hawaii is able to supply it. Perhaps this situation reflects the general American attitude to spas and the wellness industry, where wellness treatments rather than hot spring bathing form the core of interest.

The popular concept of Roman bath culture has been promoted even in countries in the southern hemisphere. The Aquarius Roman Baths (2005) in Launceston, Tasmania (Australia) have created a bathing experience using technology from the 21st century designed to replicate the imputed Roman luxurious indulgence of body and mind. Tasmania most certainly has no history of Roman occupation, but uses the reputation of Roman bathing culture to attract customers and convince them that this spa is an experience not to be missed. By way of contrast, and not only by location, to the Roman design model is the *Ananda Spa* in India, some 260 km north of New Delhi. The spa is located within the sprawling grounds of a former palace estate and offers healing powers, superb architecture and ancient traditions, and is regarded as one of the best in the world. The surroundings are stunning, including the restored palace with 70 deluxe rooms to accommodate visitors on their purification program. The Ananda Spa also features a special restaurant serving 'rejuvenation cuisine' (Silverkris, 2005), which adds to the variety of spa cuisine adopted by many resorts and hotels.

On the other hand Germany, which had restored the ancient bathing culture in the late middle ages (see Chapter 3) and gradually turned it into a health and welfare medical tradition supported by the state that forms a significant sub-set of the European (including East Europe and Russia) tradition, experienced a decline in hot spring 'health holidays' (Kur) in the late 1990s. Indicating the importance of hot and mineral springs to health and welfare medical traditions, this seems to have been a rather sudden side effect of the restructuring and redefinition of government social system support legislation that in turn caused direct cutbacks of public contributions and subsidies towards medical rehabilitation.

This policy change resulted in a struggling national health system by 1997, and caused many established health and medical spa facilities to face reduced numbers of clients/patients (Politikerscreen.de, 2002). By 1999 over 120 such health clinics had closed down according to the German Health Spa Association (Deutscher Heilbäderverband, 1999). In the year 2000 however, another reform in legislation reversed most of the drastic effects of 1997 with the aim of increasing the efficiency of the German health sector (Politikerscreen.de, 2002), and this brought back direct subsidies, although more limited, to medical rehabilitation, which include the use of health and wellness spas. In the meantime the growing wellness trend had supported hot spring facilities during this crisis and caused many *Kurhaus* facilities to re-evaluate their marketing and/or closure strategies.

Other European countries that relied on visitors being subsidised by their respective National Health Insurance systems also experienced a downturn of business in their spa resorts over the last decade of the 20th century. Communities who in the past could rely on regular income from the state through visitor numbers to their spas were forced to accept that demand was declining, and many resort facilities as well as other industry-related businesses had to close their doors. However, this has changed in the wake of the wellness movement, and the new environment has encouraged many hot and mineral spring spa towns to reinvest in their natural resources and combine the use of healing waters with new and upgraded wellness resorts and retreats. Golf courses, conference venues and many other non-core business offers have been combined under the spa and wellness umbrella without appearing mismatched as a result.

Historic spa towns that were still thriving despite the downturn in interest before the current wellness boom took hold may have done so for one or more of the following reasons:

(1) They continued to receive sponsorship and support from local and state governments in some form.
(2) They continued to receive sponsorship from medical and/or health associations (varies by country).
(3) They continued to receive sponsorship through the local travel industry as an attractive destination package (e.g. nature, hot springs, climate, landscape).
(4) They continued to receive support from the local community in order to help protect community identity and employment.
(5) They had historical value, great architecture or were heritage listed.
(6) The mineral content of their thermal spring water had the reputation of being beneficial or of curative value in the treatment of certain diseases.
(7) They were located in a country that has always been a trendy destination.
(8) They were located in a country that has always been a safe destination.
(9) They were easy to access.

However, many of these factors also mean that countries and areas without a thermal legacy have found it easy to tap into the wellness market – they start with a 'clean slate' instead of having to consider how to redevelop or revive their former spa resorts including their not always attractive architectural heritage, and they can provide artificially heated water as and when necessary. Also, the word 'spring' is often used in the name of a spa and wellness location/destination, despite the fact that no natural springs, hot or cold, can be found anywhere nearby. The subliminal attraction of the reference to springs seems to attract the attention of potential visitors, but this may be under false pretences in some cases.

The Wellness Concept: A Worldwide Bestseller

The wellness concept is subject to different interpretations. In Europe the original thought can be generally traced back at least as far as the Greek and Roman cultures, where certain parts of the population (generally males, athletes, soldiers and wealthy people) with an interest in health, fitness and hygiene as well as socialising made use of public bathhouses and fitness temples to ensure wellness. The wellness concept as currently articulated similarly aims to prevent illness through informed health promotion, education and encouragement, and includes a holistic approach to nutrition as well as mental and spiritual balance (Cohen & Bodeker, 2008; Foster & Keller, 2008; Westgate, 1996). The adoption of this approach in the 21st century is a very personal decision however, including a change in lifestyle to achieve a balanced well-being that includes physical, mental and spiritual wellness (see Figure 2.2 for a list of the more important aspects of this lifestyle change, also see Smith & Puczko, 2008).

The term 'wellness' became a catchphrase in America in the 1950s through the pioneering work of Dr Halbert Dunn, whose research in preventive medicine started a new ambitious health movement in the United States. The core idea was to prevent illness through a health-conscious lifestyle and use the individual potential of vitality (DWV, 2006). This lifestyle and preventive health management approach can include some or all of the more widely known well-being tools that have been identified to date (see Figure 2.2). Dunn's idea was picked up during the late 1970s by other doctors in America who used the term wellness to campaign for preventive alternatives to the traditional health system and for a healthy lifestyle (DWV, 2006). A common definition of the term *Wellness* derives from this campaign: a combination of good health or fitness and experienced well-being (*well*-being + fit-*ness*). However, this commonly accepted American origin of the word 'wellness' is strongly rejected by the *German Wellness Association* (DWV,

```
Wellness literature, CDs and music
Spa holidays and travel
Stress management/reduction of tiredness, and chronic fatigue
Regaining of energy, revitalisation and stimulation of circulation
Relaxation and re-establishment of the body's equilibrium
Regeneration and re-invigoration
Physical and mental restoration
Stimulation of loss of body mass, weight loss management
Beauty treatments from basic facials to cosmetic surgery
Elimination of toxins from the body/organism
Wellness and holism (holistic medicinal products) shops
Vitamins and other supplements
Herbal teas, Massages and Aromatherapies
Organic food (now termed spa cuisine)
Sheer wellness indulgence to reach an overall state of wellbeing
```

Figure 2.2 Common tools for achieving a heightened state of well-being
Source: After Dunn (1961).

2007), who argue that the term wellness has been around for centuries in Europe in describing a healthy condition. A study of the English etymology confirms this, as the word 'well' was used in the form of *weal* and *wealnesse* was a term used in the 17th century for the state of well-being (Tremplin, n.d.). Further arguments relate to the term of 'medical wellness', which can be interpreted from two viewpoints: medicine as well as alternative medicine. This allows for two different definitions:

- *Wellness (alternative medicine)*: Wellness is generally used to mean a healthy balance of the mind, body and spirit that results in an overall feeling of well-being. This approach discusses wellness from an alternative medicine perspective where wellness means being much more than just disease free.
- *Wellness (medicine)*: Here, wellness refers generally to the state of being healthy. The aspects of wellness that fit firmly in the realm of medicine are discussed in Reference.com (n.d.) or in Cohen and Bodeker (2008).

In standard dictionaries wellness is described as the quality or state of being healthy in both body and mind. It is the result of deliberate effort as well as an approach to healthcare that emphasises preventing illness and prolonging life, as opposed to the emphasis on the treatment of diseases in the current medical tradition (Cohen & Bodeker, 2008: 3–25). However, as the term wellness is used in many different contexts the meaning of the term can vary from country to country. In Germany the term wellness has also been applied to many common consumer items from 'wellness yoghurt' to 'wellness socks' and 'wellness cars' to 'wellness muesli bars' (BioFach Trendreport, 2004), as much as to health and wellness spa treatments. Many products are labelled with this term without having special distinctive qualities in the sector of health or nutrition (Tremplin, n.d.).

The most common interpretation relates to health and lifestyle choice and the range of possibilities of how to achieve and maintain wellness (see Figure 2.3). Fitness and wellness are closely related, with fitness more dominated by sporting activities. The wellness philosophy extends the sports dimension into many other

Health & Wellness Tourism	Health & Wellness Spas	Lifestyle Management	Body & Soul Benefit	Therapeutical Value
			Medical Treatments	Cultural Settings
		Prevention of Illness	Cosmetic Treatments	Natural Settings
			Physical Activities	Socialising
	Hot Spring Spas	Relaxation, Stress Management	Body & Soul Benefit	Renewable Resource
			Medical Treatments	Cultural Settings
		Rehabilitation and Recovery from Illness	Beneficial Minerals	Natural Settings
			Therapeutical Value	Socialising

Figure 2.3 Components of health and wellness tourism
Source: The authors.

aspects of lifestyle quality by embracing holistic aspects, therefore constructing a nearly inexhaustible multi-functional potential. The recent extension of the wellness concept into mental and social criteria within a new definition of the wellness message is only one example of this change according to the German Wellness Association (DWV, 2006), while Cohen and Bodeker's *Health Spectrum* model (2008) shows how the spa experience may be integrated into both complementary (eastern holistic) and medical traditions in the search for perfect health.

Environmental sustainability on a personal level

In a more general sense, the wellness concept is related to ensuring personal environmental sustainability in our daily lives. As we are part of the environment we need to be sustained too and the wellness movement seems to have materialised at the right time to reinforce this point at the individual level. During the early 1990s, the trend towards visiting spa and wellness facilities started to develop quickly and created a renewed popularity for health retreats and resorts both with and without natural hot and mineral springs. With the wellness movement taking a firm hold, for ailing hot spring spas this meant an unexpected revival and many spas underwent modernisation and redevelopment of their facilities after years of decline. Until the wellness boom many mineral spring spas, hot or cold, struggled to survive especially in countries with warmer climates. However, with this new recognition of the importance of health and wellness, people consider exposure to elements such as the sun and sea as not being sufficient for their attainment. For those who enjoy a sun tan, the health and wellness spa industry also offers 'safer' ways of achieving a tanned look.

Consumer Expectations and Growing Health Awareness

A very basic philosophy that can be encountered in many countries is provided by Valenza (2000) in summing up the interaction between humans and hot or cold mineral springs:

> Taking the waters embodied a basic and important but fleeting relationship with the natural environment. People searched for the healing powers of nature and found them in mineral springs. They sought companionship, leisure and alleviation of bodily pain in an inspiring and comforting environment. (Valenza, 2000: 6)

The wellness movement has also brought an increase of relevant information and literature relating to the 'Spa Experience'. Books, magazines and DVDs, as well as the internet triggered a heightened awareness towards long-term benefits by taking care of body and soul and achieving spiritual harmony at the same time as physical well-being. This information supply has gathered some momentum and now appears to multiply at an exponential rate. This is partly due to the fact that it is not an easy task to choose from the wide variety of spas, as every spa visitor has different expectations. The health and wellness spa industry has to endeavour to cater for most of these expectations in order to attract increasing numbers of clients.

The different categories of spas are directly linked to these customer expectations by some of the more common elements listed below:

- natural environment and scenic beauty;
- time-out in a peaceful and calming setting;
- relaxation in comfort and quality;
- benefits for health and well-being;
- feeling safe and cared for;
- thermalism, balneology, hydrotherapy;
- serviced by professionally trained and qualified staff; and
- value for money.

Expectations and customer demands are the foundations on which the spa and wellness industry is currently building a vast supply of facilities for every taste and income level. Rest and recreation or time out are needed more often these days in order to cope with mounting stress levels in a fast-paced professional as well as private environment. The time span of treatment in which a healthier lifestyle might be achieved should preferably last for a few weeks in order to get the full benefit from it. But some people only have a few hours during which they need to receive as much benefit as possible and therefore cram every suitable treatment into a shorter time period, hoping that this will help to achieve better health, better looks and a more relaxed mental state to return to jobs and family.

Individual motives for using spa and wellness facilities are numerous; they range from a genuine need for some time-out and a well-deserved rest and recreation period to the desire to achieve longevity through rejuvenation. Reasons for visiting a spa are not necessarily the same as the expectations of benefits and results. A list of examples for both is shown in Figure 2.4.

In the Western world the majority of followers of the wellness movement appear to come from the generations of baby boomers, who in the early 1990s (1) started to reach an age where many of them became concerned for their health and

Reasons for Visit	Expectations of Results
Balneology	Feeling better physically and mentally
Beautification	Increasing fitness
Change of lifestyle	Improve overall health
Detoxification	Maintenance of good health
Hydrotherapy	Prevention of illness
Medical benefits	Purification
Physical treatments	Rejuvenation
Rehabilitation	Relaxation
Socialising	Recovery
Stress management	Safe environment
Thermalism	Stimulation
Wellness/wellbeing	

Figure 2.4 Reasons for visiting a spa facility and expectations of results
Source: The author.

well-being and (2) were in a financial position to ensure that they regained or maintained their health and fitness. One of the reasons for this may be the concern (e.g. in the United States) that the demographic bulge of citizens born between 1946 and 1964 would overload the Medicare system when this generation starts to collect their benefits (Mosquera, 2003). In Australia the baby boomer situation looks somewhat less gloomy: it is often said that this generation appears to be the richest, healthiest, best-educated and most self-centred generation of modern times. Whatever the reason for their changed approach to health and wellness, including tourism based on this, they simply are too big in numbers and too aware of their influence for the market to ignore.

At the same time however, the wellness label has been used to excess in some countries in trying to influence this market. No longer applied only to spas and other forms of wellness facilities, in Germany any item with a wellness sticker seems to sell better, even at a higher price. A 20% 'wellness fee' is quite common and consumers do not seem to mind paying. The wellness label has also been used as a practical accessory to add value to inferior facilities and products as well as in attempts to get rid of old stock. In summary, the term wellness is used by all and sundry like a guarantee for quality, but in many cases without appropriate legislation to protect the consumer.

The Diversity of Spas

One of the key elements in health and wellness facilities is water. Be it a part of the wider landscape (rivers, lakes and waterfalls, the ocean), decoration in the background of health facilities (pools, fountains) or an active treatment component (natural hot and mineral springs), water is an important component of health and wellness spas. More and more spas without natural hot and mineral springs are investigating ways of tapping into geothermal or other water resources that may possibly be available underground in order to enhance their business (Davidson, 2008, personal communication; Ellis, 2008). Also, a trend towards natural looking environments or settings has long been evident in many spa hotels and resorts. Swimming pools and whirlpools are built to look as natural as possible, with rock pools the most typical and widespread design commonly used for leisure settings in many countries.

Classification of spa types or categories including natural hot and mineral springs shows that the list of activities and claimed benefits is extensive, but with some overlap in the details being unavoidable due to different interpretations of the same resources according to country or provider. The outline list provided here is in alphabetical order, not in order of popularity or importance for health and wellness. Also listed are spa-related items such as spa fashion and food:

(1) *Adventure spas*: rugged relaxation that offers activities such as skiing, hiking, mountain trekking, rock climbing, canoeing, kayaking and white water rafting, combined with resting in hot spring water afterwards, and delicious spa cuisine and wines.

(2) *Airport spas*: attractive for long-distance travellers in transit, these offer short massages and refreshing treatments. Recognising that air travel is stressful, more airports are adding spas and wellness centres for travellers (Brown, 2006). Relaxed departure and treatment for jetlag and dehydration for travellers as well as crew members should prove beneficial.

(3) *Amenity spas*: located at a resort or hotel, this is usually a facility that has expanded from an exercise or workout area. Facilities and exercise equipment are free for guests to use, and outside guests are welcome for a membership fee (Leavy & Bergel, 2003).

(4) *Bed & breakfast spas*: accommodation catering for more intimate relaxation. Usually offer some fitness equipment and beauty treatments. Similar to inn spas but on a much smaller scale or outsourced to nearby day spas.

(5) *Boot camp spas*: demanding road to wellness including marathon hikes, fitness classes, pool workouts and power yoga with the result of a leaner physique.

(6) *Boutique spas*: day spas that claim to be special sanctuaries to refresh body, mind and soul. They offer a relaxing atmosphere, a luxurious interior, and professional, licensed and certified technicians who administer treatments.

(7) *Casino spas*: spas with a casino on the premises. These spas tend to be luxury oriented and often do not admit guests under 18 years of age (Spafinder. com, n.d.).

(8) *City hotel or urban spas*: located in metropolitan hotels, some of these spas are open only to hotel guests, while others are accessible to the general public (Spafinder.com, n.d.).

(9) *Club spas*: these are basically fitness centres with regular clients, which increasingly cater for beauty and wellness.

(10) *Corporate spas*: men's spas for relaxation and rejuvenation while they are at work – mixing business with pleasure.

(11) *CosMediSpa*: cosmetic treatments on a medical level; beauty spas offering from basic treatments to cosmetic surgery (Spafinder.com, n.d.).

(12) *Cruise ship spas*: a more recent addition to the offers of relaxing marine getaways, which includes spa and wellness elements and a health food/spacuisine.

(13) *Cultural spas*: these combine local history with native traditional treatments, and encourage immersion in the local socio-cultural settings, for example Sukko Cultural Spa and Wellness Centre in Thailand (Altman, 2000).

(14) *Day spas*: also known as beauty spas – formerly known as beauty salons, recreated to suit current market demand, they do not require overnight stays – treatments are administered during normal business hours (Brown, 2006). They provide beautifying, relaxing or pampering experiences that can last an hour or may take a whole day. Can be freestanding or connected to health clubs, hotels or department stores (Spafinder.com, n.d.).

(15) *Dental spas*: similar to or included in medical spas, these establishments provide professional medical treatment in a relaxing atmosphere with additional treatment offers.

(16) *Destination spas*: assist in leading a healthier lifestyle through spa treatments, exercise and educational programming; a spa cuisine is served exclusively

(Brown, 2006); other facilities include conferences and wedding receptions as well as treatment for depression (Spa Life, 2006) and spa honeymoons for bonding experiences (Brown, 2005). These are establishments that focus exclusively on lifestyle improvement, health enhancement and self-renewal in the company of like-minded people (Spafinder.com, 2006).

(17) *Eco spas*: provide visitors with a serene 'green' spa experience. These environmentally friendly destinations believe that personal health begins with global health – this extends to the way in which they create spa products (all organic ingredients), solar power and waste water systems (Brown, 2005). These spas are set in a natural or protected area and have a major commitment to incorporating environmentally friendly practices such as organic gardening, water conservation and ecological building design. They also encourage sensitivity to the natural environment and wildlife through education of spa-goers, and may also promote the well-being of local people and culture by preserving indigenous healing traditions and ingredients (Spafinder.com).

(18) *Family spas*: benefit the health of the whole family with educational programs for the younger generations on how to take better care of themselves (SpaAsia, 2005).

(19) *Fertility spas*: some hot springs have a reputation for increasing fertility and are visited by women hoping to fall pregnant.

(20) *Fitness spas*: the result of melding spas and fitness clubs into one location (The Spa Association, 2005).

(21) *Flight spas*: passengers (who can afford it) arrive at their destinations refreshed, recharged and rejuvenated. Available on some jet charter flights (AsiaSpa, September/October 2005) and possibly on some private jets.

(22) *Health spas*: can be an all-inclusive resort or hotel that offers health-enhancing programs and spa treatments. Includes fitness facilities indoors and outdoors as well as holistic and new-age health elements, spa cuisine and spiritual supervision by trained staff. Health spas can be totally fitness oriented but also a combination of health, wellness, leisure and fitness components. The spa itself defines the term it wishes to use. Health spas can also be medical spas.

(23) *Health resorts*: combine the very best in medicine and healthcare with the most rejuvenating spa treatments and hospitality. Some health resorts advertise healing of the body and energising the spirit and may provide spiritual healing to deal with stress, as well as help to cure disease.

(24) *Holistic spas*: holistic treatment includes psychotherapies, herbal medicine, homeopathy, hypnotherapy, acupuncture, iridology, reiki, naturopathy, Ayurveda, sound healing, aroma therapy, massage and hydrotherapy (SpaAsia, September/October 2005).

(25) *Hospital spas*: hospitals are turning to spa treatments to ease the discomfort of their sick and terminally ill patients. Pain management practitioners have become firm believers in spa treatments (Leavy & Bergel, 2003).

(26) *Hot spring spas*: most of these are known for their curative powers and therapeutic benefits.

(27) *Inn spas*: accommodation with fitness facilities and available beauty treatments. Similar to hotel spas and resort spas but possibly on a smaller scale or outsourced to neighbouring establishments.

(28) *Longevity centres*: emphasise prolonging and improving the quality of life, especially at a time when the baby boomers insist on preserving their youthful appearances and living a longer healthier life (Leavy & Bergel, 2003).

(29) *Maternity spas*: offer pre- and post-natal massage, and aroma therapy for mother and baby during pregnancy and childbirth (Discover Spas, 2006).

(30) *Medical spas*: offer treatments under medical supervision and, depending on the facilities, cosmetic surgery is performed by professionally trained surgeons. Medical spas can also be day spas that perform high-tech treatments such as laser resurfacing, photo facials and Botox alongside traditional spa services (Brown, 2006). A destination or day spa that offers traditional and complementary medical services supervised or administered by medical professionals. A spa may specialise in diagnostic testing, preventive care, cosmetic procedures or a combination (Spafinder.com, n.d.).

(31) *Medi spas*: blend traditional medical expertise with spa luxury and innovation. Medi spas are becoming trusted venues for executive physicals, health and wellness programs, cosmetic treatments, dentistry and dermatology (Brown, 2005). Any facility, usually a day spa, that offers both medical treatments and spa therapies (Spafinder.com, n.d.).

(32) *Mineral spring spas*: can be cold, warm or hot water, with curative powers due to beneficial mineral content and can also be taken internally. Natural mineral and thermal waters are used in thermalism including hydrotherapy and balneotherapy.

(33) *Mobile spas*: the spa that comes to the customer, dial a treatment. Therapists visit complete with massage tables, pedicure carts, etc. They offer relaxation in venues from movie sets to hotel rooms and offices (Brown, 2005). A spa with or without a fixed facility that employs professionals who can travel to a client's home, office or another preferred location to perform treatments (Spafinder.com, n.d.).

(34) *Residential spas*: (see spa communities) living at the spa with all the facilities and treatment options close by.

(35) *Resort spas*: spas located within a resort or hotel, a guest amenity – not the sole or primary attraction (Brown, 2006), and not a spa resort. A spa facility offering treatments and services at a vacation destination that also offers activities such as golf, tennis, horseback riding, skiing, water sports and children's programs (Spafinder.com, n.d.).

(36) *Retreats*: there are various retreat types incorporating spa and wellness facilities and treatments: body mind health retreats, business retreats, health retreats, meditation retreats, mountain retreats, spa fitness retreats, spiritual retreats, yoga retreats.

(37) *Retreat spas*: located in scenic, secluded surroundings removed from the hustle and bustle of big cities or as an added feature at a hotel or country

club. These spas offer traditional spa services that invigorate the body and mind.

(38) *Seaside spas*: holiday resorts and hotels with spa facilities or a spa resort near the coast.

(39) *Spa communities*: provide aging baby boomers with a healthy lifestyle, centred on spa going. More premier spas are offering residential properties built around healthy living activities and amenities such as hiking/biking trails, workout rooms, fitness classes, healthy cuisine, spa treatments and health education (Brown, 2005).

(40) *Spa cuisine*: spa-inspired food is gaining increasing popularity by offering a large variety of diet options and of course cook books to replace the more recent diet literature.

(41) *Spa fashion*: comfortable clothing suitable for yoga classes as well as for day and evening wear with fashionable accessories from spa shops.

(42) *Spa resorts and hotels*: accommodation specifically for spa guests and offering a variety of treatments and activities for health and wellness.

(43) *Thermal spas*: warm and hot spring waters are used for thermalism including balneological treatment and bathing.

(44) *Urban spas*: these help maintain a healthy equilibrium in big cities and usually have at least 10 treatment rooms with different relaxing themes. The client is supposed to feel as if he or she is not in the middle of a metropolis but in a virtual environment more conducive to relaxation. Very popular in large cities like Shanghai, Tokyo or New York.

(45) *Weight loss spas*: spas that offer weight management programs including indoor and outdoor exercise under supervision and guidance to raise fitness levels and improve well-being through managed weight loss.

(46) *Wellness centres*: one-stop wellness centres are on the rise. Consumers can find spa and medical services all under one roof (Leavy & Bergel, 2003).

(47) *Wellness music*: for harmony and relaxing to reach a total state of relaxation (Nüchtern, 2002).

(48) *Wellness spas*: these focus on increasing and maintaining the overall wellness of their visitors through classes, workshops and activities that teach one to achieve and live a healthy lifestyle (The Spa Association, 2005). These spas appear to overlap into MediSpas and beauty spas.

(49) *Yoga spas and retreats*: provide meditation lessons, sound therapy sessions, restorative posture classes, finding a balance for body, mind and soul to increase physical health.

As mentioned earlier some of these spa types are related or similar because they have been defined by people from identical backgrounds but from different countries. Nevertheless, there is a large variety of spa types, and within the individual spas there are specialisations meant to make them unique and distinct from their competition and thus more attractive. The International Spa Association (ISPA, n.d.) lists 10 spa domains (Figure 2.5) with water heading the list. The order of criteria is not mandatory, but facilitates a broad categorisation of the different

> **10 Spa Domains**
>
> 1. **Waters:** The internal and external use of water in its many forms.
> 2. **Nourishment:** What we feed ourselves: food, herbals, supplements and medicines.
> 3. **Movement:** Vitality and energy through movement, exercise, stretching and fitness.
> 4. **Touch:** Connectivity and communication embraced through touch, massage and bodywork.
> 5. **Integration:** The personal and social relationship between mind, body, spirit and environment.
> 6. **Aesthetics:** Our concept of beauty and how botanical agents relate to the biochemical components of the body.
> 7. **Environment:** Location, placement, weather patterns, water constitution, natural agents and social responsibility.
> 8. **Cultural Expression:** The spiritual belief systems, the value of art and the scientific and political view of the time.
> 9. **Social Contribution:** Commerce, volunteer efforts, and intention as they relate to well-being.
> 10. **Time, Space Rhythms:** The perception of space and time and its relationship to natural cycles and rhythms.

Figure 2.5 Spa domains as determined by ISPA
Source: International Spa Association (n.d.).

types of spas, with more spa types being planned and established. The wellness industry is extremely adaptable and is watching the market closely while keeping potential customers informed with relevant information.

Information overload?

Wellness literature is everywhere in the modern marketplace for health and wellness spa tourism. In fact there is so much that it is becoming increasingly difficult to judge the quality of the information, let alone make an educated decision in relation to the tempting propositions (see Chapter 8). To help the potential customer find what he or she is looking for is equally difficult, because many people new to the health and wellness boom do not know themselves what might be best or, indeed, what they are actually looking for. In this situation basic information explaining spa and wellness terminology can help a lot and some of this can be found on the web simply by using the keyword 'spa glossary'. Looking through a glossary should point the potential spa and wellness client in the right direction as well as educate the client on treatment terminology. The next step could be to check with local spa and wellness providers to get an idea about prices and time allocation. From checking with the local day spa it is only a small step to investigate other opportunities, but for the more reluctant spa visitor the first step is probably the biggest.

Alternatively, the potential spa-goer in many European countries (e.g. Germany, France, Austria and Hungary) can obtain such information from their personal GP (general practitioner), who will usually recommend or even prescribe individual treatment methods, which are then administered by trained medical staff at health and wellness centres. Under the wellness umbrella in Europe there is room for a large variety of treatment options. Many of them are non-medical treatments and it is generally up to the individual to make up his or her mind as to the benefits, based on the information provided.

Having noted this plethora of sources, the literature search for this volume has shown that the majority of publications in print referring to spas and wellness are very recent. Many coffee-table books appeared around the mid–1990s, with a noticeable increase at the beginning of the new millennium, and adding to the variety of information they contain are glossy 'spa magazines' informing the readers about everything luxurious and beneficial for their health and well-being. A few researched examples are Spa (Canada), AsiaSpa (Hong Kong), SpaAsia (Singapore), Spa Life (Australia), Spa World (UK), Spa Finder (USA) and Haus & Wellness (Germany), all of which have only been published for a few years. Other countries offer their own magazines and new publications will certainly be available as the health and wellness spa tourism revolution gathers even more momentum (Chapter 8).

In European countries such as Germany however, market strategists suggest that the wellness movement has reached its peak, because the term wellness has been attached to too many consumer items through the marketing imperative and is losing its credibility. To be taken seriously genuine members of the health and wellness spa industry need to develop their focus further and communicate this to their clients on a face-to-face basis to distinguish themselves from dubious providers. The recommended new key factor for wellness marketing is therefore a health-oriented lifestyle with clear focus as well as foresight (DWV, 2006).

Current International Trends in Spa and Wellness Tourism

The trend of indulging in a relaxing environment has turned into a global movement but one with a significant difference from the original concept of health and natural hot and mineral spring spas, which mainly specialised in rehabilitation. The new emphasis lies in the prevention of disease and in the maintenance of good health instead of cures, with high expectations regarding health improvements even if there are no specific health problems. Mind and soul are also catered for along with the body in many spas using a holistic approach of creating harmony for those in need, including new-age treatments as well as the more traditional rehabilitative therapies. The main centre of attention at present appears to be natural healing methods incorporating Asian treatments accompanied by the esthetic appeal of Eastern lifestyles and culture, which are in great demand. Therapies of Asian origin are often combined with European balneotherapy and hydrotherapy as well as sport and fitness facilities to offer a diversity of options in order to attract as many customers and clients as possible. Nearly all spas cater for beauty aspects with special signature treatments to ensure that there are no missed opportunities.

The worldwide consumer focus is 'back to nature' and a natural lifestyle paired with a high disposable income and the intention to spend it on personal rewards instead of saving assets and funds for the next generation. As mentioned earlier, in the Western world a majority of followers of the wellness movement seem to come from the generations of baby boomers. This is confirmed through research by BioAnalogics (2001), which states that the wave of retiring baby boomers is providing positive news for the wellness industry through the presence of healthier, more active, more vigorous and more influential individuals than in any other older generation in history. This makes the baby boomers the core market for the wellness industry with a growing interest in new age remedies and alternative treatments. This particular consumer group is in search for new ways to escape work-related stress, family pressure, growing health concerns or just plainly enjoying retirement, and is willing to achieve this by spending time in spa and wellness resorts and hot spring spas of their choice. With this particular focus group in mind the new health and wellness spas and hot spring resorts of today include golf courses and other extensive sports facilities as well as a dedicated beauty industry and boutique shopping as additional attractions.

Wellness holidays and time-out are now a mega-trend with room for continuous growth in the future (Figure 2.6). As encouragement the spa industry now involves awards for the best resort spas, wellness summits, spa conferences, international spa and wellness trade fairs, and spa academies. The Philippines for example has a spa therapy school (Sanctuario School of Spa, Manila) that teaches

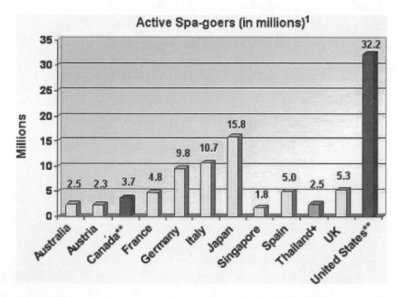

Figure 2.6 2006/2007 spa visits according to projections based on population figures for adults 18 years and over, derived from the US Census Bureau's International Database. Survey results (except for Canada and the United States) are based on the 2007 ISPA Global Consumer Report. The Canadian and US results are taken from the 2006 ISPA Spa-goer Study conducted by the Hartman Group
Source: ISPA (2007).

the ancient art of oriental healing through those who practise it. The new trend in spa suites as an ultimate personal luxury within a garden spa concept by far exceeds the almost spartan nature of the usual massage room. In recreations of Royal Thai Salas, guests are treated to private courtyards with massage platforms and lily ponds (Chapman, 2005). Spa suites have become so luxurious that they far exceed appointment levels of the average hotel room and are seen as changing the future of hotel and resort design as we know it.

Medical tourism is another fast-growing sector in the health and wellness spa industry (PATA, 2005). Before around 2000 it was hardly mentioned by the media at all, as a search of the LexisNexis database of major world media sources shows (Table 2.1; Eades, 2010). According to LexisNexis, the number of articles in the world's media that mentioned it rose from practically zero around 1990, to around 50 a year by 2000, and over 2300 at present. Much of this rise has come just in the last five years, from 2003–2008.

Table 2.1 Number of references to 'medical tourism' in major English language news sources 1992–2008

Year	Number
1992	8
1993	14
1994	26
1995	14
1996	12
1997	35
1998	103
1999	26
2000	49
2001	95
2002	151
2003	234
2004	548
2005	737
2006	1349
2007	2335
2008 (January–August)	1850

Source: Eades (2010).

Many destinations in Asia provide foreign-trained doctors and advanced medical services, including top-class hotels for the recovery period. Including flights the price for major surgery is still lower than in the countries of origin of the medical tourists if they come from the USA and Europe. An indication of this trade can be seen in the following list (PATA, 2005):

- India, over 150,000 medical tourists per year;
- Thailand, up to 1 million medical tourists per year;
- Malaysia, over 85,000 medical tourists;
- Singapore, targeting 1 million foreign patients by 2012.

The incentive here is a lower cost (50–70%) for cosmetic and other surgery combined with shorter waiting lists and the welcome from countries catering for the growing demand, but this is also combined with healing practices that use spa facilities and hot water.

In fact, water, wellness and the health of humans have always been closely linked, on the whole quite obviously but sometimes also in rather obscure ways. It looks as if old-fashioned water treatments have made a significant comeback and the internet, current magazines and recent books indicate that anything involving water in any form or at any temperature has been embraced by the spa industry again and is up and running.

> Many people's lives continue to become more complex and fast moving, as they try to balance the demands of careers, families, and self development, while being bombarded with aspirations and role models and surrounded with pressures. No wonder increasing numbers or people are taking the waters or are searching for waters that heal. (Ryrie, 1999: 26)

With the increasing possibilities for changes in lifestyle there is also an increasing anxiety and concern to miss out on something important. The addictive character of wellness-related offers and their compact timing potential fit into situations where time is rare and the fear of 'missing out' is great (Nüchtern, 2002). Because of the internet much more spa and wellness-related information is being made available for people to make their decisions at home, not at travel agencies. With this growing wealth of information it may become increasingly difficult to choose, as there is such a diversity of offers catering for every taste and demand. Escapism is one of the reasons for visiting a place where relaxation, recharging and reviving are priorities combined with a change of scenery to help achieve well-being. Spa facilities advertise the great escape to a tropical oasis with ancient therapies and modern comfort as a way of unwinding and renewing mind and soul. The Australian Spa Life magazine features a directory for spa escapes. Selling points range from aroma therapy to Zen Buddhism, including much water, serenity, tranquillity, nature, and lately, safety considerations. The prime condition is that the client is leaving the everyday world behind – unfortunately the client has return after escaping for a while, but anticipates doing so in a stronger condition.

Emerging types of spa and wellness facilities

Corporate spas and wellness

Men are also gradually becoming more adventurous and willing to experiment with spa treatments. For them it greatly depends on the right first impression, or it is back to the 'no frills' gym for the more macho types. However, with the new corporate spas it will be easier for the reluctant ones to try first together with colleagues and friends. The practice of male corporate relaxation using hot springs has always been used in Japan, where groups of company employees go out together and share a relaxing bath in an *Onsen* with food, drink and general merriness along with reduced inter-personal boundaries (to a certain degree). This Japanese way of using thermal springs for health and wellness is a model that has already found followers in the world, and typical Japanese bathing facilities have been established in many countries (e.g. Maruia Springs – New Zealand, Sparadise and Peninsula Hot Springs – Australia and Ten Thousand Waves – Santa Fe, New Mexico).

Eco spas and geo-wellness

Eco spas will be more in demand in the future in line with the rising awareness about sustainable development and management on a global scale. Geo-wellness along with pristine nature is a major draw card in the wellness tourism industry, with water and intact natural environment as its main features. This means that many older hot spring spas will be back in business, using their unique geothermal resources to create more aqua parks and water landscapes to attract visitors. Eco spas with an indigenous cultural influence and traditional medicinal ingredients also combine well with cultural spas. A growing number of spas might jump on the eco spa bandwagon – both from an operational and a marketing standpoint (Brown, 2005). The trend to involve nature on several levels gives rise to the term 'geo-wellness', relating to our natural environment as a significant element in the quest to find well-being for body, mind and soul.

Weight management and detox spas

Rising health awareness will create future opportunities in the area of weight management, especially in societies with a high percentage of obesity. Detox spas will attract more clients who want to detoxify their bodies in a pleasant environment and learn about lifestyle management. To quit smoking or alcohol while receiving beneficial spa treatments to regain health and fitness could be the best way of starting a new healthier life. The return of the 'fat farm' looks likely in conjunction with serious detox facilities. People who want to lose weight in a controlled environment and get rid of addictive habits such as drugs, alcohol and smoking do not have to go into rehab – they take a wellness holiday at a trendy spa. However, according to Leavy and Bergel (2003) the fat farms of today and tomorrow will not be run like boot camps anymore, but will be in line with destination spas and health spas, although 'outsiders' may not be accepted to attend the facilities.

Medical wellness

The aspects of holism are widely incorporated in the field of medical wellness. In Germany the term medical wellness is seen as a serious trend, which in conjunction with holistic wellness concepts gives rise to an expectation of increased numbers of visitors over the next three to five years. Medical competence and qualified staff are seen as essential elements for success (DWV, 2006).

One important trend indication is the emphasis on the combination of physical well-being and focused self-motivation, which gives new impulse to the wellness industry. Included in these modifications of the current emphasis of the physical side is the increased focus towards mental and spiritual fitness, resulting in higher energy and vitality and thus leading to a higher quality of life. Another new trend in the German wellness scene is the experience of togetherness. Social group experiences of a positive nature in the age of globalised contacts are *en vogue* (DWV, 2006).

Air travel wellness

Wellness during travel has become a growing concern of the industry. Treatments for a relaxed departure, jetlag and dehydration are already the wellness contributions of airport spas at many airports worldwide. The services offered range from fast and uncomplicated treatments like short massages to luxurious indulgence. Airport spas make a lot of sense for international travellers. Long times in transit, early check-ins and delayed departures create a large consumer potential with a variety of demands. But the actual travel time in the air can be even longer and more stressful for passengers. While air travel wellness in the form of making spa facilities available before or after flights (Virgin Touch Spa, Qatar Air Premium) is now being considered by more airlines, on-board services (of course only for passengers in business and first class) in the shape of fancy 'spa kits' filled with exclusive designer cosmetics to keep fresh during long flights are becoming generally available. The economy travellers have to make do with so-called spa kits that are supplied by a number of airlines (e.g. JAL, Qatar, Cathay, Singapore) and usually include nothing more than a hairbrush, eye mask, toothbrush and paste, socks and earplugs. Some spa kits also include moisturisers, lip balms and hot towels. This is supposed to help one stay refreshed during long flights, but has really nothing to do with health and wellness spas other than through the name.

With more people flying more often to further destinations some cabin space may as well be allocated for spa on-demand treatments. Some private jet charter companies already offer Flight Spa Services to their rich and famous customers. Hollywood celebrities and oil and corporate tycoons are now purchasing wide-bodied jets and fitting them out like luxurious hotel rooms: among conference rooms and movie theatres there is of course a spa on board (Spa Asia, November/December 2005). Making spa facilities available on commercial airlines could encourage a lot more people to travel, knowing that they have an opportunity to arrive in a more relaxed and refreshed condition after long transcontinental flights.

Wellness food

Spa cuisine will further specialise to complement every health program and diet and will continue to play an important role in reaching physical well-being. The new types of health food have undergone many refinements and are now offered as nourishing taste sensations, which help the body shed excess weight by keeping a healthy balance. But apart from the spa cuisine offered at restaurants and resorts there is a developing trend for healthier food in general among people who have started to manage their personal well-being. New shops with a variety of healthy, organic food and large selections of vitamins, minerals and herbal teas, to name just a few, are opening even in smaller towns to cater for a growing demand by health-conscious consumers, with or without associated spas.

Home spas

Home redecorations will incorporate more wellness elements to achieve an environment that encourages relaxation and assists in maintaining well-being. In the past swimming pools and home gyms were common, but the wellness movement now extends into the design of internal living spaces to create a more permanent feeling of well-being. This is partly due to the fact that consumers are becoming more educated and aware of possibilities to deal with stress and pressure and thus are able to manage their lifestyles.

Budget spas

Future spa development will tap into a large market of potential customers who need to be convinced that they receive value for their money, but perhaps not in extremely luxurious facilities. Spa franchises will branch out to reach the greater mass of budget customers and not only cater for selected groups of affluent clients who expect the highest standards of luxury environments. There will always be a budget version that caters for a majority who do not expect extravagance but effective treatments at a reasonable price. Brand names always come with a price tag. For many people the prestige image is not a priority, and they will refuse to pay for a name attached to something they can get 'next door' at the same quality, but without the expensive packaging. Once the spa industry can rid itself completely of the reputation of 'only for the rich and famous' the wellness boom will find new ways to cater for the widest variety of clients possible.

Summary: The Wellness Movement in the Future

The current lifestyle of many people is resulting in a lack of fitness and obesity caused by physical inactivity and poor eating habits – a cycle that is very hard to break without help and motivation. With more education and awareness regarding a healthier lifestyle many people worldwide will gain from the wellness boom over time. There are millions of future customers for products of the wellness industry, whether it is a holiday at a hot spring spa, a wellness resort or day spa, or just buying vitamins at a pharmacy. Already a US$250 billion business, Pilzer (2002) predicts that sales of vitamins and other health-related items will grow to over $1 trillion annually within 10 years. With so much room for expansion over the next decade hopefully we will be seeing more fit and healthy people as a result of the wellness revolution, as Pilzer describes this mega-trend. And he is not the only one looking at the big picture in immense financial figures. The India Times (2004) published a similar prognosis about organic lifestyles, wellness homes, wellness offices and wellness travel, 'holism shops' and wellness stores, which will create the next trillion dollar fortune for the new millennium. The fact that a health and wellness revolution is underway is also confirmed by McDermott (2004) and Crossley (2003) in articles about business opportunities and emerging markets in the health, nutrition and fitness sectors:

> A key factor expected to drive growth is increased health awareness in both developed markets, such as North America, Japan and Western Europe, and also in emerging markets, such as Eastern Europe and Asian markets including China, Indonesia, India and the Philippines. Health awareness is expected to underpin the continuing consumer trend towards self medication, as preventive medicine is deemed the more economic and convenient option over the increasingly high costs associated with visits to healthcare professionals. (Crossley, 2003: 1)

Fitness centres of the past have expanded and now include more upmarket wellness facilities and, in some cases, medical facilities due to the increased demand for wellness-related activities. Ordinary beauty salons which changed their branding to 'day spas' and hot spring resorts were granted a new lease of life; consequently resulting in a boom for spa hotels and resorts and hot spring spas worldwide. These trends build on existing spa centres with a vast extension into anything even remotely related to health and well-being. Pharmacies are offering more variety in supplements with a tendency towards natural healing. People are spending fortunes on vitamins and herbs in health boutiques, which have evolved from former health food shops.

Wellness, however, is more than hot springs and thermalism, spas, medical tourism, and sauna and fitness facilities. It is a comprehensive multidimensional lifestyle concept (Adams, 2003) incorporating all of these and more, which is invoked by many people in order to find a way out of deteriorating eating habits, lack of fitness and resulting declining health. Wellness is about balance in multiple domains, is relative, and is subjective and perceptual (Adams, 2003). However, market research into current industry trends is already demonstrating clearly a strong consumer focus towards a healthier lifestyle based on these factors, thus giving confidence to further spa and wellness developments. Therefore in conclusion, it appears safe to assume that the wellness industry has indeed a very bright and prosperous future, mainly due to the as yet untapped market segments of people who are just learning about opportunities for improving their health.

Chapter 3

Use of Natural Hot and Mineral Springs Throughout History

PATRICIA ERFURT-COOPER

Introduction

Ancient health and wellness spas were frequently linked to natural thermal springs and this association was often based on belief in the healing powers of water. This chapter describes the historical use of natural thermal spring water over time by providing examples of hot spring locations selected from over 60 countries. In order to demonstrate not just the magnitude of human use of thermal springs since the beginning of recorded history but also the significance of their benefits for health and well-being, it was deemed essential to include as many countries as possible.

The history of hot springs and their use as thermal spas has worldwide origins and dates back to the earliest civilisations (LaMoreaux, 2005). The first human interactions with geothermal phenomena such as hot springs are placed in the realms of prehistory and cannot reliably be documented due to a lack of written records. Any knowledge and information about the use of natural hot springs and the various bathing customs from these times have been passed on through oral transmission from one generation to the next, if it exists at all. Attempts to pinpoint the origin of the first organised bathing cultures for this book therefore proved difficult, as did the identification of many ancient customs and traditions related to the use of thermal springs for health and wellness spa tourism. Much of the historical analysis is therefore informed guesswork, leaving considerable room for speculation.

The maximum acceptable timeframe backed by written records reaches back to approximately 3000 BC (Table 3.1), but fixing even this point proved to be difficult due to conflicting dates and the absence of reliable data. (*Continued 59*)

49

Table 3.1 Historical timeframe of hot spring use worldwide

3000 –1700 BC	Indus Valley, Pakistan	The Indus Valley civilisations (e.g. Mohenjo-Daro and Harappa) are likely to have used thermal springs at that time, as the Indus Valley includes areas abundant with natural hot springs, which are still utilised for various purposes
1680–1193 BC	Anatolia, Turkey	The Hittite Empires are said to have used hot springs for recreation and therapeutic treatments (Özgüler & Kasap, 1999)
1430 BC	Lipari – Sicily, Italy	Stone-lined ponds with thermal spring water channelled into them were probably used for therapeutic thermal bathing (Cataldi *et al.*, 1999)
1050–771 BC	Huaqing, China	Huaqing Hot Spring was the favourite thermal spa of emperors of various dynasties (Schafer, 1956) and appears to have been reliably documented
1000 BC	Meso-America	The Maya Empire dates back to about 1000 BC and included Mexico in the Yucatán Peninsula, Guatemala and parts of Belize and Honduras. Due to the many hot springs in these countries it is assumed that they were used by the Mayas for various purposes as they were a highly advanced people
c. 1000 BC	Western Europe	West European tradition based on worshipping of sacred and healing springs
8th century BC	Italy	Pompeii was founded around this time and thermal water was used to heat buildings and baths within the city
7th century BC	Greece	Homer mentions thermal waters as do several classical authors later, e.g. Hippocrates (460–377 BC), Plato (427–347 BC), Aristotle (384–322 BC) and Pliny the Elder (23–79 AD) (Cataldi *et al.*, 1999)
8th century BC	Loutraki, Greece	The thermal waters of Thermae (Loutraki today) were 'revitalised' around this time for athletic games held at Corinth (Fytikas *et al.*, 1999)
863 BC	Bath, England	The legend of the founding of Bath tells that Bladud, father of King Lear, was cured of disease by immersion in the warm springs found there
750–500 BC	Italy	North of Rome the Etruscans used thermal bathing and other hydrothermal by-products (Cataldi & Burgassi, 1992)

(Continued)

Table 3.1 *Continued*

c. 700 BC	Japan	Dōgo Onsen in Ehime Prefecture on the island of Shikoku is one of the oldest and best-known *Onsen* hot springs in Japan and may have been used approximately 3000 years ago or even as early as during the Jomon and Yayoi periods as per the following websites: www.japaneselifestyle.com.au; www.japannuclear.com; www.jnto.go.jp
c. 420 BC	Greece	Hippocrates of Kos was the first author who systematically classified the waters and their distinctive properties (Fytikas *et al.*, 1999)
5th century BC	Greece	Hippocrates of Kos treated patients from all over the Mediterranean by using thermal balneology in his famous Asclepian Centre (Cataldi *et al.*, 1999: 89)
5th century BC	Spain	Archaeological evidence indicates that the thermal springs of Archena may have been used by early Iberian settlers (Balneario de Archena, n.d.)
500 BC	Guatemala	The Maya kingdoms may have used hot springs (Altman, 2000: 40)
3rd century BC	India	Megastenes, an ambassador from Greece, mentioned the medicinal value of Indian thermal springs (Chandrasekharam, 1999; Kalota, 1978)
3rd–2nd century BC	Greece	Greece and other Mediterranean countries traded in geothermal by-products, e.g. kaolin, sulphur, pozzolana, iron oxide, etc. (Cataldi *et al.*, 1999)
2nd century BC	Turkey	Hierapolis was established by Eumenes, King of Pergamon, and in 133 BC the city was bequeathed to the Romans who built large baths around the thermal springs
1st century BC–14th century AD	Roman Empire – later Byzantine Empire	Roman soldiers visited hot springs for thermal bathing on military expeditions (Cataldi & Burgassi, 1992)
c. 120 BC	Aix les Bains, France	The Romans constructed comfortable thermal baths later called *Aquae Gratianae*
84 BC	Aedipsos, Greece	Roman general Sulla underwent thermal treatment after which he backed the construction of a 'hydrotherapeutic thermal establishment', the Thermae of Sulla (Fytikas *et al.*, 1999)

(Continued)

Table 3.1 *Continued*

49 BC	Lisbon, Portugal	The Cassian Spas under Quinto Cassio and Lucio Cassio were built while they were representing Julius Caesar (Picoto, 1996)
1st century BC	Jordan	Jordan Valley Springs were described in classical literature by Roman and Byzantine historians (between 1st century BC and 6th century AD) as having healing properties, especially for leprosy (Cataldi *et al.*, 1999: 39)
1st century BC	Pompeii, Italy	The Forum Thermal Baths were established under the Roman dictator Lucius Cornelius Sulla (138–78 BC)
c. 1st century AD	Palmyra, Syria	The sulphur springs Efca were used for health purposes in 'Biblical Times', and are still in use today
1st century AD	North America	Yellowstone National Park – Shoshone Indians are said to have lived around the hot springs and used them for healing. It is assumed that other tribes also made use of thermal hot springs where available and that their use goes back much further than has been documented
1st century AD	Croatia	The first Roman thermae is built in Varaždinske Toplice and named *Aquae Iasae*
43 AD	Bath, England	The initial development of the thermal bath is thought to coincide with the Roman invasion of Britain in the year 43 AD
50 AD	Austria	Baden near Vienna was founded by the Romans and named *Aquae* (www.baden.at)
70 AD	Bath, England	The Romans built a more sophisticated bathing complex including temples at Bath and named it *Aquae Sulis*
81 AD	Vizela, Portugal	Roman baths were built under the reign of Titus Flavius (Picoto, 1996)
2nd century AD	Middle East	The springs at Hammat Gader were first exploited by the Romans who converted the site into thermal baths around the 2nd century AD (Archaeological World, 2006)
2nd century AD	Israel	Tiberias – Romans first exploited the hot springs and converted the site into thermal baths (Israeli Foreign Ministry, n.d.)
5th century AD	Caucasus, Georgia	The city of Tbilisi founded by King Vakhtang on the site of a hot spring with healing powers

(Continued)

Table 3.1 *Continued*

552 AD	Japan	Introduction of Buddhism and purification through immersion using thermal springs (Hotta & Ishiguro, 1986; Von Furstenberg, 1993)
c. 700 AD	Japan	Yamanaka *Onsen* hot spring of Kaga was founded near a temple
765 AD	Germany	First written record of Aachen, previously named by the Romans *Aquis villa*
870–930 AD	Iceland	The time of settlement and according to the Sagas thermal spring water was used for washing and bathing (Hróarsson & Jónsson, 1992)
c. 800–1200 AD	Kyushu, Japan	Yamaga *Onsen* in Kumamoto Prefecture is thought to have a history of 1200 years, discovered during the Heian Period (794–1192)
1137 AD	Cieplice, Poland	Cieplice Śląskie was mentioned in historical records and is regarded as Poland's first health resort (Omulecki *et al.*, 1996). However, the legend says that the hot spring was accidentally discovered by Prince Boleslaus the Tall in the year 1175 AD while chasing a wounded deer, which regained its strength from the warm water (www.ceti.pl)
1178 AD	Hungary	A hospital was built on today's Hotel Gellert site (Altman, 2000)
12th century AD	Hungary	Budapest – Knights of the order of St. John engaging in curing the sick settled in the area of today's Lucác's Bath
1281 AD	Cieplice, Poland	Historical record of the use of thermal spring water by the Knights of St. John of Jerusalem to cure diseases (Cataldi *et al.*, 1999: 275; www.ceti.pl)
c. 14th century AD	Belgium	A health resort was founded in the city of Spa
1300s AD	New Zealand	Maori have used healing hot springs since their colonisation of New Zealand
1349–1350 AD	Czech Republic	Discovery of Karlovy Vary [Karlsbad] according to legends during a deer hunt with emerging settlements close to the thermal springs (Altman, 2000)
1359–1389 AD	Turkey	Bursa – the Ottomans built a large complex of domed baths during the reign of Murat
14th–16th century AD	Europe	Early development of spas on sites of ancient medicinal hot springs

(Continued)

Table 3.1 *Continued*

1417 AD	Italy	Ugolino de Montecatini (1348–1425), the founder of balneology in Italy, recommended the use of the mineral waters of Montecatini (Altman, 2000, www.tuscany-charming.it)
1458 AD	Korea	Oonyang Spa in use (Altman, 2000)
1485 AD	Portugal	Caldas da Rainha hospital is founded by Queen Leonor, after discovering natural hot springs with healing properties
15th century AD	Germany	Annual visits to curative hot spring centres en vogue among wealthy citizens
15th century AD	Budapest, Hungary	Early records about miraculous springs at the site of the Hotel Gellert, which was built much later and opened in 1918
1500s AD	America	First recorded history of European style hot spring spas in North America
1502–1533 AD	Peru, South America	The hot springs of Cajamarca were used by the Inca ruler Atahualpa and his court, as oral history indicates
1522 AD	Karlsbad, Czech Republic	The water of the Mill Spring was used in the 16th century mainly for bathing (www.karlsbad.cz). Around 1522 the drinking cure of Karlovy Vary was introduced (Altman, 2000)
1541 AD	America	Spanish explorer Hernando deSoto is claimed to be the first European visitor of Arkansas Hot Springs, then named the valley of the vapours
1545 AD	Brazil, South America	Caldas Novas Hot Springs first mentioned in Spanish publication
1550 AD	Peru	First European (Spanish) written record of hot springs and their use
1558–1603 AD	Bath, England	During the Elizabethan era Bath was revived as a spa with improvements to the thermal baths (Ros, 2006) and began to attract members of the aristocracy who spent the fashionable 'Saison' in Bath
1565 AD	Budapest, Hungary	Construction of Király Thermal Bath started by Arslan, Pasha of Buda
16th century AD	Budapest, Hungary	Budapest – Rudas Thermal Bath was built under Turkish occupation
1697 AD	Taiwan	Hot springs first mentioned in a manuscript (Beihai Jiyou), but not fully developed until 1893

(Continued)

Table 3.1 *Continued*

17th century AD	Spa, Belgium	Town of Spa developed further
17th century AD	Europe	Spas in existence throughout much of the European continent
17th century AD	China and Japan	Physicians evaluate and classify several medicinal springs
1700 AD	Nantali, Finland	Thermal springs with healing properties were known and used
1709 AD	Japan	First Japanese medical study of hot springs
1722 AD	Caldas Novas, Brazil	*Bartolomeu Bueno da Silva* discovered thermal springs in the area while searching for gold, and settlers made use of the hot springs
1737 AD	Belgium	'Demonstrations on the usefulness of the Mineral Waters of Spa' published
1741 AD	France	First thermal baths were built in Avéne
1776–1784 AD	France	Aix les Bains – Victor Amedée II, King of Sardinia, established the thermal baths, called the 'Etablissement Royal des Bains'
1790 AD	America	Saratoga Hot Springs (New York State) began offering spa treatments and accommodation
Early 18th century AD	Hungary	First water analyses were carried out in Budapest on the orders of Maria Theresia (Archduchess of Austria, Queen of Hungary and Bohemia)
19th century AD	America	Hot spring therapy became popular
19th century AD	Azores, Portugal	Spa resort of Furnas is already a popular tourist destination; however, locals may have used the thermal springs since the islands were first settled during the 15th and 16th centuries
Early 1800s AD	Austria	Baden near Vienna redeveloped bath traditions and established Spa town policies
1826 AD	Hawaii	An early missionary and historian, William Ellis, describes the use of a hot spring-fed crater lake in the Kapoho area (Woodruff & Takahashi, 1993)
1832 AD	Arkansas, USA	The hot springs area in Arkansas became the first national reserve in the United States
1834 AD	Chile	*Jahuel* Hot Springs, which is considered one of Chile's oldest thermal centres, was visited by Charles Darwin in 1834

(Continued)

Table 3.1 *Continued*

1859 AD	New Zealand (South)	Hanmer Springs discovered and in use since then
1862 AD	Australia	The first discovery of the Hepburn Mineral Springs by white settlers (Menadue, 1972)
1873 AD	Namibia, Africa	The potential of the hot springs of Warmbad (Bela Bela) was discovered by white settlers, but the thermal waters were known earlier to local tribes who used it for their curative benefits
1876 AD	Uganda, Africa	HM Stanley, African explorer, visited Mtagata Hot Springs in Uganda – local inhabitants appear to have used thermal springs for their curative properties (Cataldi *et al.*, 1999)
1878 AD	New Zealand	Rotorua – the Priest Spring is discovered by a catholic priest, who cured his arthritis in the hot spring
1879 AD	Australia	Helidon Spa in Queensland was first developed (Anon, 1910)
1882 AD	Canada	Banff Hot Springs discovered and used by European visitors
1884 AD	Hungary	Budapest – Lucac's Bath Spa Hotel was built
1891 AD	Bulgaria	The first 'Law for the preservation of mineral springs' was enacted in Bulgaria and springs were declared a national property by law (Tsankov & Kamarashev, 1996)
1891	Kyrgyzstan	The *Issyk-Ata* sanatorium in Kyrgyzstan was built in the year 1891 as a thermal health facility
1892 AD	Portugal	The first official regulation concerning the Portuguese waters is published (Picoto, 1996)
1895 AD	Australia	Moree/NSW – the first bore into the Great Artesian Basin at Moree was completed with the water gaining fame for its use in Moree's hot artesian baths, which are said to heal numerous ailments (www.heritageaustralia.com.au)
1895–1945 AD	Taiwan	Taiwan's hot springs developed under Japanese occupation
Early 1900s AD	Australia	Hepburn mineral springs reserve (Victoria) popular with visitors 'Taking the waters'

(Continued)

Table 3.1 *Continued*

Early 1900s AD	Turkey	Kangal healing springs first attracted attention when a shepherd hurt his foot only to see it healed by the water of the spring (www. psoriasisfishcure.com)
1911 AD	Czech Republic	Karlsbad reached the highest number of spa guests in its history with 70,935 people cured in the year 1911 (www.karlovyvary.cz)
1925 AD	Hungary	Hajdúszoboszló – thermal springs with healing powers were discovered while drilling for oil (www.hajduszoboszlo.hu)
1929 AD	Bulgaria	The Bulgarian Balneological Society was set up and united specialists from different scientific fields (Tsankov & Kamarashev, 1996)
1931 AD	Japan	Japan began more scientific research programmes in hot springs
1940 AD	America	Most American hot spring resorts went into decline
1940s AD	Tbilisi, Georgia	Establishment of the Tbilisi Balneological Health Resort
1945 AD	Taiwan	Hot spring culture went into decline
1970 AD	France	Aix les Bains – restoration and enlargement of the thermal baths
1975 AD	Tunisia, Africa	The Tunisian Office for Thermalism (*Office du Thermalisme*) was established and located in the capital Tunis
1976 AD	Iceland	A geothermal power station was built in Svartsengi and shortly after an employee noticed the healing properties of the (clean) waste water, which had created a large warm lagoon (Ólafsson, 1996)
1978 AD	Bath, England	The old thermal baths closed down and bathing was prohibited due to public health concerns over the purity of the spring water
1979 AD	Hungary	Budapest – Daytime Hospital with complex thermal bath facilities was established in the Lucac's Thermal Bath
1982 AD	Huaqing, China	Ruins of the imperial hot spring pools in Huaqing are discovered and restored
1987 AD	Blue Lagoon, Iceland	The first public bathing facilities opened

(Continued)

Table 3.1 *Continued*

1989 AD	Czech Republic	Karlovy Vary or Karlsbad – new era of development of balneology in the Thermal Spring Valley
1994 AD	Portugal	Forty health spas using natural thermal and mineral waters are in operation. Of these 17 are permitted by government regulation to treat dermatologic diseases (Picoto, 1996)
1994 AD	Hainan, China	National Mineral Storage Resource Committee verified and approved thermal springs in Guantang as suitable for tourism and medical treatment, but the thermal spring was well known as early as the interim between the Qing Dynasty (1644–1911) and the Republic of China (http://eprints.qut.edu.au; www-chaos.umd.edu; www.wanquanriver.org)
1995 AD	Japan	Hospitals integrate spa medicine using thermal springs
1997 AD	Argentina	After successful drilling for thermal water the first thermal spa in the northeast of Argentina was opened in 1997
1999 AD	Taiwan	Hot spring culture makes a comeback due to large-scale promotion
2004 AD	Mývatn, Iceland	In the northeast of Iceland the Mývatn Nature Baths (*Jarðböðin við Mývatn*) opened
2005 AD	Victoria, Australia	The first stage of the Peninsula Hot Springs Centre, a new development with natural hot springs, opened on the Mornington Peninsula south of Melbourne. Further expansion is currently underway (www.peninsulahotsprings.com.au)
2005 AD	Blue Lagoon, Iceland	A new clinic for psoriasis sufferers opened using natural geothermal seawater
2006 AD	Bath, England	Opening of the new Thermae Bath Spa

Notes: Tracing back the use of hot springs to *pre*-prehistory is largely dominated by speculation and guesswork. In many countries indirect proof of the use of geothermal resources by ancient peoples is suggested by the location of sites in areas with geothermal manifestations. It can be therefore argued within reason that native peoples used natural hot springs and their geothermal by-products (Calderón, 1999). Anything beyond written records and reliable oral transmission is only supported by the logical preference of humans to settle near natural hot springs for their various benefits. Despite the lack of concrete evidence in some cases it can safely be assumed that wherever people came across natural warm water, they would have made use of it for cooking, bathing or healing.

Because of the presumption of the early prehistoric use of natural hot springs, which provides no written proof, the main focus is on historical facts, where these can be established beyond reasonable doubt. However, the first civilisation on this list is an exception, as their history is largely undecided and their decline is not sufficiently explained to date. But extensive research of hydro-geological data from Pakistan has led to the conclusion that the presence of clusters of thermal springs in the Indus Valley should be taken into serious consideration when analysing the history of the Indus Valley civilisations.

Nevertheless, careful evaluation of existing records shows that the history of natural thermal spring use has global roots and that only very few countries (Denmark and Sweden are among the rare examples) have no direct access to geothermal springs. We may reliably attribute hot spring use to the Hittite Empire (1680–1193 BC; Özgüler & Kasap, 1999), and probably to the Indus Valley civilisation (3000–1700 BC), while the Minoans of Crete, the Sicilians, Egyptians, Chinese, Japanese and Meso-Americans used hot and thermal springs at about the same time as the Hittites or earlier.

Between different countries the customs, culture and traditions regarding the use of water show similarities at a basic level given that the resource is ubiquitous. However, individual regions and peoples developed and used their bathing facilities in a range of ways most suitable to their own needs. In an almost culture-independent way many hot springs became renowned for their miraculous healing powers and these still have at least one story or legend covering the original healing event, which is often used as 'cultural–historical' back-up for promotional material in tourism. To substantiate this several legends will be used as reference throughout this chapter in order to provide some insight as to why many hot spring areas have not lost their reputation and appeal for health and wellness tourism across the ages.

Some hot spring destinations offer a wealth of historical, cultural and geoscientific information (some of it available in published sources), but many do not. Many of the quoted sources in this chapter derive from the internet because a large number of hot springs can only be researched using this medium given that existing information on them is either of a marketing nature or anecdotal, which lends itself to this form of communication. Few discussions are currently available in the academic research literature, and what there is concentrates either on a relatively few commonly known thermal centres (generally from a Eurocentric point of view) or on the nature of health and wellness tourism from a sociological/psychological standpoint. This chapter documents and analyses the actual experience of over 60 countries that have natural hot springs. Not all of these have a history of hot and mineral spring use going back thousands of years and not all of them have reliable recordings of past hot spring use, but this does not mean that local people did not make use of the thermal resources in their immediate neighbourhood where these existed, or that their experience is not important in informing our understanding of health and wellness spa tourism.

Thermal Spa History: European Origins

Social bathing in thermal spring waters has origins in many countries. Before the Romans, who seem to be given all the credit at least in Europe for the introduction of 'civilised' thermal bathing facilities or *thermae*, other ancient civilisations indulged in the use of natural hot and mineral springs for personal well-being and hygienic reasons. In Europe, the Greeks and Turks made use of local geothermal resources as did the peoples of Jordan, Israel and Iraq. The Jordan Valley hot springs for example are mentioned in a number of classical works by Roman and Byzantine geographic historians and chroniclers (*Strabo, Pliny the Elder, Josephus Flavius, Origen, Ptolemaeus, Jerome, Epiphanius, Eusebius* and *Antoninus of Placentia*) between the 1st century BC and the 6th century AD. According to Jaffé *et al.* (1999) all these writers discussed the Jordanian hot springs in detail for their curative powers and their reputation for the successful treatment of various illnesses.

Rome

Although large parts of the bathing culture and the use of hot water and thermal springs in the European tradition have been attributed to the Romans, this is mainly due to their presence in many countries other than their own during the time of the maximum use of these resources in the empire, rather than their actually inventing the tradition. However, the ruins of thermal baths throughout the empire (and their re-use in later traditions) not only gives an impression of the extent of these establishments, but also demonstrates how strong their influence was. Thermal bathing facilities found in the occupied provinces from Wales to the Euphrates were designed by the Romans to their specifications, which means they could be used to provide recreation and therapeutic benefits for the military as well as for the civilian population. The Romans preferred to utilise natural hot springs if they were available nearby as they did in the case of Bath in the United Kingdom and Aachen in Germany as well as in many other locations in the European continent, although they would heat the water if necessary. Their bathhouse culture and architecture is widely distributed and many of the historical Roman 'spa towns' and resorts are still in use or have been maintained and restored in the recent past. Examples of these are *Bath* (UK), *Trier*, *Aachen* and *Baden* (Germany), *Aix les Bains* and *Rennes les Bains* (France), *Teplice* and *Karlovy Vary* (Czech Republic), *Bagno di Romagna* (Italy), *Kyustendil* (Bulgaria), *Budapest* (Hungary), *Archena* (Spain) and *Chavez* (Portugal), to name a few (Table 3.2). Some of these will be described in more detail in this and later chapters.

The Roman use of thermal springs originally derived from the Etruscans (Melillo, 1995) as well as from the Greeks during their conquering days, putting the experience of these peoples to use for their own benefits. Later the custom of thermal bathing took hold in the whole of the Roman Empire. Cataldi and Burgassi (1992) outline the rise and decline of bathing and other uses of geothermal resources in the Mediterranean Sea area and start their approximate chronology between the 8th and 6th centuries BC, stating that the Etruscans were using hydrothermal products and practising thermal bathing well before the Romans extended their reign over the whole of Italy as well as over neighbouring countries around the Mediterranean. Thermal balneology or thermalism was then developed systematically by the Romans from the 2nd century BC, often determined by the location of existing hot and mineral springs. While the Romans were known to have used artificially heated water as well in their thermae and bathhouses, they preferred natural hot springs and are known to have strategically planned their settlements in close proximity to these special natural resources (Aquae Sulis – Bath, Aquae Granni – Aachen).

The Romans acquired a great deal of existing local knowledge about the use of hot and mineral springs wherever they went, and the 1st to 3rd centuries AD saw

Table 3.2 Examples of Roman spa towns still in existence as thermal spring destinations today

Historical Roman spa towns and their Latin names	
Aachen (Germany)	*Aquae Grannii or Aquis Granum*
Aix les Bains (France)	*Aquae Gratianae (Aquae Allobrogum)*
Aix en Provence	*Aquae Sextiae*
Baden Baden (Germany)	*Aurelia Aquensis or Aquae*
Baden (Austria)	*Aquae*
Baden (Switzerland)	*Aquae Helveticae*
Baden (Germany)	*Aurelia Aquensis (Aquae Aurelia)*
Badenweiler (Germany)	*Aquae Villae*
Bath (England)	*Aquae Sulis*
Budapest (Hungary)	*Aquincum*
Caldes de Malavella (Spain)	*Aquae Voconis*
Caldes de Montbui (Spain)	*Aquis Calidae*
Chavez (Portugal)	*Aquae Fluviae*
Chaudfontaine	*De Calida Fontana*
Chaudes-Aigues (France)	*Calentes Aquae*
Cutilia (Italy)	*Aquae Cutiliae*
Hammam R'Irha (Algeria)	*Aquae Calidae*
La Chaud (France)	*Calidum*
Trier (Germany)	*Augusta Treverorum*
Varazdinske Toplice (Croatia)	*Aquae Iasae (Aquae Viva)*
Vichy (France)	*Aquae Solis*
Villa Fasila (Spain)	*Aquarius Vicus*
Wiesbaden (Germany)	*Aquae Matticae*

the height of their use in their empire (Figure 3.1). From the second half of the 4th century AD the use of geothermal resources in Western Europe declined and continued to fall rapidly during the 5th and 6th centuries, entering a long period of inactivity extending beyond the end of the first millennium AD due to the decline of the Western Roman Empire. This was punctuated only by the survival of specific spring use in particular places, notably Llandrindod Wells in Wales (Gregory, 1992: 59, 80). In the Eastern Roman or Byzantine Empire thermal springs

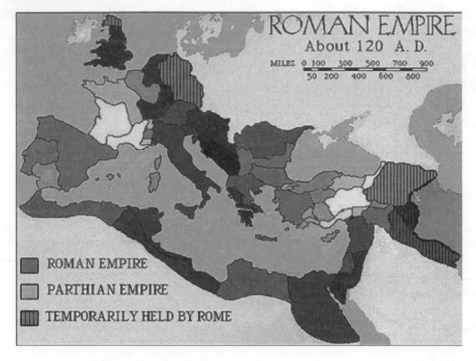

Figure 3.1 The extent of the Roman Empire
Source: http://intranet.dalton.org/groups/Rome/RMap.html (Author subscription to educational resource).

remained in use over a considerably longer period of time, eventually being taken over by the Turks and other successor states. In the long list of architectural remains the Romans left behind, one of the main features seems to have been the inclusion of at least one bathhouse or thermae in each settlement, where Roman colonists and soldiers would relax and recover from the unpleasant duties of a life spent occupying other countries.

For the Romans thermal waters were so popular that the wealthy and powerful had hot spring water brought to their private homes from distant springs. This was also the case in Japan and China because the curative powers associated with thermal springs created a high demand for hot spring water containing naturally occurring minerals (Talmadge, 2006). However, this practice of 'home delivery' could only be afforded by very rich citizens, mainly of the aristocracy. The Romans (as did the Japanese) initially reserved their domestic and foreign bathing facilities mainly for members of the army, using natural hot springs to soothe and heal injuries from the battlefields. A brief insight into the history of bathing (Register, 2008) can be gained by observing that around 43 AD the Roman public began to use thermal baths as a way of providing rest and relaxation, and by the year 300 AD there were over 900 baths throughout the whole empire. The following quote provides an interesting comparison with modern-day spa facilities and their use (Box 3.1):

Box 3.1 Roman bathing tradition

A visit to the bath would traditionally last several hours and include exercise, bathing and socialising. Roman baths were very social places and, in addition to a gymnasium area for exercising, the largest baths often included gardens, a library or reading room, restaurant, bar, marketplace, even museums or theatres that featured jugglers, acrobats and recitals. Bathers moved from room to room at a leisurely pace, enjoying the company of fellow Romans and all the amenities the baths offered. (Spa Life, n.d.)

Roman bathhouses were staffed with male attendants (balneators) who were knowledgeable in balneological treatments as well as trained to take care of the grooming of customers, including hygienic applications. These balneators were called upon to assist with washing, scrubbing, hair extractions and massaging of the Roman elite (Figure 3.2).

Greece

Greek mythology is rich in legends where thermal springs are connected with Greek deities like *Artemis Thermia* (Diana), the patron saint of all springs. This connection also included the Nymphs (Naiades), who were in charge of the spas. Apollo was also known as *Thermios Apollo*; according to legend he used thermal springs for their curative properties to heal the sick (Katsambas & Antoniou, 1996). Not only were sources of water in Greece usually linked to the divinities of the Earth, with temples dedicated to *Asklepios* (Aesculapius) also offering thermal baths (Melillo, 1995), but the importance of both drinking and bathing in water for health was emphasised by early Greek writers such as *Homer, Hippocrates of Kos* (460–377 BC) and Asklepios (Altman, 2000; Bullard, 2004). Homeric poems from the 7th century BC describe several different types of baths (cold and warm), providing evidence for their utilisation in ancient Greek civilisation.

During the pre-Hippocratic period (5th–6th centuries BC) medicine was practised at Asclepeia, the temples of *Aesculapius*, God of medicine. Treatment was carried out by the priests of the temples, which were purposely built in the vicinity of hot springs to be able to include hydrotherapy in the therapeutic process (Katsambas & Antoniou, 1996). Several classical authors such as *Plato* (427–347 BC), *Aristotle* (384–322 BC) and *Pliny the Elder* (23–79 AD) also refer to the beneficial use of thermal water (Cataldi *et al.*, 1999). In the 5th century BC Hippocrates of Kos treated patients from all over the Mediterranean by using thermal balneology in his famous Asclepian Centre (Cataldi *et al.*, 1999: 89; Monti, n.d.). Hippocrates also authored an encyclopaedia on all aspects of medicine and a systematic classification of thermal waters listing their individual distinctive healing properties and other useful medical/therapeutic criteria (Fytikas *et al.*, 1999; Katsambas & Antoniou, 1996).

Figure 3.2 The 'Balneator' with his tools of the trade (a set of strigils and sponge) depicted in a painting by Lawrence Alma-Tadema in 1877
Source: Alma-Tadema (1877).

The ancient Greek city of *Thermae* (now called Loutraki – the name Thermae comes from *Artemis Thermia*, the protectress of hot mineral springs) is famous for its natural mineral waters and thermal springs and was one of the first health resorts in history as a therapeutic and tourist town (Loutraki City Guide, n.d.). The thermal waters and their healing properties were first mentioned by the Greek historian *Xenophon* in his narration on the Corinthian or Boeotian War (396–371 BC; Loutraki City Guide, n.d.). Excavations of this area verify that later the Romans built magnificent thermal complexes at the site for their recreational purposes. Today Loutraki is known as the metropolitan centre of thermalism and health tourism in Greece, and the medicinal waters, which are described as 'the waters of life', are seen as a symbol for a natural healthy lifestyle (Municipality of Loutraki, n.d.).

According to *Plutarch* (Ploutarchos) healthy people also visited thermal spas and health resorts for leisure and recreation. *Edipsus* (Edypsos) was one of these places (and still is today), which offered very efficient spa facilities and at the same time was a popular recreational and vacation centre in the ancient Mediterranean world (Katsambas & Antoniou, 1996).

Turkey

Turkey has a long tradition of using thermalism or hot springs for health benefits and personal well-being, dating back to the period between 1680 and 1193 BC when the Hittite Empire used such springs for recreation and therapeutic treatments in the geographic region of Anatolia (over 700 hot spring areas are useable today). Bathing therefore is an old and important Turkish tradition and even today every city or town in Turkey has several public baths, warmed either by hot springs or by central heating (Özgüler & Kasap, 1999), a practice similar to Japanese customs.

During the 2nd century BC the city of *Hierapolis* was founded, probably by the Hellenistic ruler *Eumenes II* (Current Archaeology in Turkey, 2007), although there appears to be a traditional thought that Apollo was the original founder of the sacred city of Hierapolis (Sacred Destinations, 2007). It is also believed that the name Hierapolis may derive from Hiera, who was the wife of a legendary ancestor of the kings of Pergamon. However, Özgüler and Kasap (1999) suggest that the name Hierapolis, which means Holy City, was chosen for the many temples throughout the city. The hot springs at Hierapolis (today called Pamukkale, and World Heritage listed since 1988) still draw vast numbers of visitors who seek the benefits of their healing properties, with which the springs have been attributed at least since the Greeks were in control of the area, and for the visual attraction of the white travertine terraces (Geology Chapter, Figure 5.4). After the Greeks and Romans left Turkey many of the thermal establishments in the city of Hierapolis were ruined by wars, earthquakes and negligence. However, the Turks gradually restored and redeveloped the Roman ruins with typical Turkish architecture (Özgüler & Kasap, 1999), while the remains of a large 2nd century AD Roman bath for example now serve as a museum.

One of the historical and popular showpieces often used in travel advertising with respect to Turkey is the sacred thermal pool in Pamukkale. This 'sacred pool' is constantly fed by natural hot springs with water at a pleasant temperature and beneath the surface is littered with fragments of ancient marble columns (Sacred Destinations, 2007). However, the pool is presently located within a private hotel complex (Turkish Odyssey, 2004) and can only be accessed against a fee for a period of 2 hours unless the visitor stays at the hotel.

In *Bursa* the Ottomans built a large complex of domed baths during the reign of *Murat* (1359–1389 AD), which today is one of Turkey's most popular hot spring destinations. On the other hand, the unusual *Kangal* hot springs were first noticed by local inhabitants in the early 19th century when a shepherd with a foot injury healed his wound in the thermal waters of the spring. Following this rather miraculous healing more people took an interest in the location and started to construct pools and simple buildings (Blue World Travel, 2006; Kangal Hot Springs, n.d.). The springs of Kangal are said to have no equal in the world for the treatment of psoriasis. Small fish inhabiting the hot springs assist in remarkable relief from this severe skin disorder by removing the dead skin and thus encouraging the growth of new healthy skin (Wave, 1999). China, Korea and Japan also offer this particular 'fish cure' for skin afflictions.

Northern and Western Europe

European bath and spa towns have experienced centuries of use and disuse, boom and bust, sacking and looting, as well as plagues and diseases, fires and floods. Many hot spring areas were well known by local inhabitants before the Romans arrived, but although the locals recognised these natural resources to a degree for their therapeutic potential they rarely built thermal baths for their recreational use as did the conquering Romans. The first decline in thermal spring use in Northern and Western Europe came with the fall of the Roman Empire c. 500 AD when most of the thermal spa centres fell in disrepair. As Altman (2000: 41) puts it the locals were not always in favour of the 'widespread and notorious revelry that often took place at Roman springs'. This decline of thermal bathing lasted nearly a thousand years in some parts of Europe, to a large degree encouraged and maintained by the attitude of the Christian church towards hot spring facilities as centres of loose morals and a breeding ground for venereal diseases. So, despite the fact that the main function of thermal water bathing was for healing purposes and for hygienic reasons, the use of water in general was frowned upon and considered immoral and dangerous (Maier & Fiedler, 2004). However, during the 15th century some thermal springs (e.g. *Bad Wildbad* in Germany) were frequented by clerics and aristocracy alike in spite of any possible risk to their morals (Rumpf & Sollner, 2006). Later, on the return of classical culture during the 18th and 19th centuries the hygienic nature of bathing was rediscovered and sanctioned as an important element for health and wellness. Thermal spas became the place to go and be seen in many countries at this time (Ascensio, 2002). Since then thermal cures have been prescribed by physicians for their therapeutical benefits. The main afflictions treated are rheumatism, arthritis, infertility and skin problems, which in turn has resulted in a whole new type of medical science to develop, including balneology and hydrotherapy, which has been taught for centuries at most medical schools in Europe (Leavy & Bergel, 2003).

Despite the challenging past, many ancient spa towns still exist in Europe today, reflecting the history of natural hot spring use and the strength of the European spa scene. In many areas in the past visits of royalty and their consorts were used to advertise the benefits of hot spring resorts and spa centres, while these days anybody famous will do – actors, politicians and 'socialites'. But even with these additional 'attractions' the reputation of thermalism as being beneficial for health and well-being is upheld in the European tradition by qualified medical specialists experienced in the application of treatments using natural thermal springs. The following paragraphs provide a short overview of the historical background of various thermal spa locations in Europe, which are reviewed and analysed in order to highlight the significance of natural hot springs for human use over time.

The recorded thermal spa history of *Germany* spans nearly two millennia. Around the year 77 AD Pliny wrote about thermal spring areas he visited in Germany, including *Aachen*, *Wiesbaden* and *Baden Baden*, while travelling through Western Europe (Freedman & Waugh, 1996). Aachen (*Aix-la-Chapelle* – city of the waters) was one of the places chosen by the Romans for settlement because they appreciated the hot springs, and called the city *Aquae Granni*, after the Celtic god of water and healing *Grannus* (Mielke, n.d.). Aachen was settled by Celtic tribes until the Romans arrived in the 1st century AD, and in the course of their occupation the Romans established thermal baths for their military forces. Although not reliably documented, it is assumed that the Celts had already used the hot springs for their purposes before the Romans discovered them. When centuries later the spread of Christianity discredited the benefits of thermal bathing, Charlemagne, King of the Franks (742–814 AD), also called Carolus Magnus or Karl der Grosse, kept the bathing culture alive during the early Middle Ages (Mielke, n.d.). Bathrooms were reintroduced as a feature in some castles and monasteries built near thermal springs, which reduced the effort of producing hot water significantly (Die Welt des Bades, n.d.).

During the 15th century AD annual visits to curative hot spring centres became popular again among wealthy citizens throughout Germany. The thermal history of *Wiesbaden* for example also goes back to the Romans, who developed the town into a centre for thermal pleasures including therapeutic benefits, and from the later middle ages two thermal baths offered visitors healing waters for health and wellness. From 69–79 AD the first development of public thermal baths took place under Roman occupation near the natural hot springs of what is now known as *Baden Baden*. At the time the Romans called this settlement *Aquae*. Between 213 and 217 AD under Marcus Aurelius Antonius, the thermal baths underwent major expansions but were nearly completely destroyed during the 3rd century AD by the barbaric Alemannen. Today only about 10% of the original bathing facilities, which were rediscovered in 1847, can be seen, but the town has offered thermal spring water to visitors and locals for centuries (see Chapters 7 and 9). The Roman bath ruins have been turned into a museum, which can be viewed daily (Baden Baden, n.d.).

Austria has several natural thermal spring locations that have historically been used for health benefits and recreation and today has a thriving thermal tourism industry with many hot spring spa centres. The town of *Baden* has been a well-known health resort for nearly 2000 years since the time of the Roman occupation, when the town of Baden was also named *Aquae* in honour of the thermal sulphur springs and their beneficial mineral content; however, it was primarily set up as a thermal bathing facility for the Roman military, not as a normal health resort. The main spring of Baden is called the Roman Spring or the Source Spring (*Ursprungsquelle*), a name that is still used today. Altars were built near the springs and visitors showed their gratitude for successful treatments through devotion to individual gods and goddesses. In a continuation of the bathing tradition, the recently built new spa bathhouse is called 'Römertherme' in reference to the Romans, and is within close proximity of the recently renovated medieval 'Kurhaus', which now serves as a modern health centre. Fourteen sulphur springs form the core of the thermal resource in Baden, delivering some 4 million litres of water a day (Baden Austria, n.d.).

During the 16th century thermal springs with healing properties in the Tyrol region were considered a treasure equivalent to the local silver mines and hunting grounds, although the 18th century brought a decline comparable with other European countries (Kuntscher, 1990). The use of hot springs in the area of what is today called *Warmbad Villach* in Kärnten goes back to the Celts and Romans. During the 16th century the famous physician *Paracelsus* mentioned the healing properties of these hot springs in his book on bathing for health and wellness (Rumpf & Sollner, 2006).

It seems that each German-speaking country has one town called Baden, with *Switzerland* the example discussed in this chapter. The discovery of the thermal springs in the Swiss town of *Baden* is thought to go back as far as 58 BC. A legend tells of a young man who was looking for his goat that had gone missing. When he found the animal it was standing near a rock from which hot water sprang forth. The young man then thought of helping his paralysed wife have a bath in the hot water, and according to the legend she was miraculously healed (Lüscher, 1946). The Romans also knew about the healing properties of the thermal springs of Baden and used them for their benefit after they built an impressive thermal spa centre and gave it the Roman name *Aquae Helveticae*. In more recent times the warm sulphuric waters of Baden have been promoted as a centre of healing through thermalism, indicating successful healing for at least 2000 years (see Figures 3.3 and 3.4).

The Swiss spa town *Bad Ragaz*, a former rural village, has an interesting thermal treatment history; more than 600 years ago the first spa tourists were wrapped in strong fabric and lowered on a rope into a deep gorge (*Taminaschlucht*) that contained hot spring water. This gorge is now accessed via a bridge hewn into the rock face. Bad Ragaz is famous for its spa centres, focusing on the prevention of illness and curing existing medical conditions with the help of highly specialised medical personnel (Rumpf & Sollner, 2006).

France is another European country with a long thermal history and has maintained this supported by the medical elite, who have continued to back the continued survival and further development of thermal facilities (Weisz, 2001). A classic example for the Gallo-Roman spa town heritage is *Aix-les-Bains* (see Figure 3.5). Originally established around 120 BC the baths were constructed in keeping with the architectural style then in fashion (Lund, 2000c). From 1776 to 1784 AD *Victor Amedée II*, King of Sardinia, re-established the thermal baths in Aix les Bains and called them 'Etablissement Royal des Bains'.

Gréoux-les-Bains is a small 'ancient Roman' town with thermal baths and has not lost its popularity over time. According to current information (Provence Beyond, n.d.) the first records of the town refer to the Roman *Nymphhis Griselius* in the year 1084 AD. Like so many other locations with cultural history Gréoux-les-Bains was destroyed several times by barbarian invasions. However, the site of the old Roman baths is now a modern thermal establishment in the spirit of the Roman tradition and the town of Gréoux-les-Bains is an attractive tourist destination favoured for its Provençal location and its hot springs.

Figure 3.3 Advertisement for the thermal centre Baden, Switzerland from the year 1944 claiming specialised treatment for treating rheumatism, sciatica, gout, gynaecological problems, respiratory diseases and rehabilitation after accidents and injuries
Source: ThermalBaden (n.d.).

La Bourboule (see Figure 3.6) and *Vichy* are well-recognised examples of French traditional spas that were established in response to a growing demand for thermal treatments in a stylish environment that offered sophisticated entertainment, therapeutic treatment and five-star accommodations during the 19th and 20th centuries (Mackaman, 2007). The construction of palaces, casinos and opera houses in the vicinity of thermal spa towns was common in France at the beginning of the 20th century. In the year 1913 Vichy had 108,963 visitors and by the year 1921 the town offered 26 first-class hotels and 48 second-class hotels (Office National du Tourisme, 1921).

Figure 3.4 Modern thermal facilities in Baden, Switzerland
Source: ThermalBaden (n.d.).

Figure 3.5 The 'Bathing Establishment' of Aix-les-Bains and the Campanus Arch in 1921
Source: Office National du Tourisme (1921).

The Mediterranean island of *Corsica* is another French location that also has a long tradition of natural hot spring use. During the 8th century AD a medical study on the hot mineral springs in Corsica was undertaken under the patronage of Carlo Fabrizio Giustiniano, Bishop of Mariana; this work generated a comprehensive list of available geothermal resources suitable for medicinal purposes. Prior to this, the Phoenicians, Etruscans, Greeks and finally the Romans between

Figure 3.6 The thermal establishment of La Bourboule in the year 1921
Source: Office National du Tourisme (1921).

238 BC and 400 AD settled on the eastern coast of Corsica and developed their bathhouses in order to take advantage of the beneficial effects of the thermal waters. This has been confirmed by the discovery of the remains of magnificent thermal baths, coins and old pipe works. Centuries later, in the year 1909 a study of the thermal waters of Corsica was published, thus demonstrating the continuous interest in thermalism by the people of the island (Corsica, 2003).

The City of *Bath* in *England* represents a classic example of a long tradition of use of natural hot springs and for centuries has also exercised an attraction as a centre of religion, healing and pilgrimage (Bowman, 1998). The native Britons commonly attributed divinity to water, which included not just rivers and streams but natural springs as well (Ottaway & Cyprien, 1987). Bath's history is also closely linked to the Roman occupation when the springs were used to cater for the battle-weary legions. But the use of these hot springs may go back even further than the Roman occupation; there is a legend that tells of the mythical Celtic King Bladud (*c.* 500 BC) who was suffering from leprosy. Because of his skin condition Bladud left the court and became a swineherd. Some of his animals were diseased, but recovered after wallowing in the warm waters of the swamp at what later became the City of Bath. Bladud followed their example and was cured. This laid the foundation for Bath's reputation for healing hot springs (Bowman, 1998; Bullard, 2004; White, 2000), and from then on it is assumed that the site of the original hot springs of Bath was treated as a sacred site by the Celts, with a shrine dedicated to the goddess Sul.

The Romans knew the springs as *Aquae Sulis* (meaning the waters of Sul) and identified them with their goddess Minerva (Bowman, 1998; Gray, 2003; Havins,

Figure 3.7 Roman bathhouse reconstruction, Bath, England
Source: Photograph courtesy of M. Cooper.

1976). The development of this thermal bath is thought to coincide with their invasion of Britain in the year 43 AD. However, the establishment of a more sophisticated bathing complex including temples did not occur until the year 70 AD (White, 2000). The bathing complex at Bath was a rather generous establishment (see reconstruction in Figure 3.7) compared with the others developed in England and Wales, because the springs delivered virtually unlimited amounts of hot water that attracted not just local visitors but also many religious pilgrims from far afield. After the Romans left Britain the baths of Aquae Sulis were deserted in time, as the Saxons did not show much interest in hygienic pleasures, possibly because they disliked and distrusted anything Roman (Havins, 1976).

During the Elizabethan era from 1558 to 1603 AD Bath was revived as a spa with improvements to the thermal baths and the urban infrastructure (Ros, 2006), and began to attract members of the aristocracy who spent the fashionable 'Saison' in Bath and nearby surroundings (Figure 3.8). From then on declines and revivals alternated, until the spa baths were redeveloped during the 18th century and made the City of Bath again a main attraction for health and wellness spa tourism. In 1978 the old thermal baths finally closed down and bathing was prohibited due to public health concerns over the purity of the spring water. A few years later new boreholes beneath the King's and Cross Springs were drilled to establish a supply of uncontaminated clean water for the planned new development of the resort under the title of the *Bath Spa Project*, which made it possible to reopen the hot springs once more for public use in 2006 after 28 years (Haley *et al.*, 2005; White, 2000). In 1987 the City of Bath was placed on the World Heritage list, which has

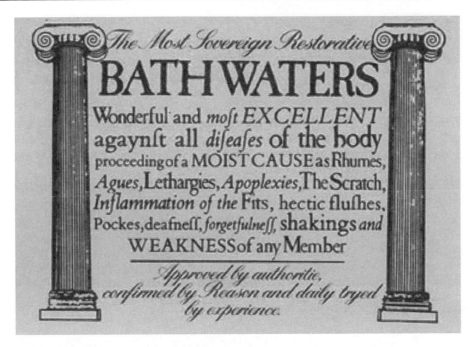

The Most Sovereign Restorative

BATH WATERS

Wonderful and *moſt EXCELLENT*
agaynſt all *diſeaſes* of the body
proceeding of a MOIST CAUSE as Rhumes,
Agues, Lethargies, *Apoplexies,* The Scratch,
Inflammation of the Fits, hectic fluſhes,
Pockes, deafneſſ, *forgetfulneſſ,* shakings *and*
WEAKNESS of any Member

Approved by authoritie,
confirmed by Reason and daily tryed
by experience.

Figure 3.8 Advertising a few centuries ago
Source: Thermae Bath Spa (n.d.), courtesy of Giles White.

proved an additional attraction for tourism (Lee, 2005). For a complete spa history of the City of Bath the following URL (www.thermaebathspa.com) is highly recommended, as it provides an excellent timeline compiled by Giles White, spokesman for the Bath Spa Project (see also Lee, 2003).

Elsewhere in the United Kingdom some spa towns with familiar names remain (e.g. *Llandrindod Wells* in Central *Wales*), but Bath is the only one with genuine hot springs. However, it is still possible to 'take the waters' in places such as *Harrogate*, *Buxton, Leamington Spa* and *Tunbridge Wells* although the popularity of these places for health purposes and social gathering has suffered a significant decline over the years, especially since funding of medical treatments using thermal spring water was discontinued in 1976.

The town of Spa in *Belgium* takes a special place in more recent spa history. It was here in the 14th century AD that a health resort was founded after the discovery of a thermal spring with apparent curative properties, and henceforth the name of Spa was connected to hot spring facilities worldwide. During the 17th century the city of Spa developed further, building on its reputation for hot springs with medicinal benefits. The popularity of thermalism with health and wellness tourism gradually increased in Belgium over the following centuries and became accessible to a larger market. In the year 2004 the new 'Thermes de Spa' opened (Cordes, 2004), offering large-scale thermal pool bathing and hydro entertainment to the public.

Nordic and Scandinavian countries

Iceland is a country rich in geothermal resources and hot springs have been used widely at least since the beginning of the 20th century. Reference to bathing in hot springs is frequently made in the Icelandic sagas, which were written in the 12th–13th century AD (Fridleifsson, 1995), but before that not much had been recorded about their use. However, it may be assumed that if natural hot springs at acceptable temperatures are available close to settlements, especially in a cold climate, people would have utilised them for washing and bathing. At the time of the conversion to Christianity, which was introduced in Iceland in the year 1000 AD at the annual assembly of the Icelandic parliament, many people were baptised on the spot in the cold water at the parliament site. Others, however, preferred the warm geothermal waters of natural springs for their baptism that they knew they would find on their way back home (Hjálmarsson, 1993). This is confirmed by Frazier (2000), who states that the early Christians preferred warm springs for baptism; while it is not clear which country Frazier is referring to, most likely in a cooler climate like Iceland hot springs would have been a preferred option.

Bathing pools in Iceland were neither elaborate nor luxurious; nature prevailed, and the temperature of the hot spring water was enough luxury for the tough Icelanders. However, Snorri Sturlusson (1178–1241 AD), one of the saga authors and historians, is legendary for having created a circular rock pool, *Snorralaug* (see Figure 3.9), on the farm where he lived. This pool has a constant warm water

Figure 3.9 The legendary circular pool 'Snorralaug' on the farm where Snorri Sturlusson (1178–1241) lived, Iceland
Source: Snorralaug (2008), Wikimedia image released by the copyright holder Tommy Bee into the public domain.

supply from a nearby hot spring and it is generally accepted that he built this specially designed outside thermal bath himself; however, according to Fridleifsson (1995) there is no absolute proof for this, despite the fact that Sturlusson was known to be a builder as well. Nevertheless, Snorralaug is considered to be of great historical importance for Iceland.

In recent times Icelanders have constructed thermal swimming pools sourced from hot spring water in every town for the benefit of the population as well as visiting tourists. On the Reykjanes Peninsula just outside of *Keflavik* the Blue Lagoon has been artificially created using waste water from the *Svartsengi* power station built in the year 1976. The water's therapeutic value was recognised shortly thereafter when one of the employees noticed a remarkable improvement of his psoriasis after bathing in the warm waters of the lagoon (Ólafsson, 1996). As a result this facility has been developed as a wellness centre as well as for bathing (see Chapter 9).

Even *Greenland* has thermal springs warm enough for a bath in the middle of a wilderness surrounded by icebergs floating in the sea. Although most thermal springs are found on *Disko* Island on the western side of Greenland, their temperature is not high enough for a swim. Eastern Greenland's 'hot springs' are slightly warmer, but the only ones warm enough to be used for a swim all year round are in the southeast of Greenland on the Island of *Uunartoq* (South Greenland, n.d.). Reliable historical records could not be identified for this book, but considering the travelling Norsemen and their record in Iceland it may be assumed that they made use of hot springs wherever they came across these natural providers of warmth. Near the hot springs of Uunartoq the remains of a nunnery have also been discovered (Uunartoq, n.d.), which could indicate that approximately a thousand years ago during conversion to Christianity religious groups would have used the hot springs for bathing, washing and possibly medicinal purposes. Further spa development to attract tourists for health and wellness is not likely to take place in Greenland, most possibly because of the close vicinity of Iceland, where a considerable hot spring tourism industry is already in place.

Not much information is available on the thermal spring area of *Naantali* in *Finland*. However, the healing effects of the thermal waters there have been known since 1700 AD and by the end of the 17th century the first thermal spring facility had been opened. During the 18th century the aristocracy and courtiers of the Russian Empire selected this Finnish island in the Baltic Sea as a fashionable holiday destination. This tradition still lives on in the new millennium as high-ranking politicians and government leaders as well as other 'noble' citizens of Finland regularly spend their holidays at the summer residence *Kulturanta*. Today the thermal springs are controlled by the Naantali Spa Hotel, which was built in 1984 (Royal Spas of Europe – Naantali, 2001).

The Mediterranean countries and Portugal

Italy has one of the longest recorded histories of hot spring use of the Mediterranean countries, due to the Roman and Etruscan traditions of employing geothermal resources wherever available. A large percentage of Italy's currently existing thermal spas were frequented for therapeutic purposes and their healing qualities by ancient Greeks and Romans (Andreassi & Flori, 1996) and in the time between 750 and 500 BC the Etruscans from north of Rome used thermal bathing and other hydrothermal by-products (Monti, n.d.). This section gives the details of only a few of the more important known springs.

In *Lipari* on the island of Sicily stone-lined ponds with thermal spring water channelled into them were probably used for therapeutic thermal bathing as far back as 1430 BC (Cataldi *et al.*, 1999) and the hot sulphur springs near Catania have been used for thermalism as well as for rest and recreation since Roman times. They still have a reputation for their healing properties, their relaxing environment and beneficial climatic conditions (Catania, n.d.). Other noteworthy spas are *Montecatini* and *Salsomaggiore*. Many of the original natural spring bathing sites have been popular for centuries despite the fact that the scale of bathhouse architecture may have changed over the years. The thermal baths of Montecatini were known in the 14th century, and in the year 1417 AD *Ugolino de Montecatini* (1348–1425), the founder of balneology in Italy, recommended their use (Altman, 2000) for medicinal purposes. Around 1771–1772 *Pietro Leopoldo* ordered the construction of baths at Montecatini at public expense. From 1773 the Montecatini spa waters became famous worldwide for their beneficial effects on the human body, but they achieved their highest international fame in the last years of the 19th century (Altman, 2000).

On the island of *Ischia* hot springs are a common sight and some of them date back to the Romans. They were mainly exploited during the 16th century by the Calabrian doctor *Giulio Iasolino*, who made Ischia one of the richest thermal areas in the world by attracting wealthy patients (Rando, 2003). Traces of history of the region of *Abano* and *Venice* also indicate that the original settlers of this area from around the 9th century BC considered local thermal springs to be of religious and cultural importance; however, written records only date back to the 12th century AD. Since then Abano has become a prominent thermal centre, which has seen many improvements, redevelopments and modernisations to cater for an ever-increasing demand (Royal Spas of Europe – Abano, 2001).

Hot springs with therapeutic properties have been used as religious centres and sites for pilgrimages in *Spain* since ancient times, with different cultures including the Roman and the Arabic leaving a legacy of thermal developments (Ledo, 1996). The earliest reliable records relate to the Roman presence, which began during the 2nd century BC. The Romans, attracted by thermal waters, established a municipality which they called *Aquae Calidae*, now known as the spa town *Caldes de Montbui* (Caldes de Montbui, n.d.). Another location where thermal springs played an important role in the establishment of an urban centre is *Aquae Voconis*. Set up during the 1st century AD this town is today called *Caldes de Malavella* and has evolved over time into a modern spa town popular for its thermal treatments (Caldes de Malavella, n.d.).

The history of the thermal springs of *Archena* possibly reaches back to the 5th century BC when Iberian settlers inhabited the area. When the Romans arrived they immediately recognised the potential of the natural hot springs and introduced their own thermal bathing culture to assist the healing of the war-inflicted injuries of their military personnel. In the year 1785 AD *King Carlos III* ordered Archena to be redeveloped and the town acquired increasing importance as a thermal spa centre, which to this day is in the continuous process of extending its facilities due to the popularity of thermal spas (Balneario de Archena, n.d.; Royal Spas of Europe – Archena, 2001). Many other hot spring destinations in Spain have a long history. The *Castilla-La-Mancha* includes over a dozen thermal centres with a rich past in hot spring use (Termatalia, 2007).

Galicia has more than 300 mineral-medicinal thermal sources registered, of which 20 are used by spas. The Galician thermal sector presently includes 20 spas in various provinces, for example *Caldas de Reis*, *Pontevedra* and *Ourense* (Cabanillas, n.d.). There is a long natural hot spring history in Spain, but for the purpose of this book only a few examples were chosen to present a general overview and prove the significance of 'termalismo' in this country.

Although the therapeutic qualities of thermal water have been known in *Portugal* for a long time it was only in the 18th century that King *Dom João* officially recognised the therapeutic effects of thermal water (Portugal, n.d.). Portugal's thermal past, like many other European countries, is strongly connected to the Roman bathing culture, which was imported during the Roman occupation. The area around *Chavez* is rich in thermal springs attributed with healing properties due to their specific mineral content. These springs *'Caldas de Chavez'* were used by the Romans for rest and recreation and were then called *Aquae Flaviae*. Today a modern thermal centre is treating health seeking tourists for a variety of illnesses, including rheumatism, digestive problems and high blood pressure. Other facilities such as the *Termas de Vidago* in the *Duro* region have recently undergone modernisation and like the *Termas de Pedras Salgadas* are located in a large park with an atmosphere of nostalgic luxury. Most thermal springs in Portugal are also bottled and consumed as a health-enhancing drink with a high natural mineral content (Michelin, 2002).

Caldas da Rainha in the Central Coast Region is named after *Queen Leonore*, who in the year 1484 AD noticed some peasants bathing in smelly, steaming ponds by the roadside. When told that these waters were beneficial in treating rheumatism the Queen is said to have stopped to take a bath herself. After realising the curative value of the hot springs a year later a hospital was established by the Queen from her private funds and under her personal management. Later a large park was added as well as a church. Today Caldas da Rainha is a popular thermal spa destination for health tourists (Michelin, 2002).

The Azores and Madeira island groups belonging to Portugal also have many hot springs due to their active volcanic environments. Historically they have been used by the local population, but reliable records are not available for the time before these islands were populated by Portuguese pioneers around the 15th century (The Azores, 2007), although the island group was mentioned earlier in a letter written by *King Alfonso V*, King of Portugal, in 1439 AD in a discussion about settlement rights (Santos, n.d.).

Mediterranean middle eastern countries

The country today called *Israel* was known as Palestine at the time of the development of the hot spring towns of Tiberias (*Tuberiya*) and *Hamat Gader*. The ancient hot spring area of Hammath outside the city of Tiberias has been a popular therapeutic spa and health tourist destination for over 2000 years, probably being first established during Roman times (Tiberias, 2007; Wolf, 1996). The town of Tiberias was founded around 20 AD as the capital of Galilee and named after the Emperor Tiberius (Jaffé *et al.*, 1999). Built as a spa for recreational purposes, it was developed around 17 natural mineral hot springs over 200 m below sea level. However, Tiberias was essentially a Jewish town, gradually assuming great spiritual and religious importance. It is therefore not surprising that, while the baths essentially were frequented for health benefits, religion exerted a strong influence on balneological practices. The moral consequences of mixed religious groups bathing in thermal waters appear to have been of considerable concern for the rabbis, who strongly opposed thermal bathing in spas where statues of 'foreign' deities were on display. Restrictions like this caused many spa visitors to travel the short distance to Hamat Gader where amusements of all kinds (including prostitution) were catered for and similar restrictions were not in place (Jaffé *et al.*, 1999). Later, during the Turkish period the site was developed into public baths and the first 'modern' spa was established in 1929 in the *Tiberias Hot Springs National Park*.

Today the Tiberias Hot Springs health and vacation resort is Israel's largest and most sophisticated mineral spring site and attracts thousands of domestic and international visitors each year (Israel Tourism & Leisure Division, n.d.). The new spa *Khamei Tveriya ha-Tsi'eera* (Young Tiberias Springs) offers personal therapeutic pools, cosmetic mud pools and treatment rooms (Larson, 2006). On the other hand, the curative properties of the thermal springs of Hamat Gader have been famous since ancient times and were described by the historian *Eunapius* after he visited the springs in the 4th century AD (Hamat Gader, 1999).

Hamat Gader (hot springs of *Gadara* or *Gedera – El Hama*) is located on the eastern shore of the Sea of Galilee in the Yarmuk Valley close to the border with Jordan and Syria, about 20 km from Tiberias. And like Tiberias Hamat Gader also lies below sea level by approximately 150 m. The springs at Hamat Gader were first exploited by the Romans, who converted the site into thermal baths around the 2nd century AD (Archaeological World, 2006). The curative powers of the springs at Hamat Gader were well known when the baths were built as the hot springs had already been used for thermal treatments by Herod the Great. However, in comparison with the hot springs of the neighbouring Tiberias some sources claim that due to the practice of mixed bathing the spa of Hamat Gader had 'a reputation for licentiousness and frivolity' (Jaffé *et al.*, 1999). Hamat Gader is not to be confused with *Gadara*, now called Um Qais in *Jordan*, also close to the border and known for the *Al Hemma* hot springs, which were frequented by the Romans as well.

During the 5th and 6th centuries AD in the Byzantine Empire period the baths became more popular until an earthquake damaged the structures in the 7th century (Hamat Gader, 1999). Restoration followed but in the 9th century the baths were finally abandoned. An inscription from the reign of *Empress Eudocia*

(421–460 AD) on a marble slab praises the thermal baths of Hamat Gader, and refers to 16 buildings, including halls, pools and fountains. Extensive excavations have recently exposed a large portion of the baths complex, and the remains of the structures have been restored and opened to visitors who can enjoy the natural hot springs and benefit from their curative properties at the successfully functioning balneological establishment (Israeli Foreign Ministry, n.d.; Jaffé *et al.*, 1999; Jordan Touristic Sites, n.d.).

The Dead Sea, which borders Jordan and Israel, is thus possibly one of the oldest thermal health resort regions in human history (Abels *et al.*, 1996; Zúñiga, 2006), and has been referred to by many writers and historians for its medicinal properties. The unique qualities and mineral content of the thermal waters, which attracted people in the past, as well as the beneficial climate, are still used for the treatment of various health conditions.

Historical events in the Middle East followed by significant geopolitical alterations in the recent present have changed the original names of the regions we know today as Jordan and Israel. In the past, under the Roman influence and later Byzantine presence people may have had no problems sharing the hot springs of Hamat Gader and Tiberias, as they belonged to the same country. The use of Jordan's thermal springs has been recorded, like those of Israel and Palestine, since Roman times when several hot spring areas (apart from the above discussed Tiberias and Hamat Gader) were utilised as health spas and facilities for recreation. The baths of *Hammamat Ma'een* some 50 km southwest of Amman the capital were already popular at this time as a treatment centre, and today as a resort complex with tourist facilities attracts visitors seeking thermal water treatment for health and wellness (Health Tourism in Jordan, n.d.; Jordan Touristic Sites, n.d.). Other places such as *Afra*, *Zarqa' Ma'in* and *Al Himma* offer thermal baths with curing properties in scenic regions together with historical architectural remains. Health and spa tourism in Jordan is mainly focused on the Dead Sea, which is fed by the River Jordan and over 50 hot sulphurous springs. The curative powers of the Dead Sea are mentioned in the Bible and were recognised by the Israeli King Herod over 2000 years ago. It is one of the most famous sites for *climatotherapy* (Routh & Bhowmik, 1996) today, because it is relatively free from various types of pollution (Oumeish, 1996) and thus represents a favourable destination for health tourism.

In *Syria* the principal source of hot and mineral spring water in the ancient Biblical city of *Palmyra* was a spring named *Efca*. This thermal spring is sulphurous and radioactive, and is believed to have curative properties. Similar springs emitting from karst caves were the source of water for several other known Biblical sites such as *Jerusalem* [*Gihon* Spring], *Shobek*, *Hazor* and *Gezer* (LaMoreaux, 2005), to name only a few.

Yemen's hot springs and natural spas are used to attract visitors seeking therapeutic tourism. There are a number of natural baths such as *Al-Shaarani* in Aden, *Al-Asloum* in Hazim and *Burhan* in Qafir. More and more people have been visiting a place called *Ibb* during the past four years, which hopes to encourage an economic revival for the area (Yemeni Times, 2004). However, the use of the hot springs in Yemen is low due to a lack of awareness of their existence resulting from negligence in promoting the importance of therapeutic tourism by officials and citizens alike (Yemen, n.d.).

Mediterranean North Africa

Every country bordering on the Mediterranean Sea was at some stage under the control of the Roman Empire (see Figure 3.1). This included all of the North African countries, and the Romans searched for available thermal resources as soon as they arrived in order to establish their preferred type of bathing facilities. Many local areas still bear witness of their presence nearly 2000 years later. Subsequently, the many African countries that came under Islamic rule also had their own bathing culture, which included visits to the local *Hamam* in a very similar way as the Romans visited their bathhouses. The influence of the Greeks also reached far into the North African countries and influenced the local ways of life with regard to health and wellness, and this was often in relation to the use of thermal springs with curative properties.

In *Tunisia* the history of hot spring use has also been recorded for at least 2000 years. The thermal waters of the resort *Hammam Bourgida* in Ain Drahim were already used for Arab baths in antiquity (Termatalia, 2006). Under the earlier Roman occupation thermal baths were established in Tunisia, which influenced the traditional way of using hot springs in this country. The largest and most imposing thermal baths were the famous *Antonine Baths* in Carthage, which were completed in 120 AD after 12 years of construction work and covered 3.5 hectares (Salloum, n.d.).

Ancient Roman baths are found in several other locations, but later were often turned into hamams (the customary form of bath in many Arab countries) after the Romans left North Africa. However, the Greeks left traces too, with the *Hammam Jedidi* for example found to have been under the protection of Aesculapius and Hygeia, as evidenced by four statues depicting these deities found in an ancient pool within the complex (see Chapter 4). Some thermal springs (not exploited by the Romans) were noted by Arab authors in the 11th and 12th centuries AD (e.g. *El Hamma Gabes*) and reference was made to their therapeutic benefits (Office du Thermalisme, n.d.). In the year 1975 (14 June) the then President of the Republic of Tunisia, *Habib Bourguiba*, established the Office for Thermalism located in the capital Tunis. This office was placed under the Ministry for Public Health in cooperation with the state-run Tourism Organisation, with the main purpose of developing the thermo-mineral tourism sector as well as the mineral water industry (Nouira, 1975). The Office of Thermalism is state financed, administered with the assistance of a medical committee, and responsible for policy making. However, the hot spring sector itself is privatised with over 80 thermal spring locations in Tunisia attracting approximately 2.5 million visitors annually seeking thermal treatments. The *Hammam Sidi Abdelkader* (Gabes) alone is said to receive over 1 million visitors each year (Office du Thermalisme, n.d.).

Egypt was known for therapeutic tourism during the Greek era when Socrates recommended Egypt's climate and its thermal waters for health and well-being. South of Cairo and east of the river Nile is the *Helwan* bath, which is fed by a hot sulphur spring (31.6°C) and has been used for curing skin disorders since at least the 7th century AD (Lund & Freeston, 2001), although it is likely to be far older.

In *Algeria* the principal uses of geothermal waters are for bathing and balneology, although some space and greenhouse heating occurs. Ancient Roman pools and modern thermal resorts are close together, in the north of the country, where there are eight hot springs used for medical purposes involving the treatment of rheumatism and skin disease (Fekraoui & Kedaid, 2005). Among the 240 hot springs and hot water wells recorded in the north, there are 10 geothermal major spas and over 150 smaller ones. As noted, eight of the major spas are public and considered as thermal resorts; they offer a number of services such as physical re-education, massages and other health care given by a medical team. The most popular major spa resorts are *Hammam Meskhoutine, H. Guergour, H. Bouhanifia, H. Bouhadjar, H. Bougharara, H. Righa* and *H. Salihine*. Apart from H. Meskhoutine, the temperatures, mineralisation and flow rates are quite low (Fekraoui & Kedaid, 2005: 3).

Central and Eastern Europe

Thermal spas in Central and Eastern Europe have a history that goes back again to Greek and Roman times, when pilgrimage was the equivalent to modern tourism and the healing powers of thermal and mineral springs were sought to improve one's health in the same way. In more recent times, after World War II in many western European countries the spa industry stagnated, but in Central and Eastern Europe health spas based on thermal and mineral waters developed under the sponsorship of the state or the trade unions. While the 'healing combinats' (Bacharov, 2004: 43) that were supposed to offer rest and recreation for everybody could not compete with more luxurious western European style resorts, their purpose was to give every worker access to 'time out' in order to increase the health and motivation of the general workforce. This was very much in contrast to earlier periods of the western European spa scene, which is described by Bacharov (2004) as having a 'cultural and elitist atmosphere' emphasising both healing and entertainment only for the more affluent social classes.

Evidence from the Neolithic era indicates that Celtic and Dacian peoples settled near thermal springs in *Hungary* and practised basic forms of balneology long before the Romans arrived (Cohut & Árpási, 1995). Regarding the original name of the Hungarian capital Budapest there are conflicting theories. The Romans used *Aquincum*, after the Celtic name *Ak Ink*, which means 'abundant waters' (Mineral Waters of Hungary, n.d.). But other suggestions are that *Aquincum* may derive from the Latin *Aquae Quinque* referring to 'five springs' water (Thermal Baths, n.d.) and was initially known as the Roman spa complex *Aquae Calidae Superiores et Inferiores* (Cohut & Árpási, 1995). Centuries later after the Romans had left, the Hungarian capital was further developed under Turkish rule (16th–17th century AD) and bathhouses in various shapes and sizes (see Figure 3.10) from these times influenced the bathing culture and left a thermal heritage, which is still a part of city life and welcomes guests today (Royal Spas of Europe – Budapest, 2001c; The Age, 2005). The Hotel Gellert (see Figure 3.11) is a landmark in Budapest from

Figure 3.10 The 16/17th century Turkish Bath Király Fürdö in Budapest. Not very inviting from the outside, very interesting inside
Source: Photograph courtesy of P. Erfurt-Cooper.

earlier times and its thermal bath facilities are popular today with locals as well as with international health and wellness spa tourists.

The currently popular thermal spa destinations of Hungary were established mainly during the 18th century, and were made popular by visiting emperors and kings, who declared the thermal waters as beneficial and set up their summer residences nearby. Hungarian spa towns such as *Budapest* and *Hajdúszoboszló*, due to their significant therapeutical benefits for health and well-being, are still increasing in popularity (Hungarospa, n.d.). Thousands of tourists, domestic and international, visit the country every year, looking for recreation and entertainment as well as convalescence from ill health.

The use of warm spring water in *Poland* was first recorded in the 12th century and several spa towns, usually situated around natural thermal springs, developed over time (Kepinska, 2002; Omulecki *et al.*, 1996). The town of *Cieplice* for example has been known under several names, which were all related to the presence of hot springs: in 1281 AD as *Callidus fons*, in 1288 AD as *Villa Warmbrona* or

Figure 3.11 The entrance to the thermal bath at Hotel Gellert in Budapest
Source: Photograph courtesy of P. Erfurt-Cooper.

Bad Warmbrunn and in 1318 AD as *Cheplevode*. Cieplice is the oldest Polish health resort and the only one in Poland with thermal spring temperatures of up to 73°C (Cieplice Śląskie-Zdrój, n.d.).

The origins of Cieplice are not certain, but like in many other countries a legend about a hunting trip is closely connected to the discovery, which is said to have happened accidentally. In the year 1175 AD *Prince Boleslaus the Tall* was chasing a wounded deer, when he saw the animal drinking from a stream. This water gave the deer back its strength and it escaped. Close examination of the water showed that it was warm and smelling of sulphur, which made the Prince decide to build a hunting lodge near the spring. Today, Cieplice has over a dozen spa hotels and sanatoriums offering thermalism combined with other wellness treatments (Cieplice Śląskie-Zdrój, 2007). Although Poland's thermal and mineral health spas experienced a decline in clients during the 1990s (visitor numbers decreased by 50% according to Bachvarov, 2004), many of the traditional thermal centres have continued to attract visitors up to the present.

Despite the fact that the thermal baths of *Croatia* have been completely destroyed half a dozen times over two millennia, the spa of *Varazdinske Toplice* has become a large and well-organised rehabilitation centre including a hospital for medical rehabilitation with 1100 beds, and employs three physicians and numerous physiotherapists. For more than 2000 years the sick and the infirm have sought comfort and healing at these hot springs known in Roman times as *Aquae Iasae*. The first public thermal baths (including a basilica and temples) were built by the Romans in the 1st century AD on the mountain side around the thermal springs. Their main purpose initially was to serve the rehabilitation of wounded soldiers. After the fall of the Roman Empire the thermal baths were destroyed in the late 4th century, but rebuilt and used until in 1540 the Turks burned the place down again. This happened several times through various invaders, but reconstruction followed every time (Gamulin, 2001).

The *Czech Republic* has several spa towns with a long tradition of therapeutic success through thermalism. One of the leading thermal centres is Karlsbad or *Karlovy Vary*, named after its founder *Karl IV*, Roman Emperor and King of Bohemia (Lund, 2000a). The first settlements mentioned in the area of Karlsbad go back to the mid 14th century, but archaeologists believe that people have lived near the thermal springs much earlier (Burachovic, n.d.; Kouba, n.d.). Over the following centuries Karlsbad developed into an attractive spa centre, which is popular with health and wellness seeking tourists who appreciate the traditional atmosphere offered at a reasonable price.

Slovakia's thermal springs (over 1100) were used by the Romans and many therapeutic centres are using thermalism for health and well-being today. *Piestany* is one of the leading Slovakian natural hot and mineral spas with a history of thermal spring use possibly going back even further than the Romans to the Celtic, Germanic and old Slav civilisations (Lund, 2000a). Stone Age settlements near the thermal waters indicate earlier human use, and many tales and legends about the healing properties of the springs are still being told. However, the town of Piestany was only recorded in official documents in the year 1113 AD with the thermal spa mentioned even later in the year 1412 AD. At present around 3000 patients can be treated every day (Lund, 2000a) using hot spring water, which reflects the popularity of this type of treatment as well as being an obvious success factor in health and wellness spa tourism.

Like its neighbouring countries *Slovenia* has a centuries-long tradition as well as experience in using natural hot and mineral springs for thermal treatments and balneology. Archaeological evidence dating back to the Roman occupation shows the origins of a cultural diversity in relation to thermal baths. Written records from the year 1147 AD document the use of thermal springs for their healing qualities (Slovenija, 2006).

The name *Romania* is closely linked to the presence of the Romans in the country, and the Romans are also said to be responsible for starting to use the local thermal springs after they conquered *Dacia* in 106 AD. However, traces of settlements near Romanian thermal springs suggest that these springs were used by the Dacians long before the Roman arrival (Cohut & Árpási, 1995), although there are no written records from this time to verify this. The thermal springs of the *Aqua Herculis Spa* (the legend states that Hercules stopped here to bathe and rest) were developed by the Romans to suit their needs and were used by them for the duration of their occupancy of the region. After the Romans left, the area was invaded by barbaric peoples, which caused the decay of the spa complex (Cohut & Árpási, 1995). Over time the spa recovered and was frequented by royalty, which made it an attractive destination for the general public as well. Today *Baile Herculane Spa* is still popular for health and wellness treatments through thermalism. In modern times, the spa has been visited for its natural healing properties: hot springs with sulphur, chlorine, sodium, calcium, magnesium and other minerals, as well as negatively ionised air. During the period 1950–1990 mass tourism facilities were built as this location was especially popular with retirees who would spend their state-allotted vacation vouchers there, hoping to improve their health. Today, they share the town with a younger crowd, attracted by the beautiful mountain setting (Cohut & Árpási, 1995), especially since interest in geotourism is increasing and people of all ages are combining geothermal experiences with different aspects of tourism to add value to their experience.

Like in many other European countries *Bulgaria's* thermal spa history is closely linked to Roman influence. Several spa centres were established during Roman times with a number of these still following the tradition of hot spring use for health and wellness. Although Bulgaria is a relatively small country, it has several hundreds of hot springs (the numbers fluctuate between around 570 and more than 800, depending on the information source), which represent a great variety of physical and chemical characteristics. The reputation of their curative properties has been appreciated for therapeutic purposes since the dawn of civilisation (Tsankov & Kamarashev, 1996). The ancient hot spring areas of *Pautalia* (*Kyustendil*) and *Serdika* (Sofia) are thought to have been used by the Thracian tribes since Neolithic times (4000 BC) with traces of Thracian settlements found at locations with natural thermal water (Spa Temptations in Bulgaria, n.d.; Tsankov and Kamarashev, 1996). This strongly supports the long-standing significance of hot springs for human use.

The popular spa destination Kyustendil is an old national balneological resort town and the ancient Thracian name *Pautalia* means 'town of springs'. Between the 5th and 4th centuries BC Kyustendil developed from a Thracian settlement into an important trade centre with a balneological resort. Several centuries later, during the 1st century AD, the Romans transformed it into a fortified town called *Pautaliya* (Kyustendil, n.d.). Thermal spa resorts in Bulgaria today still represent active treatment centres for health and recreation; out of approximately 230 thermal spa resorts, a quarter are promoted as balneological resorts (Vassileva, 1996).

Russia and the former Soviet Union

Spas remain very important in the *Russian* medical system (Simkins, 1986). The hot spring town of *Sochi* for example is officially recognised as a health and wellness centre and was developed under Stalin as a holiday destination for working class people (Sochi, n.d.). By the end of the Soviet era about 2500 state-run health spas could be found in Russia with a capacity for up to 500,000 visitors at a time (Oddy, 1999). However, after the collapse of the USSR in 1991 many of these health spas went into decline.

The capital of Georgia, *Tbilisi* was named after the 30 or so hot springs the city is still famous for after more than 1500 years (tbil-i means warm in Georgian). Several websites and travel brochures briefly describe the history and mythology of the discovery of these hot springs, but unsettled political conflicts (Oxford Analytica, 2007) and the resulting instability and security issues do not encourage international tourism on a large scale, although the city's thermal facilities are of course enjoyed by the local population and domestic health and wellness tourists. The original founding of the capital goes back to *King Vakhtang Gorgasal* in the 5th century AD on a site that is thought to have been inhabited since Neolithic times. The Georgian legend narrates that while King Vakhtang Gorgasal was on a hunting trip a pheasant was caught by the king's falcon. The injured bird fell into one of the hot springs with healing properties and recovered instantly. Thus impressed, the king ordered the city of Tbilisi to be built on this site (Lerner, 2001). This legend is repeated in various ways, including the hunted bird being boiled in the hot waters or the animal being an injured deer instead that became well again after jumping in the curative thermal waters. However, the main concept is that King Vakhtang was led to the springs by an animal during a hunt. This theme has many parallels in as many countries all over the world.

Due to its location, Tbilisi has faced many invasions (some sources claim as many as over 40 invasions in the period between 627 and 1795 AD). However, the city was rebuilt every time, as indicated by archaeological excavations. The natural hot springs of Tbilisi played an important part in the legend surrounding its birth and its continual reconstruction, and they still attract tourists to the city because of the Tbilisi Balneological Health Resort (*Tbilisis Balneologiuri Kurorti*) operative since the 1940s (Gujelashvili, 2007).

Other areas in Russia and the former Soviet Union are known for their natural hot springs used for thermal bathing, cooking and washing. The *Crimea*, due to its proximity to Mediterranean neighbour countries, was under the influence of the Roman Empire from the 1st century AD (Svalova, 2000), which of course built *thermae* in the region as needed, leaving behind archaeological remains of buildings, water pipes and other infrastructure. And at the far eastern end of Russia bordering on China and also close to Japan is the *Kamchatka Peninsula* with an abundance of natural hot springs. These natural thermal waters are used by tourists who enter this remote wilderness dominated by active volcanoes. Most visitors are interested in volcano viewing and/or hunting as much as in hot springs. It cannot easily be determined when and by whom the natural hot springs here were used in the past, as the population figures are extremely low in this part of the world. However, anybody who comes across warm water in a cold climate is likely to find a way of using it.

Thermal Spa History: Asian Origins

The Asian region developed a similar though independent tradition of hot spring bathing. The Indus Valley and Chinese civilisations made use of the abundant supply of hot water and mineral springs in their territories at least from

3000 BC, making their utilisation of this resource perhaps the earliest in recorded history. Similarly, the Japanese Island's abundant hot water meant that an indigenous bathing culture developed very early in human settlement terms.

South Asia

The Indus Valley in *Pakistan* is generally considered to be one of the cradles of ancient civilisation, with excavations revealing that *Mohenjo-Daro* and *Harappa* were settled in this region approximately 5000 years ago, most likely because of their close proximity to water. Most buildings in the cities of the Indus Valley civilisation included bathrooms, lavatories, drainage, freshwater wells and tanks, which indicates that adequate water supplies must have been available (Pakistan Water Gateway, 2007). At Mohenjo-Daro archaeologists also unearthed what they believe to be the remains of a large public bath, swimming pool or possibly a water tank (Danino, 1999; Kenoyer, 2005). This of course raises questions about the source of the water needed for these extravagant structures in an environment that relies heavily on seasonal rainfall. Domestic buildings in Mohenjo-Daro all had access to freshwater, drainage as well as internal bathrooms. These are all signs that there must have been an abundance of water to supply highly civilised amenities of this type.

Based on the evaluation of hydrogeologic data it is evident that in many areas of the Indus Basin natural hot springs are abundant (Bakht, 2000) and most likely always have been. This makes it more than likely that natural hot and cold springs would have supplied the cities of Mohenjo-Daro, Harappa and many other Indus Valley settlements with fresh hot and cold water. More importantly it would have allowed for the constant flow of pristine and unpolluted water needed to keep amenities like the baths from turning into stagnant ponds growing algae. In all likelihood the populations of Mohenjo-Daro as well as many other settlements would have appreciated their access to natural hot springs and would have used them for health and wellness purposes (see Chapter 5).

In the ancient *Indian* tradition of *Ayurveda* water was described as the main element to cure many illnesses, and a Greek ambassador travelling in India in the 3rd century BC described Indian spring water as 'rarified water' to indicate its extraordinary powers (Chandrasekharam, 1999). Although there are over 300 mineral and thermal springs in India (Chandrasekharam, 1999; Chaterji & Guha, 1968) not much literature is available other than some geological reports, which rarely mention historical uses of natural hot springs for health and wellness. While it is therefore difficult to assign reliable dates regarding the historical use of hot springs in India, in many areas the springs are associated with certain gods, which indicates that people have been aware of these hot springs for a very long time and most likely used them for their benefits (see Chapter 4). Legendary beliefs among pilgrims refer to the discovery of springs and temples close together, which seems to support this theory (Chandrasekharam, 1999).

The hot springs at *Manikaran* in the Kullu district in the north of India for example are associated with the god *Shiva* and his wife *Parvati*. According to the legend

Shiva made the water boil after Parvati lost her ear rings while bathing in the spring-fed pond. Since then the high-temperature water has not just been used to cook food; when cooled enough it is said to have medicinal qualities useful to treat rheumatism and muscular pains. *Vashisht* hot springs, also in northern India in Himachal Pradesh, have made this village famous with almost 3000 people using the thermal waters each day (Himachal Pradesh, n.d.).

Generally hot springs in India are used for their therapeutic benefits. The *Nubra* Valley for instance has been famous for centuries for its medicinal hot springs (Nubra Valley, n.d.). Tattapani's famous natural sulphur springs have been developed into a popular hot spring tourist resort because the thermal waters have been historically known for their curative powers for various kinds of bodily ailments. Here, the hot springs are an attraction for tourists and spread out over a large area. Tattapani (which means hot water, see Table 3.3) is also a pilgrimage centre for Hindus because of its religious importance (Himachal Pradesh, n.d.; IndiaLine, 2006; Tattapani, n.d.; Tattapani Travel Information, n.d.).

Table 3.3 This table was created for interest only, due to the different language sources encountered while researching individual countries for their hot spring background

Hot water, hot springs or hot place/locations in different languages		
Latin	*Aquae Calidae*	Hot water
Spanish	Agua(s) caliente(s)	Hot water(s)
Nahuatl (Old Mexico)	Atotonilco	Place of boiling waters
Otomi language (Mexico)	Pathé	Place of hot water
P'urhepecha language (Mexico)	Puruándiro	Place of hot water
Indian language (Arizona)	Tonopah	Hot water under the bush
Greece	Thermopolis	Hot city
New Zealand – Maori	Waiariki	Warm pools
Hawaii	Waiwelawela	Very hot water
Tonga	Vai vela	Hot water
	Vai mafana	Warm water
China	Wen chuan	Warm spring
	Tangquan	Thermal spring
	Feiquan	Boiling spring
Japan	*Onsen* 温泉	Hot spring
	Yu	Hot water

(Continued)

Table 3.3 *Continued*

Hot water, hot springs or hot place/locations in different languages		
Korea	Oncheon, On-chon	Hot (warm) spring
	On-su	Hot (warm) water
Thailand	Bor-nam-pu-ron	Place of hot water
Tajik	Khodga-Obi-Garm	Holy hot water
Georgia/Russia	T'bilisi	Warm location/place
Mongolia	Alashan Valley	Valley of hot springs
	Arxan 阿尔山	Hot holy water
India	Tattapani	Hot Water
Nepal	Tatopani	Hot water
Cambodia	Te-teuk-pos	Place of boiling water
Kabardian (Caucasus)	Psekups	Hot spring
Turkey	Şifalı su	Healing water
	Içme	Hot spring
	Kaynarca	Thermal spring
Iceland	Laug	Hot spring
	Hver	Boiling spring
Jordan	Hamat	Hot springs
	Hamat Gader	Hot springs of Gedera
Arabic	Hami	Hot
Sotho language (South Africa)	Bela Bela	The boiling place
Nama language (Namibia)	Ai-Ais	Burning water
Tanzania/Swahili	Maji Moto	Hot water
Germany	Heisse Quelle	Hot spring
France	Source thermale	Thermal or hot spring

East Asia

In the Asian continent *China* provides written evidence (Clark, 1999; Schafer, 1956) that for thousands of years they have been at the forefront in utilising thermal springs for various purposes. This includes achieving therapeutic benefits as well as enjoying the pleasure of a hot spring bath during the cold season. It is assumed that the culture of using thermal water found its way from China through Korea to Japan, where its history is not recorded until after the Chinese and Koreans had migratory ties with Japan (Clark, 1999).

Yunnan Province has many hot springs and most of them were known to the local residents, who used the thermal waters for healing purposes or simply as a source of hot water (Šilar, 1968). The hot springs of the *Huangshan* area in the

Yellow Mountains (*Anhui Province*) are located in a national geopark and the Chinese have used these springs for more than 1000 years as a resort and health spa for bathing and drinking cures (Cruey, n.d.). The Baotu Spring (*Jinan Province*) is one of 72 springs in the province and its earliest mention is in the 'Spring and Autumn Annals' *c*. 600 BC. Although this spring is not a hot spring by temperature, it is a hot spring by definition and also indicates the preference of the Chinese for using natural resources for health and wellness.

The *Huaqing Hot Springs* development dates back to the Western Zhou Dynasty (1050–771 BC). It was a preferred destination for the Emperors of China, who spent long time periods at Huaqing, even attempting to run the government from palaces built at the hot springs [Huaqing, n.d.(a)]. The ruins of the Imperial thermal pools (see Figure 3.12) in the Huaqing Palace built in the Tang Dynasty were rediscovered in 1982, and after 3 years of excavation five royal pools covering an area of 4600 m² were identified (Shaanxi Huaqingchi Tourism, n.d.).

The *Tangshan Hot Springs* (about 30 km north of the capital Beijing) were used during the Qing Dynasty (1644–1911 AD) under *Emperor Kangxi*, who had a pool built at the spring source. Later emperors added an imperial lodge, pavilions, villas and temples in order to create a haven of tranquility and seclusion (Tangshan, n.d.). Another hot spring area northwest of Beijing is *Xiaotangshan*, which was first recorded in the 'Annals of the Yang Dynasty' about 800 years ago. Since that time the hot springs have been visited by royals, aristocracy and high-ranking officials of the Ming (1368–1644 AD) and Qing (1616–1911 AD) Dynasties (Bathing and Spa

Figure 3.12 Lady Yang's bathing pool at Huaqing
Source: Huaqing [n.d.(b)]. Photograph courtesy of Studio 21.

Information, n.d.). Other hot spring parks are located near the *Jialing* and *Yangtse* Rivers. The hot springs of both areas were used during the Ming Dynasty (Regenttour, n.d.); however, it is not clear whether these springs are too hot for bathing and are merely sightseeing destinations. In *Guanxi Province* the Longsheng Hot Springs National Forest Park is described as an 'ideal summer resort, a place for convalescence, a health building centre and a tourist attraction' (Longsheng, n.d.: 1).

The island of *Hainan* is abundant with geothermal resources and famous for its hot springs. The *Guantang* thermal springs in Qionghai are said to have strong curative effects [Hainan, n.d.(a)] and were well known as early as during the interim period between the Qing Dynasty and the Republic of China (*c.* 1910). Under Japanese occupation thermal spring sanatoriums were set up, but native inhabitants had long before used the thermal springs to cure chronic illnesses and skin problems. The springs were also favoured for their ability to suppress pain and soothe tense nerves, increase blood circulation and help detoxify the body. In 1994 an expert team of the National Mineral Resource Storage Committee officially verified and approved the thermal springs in Guantang [Hainan, n.d.(b)].

Many other hot spring areas can be found in different Chinese provinces:

- Conghua Hot Springs (75 km from Guanhzhou);
- Seven-Fairy-Maiden Hot Springs (Baoting County);
- Xinglong Hot Springs (Wanning-Hainan);
- Baoquantang Hot Spring (Shandong Peninsula – Jinan Province);
- Tengchong Hot Springs – Baoshan; and
- Badaling Great Wall Hot Spring – Sanlihe District.

This list is by no means indicative of the vast number of hot springs in China and their history, but it provides a brief overview of the importance of these thermal areas for local Chinese communities as well as the tourism industry.

Japan has used hot springs for many centuries although their thermal spa culture developed differently from the western world. The Japanese tradition of bathing in hot springs has aristocratic connections that date back at least to the *Heian* period (794–1185 AD), although it probably has much older origins. The Japanese warlords used thermal springs for the same purpose as the Romans did – to heal war injuries and recover from battle. During the *Edo* period (1603–1867 AD) hot spring bathing was commonplace among all levels of the population to unwind after work and socialise with friends and neighbours (Japan's Natural Hot Springs, n.d.). This custom has not changed since then (see Figure 3.13).

It is not clear whether people in Japan, a country so richly blessed with geothermal resources, used these resources during the *Jomon* period of settlement (from *c.* 10,000 years ago to 600 BC; Habu, 2004); however, considering the climate (large parts of Japan have very cold winters) as well as human nature it seems more than likely that the Japanese very early made use of thermal water wherever it was available. As in the case of most other countries the ancient people of Japan too did not concern themselves with recording the origin, progress and development of regional thermal resources and attractions. There is some indication, however, that the Japanese did have a tradition of ritual bathing by the end of the following *Yayoi*

Figure 3.13 Rural *Onsen* near Beppu in Kyushu
Source: Photograph courtesy of P. Erfurt-Cooper.

period around 297 AD as mentioned in the *History of the Kingdom of Wei* (Clark, 1999). It is not clear if this refers to the use of natural hot springs or the general use of water for purification purposes; however, Sekioka and Yoshii (1999) suggest that there is certain evidence indicating that hot spring bathing may have been practised as early as 6000 years ago on the eastern side of *Lake Suwa* (Nagano Prefecture), where ruins of ancient colonies have been excavated. At this site stones with [mineral] encrustations and smelling of hydrogen sulphide were discovered at a depth of approximately 6 m, and it is thought that these stones could have been used to frame hot spring pools used for thermal bathing.

Other discoveries of hot springs in Japan were originally apparently sometimes made with the help of animals, which the Japanese regard as messengers of the gods. Altman (2000: 40) for example describes the discovery of the healing springs at *Takeo* on Kyushu Island as being attributed to *Empress Jingu* (reigning during the 3rd century AD), who came upon a white heron bathing in the thermal waters. The *Dōgo Onsen* 道後温泉 is one of the oldest and most famous hot springs in Japan, located only a few kilometres from the centre of Matsuyama, in the Ehime Prefecture on the west coast of Shikoku Island [Dōgo Onsen, n.d.(a)]. Some sources claim a recorded history of over 1500 years, as the springs are even mentioned in Japan's oldest anthology, the *Man'yoshu*, a collection of poems written *c*. 759 AD; according to legend even *Prince Shotoku* (574–622 AD) used to partake of the waters [Dōgo Onsen, n.d.(b); Dōgo Onsen, n.d.(c)]. Other sources, including the official

Japanese Tourist Organisation (JNTO), are confident that Dōgo Onsen's history dates back some 3000 years, because the springs have always been a favourite destination of the Imperial Family and celebrities [Dōgo Onsen, n.d.(d); Dōgo Onsen, n.d.(e)], who used the baths for therapeutic purposes. But the Dōgo Onsen is not the only one claiming to be the oldest in Japan. *Arima* on the island of Honshu claims to be the oldest, but so do *Shirahama* and many others throughout Japan. Talmadge (2006: 82) explains these claims as being similar to restaurants claiming to have the best chilli in Texas or England's best fish and chips. However, Arima was among the favourites of the Imperial Family. Whatever the truth of this is, many traditional hot springs in Japan date back several centuries and the custom of hot spring bathing has a special place in Japanese culture, which is maintained by the majority of the population, especially in areas rich in geothermal resources.

Most Asian countries connected through the Silk Road have offered travellers the use of hot springs for centuries. Some examples are *Kyrgyzstan* and *Nepal* (other countries linked to the Silk Road are covered individually in this chapter and in Chapter 9, e.g. Turkey, Iran, China, India) where natural hot springs are abundant and appear to have had a historical use going back to ancient times. The *Issyk-Ata* sanatorium in Kyrgyzstan for example is a health facility for 400 people and was built in the year 1891. It is run by the government and is known to have treated patients with illnesses from 'Chernobyl radiation' (Kyrgyztan, n.d.).

According to scientists there are at least 50 hot springs in Nepal, which are locally known as 'tatopani', meaning hot water (Table 3.3). The most famous hot springs of Nepal are at the town of *Tatopani*, which attracts approximately 60,000 visitors annually who believe in the curative powers of the thermal waters. Festivals bear witness to the traditional use of these hot springs and people celebrate by taking baths to cure and prevent illness (VisitNepal, 2007).

At present there are about 43 hot springs in *Mongolia* which are used for various purposes, including several sanatoriums and health resorts (Geothermal Energy Resources, n.d.). Most hot spring destinations are located in the mountains at nearly 2000 m above sea level and some are only accessible with 4WD vehicles. Historical records are scarce, at least outside Mongolia, but there is some indication that one of the mineral spring areas (*Aurag* city) is somehow connected to *Chingis Khaan*. Several hot spring sanatoriums and health resorts are listed in Mongolian travel guides, which point out that the thermal waters are believed to cure 'aches and diseases' (Mongolia-web, 2007). Hot springs also seem to be major destinations on the trip agendas of organised tours through Mongolia (e.g. Tsenkher Hot Springs) and 'traditional treatment methods' indicate the age-old use of thermal waters for medicinal purposes (Tsenkher Hot Springs, n.d.).

Thermal springs are restricted to a few locations in *Korea* because of the stable tectonic setting of most of the southern part of the country. Citations in history books indicate that the Koreans have used natural hot springs for medical treatments and relaxation in the past; for example records mention that the royal family enjoyed thermal spring bathing from the early Three Kingdom period between 18 BC and 668 AD. Later King Sonjong (1083–1094 AD) ordered a search for new hot springs closer to the capital city, promising the finder social benefits, money and exemption from labour and duty (Yum, 1999). Governors of territories were in charge of management and maintenance of hot spring bathing facilities, which generated records and data about hot spring use and related legislation. Until the Japanese occupation of Korea in the year 1910 the hot springs were mainly enjoyed by the king, his family and the nobility. This changed with the arrival of the Japanese when the hot springs were developed into typical *Onsen* style bathing facilities (Yum, 1999).

One of the older hot springs in Korea is *Onyang* in the Province of Chungcheong, which was first discovered approximately 1300 years ago. The hot springs have been in operation for over 600 years, and according to historical records they were visited by King Sejong the Great (born 1397 AD) and subsequent members of the royal family during the *Joseon* period (1392–1910 AD) to cure their illnesses (Garcia, 2007). Other sources claim that Onyang has been known since 1458, when King Sejong cured his chronic skin disease by bathing in the springs (Hann, 1996). Also, historical records point to the existence of the *Suanbo* Hot Springs in the year 1018 AD under King Hyongjong (Koryo Empire) and these attracted scholars, politicians, aristocracy as well as ordinary people throughout the year to 'take the waters' (Suanbo Hot Springs, n.d.).

Most if not all hot springs in Korea have a longstanding excellent reputation for individual therapeutic benefits and are currently sought after for their healing powers and health and wellness aspects. Throughout Korea over 70 hot springs attract health and wellness tourists who seek the benefits of the mineral-rich thermal waters. A great number of these hot spring areas have been popular with the local people for centuries, but are now developed into state-of-the-art thermal spa resorts in order to draw international visitors as well.

South East Asia

More than 90 hot springs can be found throughout *Thailand*. One example with known human use is the *Bor Khlueng* Hot Spring in Ratchaburi province. The thermal waters of this spring are believed to soothe muscle aches and pains (Kanokratana *et al.*, 2004). Others are located at San Kamphaeng and Rung Arun in Chiang Mai, offering a complete package of health treatments. Also in Chiang Mai, in Mae Taeng district, is the *Pa Pae* Hot Spring (Pong Nam Duet). This is said to be one of the nicest because it is not over-commercialised and is set within a well-maintained park in a picturesque valley. *Fang* at the northernmost tip of the country has about 50 hot springs in a 10-acre forest setting (Kanokratana *et al.*, 2004). Other northern provinces with hot springs include Lampang (*Jae Son* Hot Spring) and Mae Hong Son (*Muang Paeng* and *Pa Bong* Hot Springs). Another well-known hot spring is in Ranong province in southern Thailand. Located in the *Raksavarin Forest Park* the private resort of the same name has been granted rights to draw mineral water from the local hot spring for commercial purposes. The resort offers a full package of health and recreational facilities. Apart from this there seems to be very little information available about the historical use of hot springs in Thailand (Kanokratana *et al.*, 2004).

In *Taiwan* hot springs are considered one of the most precious gifts that Earth has bestowed on the country [Taiwan, n.d.(a)]. They call them 'the hot tears of the Earth' and it is possible that people have used hot springs here since ancient times for their rejuvenating and therapeutic properties. More than one hundred and thirty hot springs have been discovered, with the highest concentration found in the volcanic north [Taiwan Government Information Office, n.d.(a)]. Hot springs in Taiwan were first mentioned in a manuscript (*Beihai Jiyou*) in 1697 AD, but not developed until the *Beitou* Hot Springs were discovered in 1893–94. During the Japanese 'colonial period' the occupiers brought with them their own hot spring (*Onsen*) culture and built many hot spring spas that have greatly influenced Taiwanese thermal spa development [Taiwan Government Information Office, n.d.(a)]. According to the Taiwanese Hot Spring Association the Japanese failed to realise the full extent of Taiwan's hot spring resources until after the war. However, they conducted significant research on Taiwan's hot springs while it was a part of the Japanese empire and this research data proved quite valuable for the later development of Taiwan's hot spring industry. Shortly after 1945 the relatively short-lived hot spring way of life went into decline, with the remaining facilities either falling into disrepair or supporting a red-light district (Taiwan Headlines, 2002). Not until the year 1999 did the authorities consider promoting Taiwan's hot springs again to provide health and wellness spa destinations for the tourism industry [Taiwan Government Information Office, n.d.(b)].

Wulai is one of the northern hot spring centres on the island along with *Peitou* and *Yangmingshan*, and when the wellness boom arrived in Taiwan during the 1990s these hot spring areas took this as a sign to start developing their natural resources without further delay. Wulai is said to have been settled centuries ago by the *Atayal*, who were possibly the first people to have used the hot springs, as they gave it the name Wulai after *Kirofu-Ulai* which apparently means 'hot and poisonous' [Taiwan Government Information Office, n.d.(c)]. In recent years Taiwanese hot spring resorts have increased in popularity and use their natural environment, local culture and history as well as the medical benefits to attract health and wellness tourists to the many health and wellness spas that have been established.

Natural hot springs in *Indonesia* are bountiful due to the large number of active volcanoes that provide geologic conditions for the thermal water that feeds the springs. Not much historical information is readily available, mainly due to language barriers, but judging by the amount of geothermal resources in many areas of the country it appears logical that people would have used them in the past for bathing and washing, especially since some springs have a reputation for healing properties that are said to be beneficial in the treatment of rheumatism and skin disorders (Ciater Hot Spring, n.d.). In more recent times Indonesia has developed hot spring spas and resorts with thermal swimming pools and treatment facilities in order to attract health and wellness spa tourists.

The natural hot springs in *Malaysia* are also of volcanic origin, are rich in minerals and have a reputation for being beneficial for health. Small places such as *Pedas Hot Springs* in Negeri Sembilan have long been famous for the therapeutic quality of the thermal waters and people have been visiting these springs for more than 60 years. Recently a large water park has been established to attract more visitors (Editorial Team, n.d.). However, judging by the individual websites that refer to various hot springs in Malaysia, it looks as if many locations are at this stage underdeveloped and mainly used by locals who believe in the healing powers of the water. In this way, places such as *Tambun* Hot Springs and *Telega Air Hangat* appear to attract visitors through a combination of hot springs and traditional cultural experiences (Sunway, n.d.; Virtual Malaysia, n.d.).

Oceania

The countries of Oceania, including the island communities of the South Pacific combined, have many hot spring areas, but generally they are not in a developed state as in Europe, East Asia or the Americas. Nevertheless, New Zealand and Australia are almost certainly in the forefront when it comes to hot spring use for health and wellness tourism.

New Zealand has traditionally used the thermal resources widely available throughout the North Island and to a lesser degree in the South Island for health and wellness spa tourism. Hot springs were valued from the beginning of settlement by the *Māori* (*c.* 1100 AD), who thought that certain thermal pools had spiritual guardians and thus made them central to important rituals (Swarbrick, 2006). The Māoris also used the hot springs for cooking, bathing, washing and treating ailments, and when European settlers arrived not only did they build bathhouses, but they also made the Māoris use separate pools, which sometimes led to conflict (Swarbrick, 2006). The reaction of the European settlers to the geothermal resources of New Zealand is well illustrated in the following quote (Box 3.2):

Box 3.2   European reaction to geothermal New Zealand

Amongst the manifold blessings bountiful Nature has bestowed upon New Zealand, to which hitherto very little or no attention has been paid, none deserve our consideration more than the thermal springs... (Read by J. Haast, Ph.D., F.R.S. before the Nelson Association for the Promotion of Science and Industry, May 4, 1870). (Stafford, 1986)

In 1880 the New Zealand Government started to build large thermal spas at *Rotorua* and *Te Aroha* (North Island) and *Hanmer Springs* (South Island; Haast, 1870) in order to treat medical conditions, but also to attract tourists. A thriving health tourism trade developed over time around the geothermal facilities of Rotorua, including the *Polynesian Spa* (Polynesian Spa, n.d.) and the *Queen Elisabeth Hospital* where people underwent thermal treatments (QE Health, n.d.). New Zealand does not appear to have suffered as much as some other countries from a decline in the use of thermal facilities; from the 1970s many thermal resorts were modernised to keep up with health and safety expectations, and expanded to attract more visitors. New Zealand springs are more fully described as a case study in Chapter 9.

Australia is known as a dry country with many deserts and very few obvious water resources on the surface. But parts of the Australian continent have geothermal water reserves stored in deep artesian basins which were discovered in the central and eastern inland around 1880 AD. Approximately 4700 artesian bores have been drilled in the Great Artesian Basin over the last 120 years, with around 3100 springs still flowing. In spite of this, only a few examples of direct use (bathing, swimming, thermalism) by tourists are known, although the development of geothermal attractions for bathing would make some inland areas of Australia a more attractive tourist destination (Habermehl & Pestov, 2002).

Considering the overall size of the country not many genuine hot springs have been developed so far. One of the rare thermal spring facilities that it has is located in the town of *Moree* in northern New South Wales. The hot (artesian) water was accessed by drilling for irrigation purposes in the year 1895. Once the gushing hot water was under control, a large pool was dug so that residents could enjoy 'taking the waters'. By 1898 the first Moree Baths complex (see Figure 3.14) was completed, with further extensions carried out in the year 1913 to provide more comfort in the open air bathing environment (Moree History, 1995).

Figure 3.14 Moree's hot mineral water is used by several motels and resorts as well as by the original Hot Mineral Baths
Source: Photograph courtesy of P. Erfurt-Cooper.

The *Helidon* Hot Springs in southern Queensland were originally reported and mapped by the explorer Alan Cunningham (Helidon Mineral Spa Park, 2005; Pearn & Little, 1998). The Helidon Spa was not established until 1879, but was then in true Australian fashion proclaimed as 'Australia's Wonderful Mineral Water' on a par with the finest hot springs in Europe, with its waters described as a supreme health-bringer and health-preserver but also as 'invaluable hygienically' (Stuart, 1920: 7). The Helidon springs were known to the local Aborigines for thousands of years and were regarded as sacred sites (Pearn & Little, 1998). In the year 1966 Helidon Spa claimed to have the biggest manmade swimming pool in Australia; however, in the 1980s concerns about bacterial contamination were raised. The waters required chemical treatment to counteract the risk to human health, which was seen as contrary to the ethos of natural waters and the spa went into decline (Pearn & Little, 1998).

In the southern parts of Australia the discovery of mineral or hot springs was often a result of mining operations during the search for gold in the 1850s. Even then the concentration of natural mineral springs (110 springs were officially counted) was seen as a potential natural resource; however, apart from some early developments of mineral spring spas in Victoria this industry never really took off until recently. It is understood that at least some of the springs were known to the Aborigines for a long time before the settlers arrived, although without written records this can only be speculation (Menadue, 1972).

In the year 1992, Charles Davidson, founder of the *Peninsula Hot Springs Centre* (on the Mornington Peninsula near Melbourne), was inspired by the pleasures of *Onsen* bathing in Japan. Since then he and his brother were determined to open something similar in Australia (Svart, 2006). After eight stressful years of drilling for natural hot water and building, the centre finally opened end of June 2005. This thermal spa is the only one in Victoria with natural hot water that does not require artificial heating (Webb, 2005), and is fully described in Chapter 9.

North America and Canada

For the native Indians of North America hot springs were sacred places. The Indians believed in the healing powers of the minerals in the thermal waters and most major hot springs in the United States have some record of use by local Indian tribes for rituals and ceremonies (Frazier, 2000). Thermal springs were also known as neutral ground, where warriors could rest undisturbed and recuperate from battle (Lund, 2002). Although there are no Indian architectural remains near hot springs, reliable evidence in the form of pottery and other artefacts indicates the presence of native tribes in these geothermal areas.

By the year 1888 there were 8843 hot springs recorded in the *United States* alone, of which 634 were used as spas (Bischoff, 2001). But due to lack of governmental support some thermal spring resorts that had opened in the 1880s went into decline and closed down during the middle of the last century; several other locations however (e.g. mineral hot springs and hot sulphur springs) went through major renovations and are either back in business or never had to close down. Nearly

100 years later the official count of thermal springs was 1702 in 23 states. Many unnamed springs were omitted (Berry *et al.*, 1980), which may explain the vast difference to the recorded numbers of hot springs from 1888. The use of natural hot springs in North America is described by Lund (2000b) in three stages:

(1) native Indians used them as sacred places, hot springs and neutral grounds;
(2) original development of spa facilities by European settlers; and
(3) contemporary places of relaxation and fitness.

In the current spa and wellness literature North American hot springs are widely covered by a range of guide books or chronicle type publications dealing with individual regions and usually include a brief history of the area described as well as a listing of all the known hot springs of a particular area or state. Most of these books were published rather recently, possibly motivated by the onset of the wellness trend in the 1990s (see Chapter 8). The following book titles are some examples reflecting the popularity of hot springs among the casual domestic traveller and were used to examine the state of current hot spring use in North America (Box 3.3):

Box 3.3 Sources of information on USA hot springs

Taking the Waters in Texas: Springs, Spas and Fountains of Youth by J.M. Valenza (2000), University of Texas Press, Austin, Texas.
Healing Waters: Missouri's Historic Mineral Springs and Spas by L. Bullard (2004), University of Missouri Press, Columbia, Missouri.
Glenwood Springs: The History of a Rocky Mountain Resort by J. Nelson (1999), Western Reflections, Inc., Ouray, Colorado.
Beautiful Spas and Hot Springs of California by S. Young (2003), Chronicle Books, San Francisco, California.
Colorado's Hot Springs by D. Frazier (2000), Pruett Publishing Company, Boulder, Colorado.
Touring New Mexico Hot Springs by M. Bischoff (2001), Falcon Guide, The Globe Pequot Press, Guildford, Connecticut.
Touring Washington and Oregon Hot Springs by J. Birkby (2002), Falcon Guide, The Globe Pequot Press, Guildford, Connecticut.
The Making of American Resorts: Saratoga Springs, Ballston Spa, Lake George by T. Corbett (2001), Rutgers University Press, New Brunswick, New Jersey.
(The authors)

As in Canada or Latin America it was the local native tribes who used the thermal waters for health and ceremonial purposes (Table 3.4). There was widespread faith in these medicinal waters, which has parallels throughout history in nearly every country with natural hot springs. Later the early European settlers got into the

Table 3.4 Some examples of native tribes of American Indians who made use of local hot springs for health and ceremonial purposes

Prehistoric use of hot springs by native Indian Tribes in the Americas		
Agua Caliente	California	Cahuilla Indians
Calistoga in the Napa Valley	California	Wappa, Pomos and Mayacmas Indians
Cajamarca (Inca Baths)	Peru	Inca
Crater Lake (Mt. Mazama Caldera)	Oregon	Klamath Indians
Kruzgamepa Hot Springs, Kilo Hot Springs, Chief Shakes Hot Springs	Alaska	Eskimos, Tlingit Indians
Miette (Fairmont) Hot Springs (Medicine Waters)	Canada	Nez Perce, Shoshones and Flathead Indians
Minnekahta Springs	South Dakota	Sioux Indians
Pah Tempe Hot Springs	Utah	Paiute Indians and Navajo
Glenwood Hot Springs (Big Medicine Spring – Yampah)	Colorado	Ute, Comanche and Arapaho Indians
Lake Amatitlan Thermal Springs	Guatemala	Maya
Radium Hot Springs	Canada	Kootenai and Apache Indians
Saratoga Springs, High Rock Spring	New York	Mohawks (Iroquois) and Tuscarora Indians
Sleeping Child Hot Springs	Montana	Nez Perce Indians
Valley of the Vapours (City of Hot Springs)	Arkansas	Tunicas and Natchitoches Indians, later Cherokees and Quapaws
Warm Springs	Georgia	Creek Indians and Iroquois Indians
Warm Springs	Oregon	Paiute Indians, Wasco Indians
White Sulphur Springs	West Virginia	Shawnee Indians
Yellowstone National Park, Smoking Waters (Bahguewana), Thermopolis	Wyoming	Arapaho and Shoshone Indians
Agua (Aqua) Hedionda	Mexico	Aztecs
Tequesquiatlapan (river with carbonated water)	Mexico	Nahua and Chichimeca Indians

Note: Hot springs were considered sacred sites and appear to have been respected even among warring tribes and treated as neutral ground.
Source: The authors.

habit of 'going to the springs' annually, similar to today's annual holidays at a spa resort with thermal facilities (Bullard, 2004).

The *Hot Springs National Park* (HSNP) in the northern state of Arkansas is the location for 43 thermal springs, whose importance was first recognised in 1832 when the first Federal reservation was established to protect natural resources for public enjoyment. The thermal springs of HSNP have long been valued for the recreational and therapeutic benefits of the thermal water baths, and as an attractive destination since the history of the area was first recorded. This Hot Springs Reservation developed into the *City of Hot Springs*, which was incorporated in 1876 (Yeatts, 2006: 2). However, accounts of development of the thermal springs originate sometime before 1877, indicating that some springs had been walled in and covered by masonry arches to protect them from contamination by this date (Scully, 1966).

New Mexico's first thermal health spa at *Ojo Caliente* was established in 1880, but the local history claim is that the hot springs were used long before by ancient native tribes (who built pueblos with terraced gardens overlooking the hot springs) and have possibly been the home to thousands of people (Witcher, 2002a). In the year 1525 the Spaniards, in their quest for precious metals and the 'fountain of youth', rediscovered the hot springs and named them. Ojo Caliente is suggested by Witcher to be the oldest health spa of America, but without written records this is difficult to establish.

The *Faywood* Hot Springs in New Mexico are also said to have attracted prehistoric and native American peoples, as well as Spanish explorers, buffalo hunters, miners and in more recent times health seekers of various socio-cultural backgrounds. Again there are no reliable dates for the times before the Spanish explorers arrived in North America in the first half of the 16th century. Today the Faywood Hot Springs are commercially developed as a thermal spring resort offering a wide range of activities in relation to the hot spring location (Witcher, 2002b).

Although *Hawaii* has geologic preconditions for natural hot springs which could possibly be used for thermal tourism, very little is in fact known about the use of natural springs on the islands. Warm springs near *Kawaihae* on Hawaii's western coast were mentioned by the explorer and missionary *William Ellis* in 1826 as being used by the local residents, some of whom attributed medicinal qualities to the minerals in the water (Benedetto & Millikan, 1985; Takahashi & Woodruff, 1990). But otherwise the Hawaiians appear to show no interest in using their natural hot spring resources for health and wellness, as most of their luxury spa resorts have not sought to gain access to geothermal resources.

There are approximately 110 warm and hot springs throughout *Canada* (Woodsworth, 1997), with each spring having its own unique blend of minerals, gases and temperature. The hot spring spas and resorts are mainly located in British Columbia, Alberta and Saskatchewan, and are characterised by naturally occurring, water-based health and wellness treatments (de la Barre *et al.*, 2005).

Planning for the development of hot spring facilities in western Canada started around 1883 following the first visits of Europeans in the year 1859. In 1885 the area around *Cave* and *Basin* Hot Springs (*Banff*) was earmarked for development as a national park including a European style spa (Kurillowicz, 1995). However, as a result of disagreements over the private ownership of the Banff Hot Springs the Canadian Government decided to create the Banff National Park instead, including the land with the hot springs (Lund, 2003). At the Banff Upper Hot Springs the initial Grand View Villa including a bathhouse was built in 1886 and later came under the management of the Canadian Government. This recently renovated bathhouse is used by over 500,000 visitors annually, not counting other facilities also receiving thermal water from the Upper Springs, including a sanatorium and a hotel with thermal pools (Lund, 2003).

The *Radium Hot Springs* (near Calgary, Alberta) were used for centuries by the Kootenai Indians before the first Europeans arrived (Wightman & Wall, 1985; Zieroth, 1978). After some time of private ownership the Radium Hot Springs were expropriated and subsequently included in the Kootenay National Park under the management of Parks Canada (Lund, 2003). *Miette Hot Springs*, along with other thermal sources, also seem to have been used by local tribes before the Europeans arrived in Canada. The area around the hot springs (which today supply the *Fairmont Hot Springs Resort*) was used in the ancient past by Indian tribes (such as the Nez Perce, the Shoshones and the Flathead) who set up their tepees in a small settlement near what they called the '*Medicine Waters*' (Anon, 2003).

Meso-America

Meso-America and especially the Caribbean Islands (*Lesser Antilles*) are located in a highly active volcanic region and thus provide a considerable amount of natural hot springs in many areas. These springs have been used wherever they can be accessed; however, like in other areas (where the Romans did not leave their 'thermal' mark for example) reliable records are scarce and therefore careful speculation regarding the historical timeframe of hot spring use in Meso-America has to be employed. To establish the history of hot spring use in Meso-America and the Antilles is difficult because the sources are fragmentary and incomplete as well as quite often distorted. This makes it impossible to reconstruct a reliable timeline that reflects exactly the ancient customs related to thermal bathing in natural springs for health and leisure purposes. Nevertheless, examples from some countries can be given as below.

There are 576 known natural hot and mineral springs in *Mexico* and many have been used for therapeutic benefits (Brooke, n.d.) in the ancient past. These geothermal resources are also used for commercial and industrial purposes along with the supply of 20 bathing and swimming pool sites with thermal water. Several places with natural thermal water are used for recreation as well as therapeutic purposes, with Olympic-sized swimming pools fed by thermal springs. The use of balneology or thermalism is not promoted on a large scale like in European countries, although some springs were used by the early Aztecs for health purposes (Lund & Freeston, 2001). The great Aztec leaders, including Montezuma I and II and their warriors, spent time at natural thermal spas to recuperate from strenuous royal duties. One of these, *Aqua Hedionda* as it is now called, was later developed into a fashionable spa by the Spaniards (Arriaga *et al.*, 1999; Brooke, n.d.; Lund, 2002; Salgado-Pareja, 1988).

One of the first colonial spas was built at the end of the 1700s in *San Bartolo Agua Caliente* and it is commonly suggested that the use of the thermal waters goes back before the dates officially used today (Hodgson, 2004). It is accepted by historians that the Aztec ruling class enjoyed their hot springs and built pleasure gardens around them. They also believed in the curing properties of the thermal waters and used them for health reasons (Brooke, n.d.). Here they could escape from state affairs and relax in peace and comfort, much like heads of state along with mere mortals do in the contemporary world.

In *Guatemala* thermal springs are used for various purposes, including bathing resorts and health spas, but are also used for industrial purposes such as heating and fruit drying (Marini *et al.*, 1998; Merida, 1999). Anthropological evidence uncovered at *Lake Amatitlan* near Guatemala city appears to indicate that the Maya used thermal springs as early as 500 BC (Altman, 2002: 40).

Nicaragua, especially the western side, is largely an active volcanic area with an abundance of hot springs. Because of the medicinal properties of these hot springs, some have been developed into health resorts or spas (e.g. *Baños Termales* or *Aguas Claras*). The trend towards health and wellness is stimulating development in Nicaragua in order to cater for thermal tourism using the abundant low-temperature geothermal areas (Zúñiga *et al.*, 2003).

Because *Costa Rica* has the geology of an active volcanic environment, numerous hot springs are expected here. However, they are hard to find and not many have been developed into tourist destinations. Going by Mitchell's (1994) description many hot springs are only known to local villagers or are situated on privately owned land, which makes it difficult to investigate any historical use other than guessing that native residents enjoyed them where they were accessible.

St Lucia is one of several islands included in the volcanic island arc of the Lesser Antilles located in the Caribbean. Natural hot springs have been used in the past, but the first mineral baths were commissioned by King Louis XVI of France (St Lucia, 2007) when he realised that these particular hot springs contained the same beneficial minerals as the thermal waters of Germany and France (Dabrowska, 2004). The first baths were completed in 1786 only to be destroyed a short time later during the devastating effects of the French Revolution, which affected the colonies as well. Some of the original baths have been re-established under private ownership and a further large restoration project is planned to preserve the historical value of these ancient thermal baths (St Lucia, 2007).

The island of *Montserrat* used to have a 'natural spa' known as the *Hot Water Pond*. According to legend the Hot Water Pond would cure rheumatism and other ailments if a coin was tossed in for the guardian spirit (Davison, 2003). The thermal springs of Montserrat were used by locals and visitors alike, but nobody can say for sure from when. The springs are now buried under pyroclastic debris from the devastating eruptions of the long thought to be dormant volcano *Soufrière Hills* in 1995 (personal communication with D. Lea, Montserrat).

Martinique is another island with a long volcanic history. In the year 1902 *Mount Pelée* completely destroyed the town of *St. Pierre* under a cloud of hot ash. Recent geothermal studies have revealed though that despite the volcanic activity thermal springs are not as numerous here (Sanjuan *et al.*, 2005) as in other areas near active volcanoes.

South America

The South American countries offer an abundance of thermal spring destinations due to the high volcanic activity in large parts of the continent. Most areas have a history that goes back to the times before European explorers and conquerors arrived. Some written records stem from the Spaniards when they were trying to exploit the country's natural resources in the same manner as they tried in Meso-America. Instead of precious metals and the fabled 'Fountain of Youth' they discovered thermal springs and other geothermal manifestations, which were known to the local population before the uninvited arrival of the European conquerors and 'explorers'. The largest empire of antiquity south of the equator was the Inca Empire, which at its height ruled over Northern Chile, upland Argentina, Bolivia, Peru, Ecuador and Southern Colombia. Its ruling classes and military utilised the available hot springs wherever available (Calderón, 1999: 555).

In modern South America the current preferred use of hot springs seems to be mainly for recreational purposes, including health treatments. Judging by the number of aquatic leisure parks in several Latin American countries, it is obvious that hot springs play an important role in the health and leisure tourism environment, often paired with tours of nearby national parks with volcanic attractions. Some examples of thermal spring use from the past and present are briefly examined here.

Like most South American countries *Brazil* has many thermal spring areas that are used for health, wellness and leisure tourism. It is commonly understood that these hot springs were used long before the European invasion of the South American countries. The first written references about the thermal waters of, for example, the *Caldas Novas* region in the State of Goiás were made in 1545 AD in Spain [Caldas Novas, n.d.(a)]. In the year 1722 AD *Bartolomeu Bueno da Silva* discovered thermal springs in the same area while searching for gold, and settlers made use of the hot springs as they moved further inland away from the coast. Today, the hot springs and the volcanic environment of Caldas Novas (with more than 80 hotels) are one of the most important tourist attractions of the region, drawing increasing numbers of international visitors [Caldas Novas, n.d.(b)]. Other notable thermal establishments are the *Rio Quente* resorts, the *Parques das Fontes* and the *Costão do Santinho Spa* in Florianopolis (which uses traditional European treatment methods) (Brazil Spas, n.d.).

Thermal mineral resorts exist in all parts of the Brazilian State of *Santa Catarina*, with *Gravatal, Tubarão, Santo Amaro da Imperatriz, Águas Mornas, Treze Tílias* and *Piratuba* being the most popular ones. *Balneário Camboriú* is the preferred destination for third-age tourists because of its excellent infrastructure (Santa Catarina

Brazil, n.d.). Unfortunately no information about the history of these areas could be gained, although there are local legends related to the natural springs that were used by the local population in the past.

The Incas of *Peru* enjoyed the numerous hot springs scattered throughout Peruvian territory for medicinal purposes (Prazak, n.d.). The country features over 500 locations where visitors can enjoy the benefits of thermal baths in hot springs, which are equated with good health due to their mineral content. Most hot springs in Peru appear to be ideal for easing aches and pains and are also a place for tourists to relax [Peru Hot Springs, n.d.(a)].

The most famous of Peru's hot springs are the Inca Baths in *Cajamarca*. According to historical sources, when the Spanish conquerors arrived the Inca ruler *Atahualpa* (1502–1533 AD) and his court were found in the baths of Cajamarca, which are today called *Baños del Inca*. These baths are located at more than 2500 m above sea level [Peru Hot Springs, n.d.(b)]. In ancient times this place was known as *Pultumarca* and was an aristocratic residence with several palaces surrounded by hot springs and thermal bath facilities, used as a luxury retreat for the imperial family. Today Cajamarca is one of the most important tourist destinations in Peru (Calderon, 1999; Termasworld, n.d.).

The recently refurbished thermal springs of *Aguas Calientes* (Machu Picchu Pueblo) are believed to possess curative powers and offer several pools of varying size and temperature to the health seeking tourist [Peru Hot Springs n.d.(c)]. In the same way, the seven 'sacred lakes' at *Las Huaringas* are attributed with medicinal properties, have been used since pre-Hispanic times for magical and healing ceremonies, and are visited mainly by the local population. As the Huaringas are also considered highly potent in therapeutic magic, they are regularly frequented by witch doctors and faith healers from every part of the country as well as by many local and foreign faith-healing believers. Tradition demands that one has to be accompanied by one's personal witch doctor or shaman, who can be hired locally or brought along from another area (The Huaringas, n.d.).

Uruguay is rich in thermal water resources and has developed thermal aquatic centres mainly for leisure and recreation. One example is the *Parque Acuático Acuamanía* in Salto, which presents the latest in aqua entertainment. However, the health tourism side is catered for as well; thermal facilities with qualified medical staff offer preventive as well as curative balneology and hydrotherapy (Salto Uruguay, n.d.).

Along the Uruguay River balneology is associated with oil exploration efforts that began about 60 years ago when deep wells were drilled in the Uruguayan sector of the *Chaco-Parana* Basin. Some of these thermal wells brought about the development of thermal spas, which are still in operation. In the mid-1990s the successful spa industry in Uruguay led to the proposal of similar developments on the Argentinean side of the Uruguay River. After drilling a hole of 1260 m depth, this well produced sufficient thermal water and the first thermal spa in the northeast of Argentina was opened in 1997. Other thermal wells were drilled and more are planned on both sides of the Uruguay River (Pesce, 2002).

In the *Catamarca* province of *Argentina* are hundreds of hot springs, most of them with therapeutic properties but with very few tourist facilities. Several thermal springs have names that indicate a patron saint (*Aguaditas de San José, Aguas de Dionisio*), and thus suggest a history of either cultural/religious use or therapeutic use. However, in other regions of Argentina, as a result of the country's highly volcanic topography, abundant thermal springs surface naturally along the Cordillera de los Andes. Thermal spas exist or are developing also in non-volcanic areas such as *Entre Ríos, Buenos Aires* and the *Chaco* (Leitner, 2001: 27). Many of *Mendoza's* thermal springs for instance have excellent facilities, and hiking through the mountains will reveal many more springs that are not yet commercialised (Leitner, 2001: 634). Access to many hot springs in Argentina is seasonal and some can only be reached at certain times of the year or by 4WD vehicles. Others can only be reached via hiking trails or climbing mountain sides and are located in as yet unspoilt natural settings or else on private properties with no public access.

In *Ecuador* the well-known thermal springs of *Papallacta* invite tourists for a refreshing visit (Ecuador, n.d.). Other thermal spas combined with pleasant weather and recreational opportunities have also become tourist destinations, with *Baños* attracting both domestic and international visitors to its famous hot springs. The church of the Virgin of the Holy Water (*Nuestra Señora del Agua Santa*), which is known as a place of pilgrimage, also draws visitors to Baños (Hamre, n.d.). The hot spring baths of Baños are fed by picturesque falls cascading off the mountain (Yaeger & Lepkowski, n.d.).

Chile's spas attract several visitors to their unique natural assets. The thermal springs of Chile are scattered from the arid northern desert to the southern temperate forests [Chile, n.d.(a)]. One of Chile's oldest thermal centres, *Jahuel* Hot Springs, was visited by Charles Darwin in 1834 (Thermal Chile, 2000). The Termas de Chillan and the *Quitralco* Hot Springs are thermal spas that have developed from small summer resorts into prestigious thermal resorts [Chile, n.d.(b)].

In *Bolivia* natural thermal springs and mudholes draw visitors to the natural spas of *Salar de Uyuni* (Bolivia in Pictures, n.d.).

Antarctica

Tourism in Antarctica appears to have increased at a steady rate over recent years as more people have the means and the inclination to travel to the most remote areas of the world. In recent years between 13,000 and 15,000 tourists per year have made landings in Antarctica and during the season of 2003–2004 visitor numbers increased by 45% to over 19,500 (Bastmeijer & Roura, 2004: 763).

A special area that can be reached via cruise ships who ferry their passengers in small boats to this rather hidden place is *Pendulum Cove* on *Deception Island* (see Figures 3.15 and 3.16). Hot springs seep out of the ground at the black volcanic beach and mix with the cold seawater. Apparently this creates so much interest among the cruise ship passengers that many of them strip off for a dip in the thermal water. The main attraction is probably more the unusual environment rather than the quest for health and wellness through thermal bathing.

Figure 3.15 Cruise ship passengers experiencing volcanic hot springs at Pendulum Cove on Deception Island
Source: Deception Island (n.d.). Photos courtesy of Galen R. Frysinger, www.galenfrysinger.com.

Africa: South of the Sahara

Most African countries have hot springs, which are generally known to the local population if accessible. Given the political situation in individual African countries however, relatively little development on a commercial scale has so far been exercised. And the countries with a known tradition of hot spring use do not have much to offer in the sense of reliable written records which could indicate historical dates. Therefore the following paragraphs can only give some brief examples of what is available in more recently developed African hot springs rather than a historical review.

In *Namibia*, not far from the capital *Windhoek*, are two hot spring spas, *Gross Barmen Thermal Baths* and the *Reho Spa*, both said to relieve rheumatism [Namibia, n.d.(a)]. Another trendy hot spring destination in Namibia is the *Hot Springs Resort* situated at the southern end of the Fish River Canyon and popular with hikers who soothe their bodies in the lukewarm sulphurous spring water [Ai-Ais Hot Springs Resort, n.d.(a)].

The town of 'Warmbad' (also known as Warmbaths) in Namibia was known by the local tribes as 'Bela Bela' meaning the 'boiling place', which indicates earlier use by local settlers without giving a precise timeline. Established as a bathing facility by white settlers in the late 1800s, Warmbad soon became renowned for its beneficial waters and attracted visitors mainly seeking relief from rheumatism and arthritis (Warmbaths, n.d.). The relatively close proximity of the Warmbad resort and other related facilities to Johannesburg airport (a 1 hour drive) draws international visitors as well as domestic tourists (Warmbaths, n.d.). However, other sources claim that Warmbad has fallen into decline and is hardly worth mentioning. The name 'Warmbad' reverted to Bela Bela in the year 2002 (History of Warmbaths, n.d.).

Throughout *Cameroon* are several thermal spring areas that are popular for their outdoor health spas and retreats (Bird, n.d.). *Maji Moto* (meaning hot water in Swahili) in *Tanzania* is a national park with sulphur hot springs. The area is also known as the site of one of Ernest Hemingway's hunting camps (Maji Moto Camp, n.d.; Islamic Tourism, 2004) while on a safari with his wife in 1933–1934, which resulted in the book *Green Hills of Africa*.

Natural hot springs and fumaroles are found throughout *Kenya* and have been used by the local population for worship and sacrificial offerings, especially when they were afflicted with diseases that were difficult to cure (Tole, 2002). However, more research is required to examine the historical background of hot spring use in the African countries.

Summary

Much of the European and Asian history of natural hot spring use can be traced back at least 2000–3000 years, mainly because the Romans, Japanese and Chinese left behind such an abundance of reliable evidence. Hot springs have been considered as places of healing, relaxation and worship in all parts of the world throughout known history and probably well before this. Only very few countries have no hot springs at all and even these are usually not too far away from another country that has enough thermal capacity to share.

Throughout history the most popular places for rest and recreation have been those with access to natural thermal water and related treatment facilities. Depending on their mineral content, hot springs have been, and still are, used to successfully treat a wide range of illnesses. Significantly, the success rate of healing through thermalism has maintained the high reputation of thermal springs as medicinal springs with curative powers. As a result, historical hot spring towns and spas are still in existence or have been preserved as museums of ancient thermal healing, while new facilities have been developed around the antique remains and new sources of thermal water.

Chapter 4
Cultural and Religious Use of Water

PATRICIA ERFURT-COOPER

Introduction

This chapter gives special consideration to the remarkable cultural importance of the use of water in human society, as expressed in religion and mythology. It includes examples of the special cultural relationship different cultures and civilisations have had (and still have) with natural resources like hot and mineral springs, and looks at the differences and similarities of their use for religious purposes, aiming to provide an insight and understanding of the importance of health and wellness spa treatments for tourism in a variety of socio-cultural settings.

The significance of water in culture is associated with two distinct environments – the physical and the spiritual. Both are of extreme importance to cultures worldwide, although with regional differences. Often the physical and the spiritual overlapped and resulted in 'water worship', which attributes the source of the water to certain divinities. Natural hot springs have universally been seen as extraordinary and awe inspiring, mainly because people were not sure of how to explain their occurrence. Hot springs were considered a gift of the gods, and temples and shrines were erected in their vicinity (Lee, 2004), a custom still adhered to especially in Asian countries. This lack of scientific knowledge did not, however, stop people from using thermal waters if they could access them without danger and if the temperature was acceptable. Therefore separation of the religious and mythological beliefs relating to sacred springs of geothermal origin has not been attempted for this book, as it was considered only necessary to demonstrate the importance of the spiritual side of spring use in general terms to be able to throw some light on the antecedents of health and wellness spa tourism.

Without water there would be no life at all on Earth. Water and life are inseparable, not the least because the essence of a human being is water (Emoto, 2005: 15) and it is universally held in high regard as an agent for purification and the ritual washing away of sins (King, 1966: 186). Religions worldwide include water as a medium of divine origin, and nearly all religions and cultures equate water with energy (Arvigo & Epstein, 2003: 11). In the Japanese tradition as described in the 'Records of Ancient Matters' (The Kojiki, 1982), the sacred rite most frequently mentioned in that culture is purification by water. And, as cultures grew to be more sophisticated this veneration of water became the basis for secular social activities, such as the *thermae* of Ancient Rome, the *Onsen* culture of Japan, and ultimately the health and wellness spa culture of modern times.

Water as a Life-giving Force

The importance of water to human cultures lies in the fact that it is the most flexible of elements and can be used in all its individual stages: as a liquid for cleansing and bathing, as a gas or vapour for inhalation therapy, or in its solid state as ice for various uses. Water is also a carrier of essential mineral and trace elements, depending on its origin. Life and water are inseparable on this planet (King, 1966) and water has always been a symbol of life and the key to health and longevity, as well as the key to spiritual, emotional and physical well-being with its cleansing powers recognised in most spiritual traditions (Ryrie, 1999). Perhaps the divine 'spring of life' mentioned in the New Testament of the Christian *Bible* (Gideon International Australia, 2000d) has contributed to the eternal human search for the 'fountain of youth' and has inspired people of all cultures to sample the springs of the world.

All living things contain water up to half or more of their body weight (Australian Academy of Science, 1994), and humans are about 60–70% water (Clugston, 2004). The ancient Greeks classed water as the highest of the four elements the world was made of and the Cherokee Indians for example still see water as the Earth's lifeblood (Ryrie, 1999). According to the *Koran* (King, 1966: 186; Shiva, 2002: 131) water is the source of all life and by water everything lives. Ancient cultures (Chinese, Aztecs, Incas and Africans) recognised that moving water collects, stores and transfers energy and physical and vibration information. These cultures also knew how to store water to prevent it from pollution and keep it fresh – the Chinese saved water from glaciers in jade jars and the Incas and Aztecs kept water in obsidian jars (Ryrie, 1999: 18).

In relation to hot springs, for the Native Americans thermal waters were part of healing, strengthening and affirming the life-giving connection with the Earth through water (Frazier, 2000). Buildings specially devoted to cleansing the body have also been discovered in the centres of ancient civilisation in Mesopotamia and the Indus Valley. Bathing chambers in Mohenjo-Daro (*c.* 2000 BC) are thought to have been designed for public and private use and this concept may have spread all over the ancient world through trading contacts (Schafer, 1954).

In more modern times the Thermalism Office in *Tunisia* (Office of Thermalism Tunisia, n.d.) has presented a medical view of the role of water in the body but this is still essentially referring to the culture of water use in that country: 'Water is an essential element in maintaining physical performance and intellectual capacity, helps fight against heat, hydrates the skin, enables the transportations of hydro-soluble vitamins and minerals, favours urinary waste elimination and facilitates kidney operation'. Water is also unique in that it can occur as liquid, solid or gas (Allaby & Allaby, 1999: 583). Water is described by Arvigo and Epstein (2003: 12) as having unique transformational power, especially when combined with prayer, and they reinforce the universal thought that water refreshes as well as calms and balances the body, mind and soul. Emoto (2006) confirms this and adds that water is constantly flowing with life and thereby purifying what it encounters by carrying away impurities and giving life to everything.

Somewhere in the genesis of every civilisation therefore is the idea of water as being *divine, life-giving, healing, cleansing* and *renewing*. King (1966: 186) maintains that throughout history water has therefore been associated with religious observances, legends of gods, and heroes and miraculous events; however, the locations of springs and rivers also determined the locations of human settlement by encouraging their development at points of water supply (including those based on hot and mineral springs – Bullard, 2004).

Role of Mythology and Religion

Many ancient people considered springs to be sacred manifestations (Bullard, 2004) and theists and atheists alike connect the beginning of life on Earth with water. The Bible mentions water on the very first page in Genesis 1:2 (Gideon International Australia, 2000b), signifying the importance given to this substance from the beginning of time. A similar message is found in the Koran, the Sumerian, Nile and Indus Valley creation legends, Hindu Sutras and Shinto and Buddhist texts, where water played a main role in the creation of the Earth and is one of the key substances essential for life. Divinity and water were closely linked; not just in the past, but to this day a commonality seems to exist in the association of natural springs (hot and cold) with divine beings. Ancient cultures revered water and the earliest deities were water gods and spirits (Ryrie, 1999). In many regions of the world a rich mythology is woven around the discovery of healing springs, initiating long traditions in hot spring use. Hot and cold springs attributed with healing powers were often directly connected to a patron saint and were named in honour of that particular saint. Water worship and holy wells were common in Europe (Arvigo & Epstein, 2003; De Villiers, 2000; Havins, 1976) with countless springs still continuing this tradition today. However, these same springs were used well before the introduction of

Christianity and had earlier been the sites of Celtic and other tribal shrines, under local deities and their religious codes.

The ancient Greeks had numerous water deities and related myths assigning water to love and power and symbolising birth, beauty and destruction (Ryrie, 1999). The temples dedicated to their god of healing *Asclepios* also had thermal baths (Mellilo, 1995) fed by local hot springs. Most if not all of these survived into Roman times. The Greek and Roman influence was also exposed in Tunisia (North Africa) when, during the redevelopment of hot spring pools at *Hammam Lif*, inscriptions bearing dedications to *Esculape* (Asclepios) as well as to *Saturn* were unearthed. The spa at *Hammam Jedidi* also appears to have been under the protection of Greek gods. Several marble statuettes of Asclepios and *Hygeia* (daughter of Asclepios and goddess of health) were found in a cistern and are thought to be votive offerings by recovering patients of this spa (Thermalism Office Tunisia, n.d.).

The cult of sacred springs has been described by Dukinsfield-Astley (1910) as a well-known characteristic of the Neolithic stage of European culture; however, he attributes the continuity of such ideas into the historical age as being naturally found among classes in which education has not made much progress, thus opening the doors to superstition. Although Dukinsfield-Astley noted that in some countries it is devout Christians who most often resort to the use of sacred spring water to treat their ailments, he also reported on a sacred pool that belongs to the *Hammam R'Irha* in Algeria. According to his personal observations this particular pool was used (and may still be used today nearly 100 years later) by natives who performed 'ritual acts and ablutions' leaving earthenware containers they may have used for offerings to the spirits of the hot spring.

Further afield, the spa in *Varazdinske Toplice* (*Aquae Iasae* – Croatia) bears several reminders of a religious basis for its continuing existence. The thermae in Aquae Iasae included a basilica as well as a marble slab with reliefs of three nymphs and various Roman mythological scenes symbolising the power of water (Gamulin, 2001). Three detached temples formed a capitoleum, with the largest temple dedicated to Jupiter and the two smaller temples dedicated to Juno and Minerva including a large marble statue of Minerva.

While occupying parts of Germany the Romans made use of the hot springs in Aachen and called the thermae they built *Aquae Granni* after the German deity for water and healing *Grannus* (Aachen, 2005), in accordance with their usual fashion of building temples near the hot spring spas they developed across the Roman Empire. The most well-known example of this policy appears however to be *Aquae Sulis* in the south of England, where the only genuine hot springs in England were developed by the Romans for therapeutic purposes. According to Gray (2003) the original hot springs at Bath were first used by Neolithic hunter-gatherers and later regarded as sacred by Celts (Sul), Romans (Minerva) and Christians alike each contributing shrines and temples to please their respective deities. Parts of the Roman thermal baths of the city of Bath are still in use today after recent renovations; however, access to the original pools, including the sacred spring, is not for bathing or uses other than sightseeing. The historical significance of the redeveloped Roman baths adds a special quality to the treatment in these facilities

The Romans had no natural explanation for hot water pouring out off the ground; to them the Spring was the work of the gods. A sacred place.

The Spring was enclosed within a building in the 2nd century. Pillars and statues were placed in the water. It became a dark and mysterious place.

It was still possible to throw offerings through the arched openings opposite and to enter the building by steps from the courtyard.

Figure 4.1 The sacred spring
Source: Modified from a photo taken by the author.

(Lee, 2004: 36). Figures 4.1 and 4.2 illustrate the religious and mythological significance of the old Roman baths.

Holy wells and sacred springs are abundant all over Europe and usually have a guardian spirit who is trusted to bestow blessings and cures (Arvigo & Epstein, 2003); thus bathing or drinking of the water would heal various diseases. In the Middle Ages convents and churches were built around natural springs (Von Furstenberg, 1993). The sacredness of water is also reflected in the beliefs of the Celts and the Native Americans who thought of springs and flowing water as living entities and as places where creation appeared on the surface of the Earth, so that humans could reach out and connect to the divine (Arvigo & Epstein, 2003: 9). The early Americans cherished their hot springs as sacred and used them as neutral ground and for rest and recreation after battle. They believed in the miraculous healing powers of the hot spring waters and are thought to have used them for medicinal reasons for several thousand years (Bischoff, 2001; Frazier, 2000; Nickell, 2005; Lund, 1993, 2002, 2005; Von Furstenberg, 1993). Spirituality and steam were one.

In Japan, Buddhist and Shinto priests were often led to hot springs with healing powers by supernatural creatures, which appeared as visions in their dreams

The Temple and hot Spring of Aquae Sulis were important as a place of worship.

Many people came from far and wide to pray at the Temple and make offerings to the goddess Sulis Minerva at the Spring.

Priests led the ceremonies in the Temple courtyard.

Figure 4.2 Pilgrims and priests
Source: Modified from a photo taken by the author.

(Hotta & Ishiguro, 1986). Animals from white herons to brown bears were called messengers from the gods by the Japanese people, because they came to show humans the location of healing and purifying waters and thus were given credit for the discoveries of many hot springs. In modern Japan the time-honoured traditions of water rituals are still present, with water as the key to purification (Swanson, 2001).

The *P'urhépecha*, an indigenous people who still live in the heart of Mexico in the state of Michoacán, used the hot spring area at *Los Azufres* (Lagoon of Sulphurs – now a national park) for formal religious and political rites. While this form of native religious expression was altered by the Spaniards after the Conquest of Mexico in 1519 (Hodgson, 1995), religious customs today still include the use of 'holy water'. In Peru there are seven sacred hot spring-derived lakes at Las Huaringas, which were used for magical and healing ceremonies before the Spanish conquerors arrived (Peruvian Waters, n.d.). They are still considered highly potent in therapeutic magic and are regularly frequented by Shamans and faith-healers from all over Peru. These traditions attract many local and foreign faith-healing believers, who come to witness the traditional rites carried out (The Huaringas, n.d.).

Religious and mythological backgrounds: How important are they?

Hot springs have been used for religious purposes by numerous cultures throughout time (Bischoff, 2001). In this sense springs acquired spiritual significance, symbolising renewal and purification (Bullard, 2004: 12). Cataldi and Burgassi (1999: 152) clarify why the existence of religious groups utilising springs in ancient times is not surprising: all natural springs were thought of as divine gifts and therefore sacred, being honoured with temples and statues or in other ways. The development of cults promoting the worship of divinities such as Asclepius and Sulis Minerva were based on the health-giving properties of the springs. The recurring presence of monuments to the gods in the vicinity of all ancient bathing complexes can thus be seen as an indication that while thermal springs may have been a means 'of strengthening religious sentiments and their gradual spread among people of every social class and culture' throughout history, their health-giving properties were the basis for this. The fundamental role of water for popular religious uses, covering all water places with divinities as guardians and the ritual immersion in water as sacral and social, is also described by Monti (n.d.) as facilitating rebirth through purification. Monti refers to ancient Greece, where the most important spas of *Asclepiae* and *Heracles* were situated near medicinal hot springs and patients were subjected to purification rites along with the therapeutic effects.

In Israel under *Mosaic Law* hygiene and cleanliness became central to the Hebrews when Moses, inspired by God, prescribed ablutions to his people (Gideon International Australia, 2000a; Von Furstenberg, 1993). In most Christian religions baptism is one of the main symbolic religious uses of water for purification and being reborn (Lee, 2004). Holy or sacred water of various origins is used to wash away sins and purify physically as well as spiritually. In Iceland hot springs were frequently used for baptism after Christianity was introduced in the year 1000 AD (Hjálmarsson, 1993), because they were more comfortable than cold water in a cold climate. The temperature of the Icelandic hot springs may have more than made up for the necessary 'sacredness' in order to convince the new Christians to take the 'plunge'.

But the ritual of baptism is not limited to Christianity alone; it is related to several religious customs worldwide, where bathing or immersion in sacred waters is used to cleanse and purify (Swanson, 2001). For instance the Hindu custom of bathing in the sacred river Ganges and other major rivers in India, which is associated with one of the highest levels of purification for pilgrims, attracts up to 50 million people every year (Cooper, 2009; Mircea, 1995: 11). In ancient Egypt it was the custom to use sacred water to baptise newborn children and purify them. Modern Jews have started to revive the 3000-year-old custom of using the traditional *Mikvah* bath for the purpose of cleansing and purification as well as strengthening their connection with God (Arvigo & Epstein, 2003). Going back in time to the New Testament of the Christian Bible we find that the pools of *Siloam* and *Bethesda* near Jerusalem feature in the Gospel of John (Gideon International Australia, 2000c) as locations where Jesus healed people. At the pool of Bethesda the sick and disabled waited for the water to be disturbed by an Angel, believing that the first person in the water after this would be healed. With such a substantial cultural backup the current use of water for healing purposes and the hope for a cure is understandable.

In Japan the tradition of public bathing dates back at least to the beginnings of Buddhism, which teaches that hygiene and ritual bathing not only purified the body of sin but also brought luck (Von Furstenberg, 1993). Zen Buddhist gardens offer bathers a serene background for contemplation as they enjoy the hot spring bath. The use of water is deeply manifested in the Japanese religious traditions relating to rites of purification (*harai*). In *Shinto* one of the five classifications of behaviour includes special 'purification sects, groups that perpetuate the tradition of water purification to cultivate body and mind: *Misogikyō* and *Shinshōkyō'* (Mircea, 1995, 13: 286). The Shinto ablution ritual of *misogi* involves the washing or showering of the hands, feet and mouth with pure water (Talmadge, 2006). However, *misogi* can also be performed by complete immersion in the sea or under a waterfall. The Shinto rite of *yukaji* involves the sprinkling of water with a broom made from dwarf bamboo (Frédéric, 2002). On a broader scale using Europe as an example, Mircea (1995, 11: 95) describes several types of purification rites, with water as a 'particularly potent source of purification when obtained from holy springs, wells or other sacred bodies of water' with the many holy wells of *Ireland* noted as being special places of purification.

The *Prophet Muhammad* and his followers highly valued water and the state of ritual purity. The Koran dictates that without bodily cleanliness prayer is 'of no value in the eyes of God' (Von Furstenberg, 1993); therefore, before entering a mosque, ritual cleansing and purification of the body and spirit have to take place in order to prepare for communication with Allah. Fountains and pools containing pure rainwater are located outside mosques for the purpose of ablution (Arvigo & Epstein, 2003). It is also important to bathe after being in contact with impurity in general and ill persons or dead bodies in particular, and the springs available throughout the Middle East facilitate this custom.

Lourdes in southern France is renowned worldwide for repeated visions of the Virgin Mary and the miraculous qualities of the underground springs, both having been declared authentic by Pope Pius IX in 1862 (Harris, 1999). However, it is interesting to find that the visitor numbers to Lourdes can vary between 1 and 6 million people annually, depending on the source of the data used. Wikipedia states 5 million pilgrims and tourists per annum, while *Encyclopaedia Britannica* states 3 million visitors annually. We cross-checked with other sources: O'Brien (2006) and Kralis (2004) were used as reference for this section with O'Brien confirming 5 million people each year but Kralis claiming 6 million pilgrims each year. Scheer (n.d.), however, mentions only 'more than one million pilgrims' each year as coming to Lourdes. Whatever the total number of pilgrims might actually be, immersion in the holy baths at Lourdes is only one of the daily rituals. Processions, blessings and organised prayers take place on a regular basis during the pilgrimage season to the sacred springs from April to October every year (O'Brien, 2006) and support the local tourism industry significantly.

Another indication of the eternal human fascination with water that issues from the Earth is evident in the displays of fountains which are popular all over the world. They are an attempt to copy nature, but at the same time control and direct the flow of the spring to form a perfect display. Fountains have been a focal point in town centres, often near churches, for centuries, as often they were the only source of fresh and unpolluted water of a village or town. In England and Germany the custom of well-dressing acknowledges and pays tribute to divine connections (Williams, n.d.) In some areas this has been turned into a tourism attraction with weeklong bus tours to visit the decorated wells and fountains and with competitions held between villages.

The custom of throwing money into wells or other bodies of water is another indication of the importance of water and can be observed worldwide. Whether it is the Trevi Fountain in Rome, the hot spring *jigoku* (hells) in Beppu, Japan, water-filled fissures at *Thingvellir* in Iceland or the old Roman baths in Bath, people throw coins into the water believing that it will avert bad luck and ill health. Coins have also been found in one of the pools of Siloam (Jerusalem), which are mentioned in the Gospel of John and are thought to have served as a gathering place for religious pilgrimages (Siloam, n.d.). The Legend of the Ghost of the Springs (see Box 4.1) from the Czech Republic is a similar attempt to explain and placate the geothermal forces at work in these locations. To see this custom in so many different countries suggests that it must be an important part of personal faith, although not necessarily related to a particular religion or a particular spring.

Box 4.1 The Legend of the Ghost of the Springs

According to an old legend from the Czech Republic, in Karlsbad/Karlovy Vary, named after its founder Karl IV, Holy Roman Emperor and King of Bohemia (Burachovic, n.d.; Kouba, n.d.; Lund, 2000a), the mysterious Ghost of the Springs resided exactly where the Castle Baths are situated today. This entity ruled over all the mineral water springs of Karlovy Vary to protect their sources from depletion and to protect against the negative intervention of the forces of nature. The three most important elements – fire, water and wind – continually threatened the local springs, which were under constant danger of disappearing thereby threatening the whole of Karlovy Vary.

For these reasons the Ghost of the Springs one day decided to undertake a very urgent and dangerous act, which he was able to carry out due to his strength and 1000-year-old knowledge. He entrapped the non-compliant and dangerous elements into the rock, in which he used to live, and moved underground to be closer to his springs. His knowledge had taught him that fire, water and wind cannot be entrapped forever. Therefore he releases them to the elements, under his careful control, every 2 hours. Their release commences with the ignition of the fire in the Sun yard which floats through the sky, thus shaking the rock by its touch and causing the rock to open. With the clatter of falling stones the wind runs out from the rock and enjoys its short freedom under a massive roll of thunder and lightning.

Later, when this scene reaches the last element – water, the Ghost of the Springs comes back from underground to manifest himself in the middle of the pool, show his dominant power and return all the elements back into the rock. And so calm and peace return to Castle Baths and to the whole of Karlovy Vary.

Another legend says that it was right at this spring that the founder of the spa town himself, the Holy Roman Emperor and King Karl IV, tried to cure his sore limbs. In reality small thermal springs had existed in place of the present big spring since ancient times. They could be found in the arcade of the old town hall. When the present wooden colonnade was built, the spring base got its fixed position and thermal water from it started to be used in the drinking cures marketed to both locals and visitors (Lund, 2000a).

Health and Wellness Spa Tourism and Thermal Bathing

What are the cultural attractions?

One of the main attractions of visiting a hot spring spa is surely the natural aspect – the use of fresh warm spring water in an environment that caters specifically for the individual customer's well-being. Maximum relaxation, recharging and reviving are hard to achieve without a change of scenery, where the customer can unwind and renew mind, body and soul at the same time. That is why health and wellness spa facilities, with or without hot springs, offer the 'great escape' to a destination that is a combination of natural environments, ancient and contemporary healing therapies, and of course modern comfort as a way of reaching a state of total well-being. To find out more about the specific attractions of hot springs the content of a variety of sources from different countries was analysed to present an overview of the most obvious reasons for hot spring use. Although different cultures may well have different preferences, key attractions like expected health improvements through beneficial mineral content in a natural environment are definitely a common thread in the material presented below.

The fact that hot springs occur in many areas worldwide has contributed much to their popularity as an attraction for health and wellness tourism (Figure 4.3). In times of political unrest and security concerns, customer expectations seem to focus increasingly on safe environments, where they can relax surrounded by comfort and quality. Benefits for health and well-being are closely linked to time-out in peaceful natural settings with idyllic scenery. A growing interest in new-age remedies and alternative health treatments has also led to a new consumer focus that includes choice of lifestyle management and the expectation of health improvements without mainstream medical intervention. This has led many people to reconsider the traditional use of hot springs, which in turn has led to the redevelopment of existing facilities as well as the building of new hot spring resorts. Of not insignificant value also is the fact that hot springs are usually classed as a renewable resource and generally do not require

---

Attractions of Hot Springs and Thermal bathing

1. Warm spring water (especially in cold climates)
2. Benefits for health and wellbeing
3. Healing therapies
4. Health improvements (prevention and rehabilitation)
5. Medically respected (especially in Europe)
6. Beneficial mineral content
7. Change of scenery
8. Natural environments, idyllic landscapes
9. Authentic hot spring water (expected in Japan)
10. No addition of chemicals (expected in Japan)
11. Friendly socialising
12. Relaxation and Time-out in peaceful surroundings
13. Modern comfort, luxury and safety
14. Historically significant
15. Traditional atmosphere, ambience
16. Architectural heritage sites
17. Geothermal phenomena found in many hot spring areas are tourist attractions, even if not used for bathing (geysers, mud pools, boiling ponds)

Figure 4.3 Attractions of hot springs and thermal bathing
Source: The author.

the addition of chemicals to ensure water quality, which is another drawcard for customers conscious about avoiding unnecessary contact with unhealthy substances.

In Japan the use of natural thermal water is an important part of life because that the country is blessed with an abundance of hot springs that are of historical significance having been utilised for many centuries. The Japanese hot springs (*Onsen*) maintain a traditional atmosphere even if they are found in a modernised bathhouse that everyone uses locally. This situation comes about as a result of a definite cultural preference for authentic hot spring water. The ambience of the natural environment is carefully guarded and preserved especially around out-door pools and the water is supposed to have a good 'feel' due to certain minerals, which are highly valued for their beneficial properties. Friendly socialising on equal terms in relaxing surroundings is important in Japanese society, and one of the attractions for using hot springs worldwide, because the hierarchy of society is reduced when people gather in a thermal pool.

There is another side to the cultural use of hot springs for tourism in Japan though; the city of *Beppu*, famous for its *Onsen* resorts and literally thousands of hot springs, offers a special tourist attraction – the *jigoku meguri* (Erfurt-Cooper, 2006). Jigoku is the Japanese word for hell and meguri refers to a tour or pilgrim-age to certain specific locations. This 'pilgrimage' however is not strictly religious, although each of these 'hells' have several sacred shrines on site. The jigoku of Beppu are a group of 10 small geothermal parks with different themes, utilising the individual variances of hot spring manifestations like boiling ponds, bubbling mud pools and steaming geysers to their full potential, attracting vast numbers of visitors on a daily basis. Several jigoku offer pleasantly warm foot and hand spas for their visitors and hot-spring-cooked food as well as the violent geothermal attractions. Every jigoku has at least one small shrine in a secluded corner offering the opportunity for a prayer (see Figures 4.4 and 4.5).

Thermalism in France on the other hand is a highly valued sector of traditional *medicine*. The French see their bathing places as medically respected, historically significant and of contemporary importance and thus continue to use them as part of their annual holidays (Mackaman, 2007). *Vichy*, for example, now has a vast new thermal establishment, but not one constructed in or emulating the opulent architecture of the past when it was fashionable to be seen 'taking the cure' in style as part of one's obligations within upper class society as much as it was for the health results (Lee, 2004). The emphasis today is instead on health and prevention of illness in a more utilitarian way (Von Furstenberg, 1993). Nevertheless, accord-ing to Boulangé (1982) one of the prime factors prompting the revival of indul-gence in thermal cures in France is the maintenance of a particular socio-cultural environment, which plays an important psychological role especially among elderly patients.

The appeal of individual hot spring facilities, not just in France, is thus usually enhanced through the presence of qualified medical staff and a combination of fine *cuisine*, idyllic landscapes and attractive socio-cultural activities. Lee (2004) describes a modern 'spa renaissance', which can be traced all over Europe, where

Figure 4.4 This small shrine invites visitors for prayer while at one of the Jigoku of Beppu in Japan. Next to the shrine a dragon's head sends forth hot steam
Source: Photograph courtesy of P. Erfurt-Cooper.

hot spring spas that had been left to decline have been redeveloped as up-to-date spa centres without losing their aura of a glorious past.

The preference for certain attractions related to natural hot and mineral springs has of course changed over time. What was a drawcard for some destinations a few hundred years ago may not be *en vogue* in the 21st century. The main appeal however remains the promise of relaxation and time-out, rejuvenation and possibly better health after treatment at a hot spring spa with beneficial waters. Another key factor influencing the preferences of individual groups is climate. In cold-climate countries like Iceland hot springs are extremely popular, with nearly every guesthouse or hotel offering 'hot tubs' fed by geothermal water to their guests. In Japan hot springs are popular throughout the country, but are best enjoyed on a cold day, often several times a day to keep warm (personal observation). In Germany the attraction is again (from personal experience over the years) the warmth of the water, as most public swimming pools are rather cool, even in summer. The hot-spring-fed pools in the spa towns have always been a treat and a great attraction for a day out or for a longer health and wellness holiday.

Figure 4.5 Wherever there is a shrine there is freshwater for purification purposes
Source: Photograph courtesy of P. Erfurt-Cooper.

Hot spring use in different social settings

Examples of particular historical (Chapter 3) and current social settings for hot springs are the:

- Roman and Greek Bath;
- Islamic *Hammam* (Turkish Bath);
- Japanese *Onsen*;
- European Thermal Baths;
- Russian *Bania*;
- Finnish *Sauna*;
- Icelandic *Hot Tubs*;
- New Zealand Government Bath House; and
- Australian *Artesian Springs*.

Examples of two of these are seen in Figures 4.6 and 4.7.

Figure 4.6 Takagawara *Onsen*, Beppu, Japan (17th century)
Source: Photograph courtesy of P. Erfurt-Cooper.

All the above-listed facilities were established in relation to a source of natural hot spring water. However, if no natural sources were or are now available, artificially heated water has generally been an acceptable substitute, with the exception of Japanese *Onsen*. The Greeks and Romans are possibly the most famous historically for their efforts to establish spa baths near natural hot springs (Verdel & Pittler, 2003) in many locations all over Europe, the Middle East and North Africa. In the Islamic tradition *Hammams* were initially used only by men for religious and recreational purposes as advocated by the prophet Muhammad. Women were given the right to visit Hammam later for health and hygiene reasons, but interestingly the visit to the Hammam then became so much a part of their social life that if a married woman was denied access to the bath this was a reason for divorce (Aaland, 1998). Hammams were introduced into Greece and Spain under Moorish influence and became quite popular in other parts of Europe, where they were and still are known as Turkish Baths. They even made their way to America, but do not seem to have become as popular as in Europe. Here, the arrival of private bathroom facilities did not help the case of the Turkish Bath. The few remaining establishments in America rarely resemble the original *Hammam*, but new spa resort developments occasionally include features resembling a Turkish Bath as an additional attraction. In Japan the remaining public bathhouses (*sento, o'furo*) faced a similar dilemma from the introduction of private bathrooms

Figure 4.7 Government Bathhouse, Rotorua, New Zealand in the 21st century
Source: Photograph courtesy of P. Erfurt-Cooper.

in the home, but this does not seem to keep many people away from the popular community baths, especially the older generations, who are used to their social meetings at regular times.

Other social settings can be found in America where the Native Indians have a different connection to their hot springs. They still visit their sacred waters during the tourist off-season, when few tourists are around, to have privacy for their spiritual pilgrimages (Frazier, 2000). This is somewhat in opposition to the traditional use of hot springs in Japan for example, where the company of other bathers is appreciated and often considered a necessary part of a social outing, with fine dining before or after while staying at a *Ryokan* (a Ryokan is a traditional Japanese accommodation similar to a hotel; however, the architecture and furnishings are very different from those of Western hotels, and an *Onsen* may be a central experience) to create a traditional atmosphere. In these settings the Japanese enjoy the company of colleagues and their bosses for friendly socialising with the opportunity to discuss more serious subjects on equal terms. However, foreign visitors may still cause a small distraction in the customary setting of a bathhouse where clients generally gather on a daily basis in their local social groups.

It is also not unusual in some countries to use the bathing establishments for meetings that are other than social. With respect to the Russian *Banias*, it is said that sometimes members of criminal organisations prefer to use the safe environment of the bath for gatherings, as no weapons can be hidden while taking a bath (Aaland, 1998). In Japanese *Onsen* on the other hand, members of societies with connections to organised crime (*Yakuza*) are not tolerated in public baths because of their habit of being tattooed, which is frowned upon in Japanese society.

Other cultures have also used their bathing facilities for meetings of various kinds. The Romans enjoyed political discussions in their *thermae* and the Chinese received official visitors in their baths (Schafer, 1956). Islamic *Hammams* and Finnish *Saunas* are also used for talking as well as relaxing, interspersed with breaks for meals and entertainment. The thermal baths in Budapest attract visitors all year to spend a day at one of the numerous well-maintained thermal pools, where a social gathering includes games of chess while enjoying the warm water. The Icelanders are also very fond of their hot spring tubs and nearly every town has their own public pool fed by natural hot springs. This is where people meet and talk, sometimes gossiping and sometimes discussing business. Foreigners are welcomed into these typical Icelandic environments, although most international visitors want to visit the famous Blue Lagoon in the southwest of the island.

Another distinct social setting is provided by the artesian hot springs of the Australian outback. Most of these are difficult to reach because they are very remote. Some are on private properties and used for domestic purposes, including bathing; however, because of the generally high mineral content and their high temperatures most of them were in the past left to drain from their sources into the desert, until they were capped to stop the wastage of this precious resource. Some of these hot springs now attract tourists of the more adventurous kind, but unless the traditional owners (Aborigines) have any spiritual connections or used them for their curative powers, which was not researched for this book, these hot springs do not offer much, other than their use by farmers and in recent times as outback destinations. The use of these springs is rather informal as can be imagined by the remote locations. So far only a few hot spring spas have been established in places like Moree in New South Wales (Chapter 3). In the State of Victoria the *Peninsula Hot Springs* facility near Melbourne is a recent development in an area with some older established cold-water mineral spring spas. However, because Australia has been settled by Europeans only for little over 200 years (1788) perhaps the existing hot and mineral springs have not been exploited to their full potential; hence there are possibilities for future developments in conjunction with geotourism.

The use of hot springs in New Zealand has by way of contrast a very long social history. For centuries *Maori* travelled to Waiwera just north of the eventual site of Auckland, the country's largest city, to heal themselves in the therapeutic warm waters. They (and their European successors) would immerse themselves in holes dug along the beachfront and line them with branches for padding. Caressing mineral water would then gently surround them, materialising from the Earth below. Translated from the Maori, Waiwera means simply 'hot water'. However, it was so revered that many referred to it as *Te Rata*, which translates as 'the doctor'. The special healing powers of Waiwera mineral water came to be known far and wide. European settlers quickly began to use the resort in the early days of Auckland city (from 1840 on).

In the Rotorua area of New Zealand a similar length of use is recorded. For more than 700 years local Maori (the *Arawa Confederation* of tribes) have lived on this special site, treasured by Maori as a place of healing and revitalisation. The first Europeans visited Hell's Gate (Tikitere) more than 150 years ago. As New Zealand's only Maori-owned geothermal reserve, Hell's Gate is of major social and cultural importance; the special muds and sulphurous waters have been guarded for centuries by the *Kaitiaki 'Wai Ora'* (guardian warrior) after whom the spa is named (http://www.aaa.com/ n.d.; Pfieff, 2000).

Hot spring baths have thus been known as centres of social and cultural activities in many countries for many centuries. Entertainment and socialising have always been reasons for visiting hot spring baths in the past. But even as lifestyles and morality changed over the centuries, the Earth's natural springs continued to attract an endless stream of bathers seeking to cleanse both body and spirit (Von Furstenberg, 1993).

Bathing customs in different countries

When it comes to the actual use of hot springs for recreational purposes, there are different behavioural patterns in different countries. The most orderly way of preparing for a bath must be the Japanese tradition of making sure that one is meticulously scrubbed clean before entering the bath whether it is the private tub at home, a communal bathhouse or a hot spring resort pool. For visiting foreigners not familiar with this strict rule this can be quite a challenge; however, it makes sense to enter a bath clean, especially when sharing a pool with other people.

A few examples from other countries should be mentioned here. It is generally expected that people enter bathing pools in a clean state, with Iceland being probably a close second to the Japanese. The only time prior soaping and scrubbing in Japan is not required is when the *Onsen* offers only hot water and has no cold water on tap. In German hot spring facilities it is compulsory to enter the bath only after a shower. In New Zealand this practice is not strictly followed at hot springs; many people take the option of having a shower afterwards. However, in Australia taking a shower first is usually expected, depending on the house rules, and at the hot Springs in Baños, Ecuadorian customers are also asked to shower first before entering the hot spring pools (Banos, n.d.). Frazier (2000) points out that one of the main differences between American hot spring use and European or Asian hot spring use appears to be the timing of cleaning oneself. Frazier (2000) actually recommends a thorough shower and soap scrubbing afterwards, whereas in most other countries one is generally expected to *enter* the bath or pool in a clean state. This would perhaps also depend on the environment – if the hot springs are somewhere in the wilderness people make up their own rules.

Cross-cultural adaptation

There are several ways in which cultural traditions related to the use of water have been translocated. When people migrate to other countries they take a lot of their cultural customs along with them. For many people the way they use water or supported water-related traditions in their home country is the way they want to use them anywhere else too. That can be for hygienic, health or religious purposes (ablutions, purification rituals, baptism), or for decoration inside or outside their homes or included in the environment they live in. Lakes, rivers, streams, waterfalls, oceans or special bathing facilities fed by thermal spring water are preferred locations for many, either for living or as holiday destinations. If no natural resources like local hot springs can be accessed nearby, other facilities used for wellness purposes may be a sauna in the backyard, a fitness room or a cold-water swimming pool.

Apart from the migration of people and their traditional customs there are several other methods for certain types of spa and wellness-related practice to find their way into other cultural environments. The import and export of health and wellness spa concepts on a more business-oriented scale includes the introduction of different ways as to how water use and wellness treatments are applied in other countries and can be adapted elsewhere, for example the Germany–Japan example below; but it all depends on a congruence between the use the spring might be put to and the culture accepting this (for a list of possible uses see Table 4.1). But cross-cultural adaptation can also be encouraged through travelling and travel guides, the internet and word of mouth, as well as religious and non-religious pilgrimages.

Table 4.1 Examples of different cultural spa types and how their position in the cross-cultural environment has developed. The main links are either cultural-religious or health and wellness related

Type	Hygiene	Health wellness	Internet marketing	Migration or export	Religion	Travel guides	Word of mouth
Japanese Onsen	•	•	•	•	•	•	•
Russian Banias	•	•	•	•		•	•
Finnish Saunas	•	•		•			•
Roman Thermae	•	•		•	•	•	
Turkish Hammams	•	•		•	•	•	•
Asian spa treatments		•	•		•	•	•
German Kurhaus		•	•			•	
Jewish Mikvahs			•	•	•		•

There are several examples of cross-cultural adaptation involving water and wellness traditions and treatments:

- Japanese *Onsen*: export of the concept to for example Australia, New Zealand, United States.
- *Hammams* or Turkish Baths can be found in Europe and elsewhere, for example in Hungary, England, America, Germany.
- Finnish *saunas* have been exported worldwide.
- Jewish *Mikvahs* were built wherever the need for this particular type of religious bath was required within Jewish communities (Germany, Poland, America).
- *German Kurhaus*: the concept has been reinterpreted, modified and imported by the Japanese who call it *Kuahausu* and use it as a water activity and treatment centre for the whole family.
- *Roman Thermae*: the concept is used for example, in Germany, England and even as far away from Europe as Tasmania, Australia.
- Russian *Banias* have been exported to countries like America and Europe by Russian immigrants.
- Swedish massage has been introduced to Asia, where it is used alongside Asian wellness treatments.
- Asian spa and wellness treatments including TCM (Traditional Chinese Medicine) introduced to Europe and America, where these are used together with traditional Western treatment methods.

The city of Beppu in Japan maintains a sister city relationship with Rotorua in New Zealand and both cities are well known for their hot springs and health and wellness spa tourism, which dominates both communities. In the year 2004 Rotorua contributed a downsised version of the oldest bathhouse in Rotorua to a new subdivision in Beppu called *Rotorua Town*. However, so far it cannot be judged if the facility has been fully accepted by the local community, because in this particular suburb many houses have their own hot spring water piped directly into their bathrooms (the suburb is known as *Spaland Toyomi*). Cross-culturally, the German Kurhaus model has seen more acceptance in Japan. After some modification of the concept to make it more suited for Japanese purposes, the resulting hybrid is called *Kuahausu* by the Japanese and offers aquatic entertainment as well as health and wellness facilities for every age group.

Finnish saunas and steam baths have long been appreciated all over the world, especially in cold-climate countries. They have a reputation of contributing significantly to health and wellness, especially if used on a regular basis. Turkish baths or Hammams can be found in many countries as well. Because of their benefits for religion, health and hygiene they have always played a great part in the Islamic world and still do, but are frequented by non-Islamic people as well. In the same way Russian Banias and Jewish Mikvahs can also be found, built to supply the community of immigrants with traditional facilities, be it for secular or religious purposes. They were and are a necessary element to support and motivate the community spirit of immigrants in a foreign country and to supply a comfort zone for whichever function they were designed for.

Summary

Life without water is impossible, and religion and mythology not involving a considerable water connection seem to be almost impossible. The importance of water is more far reaching than commonly thought. From a socio-cultural point of view it is not surprising that hot and mineral spring water resources, which are different from the common water sources like rivers and lakes and undoubtedly have their origin somewhere deep down in the Earth, made a distinct impression on earlier civilisations and were therefore thought to have special characteristics and to be linked to divine forces. For ancient cultures the use of sacred springs, both hot and cold, was an important part of their religious customs as well as for domestic purposes in their everyday life. While in recent times the emphasis is more on hot spring use for recreational purposes and prevention of illness through a holistic approach to health and well-being, healing springs also fit this picture perfectly and have gained renewed popularity not just through the wellness movement but also through the revival of old customs. On a global level natural springs have been used for centuries, with the search for God and good health as the main aim. However, the pursuit of pleasure, prestige and relaxation is still associated with hot and mineral spring spas (Von Furstenberg, 1993) and the quest for health and wellness has contributed much to a currently strong demand for health and wellness spa tourism.

Chapter 5
Geological Background of Natural and Mineral Springs

PATRICIA ERFURT-COOPER

Introduction

Most visitors to natural hot spring spas are not aware of the geological background that makes it possible for this natural resource to be enjoyed at many destinations throughout the world. This chapter briefly outlines the key geological processes that determine the existence of the geothermal resources that are used extensively in the health and wellness spa industry, with emphasis on thermal or hot springs. The geological components of interest and the most noteworthy locations are more fully described and analysed for those countries supplying health and wellness spa tourism. The chapter also discusses the co-location of other attractions based on the same geological processes (e.g. volcanoes and other geothermal manifestations).

For our purposes, these geothermal resources can be divided into two broad types:

- *Hot spring spas*: many of these are well known for their curative powers and their therapeutic benefits (e.g. Polynesian Spa, New Zealand and Blue Lagoon, Iceland). These may be associated with other geothermal attractions such as geysers, etc.
- *Mineral spring spas*: can be cold or warm water with curative powers and can be taken internally as well. Natural mineral and thermal waters are used in *balneology, balneotherapy, hydrotherapy* and *crenotherapy* (e.g. *Bad Zurzach*-Switzerland and *Bath Spa*; England).

Hot and cold mineral springs are widely distributed all over the world; however, clusters of them are more likely to be found in regions with volcanic activity (e.g. New Zealand, Iceland, Japan) or in areas overlying large groundwater aquifers such as the *Great Artesian Basin* in Australia or the *Guarani* aquifer in South America (Pesce, 2002). Thermal springs can manifest themselves in many different ways with some examples listed later in this chapter. Also, the mineral content of thermal springs with their special geochemistry has made them a much sought after commodity in the development of health and leisure destinations (health and wellness spa facilities) worldwide, which have been developed for a number of purposes, depending on their location, temperature, mineral content and flow rate.

Origins of Hot and Cold Mineral Springs

A spring is the natural flow of water from the ground which can occur when geologic, hydrologic or human forces cut into the underground layers of soil and rock where water is circulating, thus allowing the water to rise to the surface under pressure. The amount of water that flows from springs depends on several factors, including the size of the spaces within rocks (volume of water), the water pressure in the aquifer, the size of the reservoir basin and the amount of precipitation that is necessary to replenish the aquifer. Human activities greatly influence the volume of water that discharges from a spring through excessive groundwater withdrawals in an area, which eventually reduces the pressure in an aquifer, and can ultimately decrease the flow from all natural springs in the vicinity. Thermal and mineral spring water can originate from the following groundwater sources:

- natural groundwater (meteoric water);
- rain or lake water (seepage and replenishment);
- infiltrated seawater (seepage);
- artesian water (water confined in an aquifer and rising under pressure through artificial boreholes (Whittow, 1984: 37);
- water trapped in sediments (connate water);
- water introduced by magmatic processes (juvenile water); and
- water re-injected into the ground.

In the past, legends and myths about the origin of thermal springs have been transmitted orally from one generation to the next. In ancient times it was believed by some that hot springs formed from burning alum, sulphur and/or asphaltite, which then heated the overlying soil and the water circulating through it (Özgüler & Kasap, 1999). Modern research verifies several sources of heat supply from the subsurface:

- direct volcanic activity;
- the geothermal temperature gradient as water passes through subterranean rocks; and
- fractures and fissures in the rock formations resulting in pressure buildup that heats the water as it passes.

The natural discharge of such thermal springs (warm to very hot) is facilitated by fractured rocks and faults deep underground (a fault is an approximately plane surface of fracture in a rock body). Fault lines are sometimes marked by the emergence of springs (Allaby & Allaby, 2003), where pressure and temperature control the appearance of springs on the surface. Thermal springs are ordinary springs except that the water is warm and, in some places, hot. They occur especially in regions of recent volcanic activity and are fed by water heated in contact with hot rocks far below the surface.

Warm water, regardless of its origin, is lighter than cold water and readily rises to the surface if not confined. On reaching larger voids in the rock or soil with lower resistance, water can rise much faster than when descending and only starts to cool down on arrival at the surface. There is no restriction where thermal springs can surface. In *Uunartoq*, Greenland, hot springs coexist with icebergs floating on the sea in the background (see Figure 5.1).

In the case of volcanic hot springs surface water percolates downward through the rocks below the Earth's surface to high-temperature regions surrounding a magma reservoir, either active or recently solidified and emitting heat. There the water is heated, becomes less dense and rises back to the surface along fissures and cracks (Corbett, 2001). However, water can gain heat in other ways while underground: groundwater may circulate near a magma chamber or a body of cooling

Figure 5.1 Natural hot spring in Uunartoq, Greenland
Source: Arctic Adventure (2008); Iceland Adventure (n.d.).

igneous rock, but it can also gain heat through pressure at depth if it circles deep in the Earth along joints or faults. Hot springs are also generally more highly mineralised than their cold counterparts because as the temperature increases while the water is circulating underground it dissolves the surrounding host rocks, which release minerals in high concentrations into the groundwater (McGeary *et al.*, 2001). The rate of flow and the length of the flow path through the aquifer determine the amount of time the water is in contact with the surrounding rock, and therefore the amount of minerals that the water can dissolve. The level of dissolved minerals in the water can also be affected by the mixing of freshwater with pockets of ancient seawater in an aquifer or with modern seawater along an ocean coast. The quality of water discharged by hot springs can also vary greatly for other reasons, such as the quality of the water that recharges the aquifer and the type of rocks with which the ground water is in contact. This can be illustrated by reference to the structure and output of the Guarani Aquifer on the border of Argentina and Uruguay (Box 5.1).

Box 5.1 The development of thermal centres along the border between Argentina and Uruguay

The therapeutic use of natural thermal springs in the border region between Uruguay and Argentina goes back to the exploration of potential oil fields approximately 60 years ago. The last decade has seen a considerable growth of commercial extraction of thermal water from the groundwater aquifers that were identified during the earlier oil exploration period. Health and wellness spa facilities as well as recreational and leisure resources have been established on both sides of the Uruguay River, which contributes significantly to the local economies of the two countries from tourism.

Several thermal aquifers were identified with a potential for being highly productive and therefore able to provide a sustainable resource for the health and wellness spa industry if managed with responsibility. By the mid-1990s a successful health and wellness spa industry was established along the Uruguay side of the river. This caused investors from Argentina to propose similar developments on their side of the river with the first thermal spa opening in 1997 in Northeastern Argentina. The thermal water is extracted via flowing artesian wells springing from the thermal aquifers that are located in a low-temperature volcanic-sedimentary basin (*Source*: Pesce, 2002).

The classification of natural hot springs is not determined by the nature of the heat source (McGeary *et al.*, 2001), although it seems to be generally understood and expected that thermal waters of volcanic origin (primary hot springs) are potentially hotter than artesian groundwater (filtration hot springs). However, that is not always the case, as the artesian springs and bores in non-volcanic regions like the Great Australian Basin (GAB) for example reach temperatures around boiling point just the same as springs which originate in areas of volcanic activity.

The difference may lie in the depth of the heat source. Volcanic hot springs can acquire their temperature closer to the surface if an active heat source in the form of a magma chamber or a body of cooling igneous rock is present, whereas artesian spring water derives its heat from depth, pressure, friction and time spent in circulation underground before ascending along joints or fault lines. On the other hand, the mineral content of any type of thermal groundwater depends on the temperature and composition of the surrounding rocks as well as the duration of any lateral and vertical movement underground.

The major source of spring recharge is usually provided by meteoric water (Chaterji & Guha, 1968; McGeary *et al.*, 2001) that is of atmospheric origin either as precipitation in the form of rainfall and snow or as seepage from lakes and rivers (Allaby & Allaby, 2003). Other recharge methods include the artificial well injection into fractured 'hot rocks', which is practised in several countries where overexploitation of groundwater has led to a diminishing supply of hot water.

With respect to the temperature of the water, the normal geothermal gradient (usually from depths below 200 m) is on average 24°C/km (Allaby & Allaby, 2003). Water circulating to a depth of 2–3 km can therefore be warmed substantially above normal surface temperature. On the basis of such evidence we may define hot springs as surface seepage from a natural geothermal system that is made up of a circulating groundwater system activated by a high geothermal gradient. More generally we may characterise hot springs as those that issue water at temperatures substantially higher than the air temperature of the surrounding region, given that human beings measure the impact of temperature gradients in this way.

In Japan, according to the *1948 Hot Springs Law* a natural thermal spring cannot be called a hot spring unless it meets both the following criteria: 'hot water, mineral water, water vapour and other gases (except natural gas containing hydrocarbons as the main element) that issue from the ground with a temperature in excess of 25°C (77°F) or contain more than a prescribed amount of designated substances' (Olsen, 2002: 1). Under the Hot Springs Law (Law No. 125 of 1948) Japan's hot springs are also protected, with the objective of facilitating the proper utilisation of the natural geothermal resource (Japan Ministry of the Environment, 2003; Nipponia, 2003). Thus in Japan, arguably the world's premier hot springs using society the defining characteristics for hot springs are not just related to heat but are also used to benchmark chemical attributes and to ensure their protection, reflecting considerable experience with the nature and usefulness of hot springs.

Definitions, Terms and Classifications of Thermal Mineral Waters

Different temperature categories such as cold, warm and hot or thermal water are relative terms used according to (1) the individual's perception of what is hot or cold, (2) ambient air temperature or (3) ambient water temperature. The varying definitions and their inconsistent usage, not just by scientists and researchers from different disciplines but also by the general public, have led to considerable confusion in the quest for a universally agreed definition. Moreover, different countries use different classifications of hot springs, which can also be related to the individual languages and their translation into English rather than any objective criteria. Taking this into consideration it appears to be reasonable for this book to use the terms hot springs and thermal springs according to their relevant original references. In the case of higher temperatures not suitable for thermal bathing, the term extreme hot spring may be used to differentiate from thermal waters used for hydrotherapy and balneology. However, these extreme hot springs can be cooled to a temperature suitable for bathing and medical treatments and thus turned into a spa resource still classed as 'thermal' water. The likelihood of occasional false advertising where artificially heated tap water is offered as 'genuine' hot spring or 'thermal' water cannot be completely excluded in the search for an appropriate definition. That this occurs can mean that a 'genuine' disappointment for the uninformed visitor or tourist may result.

Although many countries have their own laws and regulations (see Figure 5.2 for example) for natural hot spring or thermal spring use, in most jurisdictions thermal springs are simply categorised by temperature, with the following classification of thermal and mineral springs the most generally accepted worldwide:

- cold springs – temperatures less than 25°C;
- tepid springs – temperatures between 25°C and 34°C;
- warm springs – temperatures between 34°C and 42°C; and
- hot springs – temperatures above 42°C.

Table 5.1 gives further insight into the variation in springs by looking at a collection of definitions and classifications from various countries with examples of individual terms used for natural hot springs. Also, what is hot in one country can be classed as warm or even cold in another. Some countries have special legislations to control the appropriate use of natural hot springs (i.e. Japan, Taiwan, Korea, Germany, France and Italy) and these laws also stipulate the temperature and mineral content necessary to be classed as a natural hot spring that could be used for medicinal purposes.

Figure 5.2 The Japanese temperature scale for the classification of springs
Source: Oyu (2004).

Table 5.1 Classifications and definitions of natural hot springs from various countries

Hot springs (Japan)	Minimum temperature of 25°C – no upper limit – used for medicinal purposes
Mineral water (Czech Republic)	Springs with temperatures from 14°C to 72°C (Kačura, 1968) – used for medicinal purposes
Mineral springs (China)	Warm, hot or thermal springs – used for medicinal purposes
Hot springs	Generic term for natural springs of at least body temperature, generally identified as pleasant bathing temperature – used for medicinal purposes
Hot spa (Greece)	Natural spring water above 28°C – mineral springs are classed as cold when below 28°C – used for medicinal purposes
Mineral water (Italy)	Natural spring water of different temperatures – cold: below 20°C, hypothermal: 20–30°C, thermal: 30–40°C, hyperthermal: above 40°C – spring water may also be radioactive (Andreassi & Flori, 1996)
Thermal waters (Spain)	Natural spring water of different temperatures – cold: 12–18°C, fresh: 18–27°C, neutral: 27–32°C, warm: 32–36.5°C, hot: 37–40°C, very hot: 40–43°C (Ledo, 1996)
Pure hot spring water (Korea)	Naturally rising hot spring water – according to Korean Hot Spring Low temperature must be above 25°C
Natural hot spring	Naturally discharging from the subsurface without a specially drilled well
Thermal spring water	Includes warm and hot springs – generally above 25°C, may be artificially heated – used for medicinal purposes
Geothermal springs	Includes thermal springs and extreme hot springs or high temperature springs – heated naturally while circulating through underground voids and pore spaces
Mineral spring water	Can be cold, warm, hot, extremely hot or artificially heated – used for medicinal purposes
Thermal mineral water	Like thermal mineral spring water and artesian water – used for medicinal purposes
Thermo-mineral spring	Like thermal mineral spring water and artesian water – used for medicinal purposes
Mineralised ground water	Like thermal mineral spring water and artesian water – used for medicinal purposes
Saline springs (Germany)	Various temperatures – very high mineral salt content – possible sea water used for medicinal purposes

(Continued)

Table 5.1 *Continued*

Artesian spring (Australia)	Naturally discharging from the subsurface – warm to hot water – 25–100°C – used for medicinal purposes
Artesian bore	Same as artesian spring, but discharging from a drilled well
Geyser	Extremely hot spring – water reaches boiling point and above – used as visual tourist attraction
Submarine hot springs	Submarine vents known as black smokers emitting extreme hot water enriched with mineral and metallic trace elements

Spring classification according to mineral content

Minerals are chemical elements or compounds that occur naturally in the crust of the Earth. From there they find their way into the circulating groundwater which can contain high concentrations of minerals and trace elements directly determined by the composition of the subsurface rock environment (McGeary *et al.*, 2001). Primary hot springs and filtration hot springs are further subdivided according to their heat origin as well as their physical distinctions including mineral and gas content, which are adsorbed via leaching and heated while circulating at great depth before ascending to the surface. Table 5.2 is a list of several common hot spring classifications according to their chemical composition.

Nitrogenous thermal waters which are only slightly mineralised represent one of the important groups of mineral waters widely used in many countries (Russia, Bulgaria, Hungary, France, Italy and Austria) for their curative properties. Barabanov and Disler (1968) identified six groups of nitrogenous thermal water types:

- hydrocarbonate;
- sulphate hydrocarbonate;
- sulphate;
- hydrocarbonate sulphate chloride;
- hydrocarbonate chloride; and
- sulphate chloride.

These waters are usually formed by precipitation and infiltration of soil waters, as well as the presence of mainly atmospheric gases in them, and the absence of accumulated organic matter in the area of their formation.

Geological and Chemical Processes Relevant to the Spa Industry

Mineral waters are solutions of natural origin that have formed under specific geologic conditions and, according to Ghersettich and Lotti (1996), are characterised

Table 5.2 Examples of different spring types according to their main mineral content

Thermal springs (warm and hot springs)	Surface seepage from a natural geothermal system – water temperature is generally higher than 25°C. Can contain any of the minerals below
Mineral springs (cold, warm or hot springs)	Chloride springs
	Sulphur springs
	Iron springs
	Carbonate springs – lead to the formation of tufa or travertine deposits around the spring (e.g. Pamukkale, Turkey)
	Alkaline springs – known as natural saunas or steam tubs
	True bitter springs – magnesium sulphite
	Acidic springs – mainly in active volcanic areas
	Gypsum springs – bitter springs
	Heavy carbon soil springs
	Mirabilite springs – bitter springs
	Mirabilite sodium chloride springs
	Nitrogenous thermal springs
Radium springs	Contain a certain amount of radioactive radium or thorium
Artesian springs (warm and hot springs)	A spring fed from a confined aquifer (artesian basin). May contain any of the above minerals
Geysers (very hot springs)	Intermittent erupting spring spouting fountains of boiling water – bicarbonates
Submarine vents	Commonly known as black smokers – sulphur

by 'chemico-physical dynamism'. The Oxford Dictionary of Earth Sciences (Allaby & Allaby, 2003: 350) defines a mineral as a natural occurring substance that has a characteristic chemical composition and, in general, a crystalline structure. The mineral content in hot springs results from the transport of dissolved minerals brought to the surface from deep groundwater reservoirs where the water is heated either by depth and pressure or by volcanic processes (Stanwell Smith, 2002). Natural hot and mineral spring waters collect their essential ingredients as they filter through rock strata: for example, calcium from limestone or magnesium from dolomite. Minor elements include fluoride and several other trace elements and iron may be present in suspension. The higher the temperature of the water, the higher the mineral content is likely to be. Geothermal water of volcanic origin can also contain elevated concentrations of sodium and bicarbonates, which gives the water a natural effervescence.

The legal classification of the mineral content of a spring varies in different parts of the world. In most jurisdictions a mineral spring contains greater than 1000 mg/l (ppm) of naturally dissolved solids (Eytons' Earth, 2004). Spring waters are classified as acidic, basic or neutral, according to the balance of hydrogen in the water and their measurement on the pH scale:

- acidic waters <7.0 pH;
- neutral waters 7.0 pH; and
- basic/alkaline waters >7.0 pH.

Description of the most commonly found minerals

Minerals have traditionally been used externally in solutions, creams and ointments to cure certain health conditions. The taking of mineral spring waters (internally by drinking) is practised worldwide with a strong revival in the wake of alternative medicine. Parish and Lotti (1996) suggest that bathing in mineral spring water could be a more effective method in treating skin conditions such as atopic dermatitis and psoriasis. In order to demonstrate the significance of the mineral content of hot springs for medical use, the following tables give an overview of the chemical composition of hot springs in general (Table 5.3) and from a selection of locations in different countries (Tables 5.4–5.10). The individual minerals and their relevance in thermalism (hydrotherapy, balneology and crenotherapy) were discussed in more detail in Chapter 2.

Table 5.3 List of the most common elements found in natural thermal springs

Main elements found in spring waters	Other substances occasionally present	Main gases in solution
Calcium	Arsenic	Carbon dioxide
Carbonates	Bromine	Hydrogen sulphide
Chlorides	Caesium	Nitrogen
Fluoride	Cobalt	Oxygen
Iron	Copper	Radon
Magnesium	Iodine	Argon and helium can occur in some of the simple thermal and thermal sulphur waters
Sodium	Lithium	
Sulphates	Potassium	
Sulphides	Radium	
	Silica	
	Zinc	

Table 5.4 Blue Lagoon chemical analysis

Blue Lagoon geothermal seawater	
Chemical analysis	*mg/kg*
Silica (SiO$_2$)	251
Sodium (Na)	7.643
Potassium (K)	1.177
Calcium (Ca)	1.274
Magnesium (Mg)	0.60
Carbon dioxide (CO$_2$)	11.4
Sulphate (SO$_4$)	31.8
Chlorine (Cl)	15.740
Fluorine (F)	0.18
Total soluble chemicals	25.800
Other elements are in trace amount	

Source: Blue Lagoon (2005).
Disclaimer: The authors cannot guarantee the accuracy of the chemical analysis.

Tables 5.4–5.10 contain the chemical analysis of a number of hot springs used in a controlled environment where they undergo constant monitoring and testing as a form of quality control to ensure constant water quality. This said, there may be some facilities where health and safety standards may not be met in a satisfactory

Table 5.5 Upper hot springs Canada chemical analysis

Upper hot springs	
Major components	*ppm*
Sulphate (SO$_4$)*	572.0
Calcium (Ca)	205.0
Bicarbonate (HCO$_3$)	134.0
Magnesium (Mg)	42.0
Sodium (Na)	6.6
Potassium (K)	4.5
Chloride (Cl)	6.5
Hydrogen sulphide (H$_2$S)	2.0

*Varies throughout the year.
Source: Canadian Rockies Hot Springs (2006 – modified for comparison).
Disclaimer: The authors cannot guarantee the accuracy of the chemical analysis.

Table 5.6 Radium springs Canada chemical analysis

Radium hot springs	
Major components	*ppm*
Sulphate (SO$_4$)*	302.0
Calcium (Ca)	135.0
Bicarbonate (HCO$_3$)	100.8
Magnesium (Mg)	31.6
Sodium (Na)	18.4
Potassium (K)	3.0
Chloride (Cl)	0.17
Hydrogen sulphide (H$_2$S)	n/a

*Varies throughout the year.
Source: Canadian Rockies Hot Springs (2006 – modified for comparison).
Disclaimer: The authors cannot guarantee the accuracy of the chemical analysis.

Table 5.7 Edipsos hot springs Greece chemical analysis

Edipsos hot springs	
Chemical analysis	*mg/kg*
Potassium (K)	5.033
Sodium (Na)	98.87
Lithium (Li)	0.056
Ammonium (NH$_4$)	0.011
Calcium (Ca)	16.425
Magnesium (Mg)	3.384
Iron (Fe)	0.075
Magnanese (Mn)	0.00013
Aluminium (Al)	0.0016
Chlorine (Cl)	186.40
Bromine (Br)	0.558
Iodine (I)	0.00040
Sulphuric radical (SO$_4$)	11.11
(HPO$_4$)	0.00032
(HCO$_3$)	1.979

Source: Edipsos Health Spas (n.d. – modified for comparison).
Disclaimer: The authors cannot guarantee the accuracy of the chemical analysis.

Table 5.8 Karlsbader Sprudel chemical analysis

Karlsbader Sprudel, Czech Republic	
Major components	*mg/kg*
Sulphate of soda	2.405
Bicarbonate of soda	298
Chloride of soda	042
Sulphate of potash	186
Bicarbonate of magnesia	166
Bicarbonate of lithium	0.012
Carbonic acid gas	966
They also contain traces of arsenic, antimony, selenium, rubidium, tin and organic substances.	

Source: *Classic Encyclopaedia* (2006 – modified for comparison).
Disclaimer: The authors cannot guarantee the accuracy of the chemical analysis.

fashion for various reasons, for example cost and lack of trained staff. The data of Tables 5.3–5.10 have been used in their original terminology and are only modified to fit the template of the table.

Mineral contents of hot springs and their potential use in health and wellness tourism

As noted earlier the most sought after ingredients of natural hot and mineral springs for spa resorts and treatment facilities are minerals and trace elements. In other words, the important feature of such tourism destinations is not just a pleasant water temperature or a natural environment, but the health-related mineral composition of the water. The desired curative effect is directly related to absorption of the mineral ingredients and metallic trace elements, which are said to have a beneficial effect on the human body, assisting in the healing process of a variety of health conditions. Scientists worldwide, but especially in Europe, have long researched the connection between minerals and other elements and the potential health benefits of thermal springs (Eyton's Earth, 2004; Ghersettich & Lotti, 1996; Jorden, 1631; Parish & Lotti, 1996).

Hot springs with high mineral content are often termed *medicinal waters* as a result of their physical and chemical characteristics, and are applied for thermal therapies in order to prevent illness as well as to restore health. Apart from different degrees of mineralisation and a wide temperature range, thermal waters contain additional factors such as varying pH levels, low level radioactivity and gases in solution. All these variables have undergone thorough examinations over time by

Table 5.9 Treuchtinger Heilwasser chemical analysis

Treuchtlinger Heilwasser	
Description	*mg/kg*
Cation	
Lithium (Li$_3$)	0.58
Sodium (Na^1)	196.20
Potassium (K$_3$)	17.90
Ammonium (NH$_4$)	0.14
Magnesium (Mg$^2_3$)	3.03
Calcium (Ca$^2_3$)	18.00
Strontium (Sr$^2_3$)	0.13
Barium (Ba$^2_3$)	0.03
Iron (Fe$^2_3$)	0.17
Anion	
Fluoride (F$^-$)	3.19
Chloride (Cl$^-$)	61.50
Bromide (Br$^-$)	0.15
Nitrate (NO$_3^-$)	0.10
Sulphate (SO$_4^{2-}$)	71.00
Hydrogen sulphide (HSO$_4^{2-}$)	0.06
Hydrogen carbonate (HCO$_3^-$)	425.00
Undissolved material	
Silica polymer (H$_2$SiO$_3$)	12.54
Mineralisation	
Total	809.72

Source: Altmühlterme (2007 – modified for comparison).
Disclaimer: The authors cannot guarantee the accuracy of the chemical analysis. Also, the German terminology was not translated, as the chemical descriptions are easy to recognise due to their similarity and their added formulas.

scientists of independent disciplines, including geochemists, biochemists and microbiologists (Fouke *et al.*, 2000; Krause, 1997; Renaut & Jones, 2003). Clinical trials have been run to prove or disprove the value of minerals in thermalism, and medical faculties in many countries employ thermal mineral waters due to their belief that they are beneficial for the health improvement of their patients.

Table 5.10 Rachel Spring, Rotorua, chemical analysis

Rachel Spring, Rotorua	
Major components	*ppm*
Na (sodium)	553
K (potassium)	41.5
Ca (calcium)	4.7
Mg (magnesium)	0.05
Li (lithium)	3.25
Rb (rubidium)	0.30
Cs (caesium)	0.40
Al (aluminium)	nd
Cl (chloride)	477
F (fluoride) – SO_4 (sulphate)	174
B (boron)	6.7
NH_3 (ammonia)	nd
HCO_3 (carbonic acid)	381
SiO_2 (silica)	358
H_2S (hydrogen sulphide)	50
pH (acidity)	9.5

Source: QE Health (n.d. – modified for comparison).
Disclaimer: The authors cannot guarantee the accuracy of the chemical analysis.

Consequences and effects of heavy mineralisation

While it is generally understood that natural hot springs with high mineral concentrations have a tendency to clog pipes and slowly coat pools (Frazier, 2000), hot spring resorts and health facilities have developed technologies to counteract the consequences of heavy mineral deposits in order to continue their use (see Chapter 7). The Government Bathhouse at Rotorua in New Zealand for example initially had many problems with blocked plumbing through mineral deposits, which contributed to extended downtimes of the facilities. This ultimately led to costly repairs and replacements of pipe work well before a reasonable use-by date. An example of a tap coated in layers of minerals is shown in Figure 5.3.

On the other hand, mineralisation can be extremely effective and often becomes a major tourist attraction in its own right with spectacular results, as is seen at Pamukkale in Turkey (Figure 5.4), at the Mammoth Hot Springs in Yellowstone National Park (USA – Figure 5.5) and formerly at the 'Pink & White Terraces' near

Figure 5.3 Tap ware rendered useless by heavy mineralisation
Source: Photograph courtesy of Rotorua Museum of Art and History.

Rotorua, New Zealand (Figure 5.6; Blomfield, 1884; Chapter 3). The thermal water sources of Pamukkale reach the surface from underground karst caverns and form the travertine terraces through precipitation of $CaCO_3$ (calcium bicarbonate) as the CO_2 (carbon dioxide) evaporates. The mildly acidic (pH 6.0) waters at Pamukkale have a temperature of 44°C and are rich in calcium, magnesium sulphate, bicarbonate and carbon dioxide (Denizli, 2007). These mineral-rich waters have dripped down over a series of terraced levels in solidified cascades, dazzling in their radiance and changing their colour according to how the sunlight strikes them (Pamukkale, n.d.). Due to extreme overuse and anthropogenic pollution of the travertine terraces, they are under environmental protection and since 1988 Pamukkale's mineral forests and petrified waterfalls are World Heritage listed (UNESCO, 2008).

Active hot springs can be divided into three general groups depending on water chemistry and the resulting mineral deposits:

- alkaline, siliceous-sinter-dominated systems;
- travertine carbonate-dominated systems; and
- acid sulphate systems (Breckenridge & Hinckley, 1978; White *et al.*, 1988).

Figure 5.4 Pamukkale's 'Cotton Castle'
Source: Denizli (n.d.).

Mixed types commonly occur within individual hot spring systems with both sinter-travertine and alkaline-sulphate transitional types indicating subsurface mixtures of the two types of water. Thermal springs may thus form siliceous sinter, travertine or other types of deposits at the surface (Kruse, 1997). Yellowstone contains numerous examples of all three types of hot springs as well as mixed types (Breckenridge & Hinckley, 1978; Bryan, 1986; White *et al.*, 1988).

Hot Springs as Visual Tourist Attractions

Hot springs come in many forms. Some emerge quietly out of the ground, but others arrive at the surface with great noise and visual effect, overwhelming in their unique natural form. It comes as no surprise therefore that geothermal manifestations such as geysers, hot rivers, hot waterfalls and boiling lakes and

Figure 5.5 Mammoth Hot Springs in Yellowstone National Park in the United States
Source: Photograph courtesy of J. Duckeck, www.showcaves.com.

mud ponds are highly sought after tourist must-see destinations worldwide. One of the most famous hot springs of the visual type was the original *Geysir* in Iceland, which provided the name for all hot springs of this kind. The visual impact of a fountain of boiling water rising above the ground for a few brief moments has attracted visitors over centuries. People today are equally in awe when watching a geyser erupt as they were a long time ago when the first geo-tourists travelled to volcanic environments to discover natural phenomena to broaden their education about the environment (the comparison is given in Figures 5.7 and 5.8).

Many geothermal landscapes worldwide offer such unique features that they are either protected by environmental laws and regulations or declared cultural or national geological heritage to stop development in their vicinity (Chapter 6). Hot

Figure 5.6 Artist's view of the White Terraces at Lake Rotomahana before they were destroyed in 1886
Source: Blomfield (1884).

Figure 5.7 One of the great attractions of Iceland is the boiling mud ponds at Námafjall in the Krafla high-temperature geothermal area in the northeast of Iceland
Source: Photograph courtesy of P. Erfurt-Cooper.

Figure 5.8 One of the boiling red pools in the small geo park Umi Jigoku in Beppu, Japan
Source: Photograph courtesy of P. Erfurt-Cooper.

springs and geysers present a powerful visual display of nature at work and are natural laboratories for studies in *geomicrobiology*, a recently established discipline that links mineralisation to certain microbes that inhabit hot springs (Renaut & Jones, 2003). Also, hot springs containing silica precipitate mineralised crusts where fluids evaporate and cool. These deposits may be carbonates, calcite tufas and travertines composed of calcite, which implies that most carbonate precipitation is rapid (McGeary *et al.*, 2001; Renaut, 2004).

Deposited in this way, *Mammoth Hot Springs* in the USA are a rare kind of spring where water flows over ancient limestone deposits instead of the silica-rich lava flows of the hot springs common elsewhere in the park. The results invoke a unique landscape with its delicate features formed by flowing water spilling across the surface and creating amazing travertine terraces (see Figure 5.5; Yellowstone National Park, 2006; see Box 5.2). The travertine-depositing thermal waters of the Angel Terrace surface at a temperature of 71–73°C. While the water precipitates over mounded travertine *terracette* pools are formed including small *microterracettes*, where the temperature reaches 28–30°C (Fouke *et al.*, 2000).

Box 5.2 Yellowstone National Park

Yellowstone National Park covers an area of nearly 3500 square miles in the northwest of Wyoming State and contains the largest concentration of geothermal features in the world (Rhinehart, 1980), with around 100 different hot springs groups totalling over 10,000 individual thermal features (Bryan, 1986). The distribution of the thermal features is controlled by the regional fault systems and the Yellowstone Caldera (Eaton *et al.*, 1975; White *et al.*, 1988). The terraced Mammoth Hot Springs are an example of the travertine hot spring type, with over 100 hot springs cascading over a number of travertine terraces (Bargar & Muffler, 1975), and are one of the most popular tourist attractions in the park.

The very much larger *Pink and White Terraces* (see Figure 5.6) were colonial New Zealand's premier tourist attraction in the 1800s. These travertine terraces were formed from precipitated calcium carbonate cascading down a hillside at Lake Rotomahana near Rotorua. The White Terraces were known as *Te Tarata* (the tattooed rock). Tourists were taken to the silica terraces in whaleboats or canoes until the terraces were destroyed in the *Mt. Tarawera* eruption of 1886 (Stafford, 1986). After this catastrophe the local tourist trade went into decline for some decades, although the hot springs at Rotorua itself continued in use.

Co-Location of Thermal Springs with Other Geothermal Phenomena

It is evident that natural hot springs generally appear within close proximity to active volcanic environments, and are quite often also co-located with mountainous and/or difficult terrain, which represent a considerable attraction for tourists as an extreme environment – a new and rapidly growing market in mainstream tourism. Tourists are looking for fresh experiences of an adventurous nature particularly in geothermally active and volcanic environments, which are known for their unusual and interesting landscapes but also for their unpredictable and potentially hostile nature. Many of these environments are world heritage listed and/or located in national parks, which adds a further dimension to their interest and demonstrates a significant contribution to the overall tourism industry. Serious thought also needs to be given to the risk factors and the potential danger of areas in the proximity of active geothermal manifestations such as extreme hot springs and geysers.

In European countries volcano tourism associated with hot and mineral springs has been widespread for centuries, with Vesuvius and the buried cities of Pompeii and Herculaneum for example generally included in the *Grand Tour* undertaken by more affluent members of society during the 18th and 19th centuries (Weaver & Lawton, 2002). The observation of volcanic environments, including the use of hot springs, was considered educational and inspirational as well as fashionable. In Iceland volcanic hot spring environments have also attracted tourists for several centuries, as has been well documented in the literature (Hróarsson & Jónsson, 1992). Geothermal manifestations including geysers and boiling ponds have been successfully advertised from the 18th century in order to attract visitors to this north-westernmost European country near the Arctic Circle. Other countries rich in geothermal resources also have a history of promoting their active environments to increase visitor numbers, for example, New Zealand, Italy, Turkey, United States, Japan and China.

Tourism in active geothermal environments can be classed as a sub-group of adventure tourism due to its potential risk factors, but overall is firmly covered under the umbrella of geotourism, which includes nature tourism and ecotourism (Dowling & Newsome, 2006). This aspect of geotourism is based exclusively on active environments (geothermal and volcanic) and their associated landscapes, which present fascinating tourist destinations with extreme and unique natural features, plus the 'value adding' of learning about geological phenomena in particularly interesting settings and often the opportunity to indulge in a hot or mineral spring bathing experience. This type of tourism is not only recreational but also of social and cultural significance, as well as increasingly being highly educational.

Reasons for visiting extreme environments are determined by the individual traveller, their specific personal interests and their level of fitness. Despite the fact that active geothermal areas may attract the more adventurous type of tourist, recreation and leisure are very important factors and generally well catered for. The principal attractions of active geothermal and often volcanic environments associated with hot springs are geological and naturalistic and include the following popular features (with some examples of locations in brackets):

- hot springs and geysers (*Iceland, New Zealand, Japan*);
- boiling ponds and mud pools (*Japan, Iceland, New Zealand*);
- hot rivers and lakes (*New Zealand, USA, Iceland, Japan*); and
- sinter terraces (*Turkey, China, New Zealand, USA*).

These natural attractions are frequently included in general sightseeing, but due to an obvious increase of interest in geotourism some tour operators have already specialised in tours focusing on visits to active geothermal areas to cater exclusively for groups with this special interest.

Other geothermal phenomena and their joint use for health and wellness tourism

While many hot springs are used solely for the purpose of serving as a drawcard for health and wellness spa tourism, the common proximity to active volcanic environments offers some kind of value adding. Being within reach of unique landscape features this inevitably leads to combinations between hot springs for thermal applications such as bathing and medical treatments, and hot springs with great visual effects. Active geothermal manifestations such as geysers and boiling ponds or picturesque sinter terraces are major attractions usually incorporated in the overall marketing strategies wherever these interesting features are available (the Blue Lagoon, Iceland and Beppu, Japan, see Box 5.3).

Box 5.3 Power and water: The Blue Lagoon in Iceland

The Blue Lagoon geothermal spa, which is world renowned for its skin healing power, is connected to the Svartsengi Geothermal Power Station by using the warm wastewater from the plant. This makes the Blue Lagoon definitely one of the most famous tourist attractions in Iceland (Icelandic Tourism Board, 2005). The large bathing pool of geothermal seawater (2/3 saltwater and 1/3 freshwater) is one of Iceland's most visited tourist destinations. The following description was taken from the Blue Lagoon (2005) website (with permission):

> The origin of the seawater is 2000 metres beneath the surface from where it travels through porous lava. This blend of sea and fresh water undergoes a 'mineral exchange' and then near the surface, concentration occurs, due to vaporization, evaporation and finally, sedimentation. Part of the seawater is transferred via pipeline towards the Blue Lagoon and allows to keep the temperatures at 37–39°C/98–102°F. New water is constantly led into the lagoon and the water is completely renewed in 40 hours. Regular samples from the lagoon show that 'common' bacteria do not thrive in this ecosystem. The geothermal seawater's special ecosystem has a self-cleansing effect. Thus additional cleansers such as chlorine are not needed. Blue Lagoon geothermal seawater is a part of a unique ecocycle where high technology and nature work in perfect harmony in Iceland's extreme environment, creating the Blue Lagoon geothermal seawater, known for its active ingredients and healing power. Its unique active ingredients: Minerals, silica and algae have been praised for their benefits on healthy skin and on skin problems such as eczema and psoriasis. The aquamarine blue colour is the result of these active ingredients: minerals, silica and algae.

The Beppu hydrothermal system, Japan

A good model of the relationship between geology, the resultant hot springs and both health tourism and geotourism is found in Kyushu in southern Japan. The *Beppu Hydrothermal System* is located at the eastern edge of the Beppu-Shimabara Graben, crossing the Island of Kyushu from northeast to southwest. Three principal types of thermal water are present in the Beppu Hydrothermal System:

- high-temperature sodium-chloride type;
- bicarbonate type; and
- sulphate type.

These diverse compositions originate from a single parent hydrothermal fluid beneath the volcanic centre, which is inferred to be a sodium-chloride type water of 250–300°C. These hydrothermal waters are formed predominantly by dilution of the parent fluid with cold groundwater in the mountainous area. The diluted hydrothermal water flows along a fault line until it rises at boiling temperature. This process has caused the shallow groundwater to be heated by rising steam and converted into bicarbonate type thermal water (Yusa & Ohsawa, 2000).

Active hot springs as tourist attractions

Volcanic environments are utilised in a range of ways as key adjuncts to springs, nature and eco-tourism (see example boxes, this section). Some overlap exists with industrial tourism, where power plants and greenhouses sourced by geothermal energy are used as tourist attractions in countries such as New Zealand, Iceland and Japan (Box 5.4). While it is not possible to determine the exact numbers of visitors to active volcanic areas, in the case of Iceland approximately 75% of the overall annual visitor numbers (356,152 visitors in 2005, 485,000 in 2007; Icelandic Tourism Board, 2005/2007) choose nature observation as their main activity (where volcanic environments including natural hot and mineral springs are the overwhelming natural feature) and at least 65% of the overall annual visitor numbers (2,421,562 tourists in 2006, Statistics New Zealand, 2006; Box 5.5) visit the geothermal centres around Rotorua.

Box 5.4 The Jigoku Meguri

For tourists in Japan who visit areas with high geothermal activity like Beppu City on the Island of Kyushu the 'extreme' hot springs called *Jigoku* (Japanese for 'hell') are a 'must see' (see Figure 5.8). These Jigoku are small parks with boiling, bubbling and steaming attractions, including geysers, mud pools and hot springs for foot baths, the last of which are very popular on cold and wet days. Eggs and dumplings are also cooked in hissing steam vents or in the boiling ponds. A special tour is recommended, the *Jigoku Meguri*, which includes all ten Jigoku. One of the unique aspects of these Jigoku, apart from their geothermal origin, is their location in the centre of a city of 140,000 people with annual visitor numbers between 10 and 11 million, mainly domestic tourists. And most of these will at least visit one of the Jigoku at a relatively low cost of 400 yen (approximately US$4.00) as well as many local *Onsen*. Hot mineral spring spas (*Onsen*) are a favourite of the Japanese and greatly appreciated as a geothermal by-product of over 100 active volcanoes in Japan.

Box 5.5 The thermal wonderlands of New Zealand

New Zealand's city of Rotorua is well known for its geothermal manifestations and the complementary sulphur smell. Surrounding areas offer high-temperature geothermal attractions that include hot creeks, hot mineral springs, geysers, sinter terraces, mud pools and geothermal power stations, which are to a large degree contained in national parks or private parks and can be visited. However, the entrance fees can be quite high compared to Iceland or Japan, where geothermal attractions are generally open to the public at very little extra charge, if any. Some free geothermal features around Rotorua like the rather inaptly named Kerosene Creek are located in somewhat hidden locations (see Chapter 2), but are very popular with 'tourists in the know' for a hot soak in a natural bushland setting. Hot spring water from geothermal activity is available to domestic buildings and most hotels offer genuine mineral pools to their guests.

In Iceland, where geothermal activity is nearly everywhere 'underfoot', tourism organisations and private operators offer visitors a tour of their 'hellish' landscapes. Day trips are popular, even half day trips are offered but transport and travel are seasonally limited. In a short time sensational volcanic landscapes can be explored, including spouting geysers and boiling mud pools, similar to Japan and New Zealand (see Figures 5.7–5.9); all that with the ever-present backdrop of layers upon layers of ancient lava flows. In the case of Iceland it can be safely assumed that most visitors sooner or later will be participating in some form of health and wellness spa tourism, even if they only enjoy the famous 'Blue Lagoon' in the middle of endless lava fields with a geothermal power station as a backdrop (see Chapter 2), the Nature Baths near Mývatn or the rather wild hot spring ponds at Landmannalaugur.

What are tourists looking for in such environments?

The main reason for visiting hot spring environments close to active volcanism seems to be the desire to experience the scenic attraction of unique natural phenomena, which is plausibly demonstrated by the difficulties tourists are prepared to overcome when embarking on excursions to places such as the Aleutians or

Figure 5.9 One of the geothermal parks which are located in and around Rotorua, New Zealand. This geyser is a regular feature erupting in a beautiful column for more than a minute at a time
Source: Photograph courtesy of P. Erfurt-Cooper.

Kamchatka. Curiosity and an educational aspect may be other important factors, as geotourism is gaining momentum and becoming the current motivating trend to visit destinations, which include not only geological features but also a diversified ecology and thus offer more than just sightseeing and photo opportunities as part of the trip agenda. Visitor types include domestic and international tour groups and individuals, people interested in nature and outdoor activities, scientists and researchers of unusual environments, and of course photographers and people who can afford the rather unique holiday experience, which can take them to any remote location worldwide. One of the key factors in using extreme geological phenomena as tourist attractions is the long-term sustainability (under responsible management) of a renewable natural resource (Buckley, 2007; Dowling & Newsome, 2006). The high number of hot spring environments with distinctive and unique natural surroundings in many countries worldwide is of considerable economic value for the tourism industry. In some regions the majority of the revenue derived from tourism is directly related to hot spring tourism and geotourism in active volcanic environments. Geo parks, national parks and world heritage sites contribute significantly to the attraction of areas with geothermal features. To attract visitors of different interest groups, tourism operators offer a diversity of tours including activities ranging from trekking, hiking, climbing, skiing on or around active volcanoes and hot springs to canoeing and fishing on crater lakes. This is combined with overnight accommodation with hot spring facilities for relaxing. In Iceland for example, a day of hiking cross country usually ends with a soak in a hot spring or a hot tub fed by natural geothermal spring water. The same goes for New Zealand and Japan, where a hot spring bath is one of the main attractions of the day, whether it is after a long day on the ski slopes or a strenuous day trekking cross country or just leisurely shopping for souvenirs and visiting the local cafés.

Summary

This chapter has briefly outlined the key geological processes that determine the existence and use of mineral waters in the health and wellness spa industry. Its emphasis has been on the location, type and mineral constituents of thermal springs. The geological components of interest and the most noteworthy locations have been more fully described and analysed for those countries supplying this form of tourism, and the importance of the co-location of other attractions based on the same geological processes (e.g. volcanoes, geysers, boiling mud pools and other geothermal manifestations) has been stressed. These notes form the background for the discussion in Chapter 6 of the physical, social and economic environments of health and wellness spa tourism.

Chapter 6

Health and Wellness Spa Tourism Environment

MALCOLM COOPER

Introduction

Tourism based on health and wellness spa facilities is not one-dimensional, passive or unsophisticated: it contains within itself multiple ideas of landscape and building appreciation, environmental and touristic sustainability, health improvement, self-involvement, active learning, facility–client relationships and the importance of the involvement of host communities that transcend the passive tourist 'gaze' experience (Smith & Kelly, 2006; Urry, 1990). While there is an increasingly enhanced appreciation among tourists and local communities of the importance of the geological resources described in Chapters 2 and 5, especially those of natural thermal water resources as a framework for health and wellness, there is also recognition that behavioural factors and social environments together with new combinations of landscapes and facilities greatly impinge on the willingness of visitors to travel to a particular location or spa resort. Health and wellness spa tourism involves an individual in a personal assessment of his or her health and psychological status (and/or vanity) as much as it does their (and providers) recognition and understanding of the physical, social, regulatory and business environments surrounding this activity. Equally, it involves communities and their governments in the creation of regulatory frameworks for the spa and wellness industry so that community health standards are not compromised. These interconnections are explored in Figure 6.1.

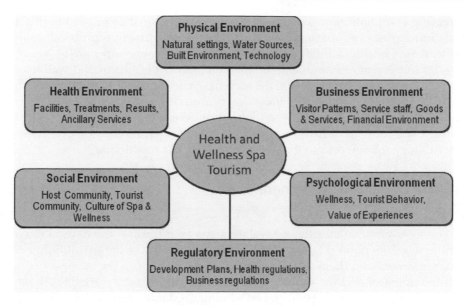

Figure 6.1 Environments of health and wellness spa tourism
Source: The author.

The physical environment is of course the fundamental resource without which health and wellness spa tourism cannot exist, and is composed of

- the natural environmental settings for the water resource;
- the geothermal or mineral water sources (in some spa traditions such as in Japan the most important criteria are natural geothermal water resources in as natural a setting as possible) themselves;
- the built environment of the spa or similar facility;
- the technologies used in both supplying and guaranteeing the quality of water; and
- the physical treatments offered to clients.

Directly associated with the physical environment is the health environment in this form of tourism. The basic facilities and treatments offered in natural hot and mineral springs-based health and wellness centres are dependent on the water resource, although this may be and often is supplemented by ancillary services such as beauty therapies, fitness activities and nutritional advice. In other situations such as medical tourism, the water resource may be secondary though still important. The *total* health environment and its results for the individual tourist are the key to both personal health and the tourism experience together.

For health and wellness spa facilities there must also be a sound operational, financial and marketing environment. Businesses that do not operate successfully cannot of course supply the market in the long term, especially in conditions of increasing competition, so a sound business strategy must be present in this as in other industries. The existence of suitable and/or attractive physical environments, water, health facilities and effective business frameworks are however not the only important environments in the development of health and wellness spa tourism. Of equivalent impact are the social, psychological, behavioural, economic and regulatory environments of the industry, individual tourists and the host community. This chapter therefore also looks at those environments of the health and wellness spa tourism industry which act as facilitators, moderators, barriers and as regulatory frameworks to its existence and proper functioning.

Physical and Built Environment

Natural settings

Wherever possible, health and wellness spa facilities use the natural environment as a selling point (Figure 6.2a/6.2b). Sustainability of the surrounding natural environment and the water resource thus becomes one of the major concerns of both the operator and the tourist, with 'eco-friendly', 'green', 'organic', 'holistic', 'natural' and 'sustainable' environments being used in marketing literature and as

Figure 6.2a/6.2b Typical outdoor settings for natural hot spring baths at *Yasaka Ashiginu Onsen* and *Yumoto Sanso Yunokuchi Onsen*, Japan. These photos (a) and (b) shows separate bathing areas for men and women, which is the most common form of Japanese customary bathing today
Source: Photographs courtesy of P. Erfurt-Cooper.

frameworks for development. If this cannot be easily achieved in a natural setting spa operators go to considerable lengths to recreate a 'natural' environment within the built form. Of course one of the most important natural settings is that of the underlying geology of the area that contains the health and wellness spa facilities as described in Chapter 5. Natural hot and mineral springs cluster in geological settings that are generally similar the world over – they are either directly of geothermal origin (USA, Japan, New Zealand, Azores, Italy, Turkey, China, Iceland, Mexico) or associated with geological faulting and artesian basins (Germany, Austria, USA, UK, Spain, Australia).

Water sources

As a fundamental factor in the health and wellness spa tourism industry, active and fossil hot and cold mineral spring systems occur worldwide and share many common characteristics that indicate common geological histories (Bowen, 1989: Chapter 5; Waring, 1965; White, 1955, 1981). Hot springs mainly occur as surface expressions of geothermally and volcanically active areas, commonly associated with rhyolite-composition volcanic rocks, although pressure at depth can heat water in the absence of volcanically active areas (Rhinehart, 1980). The latter are described as thermal mineral springs and are common in a variety of rocks in areas of geologically recent folding and faulting (Waring, 1965). Fossil springs are also present as extinct portions of modern, active systems, and may also be preserved in the geologic record as epithermal mineral deposits (White, 1955, 1981).

Natural hot springs are geological phenomena resulting from when ground water is heated (sometimes far beyond the level of human endurance) by geothermal forces, dissolves minerals in the rocks it subsequently percolates through and comes to the surface. Many are in attractive locations and are important to tourism in a scenic sense at least (e.g. the geysers of Yellowstone National Park, USA, Rotorua, New Zealand, the Valley of the Geysers in Kamchatka, the Jigoku of Japan and Haukadalur in Iceland), or are celebrated (e.g. the Blue Lagoon, Iceland and the original town of Spa in Belgium) as special attractions or even destinations in their own right (see Chapter 4). However, for the hot or cold mineral spring aficionado, the greatest pleasure comes not from just looking at the spring, but from bathing in the water and at a number of locations drinking it for its therapeutic powers.

It has been seen in earlier chapters that the terms hot and mineral springs and health and wellness spa mean different things to different people and their communities, and this can lead to differences in their social value, in the traditions covering their use and in the regulations for their exploitation. In Europe the term mineral springs is used more or less interchangeably for *natural* springs, where the water emerges directly from the ground into a natural catchment that can be used for bathing, and *developed* springs, which exploit the water through construction of man-made facilities such as pools and bathhouses. These can differ physically in many ways, even though in their utilisation they may all

Figure 6.3 Kerosene Creek near Rotorua in New Zealand is a hot stream fed by geo-thermal springs in a natural bush setting attracting many people for a bath
Source: Photograph courtesy of P. Erfurt-Cooper.

have the same outcome for the user, so the above distinction is maintained in this chapter.

Natural springs are often (although not always) on public land or otherwise accessible to the public without charge (e.g. 'Kerosene' Creek near Rotorua, New Zealand – Figure 6.3), while developed springs are almost invariably intended by the developer to make a profit, and hence visitors will be charged (and the developer/owner/lessee will be a legal position to demand) an admission fee for access to the water resource even if that water is classified as a publicly owned mineral by the country concerned (e.g. Polynesian Spas, Rotorua, New Zealand – Figure 6.4). Natural springs may also have few or no user facilities; visitors may have to change in the open, and there will be no showers either before or after the bathing experience, let alone amenities like the poolside restaurants that a developed spring may offer. On the other hand, natural springs are generally open-air and take visitors 'back to nature' in ways that a developed spring may not.

At a natural spring the ambient water temperature is purely on an as-is basis: at a temperature that is regulated solely by the relative proportions of water from the spring and surface water that the terrain imposes. As a consequence, water at natural springs can be uncomfortably or even dangerously hot. Commercial operators

Figure 6.4 Polynesian Spa, Rotorua, New Zealand
Source: Photograph courtesy of P. Erfurt-Cooper.

of developed springs on the other hand will generally ensure that the water temperature is appropriate for the majority of visitors (sometimes offering several choices of temperature in different pools) through dilution of the spring with water from a commercial supply or other methods of cooling the water, such as aeration. *This distinction is particularly important*; the visitor used to 'tame' water from a commercial spring who wades directly into a seething-hot natural spring can receive a painful, or even fatal, surprise.

Natural hot spring water may also carry disease-causing organisms that cause *Primary Amoebic Meningoencephalitis*, which is a rare but life-threatening infection caused by protozoa that inhabit some hot mineral springs. The disease is hard to catch; casual exposure via skin does not result in infection, only the inhalation of contaminated waters can cause problems, as the pathogenic amoebae migrate up the sinuses and surrounding tissue to the brain (Barnett *et al.*, 1996). If a brain infection does result, however, the consequences are extremely serious, with death nearly certain without medical treatment and all too likely even if the disease is treated. Prevention is simple: DO NOT inhale hot spring water from natural springs and avoid doing so if there is any doubt as to whether waters in a commercial spa have been sterilised. Additionally, the surface water that cools a scalding spring to usable temperatures will be prone to the same pathogens as any

Figure 6.5 Warning sign at Kerosene Creek, Rotorua, New Zealand
Source: Photograph courtesy of P. Erfurt-Cooper.

other untreated surface water. Operators of developed springs may (or may not) take steps to disinfect the water and/or lower the temperature, but at a natural spring visitors need to take care if there are warning signs indicating that the water could be potentially harmful (see Figure 6.5).

A *developed* hot spring is also not necessarily a *commercial* hot spring – one that has been developed for profit-making purposes – but will be one that has had additional facilities and/or treatments added to the spring resource. This distinction can be important where the local economic system allows for both public-interest/non-profit and for-profit development. The development regulations will often differ between the two cases (Cooper & Flehr, 2006), as may the resulting amenities, access and other facilities. For example, springs that have been developed by government departments or local communities may have fewer amenities, but also lower admission fees, than those developed for profit. In Japan, many springs are developed and maintained by local government and/or a community group and are free to the public or allow entrance for a very small fee.

By far the most sophisticated health and wellness spa tourism facility generally is of course the commercial type. Importantly, the physical environment *within* these facilities often tries to include the natural with the artificial in a blend that is designed to enhance the health experience. The most common constructs in this physical environment are:

- water availability in a number of different forms (pools, spas, specific water-based treatments) that usually require more than one type of building;
- massage and associated treatment rooms;
- beauty therapy rooms, often combined with a commercial outlet or shop for signature treatment products;
- water and waste treatment plants and, in some cases, geothermal power plants;
- associated accommodation and food outlets;
- landscaped surroundings evoking a range of physical environments; and
- access provision (usually bus and car parks).

Built environment

Variations in the built environment can best be illustrated by comparing and contrasting just three different types of facilities (see Chapter 7 for an in-depth analysis of the design of spa and wellness facilities). The first is an outdoor *rotem-buro* (hot spring bath) anywhere in Japan and in other countries (see Figure 6.2), where the pools for bathing will be uncovered, while the support facilities are generally limited to covered changing areas (often roof only) and clothes storage. There may be screens around the whole complex and associated refreshment areas, but this is not universal or even common especially in rural areas. The natural setting is as much the key to enjoyment of the facility as is the hot water.

A more developed type is situated in the alpine village of Hanmer Springs near Christchurch, New Zealand: the award-winning *Hanmer Springs Thermal Pools* (Best Visitor Attraction 2004 and 2005, New Zealand Tourism Awards – www.tourismawards.co.nz/Award-Winners/Past-Tourism-Awards-Winners.asp) offers visitors a wide range of experiences, from spa-based indulgence to family fun pools. The complex has nine open-air thermal pools, three sulphur pools and four private thermal pools, as well as a sauna/steam room. Additionally, a fresh-water heated pool and a family activity area, complete with water slides, water toys and a picnic area, ensure that the Hanmer Springs Thermal Pools & Spa offers something for everyone (Figure 6.6).

The Hanmer Springs bathing pools range in temperature from 33°C to 42°C (91.4–107.6°F), and the geothermal water is drawn from a bore adjacent to the village's nature reserve complex, providing a natural setting for the complex (Hanmer Springs Thermal Reserve, n.d.). Complementary to the bathing experience is a range of massage and beauty treatments from trained professionals at the associated Health, Body & Mind wellness facility. These treatments include Swiss and sports massage, detoxifying body wraps and aromatic facials. In addition, there is a cafe, and the thermal pools are within easy walking distance of a full range of accommodation, shops, a golf course and other park amenities. In winter, visitors to Hanmer Springs are only one hour's drive from two ski areas. For other outdoor activities, the forests surrounding the village incorporate walking and mountain bike tracks and the

Figure 6.6 Hanmer Springs Thermal Pools, New Zealand
Source: Photograph courtesy of P. Erfurt-Cooper.

region offers an exciting array of other adventure activities. The springs are open 364 days a year, and have been operated commercially for over 126 years.

Perhaps the most sophisticated developed type is to be found in the Hungarian capital of Budapest, a former Roman Empire spa town that was further developed under Turkish and Austro-Hungarian Empire rule, where the bathhouses from these times still welcome guests (Royal Spas of Europe – Budapest, 2001) as some of the most architecturally developed health and wellness spa tourism facilities in the world. While European spa towns with hot springs like Budapest were origi-nally made popular by visiting Emperors and kings, who declared the thermal waters as beneficial and set up their summer residences nearby, the subsequent centuries saw state-supported medical tourism come to the fore. The *Danubius Hotel Gellert* and the Gellert Bath make up one of the most famous spa resorts in Budapest (Figure 6.7). The complex is based on a four-star hotel opened in 1918 plus indoor and outdoor swimming pools, Jacuzzi, wave bath, thermal bath and steam rooms, as well as medical facilities and the usual range of accommodation. The medical section offers balneotherapy, electrotherapy, physiotherapy, hydro-therapy and medical massage. In this case the pool and spa are based on utilisa-tion of Gellert Hill's mineral hot springs, an aquifer of the Budapest geothermal field, noted for its calcium, hydrocarbonate, sulphate and magnesium content since prehistoric times (http://wwwdanubiushotels.com).

Figure 6.7 The Gellert Hotel and Bath, Budapest, Hungary
Source: Photograph courtesy of P. Erfurt-Cooper.

The basic design of the built and technological environment

The most common health and wellness spa facility usually incorporates the following components (Luxury Spa Finder Magazine, 2006; McNeil & Ragins, 2005) in the built environment:

- wet treatment rooms (may be male, female and/or common);
- dry treatment rooms;
- baths and showers;
- laboratories;
- reception, relaxation and waiting areas;
- locker rooms;
- retail areas;
- administrative and associated service areas, and, where provided, the following additions;
- beauty salons;
- fitness areas;
- café; and
- accommodation.

They are also usually provided within a visual environment that increasingly incorporates the outdoors, makes use of colours and textures to create a sense of isolation (peace, security) from the outside world, and pays attention to the way in which the built environment can enhance the overall experience (Nahrstedt, 2004).

Health Environment

Facilities and treatments

More and more frequently the modern health and wellness spa facility is being used to promote health as well as a healthy lifestyle among visitors and locals. Travel packages that combine medical checkups or treatment with fun and relaxing activities are enjoying a steady growth in popularity. A typical package of this sort involves the traveller being given an extensive medical check-up or treatment at a hospital before enjoying a relaxing and therapeutic stay at a hot or mineral spring resort. This type of 'tour' is common in Europe, was common in the United States in the past and is now becoming more and more popular in the Asia Pacific region. One example of such tours is offered at the *Yubara Onsen* resort in Okayama, a town in Western Japan with many hot springs. The package offers a general medical check-up and any optional tests, such as abdominal ultrasounds or respiratory tests. Trained staffs then advise visitors on the fundamentals of using hot springs for therapeutic benefit. This program is part of a project to promote the town as a destination for travellers interested in therapeutic bathing, and has received the enthusiastic backing of a local hospital, whose officials hail it as an important approach that links medical treatments with a curative environment (Japan Echo Inc., 2005).

Also enjoying a particular boom in popularity in Japan at the time of writing are medical travel package tours offering positron emission tomography scans, a new technology that is being used increasingly in the detection of cancer, with hotel accommodation (Japan Echo Inc., 2005). These packages are the result of alliances between travel agencies and medical institutions in cities throughout Japan, including *Sendai* in Miyagi Prefecture, *Koriyama* in Fukushima Prefecture and *Fukuoka* on the Island of Kyushu, and offer benefits not only for consumers – it is well known that early detection is vital in the treatment of many diseases – but also for medical institutions and the travel industry. Hospitals and clinics are as a result able to use the expensive medical equipment they own to derive commercial revenue, while travel agencies are able to tap an expanding market in the baby boomer generations (Hall, 2003; Japan Echo Inc., 2005). Other countries in the Asia Pacific region are beginning to supply such services more and more (e.g. Malaysia, India, Thailand).

The concept behind the *Spa Resort Hawaiians* (opened in 1961), a major hot spring-based health and wellness spa and family-oriented facility in *Iwaki City*, Fukushima Prefecture, Japan, and other similar facilities worldwide on the other hand, is for part of the customer base to stay for prolonged periods to maximise the therapeutic benefits of spa bathing in the European health spa tradition while the general clientele treats the facility as a giant water-based playground. The facility as a tourist attraction is therefore diversified; the majority of visitors in this case are encouraged to treat the complex as a theme park based on Hawaiian motifs and hot water bathing. Customers of the *health spa facilities* are segregated and spend their time taking part in bathing and exercise programs as well as eating foods with health benefits. These packages have been offered since November 2004, and the standard length of stay is four nights. Industry analysts predict that more and more medical travel packages and wellness resorts are expected to appear in the years ahead (Lund, 2002) as medical tourism becomes an increasingly important element of the travel industry (Luxury Spa Finder, 2006; McDermott, 2004).

As a result, notwithstanding the existence or otherwise of hot and mineral springs, such facilities are being duplicated all round the world, and their older European and American counterparts rejuvenated. In most cases their built environments contain a mixture of private treatment rooms and luxurious public spaces, some of which are increasingly sophisticated medical facilities, but all are designed to provide a range of

- spa and wellness treatments;
- wellness products;
- medical/cosmetic medical support and treatment;
- alternative and holistic therapies;
- fitness regimes; and often in recent years; and
- occupational wellness programs.

Business Environment

The business environment of health and wellness spa facilities is comprised of

- existing visitor patterns, potential markets;
- attractiveness of the core and ancillary services offered by the operator;
- local community attitudes; and
- external access, regulatory, labour and financial frameworks the business must operate under, as well as the actual spa facilities.

This section briefly outlines the business environment of the typical operator in this industry; Chapter 8 provides further details on the business environment through an examination of the marketing, management and planning associated with the health and wellness spa industry.

Visitor patterns

Estimates vary but the overall pattern of visitors to facilities offered by the health and wellness spa industry on a worldwide basis indicates that this form of tourism is increasingly popular. At the bathing end of the spectrum of visitors, in Japan some 100–150 million domestic visit *Onsen* facilities (with 19 million visiting health and wellness spa resorts), while in both Europe and America there are over 30 million visits per year to facilities offering health-related tourism

(Smith & Jenner, 2000: Chapter 2). The trend of indulging in a relaxing environment has turned into a global movement with a significant difference from the original concept of health spas, which mainly specialised in rehabilitation. The new emphasis lies mainly in the prevention of disease and maintenance of good health instead of cures, with high expectations regarding health improvements even if there are no health problems, although there is an increasing awareness of the benefits of combining medical treatment with spa tourism. Along with the body, *mind and soul* are also catered for in many spas in a holistic approach of creating harmony for those in need including new age treatments as well as the more traditional rehabilitative therapies (Kozak, 2002; Nahrstedt, 2004; Schobersberger *et al.*, 2004).

Several demographic, economic and lifestyle trends are contributing to these patterns. The ageing of developed countries' populations, a new desire for fitness, changing travel expectations combining travel with fitness and health opportunities, and the high cost of health care in developed countries are all increasingly important factors in the development of the market for health and wellness spa tourism. The main centre of attention appears to be natural healing methods incorporating Asian and European treatments accompanied by the aesthetic appeal of Eastern lifestyle and culture, which are in great demand. Therapies of Asian origin (e.g. Ayurvedic massage and skin care, yoga, reflexology, natural hot spring baths, traditional Chinese medicine and other native cures and remedies) are often combined with European balneotherapy (includes hydrotherapy, medicinal baths, peat and mud packs, Kneipp cure, drinking of medicinal waters as well as sport and fitness facilities). In these ways nearly all spas cater for beauty aspects with special signature treatments to make sure there are no missed economic opportunities.

In summary, it is estimated that there are over 100 million active *spa*-goers worldwide (ISPA, 2007). This estimate is based on the International Spa Association's research in 12 countries – Australia, Austria, Canada, France, Germany, Italy, Japan, Singapore, Spain, Thailand, the United Kingdom and the United States. Other patterns of interest to businesses in the industry discovered by ISPA were as follows:

- Women continue to dominate health and wellness spa tourism. However, men account for more than 40% of spa-goers in Australia, Austria, Germany, Japan, Singapore, Spain and Thailand.
- Baby boomers are the core market for the wellness industry with a growing interest in New Age remedies and alternative treatments.
- On average, spa-goers are in their upper 30s to early 40s or older.
- Relaxation and relieving stress are universally cited as the primary reasons for visiting spas.
- Facials, sauna/steam baths and full-body massages are among the most popular treatments worldwide.

These patterns inform the business environment of firms in the industry and those wishing to enter it. For many tourists the term 'spa' has become a household word and the health and wellness spa industry is now a leading leisure industry, generating some 250 billion dollars worldwide (Osborne, 2006; Pilzer, 2002). At the moment this market is principally split between local users and health and wellness spa tourists, but as Osborne (2006) suggests the industry can expect to see niche products and markets evolve in the direction of greater market segmentation, along with diversifying corporate investment, the entrance of new and often undercapitalised operators, the introduction of a new social ethos within the health and wellness spa facility and with the host community, new ways of delivering services and a further expansion of health and wellness spa-based advertising media (see Chapter 8).

Human resource development

The greater awareness and responsibility for personal health and well-being that is a major driver of these trends also means that the reputation of a particular facility will be an important factor in business success. One of the most important variables in this is the training and motivation of employees to deliver good service. Quality of *treatment* is dependent on high overall levels of training and motivation, not simply on the qualifications of therapists or the quality of the bathing experience, and quality of treatment is more important than cost or benefits (Osborne, 2006). Poorly trained, organised and often temporary labour presently characterises the tourism and hospitality industry, and where this pattern is replicated in the health and wellness spa sector it will need to change if businesses are to prosper in the future. Labour costs typically over 50% of revenue will not easily be a reason for de-staffing in this 'hands-on' industry, but higher guest-to-therapist ratios may be possible with concentration on group water treatments and the like in wellness traditions where these have not generally been in vogue.

Corporate environments

The health and wellness spa industry has shown rapid growth around the world over the past 2 decades, resulting in a very favourable corporate environment for investors (Idris, 2008; Tourism Queensland, 2002). Health and wellness businesses may provide day spa facilities, destination spa facilities, or medical facilities or a combination of these and other facilities, and their corporate environments may favour short-term results over long-term position, or vice versa. Whichever combination of these is taken will determine the positioning of the facility in the industry and in the local/national/international tourism market, but in general the health and wellness spa tourism industry is in a growth phase in the early 21st century and this is not expected to change in the short to medium term (Osborne, 2006).

Such a position means that investment funds are currently generally available to well thought-out development proposals, and regulatory agencies are likely to view proposals for health and wellness spa development as being suitable for many different locations. Regulatory environments are discussed in detail below, but the attitude of host communities is important when these are being developed and enforced. While health and wellness spa tourism is experiencing a rapid growth phase, more communities will be happy to support such developments, especially as spa and wellness centres now provide a significant layer of health care underpinning the normal community medical system. The challenge for this part of the tourism industry then is to stay in touch with the desires and attitudes of the local and visitor communities in terms of their political and consumer profiles, as much as with changes in products and technology (McNeil & Ragins, 2005).

One important corporate aspect of this will be to recognise and ameliorate problems before they become legal ones. Consumer litigation is now an ever-present possibility in the United States and other markets, so health and wellness spa businesses must operate sophisticated customer, staff and revenue management models to ensure their long-term survival (see Chapter 8).

Social, Psychological and Behavioural Environments of Health and Wellness Spa Tourism

Millions of consumers cannot be wrong. In fact promoting health and well-being has been a fundamental goal and rationale for both tourists and the industry since tourism began (Weaver & Lawton, 2005). It is assumed on all sides that a holiday is in itself healthy (Schobersberger et al., 2004; Walker & Page, 2003: 225), but how well founded is this assertion? The answer is that there is as yet very little scientific proof that mere vacations are in fact more intrinsically healthy than the alternative of staying home, while there is plenty of evidence to show that the act of travel itself may in fact be more dangerous to health than formerly supposed (Wilks & Page, 2003: 5–7). Nevertheless, consumer needs and wants have created readily identifiable profiles of individuals seeking to either recover from ailments or remain healthy through health and wellness tourism. The tourism types chosen increasingly include health and wellness spa therapies (Hall, 2003), or just bathing in thermal water in a relaxing environment, and it is to these particular social and behavioural aspects of the tourism profiles based on these resources that we now turn.

Wellness and tourist behaviour

The social, psychological and behavioural factors impacting on and/or creating the health and wellness spa tourism environment are outlined in Figure 6.8. Each of these will have a differential impact on the individual tourists' propensity to travel for health and wellness spa treatments and on a host community's desire and ability to accommodate them. Of critical impact are the social and psychological values that underpin the rise of health tourism. These are changing rapidly as more and more people accept the fact that health is a personal and dynamic process and wellness for all demands a widespread offer of wellness arrangement, of which health and wellness spa tourism is but one manifestation (Hall, 2003; Nahrstedt, 2004). As Hall (2003) noted in one of the first academic papers to be written on the rise of spa and health tourism, Western society has witnessed a marked trend among particular sections of the population toward more active and experientially oriented leisure activities and the desire for a

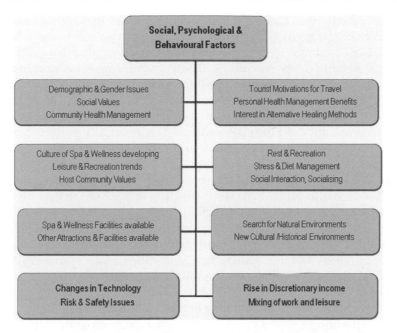

Figure 6.8 Social, psychological and behavioural factors in the health and wellness spa environment

healthy lifestyle. Cross-fertilisation with traditional Asian social values relating to the health benefits inherent in various forms of massage and hot water therapies (e.g. *Ayuraveda*) has both added to this trend and caused a shift in paradigm from indulgence to wellness at an individual level (Douglas *et al.*, 2001; McNeil & Ragins, 2005).

In part these changes in social values have been brought about by the rapid aging of the richest generation in modern times, the 'baby boomers' (Hall, 2003; Tourism Queensland, 2002). Approximately 2% of the world's population is aged 60 or above at the present time and this proportion is predicted to rise to about 30% by 2100; but these people are generally much healthier and fitter than at any time in the past and not only wish to stay that way but can afford to invest in order to do so. Demographic changes of this nature are already becoming manifest in parts of Europe, the Americas, China and Japan. With people living longer following retirement, the lifestyles and social values of the mature traveller will have a profound effect on the development and supply of tourism infrastructure, and a significant part of this impact will be felt in the health management field. We can therefore expect a further intensification of the culture of health and wellness spa across both origin and destination environments in the future. Coupled with this will be gender bias changes (McNeil & Ragins, 2005) where male clients become relatively more important, and a rising usage pattern among younger age groups following the baby boomer lead into health and wellness.

Product opportunities based on these and other social trends (increasing acceptance of technology, medical tourism, willingness to mix work and leisure, etc.) will result. Host communities can also benefit from the product combinations currently being identified. Sports clubs with spas, adventure tours and hot springs, natural environments with undeveloped hot springs, cultural and historical tours of geothermal areas, weddings (a common combination with *Onsen* bathing in Japan already), day spas within destination spa facilities, and the like will serve to bind a host community and the visitor together economically much more strongly, and will certainly expand the opportunities for tourism in an area.

Motivation for travel has been extensively covered in the tourism literature (Harrison, 2007). Many attempts have been made to profile tourist motivations and then link them to actual behaviour (Andreu *et al.*, 2005), based on the inter-relationships between needs and the motivation to satisfy these. Kozak (2002) notes that each visitor may have different motivations and preferences for different destinations, while the extensive tourism research literature based on Maslow's (Hierarchy of Needs and their satisfaction) and Plog's (Allocentric–Psychocentric personalities) theories of behavioural motivation serves to illustrate the complexity of possible motives (Harrison, 2007: 74).

From previous research it is possible to postulate a typology of likely motivations for health and wellness spa tourism based on push–pull factors (Andreu *et al.*, 2000; Crompton, 1979; Moscardo *et al.*, 1996). Push factors are origin-related and refer to the intangible desires of the individual traveller (in this case primarily a desire for wellness and/or a more healthy lifestyle), and pull factors are related mainly to the attractiveness of a given destination and its tangible tourism resources (spa and accommodation facilities, associated resources, etc.; Figure 6.9). Push factors or motivations to travel may vary from one person to the next or from one market segment to another, as well as from one particular time period to another by the same person or group. Pull factors vary by destination *and* the weight put on the various components of each destination attraction mix by the intended consumer (Kozak, 2002), which in turn can vary by level of information, prior experience, cultural and personal attitudes, and the existence of the 'word-of-mouth' effect (Cooper & Erfurt, 2003; Cooper *et al.*, 2001; Song & Witt, 2000). Customer loyalty may also be a prime motivation for repeat visitation/use of health and wellness spa facilities (Donovan & Sammler, 1994), which accounts for the increasing emphasis on relationship marketing in the tourism industry in the early 21st century (see Chapter 8 for further discussion of this form of marketing).

The tourist destination choice is based on assessment of destination attributes and their perceived utility values in relation to the push and pull factors felt (Figure 6.9), plus intervening variables such as marketing and contingency factors such as money, personal health and time (Pearce, 1993: 113). The environmental choices made in taking benefits from health and wellness spa tourism that result from the influence of these factors range from using a river bed without facilities (Figure 6.3) to those typified by the built environment of the Hotel Gellert in Budapest (Figure 6.7) and the Polynesian Spas in Rotorua (Figure 6.4).

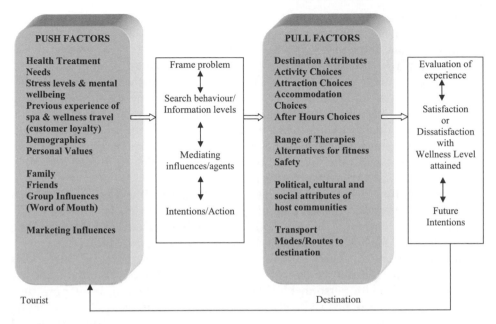

Figure 6.9 Destination choice factors
Source: After Pearce 1993.

Potential hazards and risks

An increasingly important factor in the environment of health and wellness spa tourism is the health *hazards* associated with the use of spa and wellness facilities. These include those normally associated with swimming pools and in addition others resulting from the use of hot and mineralised water. The high temperatures in some types of spas may also exacerbate the effects of alcohol or drugs, and the risk of drowning may also be enhanced by the lack of transparency in coloured or turbid spa waters. Deaths from the mineral constituents of the water itself are rare; those that do occur have been associated with a combination of high water temperature and the over-use of alcohol or drugs (the resulting drug-induced drowsiness increasing the risk of drowning), or inadequate supervision of young children. In the United States, 67% of all drownings occur in spas, hot tubs and backyard pools (WHO, 2000), and of the 700 deaths in spas and hot tubs recorded in that country since 1980 a third were of children under five years of age, emphasising the importance of the supervision of children playing with water.

The high turnover rate of users in many spas and whirlpools also poses an infection risk, involving both micro-organisms from the bathers and those present in the water. The warm, usually nutrient-containing aerobic water provides an ideal environment for many pathogenic organisms, such as *Legionella pneumophila*, the cause of legionellosis (Legionnaires' disease) and *Pseudomonas aerugionosa*, which causes folliculitis or infection of the hair follicles associated with an itchy rash (Madigan & Martinko, 2005; WHO, 2003). Also, natural hot spas may contain a species of amoeba that can cause amoebic meningitis (*Acanthamoeba*). Cases of this disease have been reported after swimming in natural spas or exposure to fountains in warm climates. Infections of the ear (*otitis externa*), urinary tract, respiratory tract, eye and wounds have also been linked to spas (Madigan & Martinko, 2005). These infections are difficult to control and require frequent monitoring of the pH (degree of acidity/alkalinity) of the water, and its disinfection and filtration. And water quality treatment itself may also present chemical hazards unless the chemical disinfection is well managed. There is also a risk of accidents around spas due to slips, trips and falls, and bathers may also pick up fungal and other infections from wet surfaces and other bathers.

There is another form of risk attached to health and wellness tourism, and that is related to its very success. Take for example the present rapidly growing attraction of medical tourism. Like many potential destinations around the world the various states of Malaysia are interested in setting up a 'medical hub' where medical/health tourism (especially from foreign markets) can be practiced, but as Idris (2008) notes while this may be far-sighted and visionary, there is at present a perennial shortage of health personnel in Malaysia. The net effect of developing such facilities may therefore be to actually reduce the opportunities for locals to obtain quality medical care in favour of the treatment of international medical tourists. A medical hub would simply exacerbate shortages of qualified medical personnel by attracting those that do exist into a more lucrative enterprise, while probably also soaking up domestic investment funds to provide the quality infrastructure expected by the foreign tourist. Idris (2008) suggests that further analysis needs to be carried out on the costs and benefits of such projects, wherever they are mooted, in order that the domestic economy and local communities are not adversely affected by the growth of health and wellness tourism.

Regulatory Environment

Water has been used for positive health for millennia though, and recreational use is not just a luxury. It provides opportunities for physical exercise, rest and pleasure, all fundamental components of the well-being essential to health. Thus the health aspects of the recreational use of water environments have attracted increasing attention from members of the public, concerned professionals and regulatory agencies. The World Health Organization program on water, sanitation and health for example includes development of guidelines for safe recreational water environments for coastal, freshwaters, swimming pools and spas (WHO, 2003); and a manual on the monitoring and assessment of bathing waters, including a code of good practice agreed with the European Commission (Bartram & Rees, 1999). In 1998, a meeting between the WHO and the USEPA (United States Environmental Protection Agency) produced the *Annapolis Protocol* (WHO, 1999). This acknowledged the limitations in establishing ways of monitoring recreational water quality and the need to agree possible alternative approaches, with particular emphasis on the control of microbiological hazards.

Development planning: Control of development and use

These concerns are translated into national and regional control systems through the political and legal jurisdictions that govern the health and wellness spa industry in any country. Common features of community-controlled spa and wellness facilities in most countries for example include

- environmental (land use) regulations;
- control of water sources and quality;
- control of wastes and discharges;
- control of treatments;
- control of visitation through pricing regimes; and
- use of oversight and/or education to modify visitor behaviour.

The *Taiwan Environmental Protection Administration* (EPA) for example is at the time of writing considering regulating wastewater discharged by hot spring hotels because emerging spa tourism has been linked to ecological damage (Regulations pursuant to the provisions of Article 18, Paragraph 3 of the *Hot Spring Act* 2003, Taiwan Water Resources Agency, 2008a; Table 6.1). According to the Taiwan EPA, nearly half the nation's 128 recreational spa sites are in environmentally sensitive areas designated by the government for protection of water resources. Officials investigating the downstream ecological impacts of several major spa recreational sites recently found that hot wastewater discharged from spa hotels along rivers has caused dramatic changes in the distribution of populations of fish, zooplankton, algae, insects and other organisms. EPA officials noted that 65% of the Nation's hot and cold mineral springs contain baking soda, but also noted that they are mostly worried by the temperature of such wastewater, which ranges from 35°C to 45°C (95–113°F, Taiwan Water Resources Agency, 2008b).

Consequently, the Taiwanese EPA is considering regulating spa hotels' wastewater discharges, at least by asking spa hotels to discharge hot spring wastewater and other sewage separately. Under the new regulations used hot spring water will have to be disinfected and filtered before being discharged into rivers, while sewage will have to be treated in septic tanks. Recycling of spring water will also be considered, but the difficulty here is that, unlike in Japan, users treat the hot water resources as a bath and often wash in it (or not at all), thus making it unsuitable for recycling without treatment (80% of used hot spring water in Japan can be reused appropriately because of the nature of their hygienic bathing tradition).

In other jurisdictions a variety of control mechanisms may be found. For the *Liard River Hot Springs Park* in British Columbia, Canada, a zoning plan has been imposed to ensure appropriate management. In this case the zones are management prescriptions to indicate appropriate activities for particular areas in the Park, and include a *Special Feature Zone, an Intensive Recreation Zone* and *a Natural Environment Zone.* The Special Feature Zone includes all lands and waters directly associated with the hot springs ecosystem. This includes the sensitive hot springs and pounded warm swamp ecosystems and the flora and fauna associated with these environments, and is subject to a high level of management protection.

Table 6.1 Taiwanese hot spring regulations

Article	Content
Article 1	These regulations are stipulated pursuant to the provisions of Article 18, Paragraph 3 of the *Hot Spring Act* (hereafter referred to as 'the Act')
Article 2	To utilise a hot spring for tourism, leisure and recreation purposes, a hot spring enterprise shall submit the hot spring for testing by an authority (institution) or organisation approved by the Ministry of Transportation and Communications, and, provided that the hot spring meets the pertinent requirements, apply to use an official hot spring logo in accordance with the provisions of these Regulations. The Tourism Bureau of the Ministry of Transportation and Communications is mandated by the Ministry of Transportation and Communications to undertake the approval of hot spring testing authorities (institutions) and organisations, the approval follow-up procedure as stipulated in Articles 3 to 5 of these Regulations, the application to register and certify the official logo, and the stipulation of the format of all documents and forms required under these Regulations. The matters thus mandated and the legal and regulatory basis thereof shall be publicly announced and published in an official gazette or in newspapers
Article 4	For the purpose of carrying out the approval of a hot spring testing authority (institution) or organisation, the Ministry of Transportation and Communications may call together the related authorities in charge and scholars and experts to review the content of the implementation plan, and when necessary may conduct on-site inspection; the same applies to the cancellation of approval. The review or cancellation of approval shall be publicly announced and open to the public on the internet
Article 5	An authority (institution) or organisation that has been approved for hot spring testing under the preceding articles shall carry out testing operations strictly in accordance with the content of its implementation plan and in accordance with the following provisions:
	(1) It shall itself attend at the site of the hot spring enterprise to take samples of the hot spring water from the storage tank at the mouth of the hot spring source and from the outlet of the hot spring water at its point of usage. (2) It shall complete testing within 20 days of accepting the application, issue a hot spring testing certificate, and submit a record thereof to the Tourism Bureau of the Ministry of Transportation and Communications. (3) Where there is a need to amend its implementation plan, such amendment shall be referred to the Ministry of Transportation and Communications for checking and approval

(Continued)

Table 6.1 *Continued*

Article	Content
Article 9	A hot spring enterprise that is in possession of an official hot spring logo identification sign shall hang the sign in a conspicuous place at the entrance to its premises, and in a suitable place shall display the following prohibitions and matters for attention when using the hot spring:
	(1) Bathers should thoroughly wash their body before entering the bath(s). (2) Persons with infectious diseases should not enter the bath(s). (3) Persons suffering from chronic disease such as heart disease, lung disease, high blood pressure, diabetes, and other obstructions of the circulatory system should enter the baths in accordance with a doctor's instructions. (4) Persons with dry or hypersensitive skin should avoid hot spring bathing. (5) Women who are menstruating should not enter the bath(s). (6) It is inadvisable to enter the bath(s) when intoxicated, with an empty stomach, or after a filling meal. (7) Do not take any pet into the bath(s). (8) It is inadvisable to be immersed in the hot spring for more than 15 minutes at a time. (9) It is inadvisable to be immersed in the hot spring above the heart. (10) It is inadvisable to enter a sauna directly after taking a hot spring bath, to avoid causing damage to the corneas. (11) It is inadvisable for pregnant women, elderly persons who have difficulty moving, and children under the age of three to enter the bath(s). (12) Persons who are elderly or in poor health should avoid entering the bath(s) alone to avoid accident. (13) After a long-distance hike, excessive fatigue, or strenuous exercise, it is advisable to rest awhile before entering the bath(s), to avoid cerebral anaemia or heat shock. (14) Anyone suffering any discomfort while bathing should immediately leave the bath and inform the service personnel. (15) Other matters as stipulated by the city or county (metropolitan) authority with due jurisdiction

Source: Water Resources Agency, Ministry of Economic Affairs, Taiwan.

Management actions are oriented to maintaining the natural resources and, as appropriate, a high quality recreational and interpretive experience (Ministry of Water, Land and Air Protection, British Columbia, 2003). The Special Feature Zone also includes all those areas within the hot springs ecosystem not designated for development and includes several undeveloped hot springs, large expanses of pounded warm swamp and associated meadows and forest, as well as all warm and cool creeks flowing through the park. No facilities or services are provided in the park but guided activities such as walking, interpretation, scientific study, photography and nature appreciation are allowed. This zone is also subject to temporary closures or permanently restricted access in order to preserve natural resources.

The Intensive Recreation Zone provides for a variety of outdoor recreation opportunities and those areas needed for park operations facilities. Improvements within this zone include those facilities compatible with the Visitor Services Plan such as the campground, day use parking and related facilities of the interpretive centre or kiosk. Possible use activities include vehicle camping, picnicking, nature appreciation and day use recreation. The Natural Environment Zone is comprised of the rest of the park, and includes the forested and open meadow areas of the park not lying within the special feature zone outlined above. The overall objective of the Liard Hot Springs Park Plan is to retain all existing undeveloped hot springs and swamp areas in their natural state and to allow natural processes to occur without interference. Management actions include the following:

- avoiding interference in water flow or channelling, or in plant or animal habitat without an evaluation of environmental impacts, and only if essential to protect the hot springs environment;
- keeping the appearance of the developed hot springs as natural as possible and minimising interference with water flow, temperature or the vegetation surrounding the springs. The optimum carrying capacity has been tentatively established at approximately 35–50 persons bathing at a time;
- redesigning the cooling water system at Alpha Pool to create less impact on the hot springs ecology;
- avoiding annual vegetation removal by maintenance staff in plant communities surrounding the hot springs;
- increasing supervision of the pool during peak hours; and
- undertaking any additional management actions as required to rehabilitate disturbed sites and to ensure minimum impact on the ecosystem by visitors.

Access and personal use of hot springs may also be controlled by regulation. Access to commercial spas and mineral springs is a simple matter: the visitor and operator are required to conform to business ethics in an economic relationship (generally involving the exchange of money for use and/or treatment). The situation is less clear-cut however with natural springs. If such a spring is located on private property it is likely that the land owner will have a legal right to control access to it, including charging for entry if he/she wishes. If the land owner chooses to assert this right the law will generally uphold it, although in countries with common land-use rights such as the United Kingdom public access may be protected even in this situation. On the other hand, natural springs in many countries are being placed off limits as a result of trespassers abusing access that land owners had previously afforded visitors, even if with limitations.

Springs on public land pose more complex access issues: in the United States for example, a general but by no means universal rule of thumb is that hot and cold mineral springs are off limits, or access is at least carefully controlled, unless specifically indicated otherwise. However, those in national forests and on land controlled by the federal Bureau of Land Management outside of a national park *are* generally available for free use unless indicated otherwise, with those under state jurisdiction generally following this pattern (see for example National Park Service, U.S. Department of the Interior, n.d.).

Health regulations

Having achieved access, health customs (and laws) at both commercial and natural springs vary substantially as to whether visitors are required to wear a bathing suit or ensure cleanliness before use. Most commercial establishments will post their own rules, which may be 'swimsuit required', 'clothing optional' or 'swimsuit required until sundown, then nudity OK' (this is commonly seen in commercial hot spring operations in the United States), or if in Japan clothing is not allowed under any circumstance, and bathers MUST wash thoroughly in a designated area before entering the bath. Commercial hot and mineral springs in most countries will also expect visitors to at least shower before entering the water, theoretically to avoid contaminants that can clog filtration systems. If entering to a natural spring however soap is not needed (since there is flowing, mineral heavy, non-recycling water) as it is considered to act as a pollutant.

The normal practice at natural springs is thus much more a local, ad-hoc matter. As a general but by no means universal rule, in most countries visitors should plan on wearing a swimsuit at springs in sight of a road unless the spring is specifically posted as accepting naturism, but will not generally be expected to do so in Japan. In the backcountry almost anything usually goes in any country, but it may be wise to err on the side of conservatism, especially as some countries prohibit nude hot spring bathing and enforce the prohibition with fines. In most there are no laws regarding nude bathing, so it is up to the visitor to decide. Local etiquette varies from spring to spring and country to country, but a general rule is that naturists are less tolerant of clothed bathers than the other way around.

Business ethics and health and wellness spa facilities

It is said soaking in hot natural spring water is as much a part of Japanese life as is karaoke, but some of the country's best-known spa resorts have recently admitted filling their baths from sources other than the geothermal ones they advertise (McCurry, 2004). At least seven of the 55 *Onsen* and Ryokan in the spa resort town of *Ikaho*, about 180 km north of Tokyo, have acknowledged that they had filled baths with tap water after mineral-rich springs started to run dry in the early 2000s. Ikaho is known for its iron-rich waters, which were first piped to the surface 400 years ago, and many thousands of visitors every year seek the purported therapeutic effects of the reddish brown water. It is no surprise then to learn that this admission prompted many cancellations from appalled tourists (see Chapter 4 for an explanation of this cultural phenomenon).

Shortly after this report surfaced several inns in the spa resort of *Shirahone* in Nagano Prefecture (192 km north of Tokyo) admitted that they had added bath salts to maintain their waters trademark milky-white appearance. These waters, which are said to have medicinal qualities reportedly started to lose their natural colour over 10 years ago (Faiola, 2004). After these admissions, the trickle of embarrassing revelations became a flood when other *Onsen* owned up to misleading guests, angering Japan's millions of hot spring enthusiasts and prompting calls for tighter regulations.

Under Japanese law however, the innkeepers have not broken any regulations. The 1948 Law on the regulation of *Onsen* facilities merely notes that anyone who discovers a source of water 25°C (77°F) or hotter can open a bathhouse. They are required to *register* the bathing facilities when they open, but do not have to renew their license should the natural spring water run dry; so there is nothing legally to stop them using heated tap water to replace it. The lengths to which some will go to keep the waters flowing reinforce the power of the centuries – old Japanese bathing tradition as McCurry (2004) notes. There are now more than 22,000 registered inns and bathhouses at 3000 resorts across the country, almost double the number of 40 years ago, yet according to Japan's Fair Trade Commission only about a third of the country's hot springs use pure, undiluted spring water from natural sources (McCurry, 2004).

Dubious business practices do not of course stop at manipulating water supplies in any jurisdiction. Unethical practices involving finance, marketing, water quality reports and the ingredients used in treatments are probably as likely in the health and wellness spa industry as in any other; however, it is not possible to document these with any degree of reliability as the basic research has not been carried out.

Summary

The existence of suitable and/or attractive physical surroundings, health facilities and effective business frameworks are important environments in the development of health and wellness spa tourism. Of equal impact are the social, psychological, behavioural and regulatory environments of the tourist industry, individual tourists and the host community. This chapter looked at the impact of the social, psychological and behavioural environments of the health and wellness spa tourism industry, which act as facilitators, moderators, barriers and as regulatory frameworks to its existence and proper functioning. It also covered the risks associated with the use of hot and mineral springs. The next chapter will cover the economics of the health and wellness spa sector of the tourism industry, and the technologies used within it.

Chapter 7

Technology and Economics of Health and Wellness Spa Tourism

MALCOLM COOPER

Introduction

We have seen that the current demand for health and wellness spa-based products and services is driven to a large degree by the aging of the 'baby boomer' generation of 1945–1954 (Chapter 2). Each reported beneficial result from wellness spas in health terms further increases the demand, as satisfied customers seek to look even healthier, live even longer and consume even more wellness products, while new customers look to the apparent benefits as portrayed by the industry and information provided by their friends and acquaintances. This chapter looks at recent developments in the health and wellness spa industry from the point of view of its technology and economics, and notes that the industry is in the throes of a huge expansion in the demand for and supply of wellness products. New products are also appearing in otherwise traditional markets. As noted in Chapter 2 some traditional hot springs in Japan have been developed into aquatic centres as kuahausu, providing separate and mixed bathing areas for men and women, with mineral pools at different temperatures, and with cold pool areas with fountains and waterslides, beauty salons, hairdressers, bowling alleys, gyms, saunas and steam rooms, massage services, restaurants and bars, relaxation rooms, music rooms and videos games, even though the main bathing attraction in Japan remains

Figure 7.1 Blending in with nature. Japanese open-air *Onsen* at Nachikatsuura in Wakayama Prefecture
Source: Chris73 (2004). A Wikimedia Commons image released under the creative commons cc-bt-sa license.

the traditional *Onsen* communal bath. New technologies are also advancing health products in the wellness industry within the hydrotherapy tradition.

The hot spring-based health and wellness industry's use of technology during its thousands of years of history has variously included open air immersion in naturally created pools and/or rivers (Figure 7.1), through simple buildings to massive building complexes incorporating many different types of use (Government Bath House, Rotorua, New Zealand – see Figure 4.8). A succession of civilisations have promoted the use of hot springs for therapeutic purposes over at least the past 5000 years (Chapter 3), and where geothermal waters have not been readily available have resorted to artificial heating to obtain the same benefits. Description of the technologies used by the health and wellness spa industry must therefore cover the simple diversion of naturally heated waters through to the building of spa resorts. In addition, it is necessary to discuss changing technologies relating to the wellness side; these are often ancillary to the use of water, but are nevertheless a critical part of the development of the industry.

In the same vein the discussion must also briefly cover the use of technologies on the business side that are increasingly central to the efficient operation of the health and wellness industry on a global scale. For example, in the past few years the industry has moved beyond the use of computers for simple research, database or email tools, and is now reporting major investments in database management, integrated channel customer contact systems and is marketing its products and services online (McNeil & Ragins, 2005; Tourism Queensland, 2002).

In terms of the socio-cultural background of health and wellness tourists that determines the design of facilities and their associated technologies, Tourism Queensland notes that *relaxation* is the primary reason for visiting a spa for 43% of day spa-goers and 61% of resort/destination/cruise spa-goers in Australia and the United States (Tourism Queensland, 2002: 2). Pampering and stress reduction follow, with weight loss, health reasons and exercise and fitness at the bottom of the list. So in fact a high proportion of clients are visiting health and wellness facilities to relax and forget about the real world for a while. Personal growth classes and activities ranked as the least important factor in choosing a spa among American spa users (Yesawich *et al.*, 1999). On the other hand, in Europe it is the health treatments available and the atmosphere and surroundings of the spa that are the most important factors in visitation (Hank-Haase, 2006). Non-traditional products such as 'Eastern' or Asian treatments and products with fitness components are also gaining popularity in all markets, while traditional products – the 'tried and true' therapies like hydrotherapy and mud baths – continue to be highly popular.

In the Asia Pacific region keeping a healthy body and mind (the holistic approach) while using natural and organic materials are the focus of new product and service technologies in spas. Services for couples such as dual massages and hydrotherapy are being requested more frequently, while healthy meal choices, integrated spa facilities and workout facilities are important in the selection of accommodations (ISPA, 2007).

From these data it is possible to suggest that the *desirable* facilities that should be provided in comprehensive health and wellness spa facilities include:

- hydrotherapy facilities;
- associated hot springs facilities;
- facilities for healthy nutrition;
- facilities for physical fitness;
- provision for relaxation, cultural activity and mental activity;
- qualified staff;
- sufficient information about health topics made available;
- nature tracks for recreation activities such as walking, cycling and jogging; and
- facilities for the aged and disabled.

This chapter examines the provision of these facilities from a technological and economic perspective.

Obtaining Water: Exploration, Development and Delivery

As we have seen in earlier chapters, mineral waters for therapeutic use are a basic requirement for recognition as a health resort or spa facility by both users and regulatory authorities in many countries (Gingerich, 2004; Hank-Haase, 2006;

ISPA, 2007). Obtaining a secure supply of such waters is generally therefore of paramount concern to the operator of a spa or wellness centre in those countries. Throughout the history of use at each site around the world various methods have been tried to ensure supply, regulate temperature and mineral content, and disposal of wastewater. At the spa resort Baden Baden in *Germany* for example, the thermal water today is produced by three sources: from tunnels intersecting several former springs, from remaining individual naturally occurring springs (piped free flow) and from two wells drilled in the 1960s into potential water bearing strata (Sanner, 2000). Thermal water is also delivered to three public drinking fountains and several private users (hotels, hospitals) within the town (Figure 7.2). Combinations of similar methods are in use at all sites around the world.

Baden-Baden's health and wellness spa resort sector has two major bathing facilities: the traditional *Friedrichsbad* (1877) and the *Caracalla Spa* (1985). Both are fed with thermal water from the natural hot springs as well as from the wells drilled in the 1960s (Figure 7.2). Thermal water is also delivered to three public drinking fountains and several private users (hotels, hospitals – Sanner, 2000), and the annual mineral water use at these sites totals 290,150 m^3. The Friedrichsbad is in the traditional hot springs district to the west of the town centre, just beside

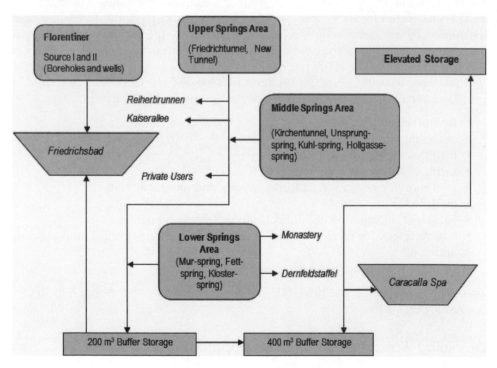

Figure 7.2 Schematic of the thermal water production and use in Baden-Baden, Germany
Source: After Sanner (2000).

the traces of the Roman bath and partly on the site of the former sinter mound of the original hot springs (Sanner, 2000: 20). Architecturally, the facilities feature a combination of Roman and Irish bathing traditions that came about through the influence of a certain Dr Barter, an Irish physician who combined the Roman approach (various types of warm thermal baths) with traditional Irish techniques involving hot air baths (Lund, 2000d). Friedrichsbad waters are used to treat chronic joint disorders such as arthritis and rheumatism. The Caracalla Spa, located in the city centre and opened in 1985, is more of a modern indoor swimming complex, comprising a large pool (at 32°C/89.6°F) with its own therapeutics area, two open-air pools (30°C and 34°C/86°F and 93.2°F), one cold and one hot water grotto (18°C and 38°C/64.4°F and 100.4°F), in a total area of more than 900 m² (Sanner, 2000: 22).

Japan is one of the world's major hot spring nations, and hot springs play a very important role as facilities for people's health and relaxation. But it is not just humans who use the bath in this country; the only recorded constant use by animals is shown in Figure 7.3. As of March 2005, there were 27,644 hot spring sources throughout the country: 5120 naturally flowing, 13,805 equipped with pumping

Figure 7.3 At Jigokudani Hot Springs, Nagano Prefecture, Japan the local 'snow monkeys' (Macaques) enjoy the open air thermal springs. The monkeys do not share the bath with tourists
Source: Wikimedia Commons (2005), GNU Free Documentation License, Version 1.2.

systems and 8719 not in use (Japan Ministry of the Environment, 2006). The total hot water from these sources amounts to approximately 3.91 million tons per day. Under the 1948 *Hot Spring Law*, the Japanese government recognises as *Onsen* only those hot springs that reach certain standards regarding temperature and mineral composition. The Hot Spring Law defines a hot spring as 'hot water, mineral water, water vapour and other gases that issue from the ground with a temperature in excess of 25°C (77°F) or contain more than a pre-described amount of designated substances'. On the basis of this law, the Minister of the Environment gives the designation of 'Hot Spring Health Resorts' to hot springs of good quality (see Chapter 10). As of March 2006, 91 such sites covering over 16,000 hectares (16,653.75 ha) had been designated (Japan Ministry of the Environment, 2006: 41).

Techniques for acquiring hot and mineral springs water for health and wellness facilities have been developed in many different parts of the world since the ancient civilisations that first mastered them (Chapter 3). In Japan an indigenous well-boring technique known as *Kazusabori* made possible many of the Beppu and other cities' *Onsen* in use today throughout Japan (Takamura, 2004). Developed in the early 1800s this method involved thrust boring with metal rods dropped repeatedly to butt the ground. Initially wells could reach about 100 m using split bamboo rods joined together to 5–6-m-long iron rods or pipes with a diameter of 3.5 cm, on the bamboo tip. Improvements to the rods, jointing and raising of the poles to provide more thrusting power by means of a wheel device allowed depths of up to 1000 m to be reached by the 1880s, although this system went out of use once rotary boring mechanised techniques were widely available in the 1950s (Takamura, 2004: 42).

In *Iceland* for example it is said that piped hot water was available by the early 13th century AD, but it was not until 1908 that a farmer in the *Mosfellssviet* area constructed a 2.3 km pipeline (steel pipe) from a hot spring to heat radiators in his house (Fridleifsson, 1999). The spring was at a higher elevation than the house though, so no pumping was required. This achievement was soon surpassed by farmer and blacksmith Erlendur Gunnarsson (1853–1919) who invented a way to separate steam and hot water from a boiling spring by his farm at an elevation 6 m below the farmhouse. He piped the steam to his house in 1911 and used it both for cooking and for heating. In 1980 boiling water began to be piped 63 km to Reykjavik from the same area (Fridleifsson, 1999).

In *Eastern Europe*, over 2000 mineral and thermal springs have been identified in the former Czechoslovakia (Lund, 2000b: 35). The recorded use of these waters has been traced back almost 1000 years to before the Roman Empire (Chapters 2 and 3). There are now over 60 spa resorts in the Czech Republic and Slovakia, visited by more than 460,000 patients annually, and about 360 million bottles of mineral water are produced from the same resources. In terms of the technology used in this area, Lund (2000b: 35) notes that the first visitors to the thermally active locations prob-ably bathed in uncovered bathing pits dug along the banks of the River *Vah*. The first wooden building housing spring-fed tub baths was built in 1778, with the first hotel accommodation constructed on the site in 1813. The spa hotel *Thermia Palace* and the balneotherapeutic centre *Irma* were completed in 1912, resulting in Czechslovakian spas becoming the meeting place of Europe's elite when it was part of the Austrian-Hungarian empire (Piestany Spa – Lund, 2000b: 36). Spas were privately owned up to the 1940s, at which time they became the property of the state and formed a treatment nucleus of medical importance in the state health system, and have remained so since the division of the country into two (Piestany is now the *Czechoslovakia State Spa and Curative Springs* in the Slovak Republic).

The collection and distribution technology used in these spas has to deliver and deal with hot gypsum–sulphuric spring water (67–69°C/152.6°F and 156.2°F) containing 1500 mg/l of total dissolved solids, as well as gases, especially hydrogen sulphide, and sulphuric mud (Lund 2000b: 36). Thermal water is used in pools and tubs, and the mud is utilised in baths and for mud packs. The surface springs flow at a rate of over 3 million litres per day and the water must be cooled from around 69°C to 35°C to 40°C (156.2°F to 95°F to 104°F) through heat exchangers for use in the pools and baths. The sulphurous mud is cured for 6 months by an anaerobic process to increase its sulphur content. It is also 'cooked' for a minimum of 48 h from 70°C to 80°C (158–176°F) for the peloids (clay particles) to gain their optimum properties before use (Lund, 2000b: 36).

There are two types of pools in this area: some have a natural bottom with a layer of mud through which thermal waters (cooled to 40–41°C/104–105.8°F) flow; the other type of pool is supplied with thermal water (38–40°C/100.4–158°F) through a system of pipelines (Lund 2000b: 36). The extracted sulphur mud is applied at a temperature of around 50°C/122°F to the patient by means of modern equipment (spray-gun) or as partial packs on hands and legs.

Technology and Design of Spas

The American Society of Heating, Refrigeration and Air-Conditioning Engineers (ASHRAE, 1999b) has suggested that the desirable temperature for thermal bathing in that country is approximately 27°C (+ or –5°C)/80.6°F (+ or –41°F). If the temperature of geothermal water is higher than this level, then mixing or cooling by aeration or in a holding pond is usually required to lower it (Lund, 2000d: 6). Also, if geothermal water is used directly in a bath then a flow through process is also necessary to replace the 'used' water on a regular basis to avoid the possible build up of contaminants; in this situation, acceptable circulation rates vary from 6 to 8 h for a complete change of water. In many cases, the raw water must also be treated with chlorine or other disinfecting additives for human use, making it more economical to use a closed loop for the treated water and have the geothermal input provide heat through a heat exchanger rather than directly through the temperature of the water itself (Lund, 2000d: 6). In turn, heat exchangers must be designed to resist the corrosive effects of added chlorine and the scaling or corrosion effects from the geothermal water.

Sizing of a pipe and pool system for usable temperature and flow rates depends on four considerations (Rafferty, 1998). These are

- conduction through bath/pool walls;
- convection from the pool surface;

- radiation from the pool surface; and
- evaporation from the pool surface.

Of these, conduction is generally the least significant unless the pool is above ground or in contact with cold groundwater. Convection losses from the pool surface depend on the temperature difference between the pool water and the surrounding air, including the effects of wind velocity. This form of loss is substantially reduced for indoor pools and those surrounded by wind breaks. Radiation losses from the pool surface are greater at night, especially for outdoor pools however during the day there will be solar gains which may offset this.

Evaporation losses contribute the greatest heat loss from pools –50% to 60% in most cases (ASHRAE, 1999a: 48.9–48.20). The rate at which evaporation occurs is a function of air velocity and pressure differences between the pool water and the water vapour in the air (vapour pressure difference). As the temperature of the pool water increases or the relative humidity of the air is decreased, the evaporation rate will increase. An enclosure can reduce this loss substantially, and a floating pool cover can practically eliminate this form of loss (as well as radiation losses).

Hot water spas require year-round humidity levels between 40% and 60% for comfort, to minimise energy consumption, and for building protection (ASHRAE, 1999b: 4.5–4.7). A successful physical design must therefore consider all of the following variables: humidity control, ventilation requirements for air quality, air distribution design, pool water chemistry and evaporation rates. According to ASHRAE (1999b) human beings' desire to use spa facilities is very sensitive to fluctuations in relative humidity, while those outside the 50–60% humidity range can increase levels of bacteria, viruses, fungi and other factors that reduce air and water quality (Lund, 2000d: 8; Table 7.1). High relative humidity levels are also destructive to building components; mould and mildew can attack wall, floor and ceiling coverings, and condensation can degrade many building materials.

Within the facility itself, the technology used to deliver the water and treatments to the patient/visitor are as varied as the number of spas worldwide. There are many sources for illustrations of the treatment technologies that might have been found in spas based on the European tradition at any point during the 19th and 20th centuries. These ranged from emersion with mild electrical stimulation,

Table 7.1 Spa temperature design conditions

Type of pool	Air temperature (°C)	Water temperature (°C)	Relative humidity (%Hg)
Recreational	24–29	24–29	50–60
Therapeutic	27–29	29–35	50–60
Competition	26–29	24–28	50–60
Diving	27–29	27–32	50–60
Whirlpool/spa	27–29	36–40	50–60

Source: After Lund (2000).

Figure 7.4 Interior of a typical Japanese *Onsen*, Akita, Japan
Source: Oobuka Onsen Akita (2005). Wikimedia Commons, GNU Free Documentation License.

through steam baths, to high- and low-pressure hoses directed at various parts of the body (see, for example, the *Slipper* and *Greville* bath systems used in the Government Bath House in Rotorua New Zealand during the 1920s; Stafford, 1988; Rotorua Museum of Art and History, 2008). Figure 7.4 shows the rather more simple system in use today in most Japanese spas.

Changing Techniques in Health and Wellness

The idea of a spa treatment specifically created to soothe tired bodies, as distinct from mere hot water use, is what underlies the development of the modern health and wellness concept. In one recent development *Singapore Airlines* has begun offering – after a lengthy flight – an explicit treatment specially made as a flight reviver. Of course, many destinations around the world have spa treatments that revitalise bodies and relax stressed minds, but the idea of a flight reviver spa treatment arose because the airline has a lot of older guests who come from Europe and Australia (Singapore Airlines, n.d.). Like all great ideas this one is becoming part of the menu of many spas worldwide (and their associated airlines), and includes aroma therapy, deep massage, with intensive spinal pressures, and hydrotherapy.

This indicates the importance of the combination of the two sides of the Health and Wellness Spa industry in recent years. Modern thermal hydrotherapy combines water treatments with a range of other therapies in a 'rest and relaxation' context, with or without medical supervision. The historical centre of *Aix-les-Bains* in France has reinvented itself in this way for example, offering in its 'Centre Well-being' programme 6- or 7-day stays or individual tailor-made packages for the visitor's well-being (Mackaman, 2007). The complex offers facilities for pure relaxation and regeneration, with a swimming pool with different swirls, a thermal-water indoor pool and a freshwater outdoor pool as well as hammans (steam baths), saunas and a gym and relaxation area. The thermal baths are hosted in a 19th century building in order to create a sense of 'being steeped in history'.

In a further reflection of consumers' growing inclination to choose products that are good for their health, travel packages that also combine medical checkups or treatment with fun and relaxing activities are enjoying a steady growth in popularity in Japan, Europe and elsewhere. A typical package of this sort involves the traveller being given an extensive medical checkup at a hospital before enjoying a relaxing and therapeutic stay at a hot spring resort. One such package is the '*hot doc*' plan offered at the Yubara *Onsen* resort in Okayama, a town in western Japan boasting numerous hot springs (see Chapter 6; Japan Echo, 2005). Japan Railways Hokkaido is marketing a similar service that combines a medical checkup with hotel accommodation in the city of Sapporo. These packages include return air or train tickets from Tokyo and other major cities to Sapporo, the biggest city on the northern island of Hokkaido, as well as a night in a hotel and a medical checkup.

The spa services industry in the United States consists of about 14,000 facilities with a combined annual revenue of over $10 billion (ISPA, 2007). The industry is highly fragmented: most spa services companies operate a single facility and, importantly, most of these are based more on the beauty therapy side of health and wellness tourism than the hydrotherapy/therapeutic side as in Europe. Demand for spa services is driven by personal income and demographic trends, and these in America have more to do with body surface (obesity, beauty) appeal than with underlying internal health (Lund, 2002). Thus the major providers of spa services are day spas (70% of industry revenue), resort and hotel spas (20%), and medical spas (5%). Other providers include club spas, mineral spring spas and destination spas. About 80% of all the spa facilities in the USA are day spas (ISPA, 2007). The medical spas that do exist are similar to day spas, but focus on services by health-care professionals, such as Botox injections and laser hair removal (McNeil & Ragins, 2005). Destinations are increasingly offering lodging and specific health regimes, such as weight loss or detoxification programmes. As a result of these patterns of demand and supply the most popular spa services are full body massages, manicures and pedicures, and facials. Other services include movement classes, food therapies, aroma therapies and (some) hydrotherapy (ISPA, 2007).

Therapeutic bathing for the 21st century

In many other countries therapeutic bathing is once more gaining ground. The concept behind the Spa Resort Hawaiians for example, a hot spring facility in Iwaki City, Fukushima Prefecture, Japan, is for health and wellness customers to stay for prolonged periods to privately maximise the therapeutic benefits of spa bathing in controlled facilities. This is though alongside a massive recreational complex containing water slides, public swimming pool, and the health and wellness spa facilities themselves. This complex houses the world's largest open-air bath (Guinness Book of Records, 2006). The wellness customers spend their time at the resort taking part in bathing and exercise programmes as well as eating foods with health benefits. Packages have been offered since November 2004, and the standard length of stay is four nights. Another packaged resort in Japan involving stays lasting several days, called *Spa Do*, was being trialled in Kagoshima Prefecture, southern Kyushu in 2004. This package includes a consultation session with a doctor, who advises travellers on ways to improve their health, while much of the time is spent taking it easy soaking and dining at local hot springs. During a trial tour in July 2004, participants had their health checked by doctors before relaxing at sand baths and hiking local trails to burn some calories, while also sampling some of the local delicacies (Japan Echo, 2005). The same article makes the point that more and more combination hydrotherapy and medical travel packages are expected to appear in the years ahead; with industry analysts predicting that medical tourism will be an increasingly important element of the travel industry, because people's awareness of the importance of preventative health and their willingness to spend time and money on it are likely to continue to grow.

Medical thermalism

Medical thermalism has a strong pedigree in Europe. On the formation of the USSR at the end of the Second World War for example, Eastern Europe's existing spas were extended and modernised as part of the former USSR's public medical treatment system. The same process occurred in both Germany and France, where the medical spa tradition still holds sway in the 21st century. The integrated health and wellness concept embodied in the European tradition is quite different from the beauty therapy-based concept of the Americas and Australia, but the two are now converging. This is not without considerable debate – wellness centres, doctors' offices with spa services, spas with medical examinations, anti-aging treatments and spiritual guidance – which ones qualify as a medical spa? But it is generating a very large subset of health and wellness spa tourism, with recent studies suggesting a total value of between USD40 and 100 billion within four years though caution as to the reliability of these figures should be exercised (The McKinsey Quarterly, 2008).

Vanderbilt (2002) considers that the medical spa facility *technically* has two very different modalities: the *doctor's office* that adds on spa services, like homeopaths, internists, dentists or plastic surgeons; and the *spa aligning itself with the medical profession* to back up its claims of therapeutic value. The latter may or may not have medically qualified employees or associates on call during times of operation. While consensus as to definition, defined purpose and guidelines for the operation of medical spas still hangs in limbo in the United States, most industry experts seem to agree that one is needed given the oversight capacity of the National Food & Drug Administration, the Occupational Safety & Health Administration and State Regulatory Boards (Vanderbilt, 2002). This is because blood-borne pathogen standards, hazards communication standards, clinical laboratory control standards, health insurance accountability standards and the procedures for purchasing many types of equipment that require qualified medical staff to be signatories all require compliance to national and state standards. Unless such compliance is forthcoming it will not be possible for a 'Medical Spa' to operate certain classes of equipment such as lasers or be accredited to offer other medical procedures desired by health and wellness tourists (clients).

In the European context as typified by France and Germany (as well as the former eastern European countries) these questions are of less importance as government has regulated this industry since before the development of modern spas (Tilton, 1981; Hank-Haase, 2006). Currently the *Ministère de la Santé* in France oversees the exploitation of therapeutic waters in France, while the *Commission des Eaux Minérales* of the *Académie Nationale de Médecine* establishes the therapeutic value of new resources and the technical aspects of tapping into such water supplies are overseen by the *Service de Mines*. Noticeable is the close connection between the health and wellness industry and the medical profession. Medical students at universities can study for the *Attestation d'Etudes d'Hydrologie* and there is an *Institut d'Hydrologie* at the national level (Tilton, 1981: 572). The therapeutic value of waters is attributed to properties including trace elements, gases, a variety of minerals including calcium and sulphur, temperature and radioactivity. Different concentrations of these ingredients have meant that different spas specialise in treating different diseases. In this situation French spas specialise to maximise client acceptability (positive outcomes) and the use of equipment. Respiratory ailments, metabolic and urinary disorders are considered to be treated best in spa water containing sulphur, calcium and magnesium, motor disorders are best treated with high water temperatures, while bone diseases are treated at spas whose waters are slightly radioactive. As Tilton (1981) notes, a health and wellness spa tourist in Europe may travel to several different sites to achieve full coverage of personal disorders and the resulting benefits. The marketing of spas in France and other European countries makes much of these variations (see Chapter 8), but is firmly supported by the medical profession and governments.

An outpatient clinic for skin diseases was opened at the *Blue Lagoon, Keflavik*, Iceland, in January 1994, specialising in the treatment of psoriasis (Gingerich, 2004), and attracting since then an increasing number of patients. Following immersion in the healing waters and the application of silica mud a *phototherapy* cabinet provides the patient with a combination treatment of immersion and light therapy. Gingerich (2004) reports that many patients show some improvement in their skin conditions and the first signs of skin healing after as little as one week of treatment, and demonstrable improvement with a 3–4-week treatment regime. In these treatments each individual is provided with follow-up recommendations for selected skin care products to extend the healing as they return to their own community and/or country.

A much larger medical tourism market exists in Thailand, and is being developed in India and a number of other countries (Tourism Review, 2008). While spa resorts and meditation centres in Thailand are packages themselves designed to help prevent health problems, many Thai hospitals and medical centres have recently begun to tap into an important revenue stream derived from attracting foreign clients with pre-existing medical problems for checkups and treatment. At present, the cost of getting a medical checkup in Thailand and India and other countries of Asia is a fraction of what it costs in Europe and America, and spa treatments are part of the package cost. Major Thai hospitals have also begun marketing themselves as regular participants at international tourism trade shows, like ITB in Berlin and the Arabian Travel Mart (Moohin, n.d.). In Bangkok and the main provincial cities and tourist centres doctors and specialists can obtain patient records by satellite and the internet from their home countries, while at the same time patient care is made more bearable for the client in spa-like surroundings. This type of health and wellness spa tourism and the linkage between the hospitals and the travel industry was recently reinforced when Thai Airways International began packaging medical checkups as part of its Royal Orchid Holidays Program (Thai Airways, 2008).

Day spas

Box 7.1 Marketing of day spas

Walk into a world of complete sensory heaven – where time is left at the door and a new journey begins – step into a temple of touch and aroma a sensory space for men and women – escape from the pressures of everyday life and transport yourself to a more tranquil world step back in time to rituals of ancient understanding – discover an exotic blend of therapies from around the world ... Bali, Tibet, Polynesia, Japan, Morocco and Thailand discover a pathway to inner peace, reflection, restoration and enlightenment – no clocks, no stress, no urgency ... (Savoy Hotel, 2008).

So goes the advertising for the 'day' spa at the Savoy, London, indicating that here is a fully artificial health environment based on something other than hydrothermal resources (although hot water can feature in many of these establishments as a therapy – Box 7.1). Accordingly, the technology that is described here involves beauty therapy products and techniques more than it does methods of immersion in or reliance on the health-giving properties of water, although the wellness intention is undoubtedly the same. Specialised packages in these environments usually include treatments such as

- remedial body massage;
- exfoliation scrubs;
- mud wraps;
- advanced facial treatments;
- laser treatments;
- weight loss programmes; and
- glamour makeovers.

Some day spa packages also include food and drink such as herbal tea and wellness elixirs. Traditional beauty therapy/maintenance treatments found in such establishments include:

- eye enhancements and treatments;
- skin treatments and facials;
- manicures and pedicures;
- make up artistry;
- hair removal;
- massage therapies; and
- spa body therapies.

And all clients are promised personalised assessments and prescriptions to suit their specific needs and a range of professional retail products for home care, gifts and perfumes are usually also available for purchase. The following description is unsourced to preserve the anonymity of the operator, but it gives a very good idea of the type of facility being now rapidly developed in many parts of the world to supplement more traditional forms of health and wellness treatments. The Deluxe Package is an all-day spa treatment (approximately 5 hrs) costing US$455 per person (Box 7.2):

Box 7.2 The ultimate spa journey

Every part of your body, from head to toe, is restored, rejuvenated and relaxed during this half day of total luxury. Your journey begins with a body polish using ancient marine crystals, followed by the layering of unique clays, pure essential oils and semi-precious stone balm. You are then enveloped in our exclusive Infrared Body Capsule to infuse the product nutrients. After the clay cleansing ritual is completed your muscles are massaged from head to toe for pure relaxation. The focus then moves to achieving skin radiance with an exclusive facial using a specially selected serum and masque. Your journey is then completed with both an express manicure and pedicure with your choice of polish.

These Spa Indulgence facilities implement leading technology in beauty therapy at the individual level, another characteristic that sets the Day Spa apart from other forms of health and wellness treatments. The total experience is usually gained in private treatment rooms, or with a friend or partner in a couple's room, not in a communal bath. On the Medi Day Spa side they often provide permanent hair reduction and skin treatments using laser technology. An indication of the importance of this market within the health and wellness industry can be found in a survey commissioned for the medical website *TreatmentAbroad.net*, which found that in 2006 more than 50,000 Britons travelled abroad for lower cost medical treatments, with the most popular procedures including cosmetic surgery (TreatmentAbroad.net, 2007). This survey, of 138 treatment clinics, also showed that British tourists spent a total of 161 million pounds (€231 million, USD328 million) on medical tourism. In terms of UK patients undergoing procedures abroad the three most popular international destinations were revealed as Hungary, Turkey and India, and the most popular service was dentistry, with more than 20,000 Britons travelling abroad for dental work. Second to dentistry was cosmetic surgery, with approximately 14,500 patients travelling outside the United Kingdom in 2006 for a variety of procedures such as breast augmentation, liposuction and tummy tucks, creating an estimated market in cosmetic surgery tourism which is in excess of 50 million pounds (€71.8 million, USD101.9 million) per year.

Associated Technologies

The health and wellness spa industry is associated with a number of other technologies that impinge on its operation and/or image. This section outlines the more important ones.

Water quality and wastewater

Water cleanliness as distinct from its quality as a therapeutic medium has been touched upon earlier in this book in Chapters 2 and 6. Water quality in spas and the wastewater that is subsequently generated are closely monitored and controlled in all countries with this type of facility in line with standards operating in the water and food supply industries. The general process is outlined in Figure 7.5.

Internal purification systems for all hot springs water utilise a range of methods, including ultraviolet light, hydrogen peroxide dosage, ozone dosage, membrane filters and copper/silver ion treatments. The entire water usage or that part destined for direct contact with the human clients of the facility is passed through a filtration system in accordance with the local regulations relating to water purification. Bacterial culture and other forms of testing are usually carried out to ensure

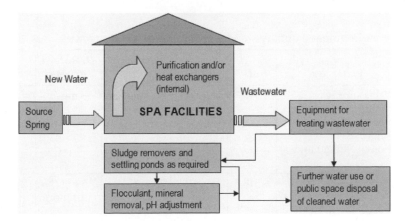

Figure 7.5 Basic technologies for water quality
Source: The author.

that all systems work properly. Often the result is of drinking water quality, and as such the waters may then be supplied to the spa client or bottled for sale.

The Japanese water quality assurance system provides a relevant case study and this will now be briefly outlined. Control of water and wastewater quality vests in the Water Environment Department of the Ministry of the Environment under various enabling Acts, the main one being Law No. 138 of 1970: *The Water Pollution Control Law*. This law and its accompanying regulations target hot springs water as well as other forms of bathing water directly given its importance to Japanese culture. Environmental quality standards for water for bathing are listed under Water Class A (Table 7.2). While not the most 'pure' water it is nevertheless of potable quality.

National and prefectural governments control water quality and pollution in Japan by setting stringent regulations for water input, water use, wastewater discharge, extension and improvement of sewerage and water reticulation systems, and by appropriate environmental impact assessment of various projects that discharge wastewater into public water areas. The following are the measurements that are required under the *Water Pollution Control Law* for hot springs facilities in Japan and these are set out in the appropriate Japan Industrial Standard for that measure (JIS B 9940-9944, JIS K 0102; Japan Industrial Standards Committee, 2008):

- pH (hydrogen ion concentration);
- BOD (biological oxygen demand);
- COD (chemical oxygen demand);
- SS (amount of suspended solids);
- n-HEX (content of normal-hexane extracts);
- temperature;
- electric conductivity;
- chlorine concentration;
- hydrogen sulphide concentration;
- calcium concentration; and
- iron concentration.

Table 7.2 Environmental quality standards for water, Japan

Class	Water use	pH	BOD	Suspended solids	Dissolved oxygen	Total coliform
AA	Water supply class 1, conservation of natural environment and uses listed in A–E	6.5–8.5	1 mg/l or less	25 mg/l or less	7.5 mg/l or more	50 MPN/ 100 ml or less
A	Water supply class 2, fishery class 1, bathing and uses listed in B–E	6.5–8.5	2 mg/l or less	25 mg/l or less	7.5 mg/l or more	1000 MPN/ 100 ml or less

Source: Okada and Peterson (2000).

In other jurisdictions similar requirements have to be met. Generally Class A level water anywhere is fit to drink and most spa operators will attempt to control their source water so that this standard can be maintained for marketing purposes as well as for safety. Most geothermal water used for health and wellness spa tourism has been classified under the relevant *Environmental Protection Authority Guidelines* as potable, for spa resorts as far apart as Bath Spa, UK; and Peninsula Spa, Melbourne, Australia; the Hotel Gellert, Budapest, Hungary; and Spa Hawaiians, Iwaki, Japan. The environmental protection systems in use around the world also control temperature. As noted earlier in this chapter under the 1948 *Hot Spring Law*, the Japanese government recognises as *Onsen* only those hot springs that reach certain standards regarding temperature and mineral composition. Mineral composition is regulated in accordance with government guidelines to some extent but the individual spring operator is free to claim benefits from mineralisation that is not considered harmful in the concentrations to be found in these waters. Table 7.3 indicates the range of minerals that may be found in geothermal

Table 7.3 Analytical results for Peninsula Hot Springs geothermal water

Analytical category	Unit	Amount
pH value	pH units	6.82
Total dissolved solids (TDS)	mg/l	3836
Total hardness as $CaCO_3$	mg/l	705
Langelier Index	mg/l	0.34
Calcium	mg/l	116
Bicarbonate	mg/l	1163
Magnesium	mg/l	90
Sodium	mg/l	868
Potassium	mg/l	64
Alkalinity as $CaCO_3$	mg/l	714
Sulphate	mg/l	20
Chloride	mg/l	1432
Iron	mg/l	<0.1
Fluoride	mg/l	0.73
Lithium	mg/l	0.15
Silica (as SiO_2)	mg/l	23
Manganese filtered	mg/l	0.08

(Continued)

Table 7.3 *Continued*

Analytical category	Unit	Amount
Ammonia as NH$_3$	mg/l	2.7
Nitrate as N	mg/l	0.03
Zinc	mg/l	0.038
Rubidium	µg/l	0.14
Tellurium	µg/l	0.238
Selenium	µg/l	71
Total cations	me/l	49.22
Total anions	me/l	44.32
Actual (anion/cation) difference	me/l	4.9

Sources: Peninsula Hot Springs (n.d.); http://www.peninsulahotsprings.com/downloads/about-us.pdf.

water using an example from the Victorian (Australia) Peninsula Hot Springs facility (Peninsula Hot Springs, 2008).

In summary, all commercial spas use water purification systems. Materials and methods used include ultraviolet light sterilisation, dosing with hydrogen peroxide, ozone and of course chlorine. In Japan, where there are high levels of boron and other non-metallic trace elements in *Onsen* water, contaminated wastewater treatment technologies (technologies for treating wastewater containing boron or other non-metallic elements) are those most often used to properly treat hot spring water. The target in this case is 10 mg/l (the nationwide uniform standard set by the *Water Pollution Control Law 1970*).

Ancillary uses of the geothermal resources

In certain places the geothermal source water may also be used for power generation and space heating, horticulture and similar uses. In the case of Rotorua, New Zealand, thermal water space heating and personal bathing supplies were available to city residents until the 1980s from the local geothermal fields, when it was determined that the draw-off of water was affecting the tourist attractions of the city (Pohutu Geyser and similar areas), and might in turn impact on the Wairakei Geothermal power station south of the city (Turner, 1985).

In Beppu, Japan, the area with the second largest flow of geothermal waters in the world after Yellowstone National Park in the United States (see Chapter 9), many homes and apartments have their own *Onsen* (indoors) or *Rotemburo* pools (outdoors). In addition, hotels, communal bath houses and Ryokan use the available water for bathing and sightseeing purposes. One such establishment, the Suginoi Hotel, has the ubiquitous hot spring baths, which are used by visitors and residents alike, but there is also a geothermal powerplant and a large indoor heated bathing and recreation area. The hot springs that supply the Suginoi Hotel are colourless and transparent, have a slight sulphur odour and the water emerges at a constant 210°C or 410°F (Kudo, 1996). The hotel, consisting of two towers, has a capacity for 2100 guests, and has 11 meeting rooms, 20 banquet halls, four restaurants, four cafeterias and a wedding ceremonial room. The hot springs are also used for *Acquabeat*, a facility that includes water slides, a Jacuzzi dreambath (*Ume-no Onsen*), flowerbath (*Hana-no Onsen*), outdoor hot spring baths, a wavepool and a thermally heated bowling alley (Kudo, 1996).

The Suginoi Hotel Geothermal Power Plant is rated at 3000 KW (annual generation 18 million KWh), sufficient to power the hotel during normal periods of operation. Opened in November 1980 the geothermal energy derived from this plant is used for many purposes as noted above such as baths, hot water supply space heating and air conditioning, as well as for power generation. Geothermal steam from three wells is collected in a steam gathering plant located beside the power house through a two-phase flow transmission pipeline. The steam gathering plant consists of a cyclone separator and a moisture separator, and supplies clean steam to the turbine. Also, waste hot water from the steam gathering plant is utilised for public use in several Beppu *Onsen* (Kudo, 1996).

Spa Economics: Current Investment Patterns and Changing Demand

Measuring the potential market for health and wellness products and services from all this hot and mineral water and associated health and wellness spa tourism activities is extremely difficult. The health and wellness spa industry is very diverse, and there has been little effort to date to measure it as a distinct market (but see ISPA, 2007). The approach taken in the final section of this chapter then is to attempt an overview by aggregation of the results of individual studies of individual markets. Among these are data from the Canadian, American, European and Japanese markets, and more briefly as a set of case studies of Asia Pacific region spa locations.

One overarching market consideration in relation to health and wellness tourism is the increasing interest in a wide variety of unusual or exotic forms of vacation travel as a whole. A 2002 *Travel Attitudes and Motivation Survey* in Canada and the USA found that: 'There were considerable increases in the percentage of respondents who reported being interested in the less common activity-based accommodations in 2002. For example, respondents were three times as likely to express an interest in staying at health spas … relative to the last two years. This suggests that the more exotic forms of vacation travel are on the increase' (Lang Research, 2002: 16–17). The survey also found that there is an increasing focus on overall health among consumers, including health and wellness programmes responding to the growing consumer demands for fitness level improvement, for healthy lifestyle education, for nutrition counselling, for healing, for preventative medicine, for solving personal problems like stress or depression, and for holistic, naturopathic, alternative or eastern medicinal practices and therapies (Lang Research, 2002).

Another important market consideration is that health and wellness tourism has been found to be an all year round activity for tourists:

> A recent survey carried out on Spas Relais Santé clientele revealed that all seasons are favourable for health and wellness getaways. Member establishments have been busy year-round. This makes us believe that the health tourism industry represents an ideal four-season tourism product. We also noticed that customers were willing to book their stay during the off season which greatly contributes to *making the health industry available any time of year.* (de La Barre *et al.*, 2005: 27)

As a result, the health and wellness spa industry is now estimated to be worth in excess of USD1 trillion per year and attracts over 100 million visitors worldwide (ISPA, 2007). ISPA (2007) notes that the most popular treatments during 2006 and earlier years include facials, saunas, and steam-baths and full-body massages, in addition to the use of hot and mineral springs wherever these are available. The ISPA research was drawn from 12 countries, including Japan, Italy, Thailand, Spain, the UK and the United States. For the United States the study revealed that as of July 2007 there were 14,600 spas in the United States, up 6% from August 2006, when there were 13,800. Of the available spa types in this market day spas were the most prevalent. In 2006, the US spa industry generated an estimated US$9.4 billion in revenue.

Individual businesses maximise their revenue through careful management. Revenue management as a tool of business is the application of decision rules and industrial organisational processes to maximise revenues and profits (Kimes, 1989). These processes can include forecasting demand through modelling systems, optimising the allocation of inventory, providing dynamic packaging, and offering dynamic pricing. One of the most familiar examples of the latter is airlines (and Petrol Stations) raising ticket prices during holiday periods and weekends, lowering them during weekdays, offering cheaper rates for advance bookings than for last-minute bookings, etc. The application of revenue management to the health and wellness spa industry will therefore likely translate into lower prices for treatments during slower times (mornings and early in the week) and higher rates at peak periods (Saturdays). Spa products, hotel rooms, special service prices and similar features can also be adjusted to rise and fall according to demand. Value-adding, packaging and dynamic pricing will also be part of the revenue maximising mix (Kimes, 1989; Witt & Moutinho, 1995).

The market research resource group Research and Markets (2007) has published a new report examining the growth rates and market opportunities available in the beauty, wellness and health therapy industries in Europe. The *European Spa Market Report 2007* is structured around spa facilities defined in sectors, including day, hotel, resort, medical and health spas. Split into nine sections, the report details facilities country by country, summarising spa visitor numbers and annual revenues on available estimates.

Asia Pacific regional trends

Table 7.4 provides a snapshot of key industry statistics by selected country in the Asia Pacific region. The data are the most up-to-date information available at

Table 7.4 Health and wellness industry by country, Asia Pacific region 2007

Category	Australia	New Zealand	Thailand	Indonesia	China/ Hong Kong	Malaysia	Philippines	Singapore	Taiwan
Total no. of spas	503	–	320	390	–	151	87	173	317
Historical growth rate (%)	129	–	–	160	–	202	74	63	–
Period	2002–2006	–	–	2003–2007	–	2002–2006	2003–2006	2003–2006	–
Day spas % of total	65	35	–	42	–	54	76	58	81
Destination spas % of total	28	–	–	52	–	40	20	14	6
Employment	–	800	5000	3000	400	500	–	700	–
No. of visitors	–	500,000+	4,000,000+	1,000,000+	940,000	120,000	–	400,000	–
International visitors (%)	–	30	78	80	40	50	–	25	–

Source: Intelligent Spas (2003–2007).

the time of writing and based on this a country by country description is provided below. Within this pattern of regional development and activity there are approximately 320 spa facilities in *Thailand* employing over 5000 people, and attracting over 4 million visitors. Thai spa industry economic benchmarks according to the Thai Ministry of Public Health (2008) include the following:

- Thai spas generated approximately 6.7 billion baht (USD200 million) in revenue in 2005, within a tourism industry worth 702 billion baht and attracting 3.3 million international and domestic visitor trips per year;
- on average, 78% of spa visitors are international tourists;
- fifty-seven percent of spa visitors are female and 43% are male;
- there were 600,000 foreign medical spa patients in 2004, generating 19.6 billion baht;
- employees are typically hired on a full time basis;
- on average, at least half of spa revenue is generated by massage services;
- almost half Thai spas are located in a resort; and
- spa facilities in Thailand contain 9.4 treatment rooms on average.

Of all the major spa markets surveyed in 2005 only Thailand had captured the high-spending international market successfully, with nearly 80% of total spa visits generated by international tourists. However, although Thailand had the highest proportion of hotel resort spas of the markets surveyed, their capture rate was the lowest. This implies their guests were not utilising the spa services offered within a particular property. When correlated against total spa visits, it seems likely guests in the Thai market visit other spa facilities outside their hotel/resort instead (Intelligent Spas, 2005).

New Zealand in contrast hosts relatively few hotel and resort spas; however, they achieved the best capture rate of the high-spending health and wellness tourism market on average compared to other major spa markets across the Asia Pacific region in 2003 (Intelligent Spas, 2004). This spa industry survey of New Zealand facilities conducted in 2003 estimated total employment had grown by 13.4% to approximately 800 people between July 2002 and June 2003. The New Zealand spa market mainly consists of day spas and salon spas based on the abundant hot spring resources of that country. Other key results include the following:

- approximately two-thirds of the spas surveyed in New Zealand were operating as partnerships;
- day spas made up 35% of spa types;
- eighty-two percent of visitors were female and 18% were male;
- thirty-three percent of visitors were international tourists;
- over 500,000 people visited spas during 2001/2002; and
- on average, 30% of spa revenue was generated by massage services.

Indonesian spas employ almost 3000 people and are typically day spas or resort spas (Intelligent Spas, 2003). Key results include the following:

- over 1 million people visited spas during 2001/2002, of which over 80% were international tourists;

- sixty-seven percent of spa visitors were female and 33% were male; and
- on average, 44% of spa revenue is generated by massage services.

Spas in *Malaysia* are also generally resort or day spas and collectively employ over 500 people (Intelligent Spas, 2003). Key results include the following:

- approximately half the 120,000 spa visitors in 2001/2002 were international tourists;
- sixty-four percent of spa visitors were female and 36% were male; and
- forty-eight percent of spa revenue is generated by massage services on average.

Hotel spas and day spas also dominate the *Hong Kong/China* spa market, which employed almost 400 people in 2001/2002 (Intelligent Spas, 2003). Key results include the following:

- over 940,000 people visited spas during 2001/2002, 40% of which were international tourists;
- fifty-five percent of spa visitors were female and 45% were male; and
- on average, 54% of spa revenue is generated by massage services.

The *Taiwanese* market during 2006 included a total of 317 spas currently open and operating (Intelligent Spas, 2007). The Taiwanese spa market is dominated by stand-alone day spas, which account for a total of 81% of spas in the country, while a total of 6% of all spas are located in hotels and resorts. Forty-eight percent of the spas surveyed were located in Taipei while the average indoor area was 457 m², containing seven treatment rooms on average.

The key differences between female and male spa consumers relating to historical behaviours and current expectations and preferences in Asia have also been determined by Intelligent Spas' field research (released 30 August 2005). Key findings from this unique study included the following:

- forty-nine percent of females compared to 65% of males stated their last visit to a spa was for relaxation;
- sixty percent of females encountered some disappointment during recent spa visits;
- seventy-eight percent of females and 63% of males preferred a female therapist to perform spa facials; and
- of those who stated they were likely to visit a resort spa, 46% of females and 39% of males said they would most likely choose a package of spa treatments during their next visit.

While Japan is not covered here due to the difficulty of equating *Onsen* with spas, it is important to note that there are approximately 3000 *Onsen* resorts, 6400 public bathhouses and 27,000 hot springs in the country, frequented by over 150,000,000 visitors in any one year (Beppu International Tourist Office, 2007).

Europe

For the German travel industry, health and wellness are very definitely important products (Hank-Haase & Illing, 2007). In 2004 5.9 million health-related holidays were taken by Germans in Germany and the country's spas and health resorts recorded a total of 12 million visitors, an increase of 1.1% on the previous year. The average stay was 5.5 days, almost double the average for Germany overall (2.9 days). Germany has 500 health and wellness spa hotels, and holistic health and wellness spa packages are offered by 68% of all German spas and health resorts. The industry is aiming to attract travellers through professional marketing services, highly developed infrastructure and products, continuous quality improvement while also tapping into new groups of holiday makers whose stays are privately rather than health-service funded, for example, in wellness and preventive healthcare.

Due to cut-backs in the German health system over the last decade more personal responsibility for health and overall well-being is necessary. This has resulted in a new market of considerable size opening up for providers of attractive Medical Spa establishments. In a nationwide survey by *ghh consult GmbH* in 2006, it was established that a likely demand of 800,000 guests contributing approximately 4 million overnight stays for the already operating facilities (Hank-Haase, 2006). Within these stays about 20 million treatments of a preventative and health supporting nature were paid for privately. This equates to an occupancy of roughly 17,000 rooms, sales of €1 billion nationwide, and full time employment for 20,000 people. One-third of all participants of every age group acknowledged the necessity for private healthcare and preventative medical actions, and also positively indicated a willingness to finance this. This willingness increases with age. Overall, the wellness market has become an important part of the German hotel industry. More than 500 hotels and resorts all over Germany have included wellness concepts of varying size in their offers. More than 4 million guests are influenced significantly in their choice of accommodation by appealing wellness facilities. A benefit of 20 million overnight stays for the hospitality sector can be attributed to this, resulting in a turnover of approximately €2.5 billion (Hank-Haase, 2006; Hank-Haase & Illing, 2007). This in turn sustains full time employment for 50,000 people in this sector, and increasingly competitive large investments are made to attract the affluent guest.

However, the research also showed that wellness developments of more than 1000 m^2 require investments in excess of €2 million. Due to the limited research in this area, little is known about the economic impact and profitability of such developments. In this respect the perceived need by the industry to stay competitive with ever grander and more luxurious concepts could result in costly consequences. Higher occupancy rates and increase in sales revenues are vital to justify these enormous investments. Only a combined increase of several factors such as overnight stays, turnover, food and beverages sales revenue and room rates will validate such an investment (Hank-Haase & Illing, 2007).

Other countries in Europe, such as Hungary, are redefining and redeveloping their health and wellness spa industry, which prior to the 1990s in many cases was part of the Soviet health system. Current developments in Hungary include:

- developing service packages in health and hot springs tourism;
- encouraging competitive investment in quality and exclusive products; and
- extending the tourism season.

In order to achieve these changes a national 10-year development plan was launched in 2002. Known as the *Széchenyi Plan*, it aimed to improve the country's existing spas and promote wellness tourism both domestically and internationally (Ministry of Economic Affairs and Transport, Hungary, 2002). Under this programme approximately €188 million was to be spent by the government on developing spas and subsidising the hotel industry to 2004. The industry itself spent in excess of €550 million on the existing 82 spas and spa hotels during the same period. The Szechenyi Plan specifically promoted the development of healthcare and hot springs tourism in Hungary as one of the six subprogrammes of the national tourism development plan. Emphasis was placed on increasing the country's tourism-related revenues, attracting three-generation target groups rather than just the elderly to hot springs and health facilities, and developing products that would be competitive on an international scale (focussing mainly on European, Russian, Ukrainian, Croatian and Israeli markets). The strategies designed to achieve these aims included:

- reconstructing existing health resorts and hot springs and improving services;
- promoting the use of known thermal resources that are not yet used for tourism;
- further developing the infrastructure of health resorts and hot springs for tourism;
- developing a regulatory framework;
- ensuring effective marketing; and
- developing human resources for health resorts and hot springs.

Summary

The health and wellness spa tourism industry based on hot and mineral springs is currently experiencing a worldwide boom. Examples of new developments abound, even in areas that before now have not shown marked interest in this form of tourism. One of these is the Saraya Islands USD1.4 billion project in *Ras Al Khaimah*, UAE (Saraya Holdings, 2008). This mixed-use residential, wellness and tourism development will consist of four interconnected islands. One of the islands, called *Al-Sahab*, will be exclusively dedicated to a spa and resort development. Similar developments are proposed for Vancouver Island, Canada, where a geothermal spa will be a key amenity within the resort, and for the city of Kobuchizawa in central Japan, where the Brazilian-based company Kurotel has joined forces with the Japanese pharmaceutical company CMIC to open the Kurotel *Longevity Center and Spa* to complement its earlier Gramado, Brazil equivalent (Spas Canada, 2000). On a worldwide basis, the Hilton Hotels Corporation (HHC) is to invest USD200 million in a strategic arrangement with Moet Hennessy Louis Vuitton (LVMH) to develop 70 new spas, which will be combined with its existing 65 spas, under two LVMH brands Guerlain and Acqua di Parma (Hilton Hotels Corporation, 2007).

The use of Sector Benchmarking Indicators (SBI) for spa operation is also becoming important in the health and wellness spa industry. As outlined earlier in this chapter and in Chapter 6, existing controls and standards are both piece-meal and limited to water quality and financial benchmarking. Green Globe, one of the world's largest environmental sustainability certification and improvement organisations, proposes to apply its ecotourism standards to the industry, using the independently verified *EarthCheck* benchmarking system. Data have been collected from existing spas to set baseline and best practice standards (Six Senses Spas, 2007), and these are intended to be the first eco-label for the global health and wellness spa industry.

Perhaps the most telling indicator of the worldwide importance of the economic development of and future technical innovation in this industry was the inaugural *European Spa Summit* which took place in Paris in October 2007. Organised by ITEC France, the summit was intended as a forum for the exchange of ideas and information on an international scale and was targeted at spa and resort developers, hotel managers, investors and spa brand owners. The first day examined spa development and conception as well as technical issues, while the second day involved discussion of spa management, strategy and profitability issues. Such a development could not have occurred even five years ago, and has to date not been paralleled in academic circles (although ATLAS and other academic organisations have held small discussion symposia).

The role of hot and mineral springs in the further development of the health and wellness spa tourism industry is being recognised in such fora as being critically important in providing not just physical well-being but also the increasingly necessary psychological/emotional and social well-being inputs to human health through its incorporation in modern spa facilities. Water-based therapies have long been understood to be perhaps the most effective treatments for the maintenance of health and well-being; these developments are reinforcing this knowledge.

Chapter 8

Aspects of Management and Marketing in Health and Wellness Spa Tourism

MALCOLM COOPER

Introduction

Local, national and global competition is increasing in the health and wellness spa industry following its resurgence in the past two decades. Paradoxically, this increased recognition and use makes it increasingly difficult for individual operators to provide a compelling reason for potential or existing customers to buy a particular local product, and therefore the probability of business success in this industry without an extensive and active marketing programme is likely to diminish over time. The health and wellness spa industry has understood this relationship for many years and has developed its own unique selling propositions (USPs – Rosser, 1961) to define the core essence of what the business is about in order to effectively communicate its advantages to the most profitable market opportunities currently available. What is noticeable about this industry though is its definition of its mission in much broader societal terms (the promotion of *wellness*) at the same time as it is promoting its products (Kotler *et al.*, 1999b). One of the most often used USPs and at the same time social messages is that of the beneficial effects of hot water in health and wellness spa therapies. This chapter outlines how the health and wellness spa industry has marketed itself to tourists using the close association of wellness with hot and mineral springs as well as beauty therapy products (including the huge bottled mineral water industry). The chapter also discusses the influence of the industry's management and human resource development on its attractiveness to tourists, and the impact of changes in the national health systems in selected countries on the growth of health and wellness spa tourism as a key aspect of the industry.

Marketing in the health and wellness spa industry currently involves appealing to the hearts and minds of the baby boomer (and younger generations) in relation to their physical and mental well-being. A mixture of messages and message types is used from word of mouth, through travel guidebooks, to their culmination in Internet and print-based 'glossy' images of ideal spa types and of wellness outcomes. Spa magazines, internet and/or print based, informing the reader of everything luxurious and beneficial for their health and well-being that is available are now very common, as are coffee-table books about 'The 100 Best Spas of the World' or equivalent market-conditioning subject matter (Table 8.1 and Figure 8.3).

Table 8.1 A very partial list of coffee-table material

Arieff, A. and Burkhart, B. (2005) *SPA*. Köln, Germany: Taschen Verlag (English, German and French captions).
Arvigo, R. and Epstein, N. (2003) *Spiritual Bathing: Healing Rituals and Traditions from Around the World*. Berkeley, CA: Celestial Arts.
Asensio, P. (2002) *Spa & Wellness Hotels*. New York: teNeues Publishing Group.
Benge, S. (1999) *The Tropical Spa: Asian Secrets of Health, Beauty and Relaxation*. Hong Kong: Periplus Editions.
Clark, A.J. (2005) *Australia's Best Spas – The Ultimate Guide to Luxury and Relaxation*. Hong Kong and Singapore: Periplus Editions.
Jotisalikorn, C. (2003) *Thai Spa: Sanfte Wellness zur Selbstanwendung*. Germany: Irisiana Verlag München.
Kunz, M.N. (2004) *Wellness Hotels: Indien, Südostasien, Australien, Südpazifik*. Germany: avedition GmbH, Ludwigsburg.
Leavy, H.R. and Bergel, R.R. (2003) *The Spa Encyclopedia: A Guide to Treatments & Their Benefits for Health & Healing*. New York: The Day Spa Association, Thomson Delmar Learning.
Lee, G. and Lim, C.Z. (2003) *Asien Spa: Anwendungen, Rezepte, Wellness-Oasen*. München, Germany: Christian Verlag.
Lee, G. (2004) *Spa & Wellness in Europa: Hotels, Anwendungen, Rezepte*. München, Germany: Christian Verlag.
Levick, M. and Young, S. (2003) *Beautiful Spas and Hot Springs of California*. San Francisco: Chronicle Books.
Maier, D. and Fiedler, H.G. (2004) *Der große Thermenführer: Wellness und Badespaß in Österreich und den Benachbarten Regionen*. Wien (Austria): NP Buchverlag.

(Continued)

Table 8.1 *Continued*

Niel, A. (1984) *Die großen k.u.k. Kurbäder und Gesundbrunnen*. Wien, Österreich (Austria): Verlag Styria.
Schweitzer, C. (2003) *Wellness in Weekendnähe: Die 100 Besten Adressen zum Abtauchen, Entspannen und Geniessen – Schweiz und Nachbarländer*. Schweiz (Switzerland): AT Verlag Aarau.
Seki, A. and Brooke, E.H. (2005) *The Japanese Spa: A Guide to Japan's Finest Ryokan and Onsen*. Tokyo, Japan: Tuttle Publishing.
Von Furstenberg, D. (1993) *The Bath*. New York: Random House.
Zeitgeist Media (2005) *Deutschland Deine Thermen – Saunen, Spassbäder, Wellness-Oasen*. Düsseldorf, Germany: Zeitgeist Media Verlag und Neue Medien.

Source: The authors.

Examples of such magazines are *Spa* (Canada), *AsiaSpa* (Hong Kong), *SpaAsia* (Singapore), *Spa Life* (Australia), *Spa World* (UK), *Spa Finder* (USA), *Haus & Wellness* (Germany), all of which have only been published for a few years. By now it is also noticeable that most of the glossy magazines and coffee-table books emphasise personal luxury and well-being to sell their products, revealing the nature of the actual water sources beyond temperature where these are used in treatment is not common. This may be because such details are not important once a decision has been made that natural hot or mineral waters are to be part of a particular experience, or it may be that some of the spas advertised are not in a position to offer genuine hot springs and cleverly exploit unspecific mineral spring terminology to advertise their facilities even though they do not in fact offer such resources (see Chapters 2 and 6). Whatever the reason for not going into much detail about the water itself, many if not most spas and resorts use natural features that copy the look of hot spring-fed rock pools and waterfalls to also market to the customer the sought after natural environment associated with water therapy-based wellness.

The continued growth of the health and wellness spa industry also means that increasingly sophisticated management will be the only way for individual businesses to compete effectively in the tourism marketplace. This is because the main difference between facilities endowed with the same or similar resources of hot or mineral springs, modern technology and attractive buildings lies in the quality of the services provided, the attitudes and competence of the staff providing them, and the perception by clients of value for money. And all these are predicated on efficient and effective management.

Another aspect of modern health and wellness spa facility operation that requires good management lies in the area of risk. There are three broad risk areas for the health and wellness spa industry: the first, the nature of extreme environments, which is basically what the geothermal part of the industry is sourced from, makes them an object both of interest and of apprehension, and is the first area of concern discussed later in this chapter. The second involves the quality of the waters themselves, and the third covers the risks associated with the ancillary services provided at most health and wellness spa resorts. The latter can include disease transmission, inadequate treatment and surgical error, misleading advertising as to the nature of services offered and the quality of the natural resource (see Chapter 6), and the financial burdens associated with some forms of treatment.

Effective management involves securing, developing and keeping trained staff. Almost always the quality of the experience gained by the visitor to any particular facility depends very much on the existence of trained and competent staff, rather than on the décor or the sophistication of the equipment available. Human resource development in this industry, as in any other, involves

- understanding of the differing roles of the spa operative and manager;
- effective leadership;
- personal organisation;
- effective time management;
- financial awareness;
- recruitment of visually competent marketing and selling staff (much of the marketing of the industry is based on visually communicated health attributes);
- generally recruiting the best operatives that can be found (and training them to an even higher level);
- effectively managing day-to-day performance;
- developing training and coaching skills;
- performance appraisals; and
- assisting staff to effectively manage client relationships.

Changes in national health systems have also had a major impact on the management of spas in western Europe, the former socialist countries of Eastern Europe, and the Americas (see e.g. Tourism Queensland, 2002 and Chapter 2). Health and wellness spa tourism has long been an important component of health care in a wide range of jurisdictions; from the countries of the former USSR to Germany and France, Austria, Italy, Israel, New Zealand, and now India, Malaysia, Thailand, and a host of other countries interested in the recent boom in medical tourism (Hall, 2003; Idris, 2008). In many of the countries of eastern and western Europe the cost of domestic visitors to spas has been in the past wholly or partly subsidised by the State as part of national health care delivery, while in other countries the lower relative cost of medical services has led to a rapid recent expansion of health tourism in part also based on the existence of hot and mineral spring resources.

Marketing

As we noted in Chapters 2 and 3, the use of natural hot and mineral springs for health and wellness spa tourism extends far back into human history, and many of its historical attributes can still be used to market spas today. Although the preserve of the wealthy and/or the military in some eras, social bathing in Europe, the Middle East and the East, in China and Japan, was distributed far and wide throughout historical times (Cataldi *et al.*, 1999). While much of the early historical analysis is guesswork the accepted timeframe is backed up by the most reliable records and reaches back to approximately 3000 BC, and careful evaluation of existing records shows that the history of natural thermal spring use has a global expression (Chapter 3). Across the world the customs, culture and traditions regarding human use of water show similarities at a basic level; however, individual regions and peoples developed and used these resources in a range of ways most suitable to their particular needs.

From earliest times, many hot and mineral springs were renowned for their miraculous healing powers and have a story or legend covering the original healing event, which in more recent times has often been used as 'cultural–historical' backup in promotional material for tourism (see Chapter 3). Some destinations are thus able to offer a wealth of historical, cultural and geoscientific information to back up their claims of importance to health and wellness spa tourism, but others are extremely difficult to research, which leads to the majority of the marketing and academic literature concentrating on the more commonly known thermal centres whenever this form of tourism is discussed.

Historical marketing and promotion

In the long list of architectural remains the Romans left behind in western Europe and the Middle East, one of the main features is the inclusion of at least one bathhouse or thermae in each settlement or military base, where officers and soldiers would relax and recover from the unpleasantness of the military life, and it was not long before many of these thermae were made available and marketed to all citizens (Register, 2008a). The Romans (as did the Chinese and Japanese, and in Europe before the Romans, the Persians, Greeks and Etruscans) initially reserved their hot water bathing facilities mainly for members of the army and the priesthood, using natural hot springs to soothe and heal injuries from the battlefields. However, as populations became more prosperous the number and range of people using such facilities increased in all areas. Around 43 AD the Roman public as a whole began to use thermal baths as a way of providing rest and relaxation, and by the year 300 AD there were over 900 baths throughout the whole empire to which at least the wealthier non-military or administrative members of society could travel (Aachen n.d.; Spa Life, n.d.). Medical tourism based on a mineral spring was also very important in history; for example in the 5th century BC, Hippocrates of Kos treated (and marketed to) patients from all over the Mediterranean by promoting thermal balneology in his famous *Asclepium* (Cataldi *et al.*, 1999: 89).

Marketing of a natural hot and mineral spring resource in ancient times of course relied considerably on word of mouth, generally with respect to imputed healing and partly with respect to magical properties (their occurrence and effects attributed to 'divine' intervention), and this information has never really been lost in relation to many of the sites that have survived through to modern times. The enduring reputations of many contemporary centres were created through this method of marketing; for example the ancient Greek city of Thermae (which is now called *Loutraki*, derived from the Greek word for spring) is famous for its natural mineral waters and thermal springs and was one of the first health resorts in history. The waters were first mentioned by the Greek historian Xenophon in his history of the Boeotian War (396–371 BC – Chapter 3), and the archaeological and historical record shows that the later Romans built large thermal complexes in the city for recreational purposes. Loutraki remains important today as the metropolitan centre of thermalism and health tourism in Greece, having been marketed in the modern era as long ago as 1847 in Italy through announcements asserting the therapeutic benefits of bathing in its natural thermal spas, an event that caused an influx of settlers to the surrounding areas of the springs, thereby creating modern Loutraki (Loutraki City Guide, n.d.).

While the widespread secular tradition of bathing declined in Europe when the western Roman Empire collapsed, the ruling classes, including the military and priesthood, kept using the known springs wherever castles and monasteries could be located (and defended) near them. During and after the reign of Charlemagne (768–814 AD) in what is now France and Germany, bathrooms were reintroduced as a feature in some castles and monasteries built near thermal springs, an innovation that reduced significantly the effort required to produce hot water for at least some of the aristocracy and clergy of the time (SGVSB, n.d.). Elsewhere in Europe, during the 8th century AD a medical study on the hot mineral springs in Corsica was undertaken under the patronage of *Carlo Fabrizio Giustiniano*, Bishop of Mariana (Young, 1909). In this study it is reported that two doctors had earlier investigated the therapeutic value of Corsica's hot springs and had generated a comprehensive list of available geothermal resources suitable for medicinal purposes. These sorts of studies served the role of marketing information in the royal and ecclesiastical Courts of the early Middle Ages, keeping the concept of health and wellness spa activity alive at least in front of the aristocracy, and by the 15th century AD annual visits to curative hot spring centres had become popular again among wealthy citizens throughout Germany, Austria, Switzerland, Italy and France (Rumpf & Sollner, 2006). Centuries later, in 1909 a study containing more precise indications relating to the thermal waters of Corsica was published, demonstrating a continuous written interest in thermalism in this part of the Mediterranean over a period of more than 2000 years (Young, 1909).

In the Eastern Roman Empire and its successor states, the same traditions and the same patterns of waxing and waning in the popularity of hot and mineral springs are apparent, although urban life did not decline as much as in western Europe. An important imperial facility, the hot spring of Hamat Gader, is located in the Yarmuk Valley on the eastern shore of the Sea of Galilee, about 20 km from the city of Tiberias. An inscription from the reign of Empress Eudocia (421–460 AD) on a marble slab praises the thermal baths that are found there; no doubt the Imperial stamp of approval did much in marketing terms for the fame of these springs among those able to travel in the Empire. Today the Tiberias Hot Springs health and vacation resort is Israel's largest and most sophisticated mineral spring site and attracts thousands of domestic and international visitors each year (Larson, 2006).

The Dōgo *Onsen* is possibly Japan's oldest but certainly one of its most famous hot springs, and is located on the western coast of the Island of Shikoku (Dogo *Onsen*, n.d.(a)). With a history dating back some 3000 years, these springs have been favourite destinations of the Japanese Imperial family and other celebrities for centuries. The springs are mentioned in the *Man'yoshu*, a collection of poems written between the 5th and 8th centuries AD in what is Japan's oldest extant anthology [Dogo *Onsen*, n.d.(c)]. Similarly, in the *Kojiki* ('Records of Ancient Matters') published in 712 AD, the more important *Onsen* of Japan are given prominence due to their association with the Imperial family, wars or religious events (Asian Info, 2000), and Dōgo is one of these. Later, while travel for pleasure was restricted during the *Edo* period (1603–1867 AD), it *was* allowed for special purposes (merchant travel, official duties, visits to the Grand Shrine at Ise and other shrines, etc. on the agreement of each Feudal Clan office (Cooper *et al.*, 2008)). Equally, while the 'work-ethic' appears dominant during this period, it is manifestly obvious that this was to some degree at least balanced by the concepts of *asobi* (play, pleasure, fun), of *tanoshimi* (delight, happiness, pleasure) and of *kaiko* (nostalgia) (Linhart & Frühstuck, 1998), which made it possible to include bathing as well as food and drink in the pilgrimage. Thus, even before the introduction of the six-day working week in Japan, the available evidence shows that travel for attendance at shrines, temples and their associated *Onsen* was commonplace and approved. Not only did the population travel to such centrally important shrines as Ise, but these places as well as local shrines offered *matsuri* (festivals) and *ennichi* (the local deity's day of worship) as reinforcement of important cultural heritage traditions, including food and bathing (Ashkenazi, 1993; Plutschow, 1996). Thus, health and wellness spa tourism in the form of religious pilgrimage marketed by religious houses and Feudal Clan Offices has flourished in Japan for centuries (Cooper *et al.*, 2008).

The premier Japanese hot spring destination of Beppu (in Oita Prefecture on the southern island of Kyushu) is at a different level however. Its history and marketing starts with a legend where two gods visited the 'ancient country'; when one got sick, the other pulled a long pipe from the seabed of Beppu Bay, opening up the 'springs' from the underground to bathe and cure the sick one (Iwata, 2006). Beppu's *Onsen* healing power is referenced throughout history. During the *Kamakura* era (1192–1333 AD), sanatoria were built in the city to treat wounded soldiers from the battles against the Mongolians (Iwata, 2006). In more recent times the spring discovery technology called *kazusabori* (well digging technique) resulted in more than 1000 new holes being dug to generate thermal water for usage during the *Meiji* era in the late 19th century (Beppu City Council, 2007, personal communication; Takamura, 2004), and transportation to the city from the rest of Japan was facilitated by the development of a seaport and train services.

The fame of Beppu also reached the international level in the early part of the 20th century, with the comedian *Charlie Chaplin* among the frequent visitors from abroad (Beppu City Council, 2007 – personal communication). This was facilitated by excellent marketing in the form of a compendium of Japanese *Onsen* put out by the Japanese Government Railways in 1922 (de Garis, 1922) in a similar fashion to those of the British and European railway companies and the new travel agents such as *Thomas Cook* and *Baedeker*. Since then its economy has rapidly developed, attracting health and wellness spa tourists from across the nation as well as overseas. Beppu City officially attracts over 11 million tourists annually (Beppu City Council, 2007 – personal communication), but only some 140,000 of these are foreigners (mostly Korean and Chinese visitors seeking the *Onsen*). Coupled with the *Onsen* bathing opportunities is the strongly marketed sightseeing product *Jigoku Meguri*, the Hell Pilgrimage. This originated many years ago with the superstition that in certain places thermal minerals were coming from hell due to the violent underground activity bringing mud, water and gas fumes to the surface. Sightseeing trips were started in the 1930s, to capitalise on the magnificent view of various minerals producing water ponds of different colours and volcanic mud flowing straight from underground (Iwata, 2006). Manipulating this daunting spectacle cleverly, the trips were marketed as experiential challenges to capture the human desire to prove psychological strength and were an immediate success as a tourism product. Over the years in response to family tourist demands the tours have incorporated other elements, such as a zoo and an aquarium housing tropical animals, crocodiles and fish to entertain children visiting along with their parents, and foods cooked on site using geothermal steam.

On the Asian mainland the Chinese tradition also provides written evidence (Needham & Liu, 1962; Schafer, 1956) that for thousands of years the country has been in the forefront of marketing and utilising thermal springs for various purposes. The latter included therapeutical benefits as well as enjoying the pleasure of a hot spring bath during cold seasons. It is in fact assumed by many scholars that the culture of thermal water use found its way from China through Korea to Japan where the marketing of *Onsen* is not recorded until after the Chinese and Koreans had established migratory ties with Japan prior to 297 AD (Clark, 1994). Although the longevity of the Jomon (prior to 300 BC) and Yayoi cultures (300 BC–300 AD) means that this assumption in respect of the use of hot springs in Japan is not likely to be particularly accurate, nevertheless the first documented use of mineral springs bathing in Japan occurs in the book *The History of the Kingdom of Wei* written in China in 297 AD (Clark, 1994).

The rest of Asia also certainly used them even if it did not market the value of hot springs as widely as other civilisations. The Silk Road Central Asian Republics, Iran, India, Pakistan, Mongolia and Korea all have historical use records going back to ancient times (Chapter 3), while the Taiwanese consider hot springs as one of the most precious gifts that the earth has bestowed on them. Hot springs in Taiwan were in fact first mentioned in a manuscript (the *Beihai Jiyou*) in 1697 AD, while Korean records mention that the royal family enjoyed thermal spring bathing from the early *Three Kingdoms* period between 18 BC and 668 AD. In India and Pakistan, legendary beliefs among pilgrims refer to the discovery of springs and temples close together, and there is even earlier evidence in the form of the Great Bath at *Mohenjo-Daro* in Pakistan, which seems to support the theory that use of hot springs for health and wellness spa therapy in that country too has a long history (Chapter 3).

The countries of Oceania and South East Asia, including the island communities of the South Pacific, have many such hot spring areas, but generally they are not in as developed a state as in Europe, East Asia or the Americas. In New Zealand the thermal waters concentrated around *Rotorua, Auckland* (Waiwera) and *Hanmer Springs* (North Canterbury) were for centuries used by the Māori for their healing powers and people travelled from far and wide to take advantage of them before European colonisation in the 1800s. After European settlement the Government built and operated big thermal spas at Rotorua and Hanmer Springs in order to treat medical conditions, but also to attract tourists. A thriving but also heavily promoted health tourist trade for tourists from Europe developed over time around the geothermal facilities of Rotorua (Stafford, 1986).

For the native populations of both North and South America as with Japan hot springs were sacred as well as useful places and this gave them added attraction. They believed in the healing powers of the minerals in the thermal waters, and most major hot springs in the United States, Mexico and elsewhere in Latin America for example have some record of use by local Indian tribes for rituals and ceremonies (Frazier, 2000). The *Incas* of Perú enjoyed the great number of hot springs scattered throughout Peruvian territory for medicinal purposes, as did the *Aztecs* of Mexico and the *Maya* of Central America. As noted in Chapter 3, thermal springs were also known as neutral ground, where warriors could rest unmolested by other tribes and recuperate from battle (Lund, 2002). After European settlement, by the year 1888 there were 8843 hot springs recorded in the United States alone, of which 634 were used as spas (Chapter 3; Bischoff, 2001). Since then there has been a cycle of decline and rejuvenation related to varying degrees of government support and/or changes in medical and wellness fashion, but at present geothermal-based spas are experiencing the same massive increase in demand as in other countries. In recent years the marketing literature related to the health and wellness spa industry involving North American hot springs is to be found in a range of tour guides or chronicle-type publications, dealing with individual regions, usually with a brief history of the area described as well as a listing of all the known hot springs of a particular area or State. Most of these books have been published rather recently, possibly motivated by the onset of the wellness trend in the 1990s.

Central and Southern Africa also has a tradition of the use of local hot springs. The town of 'Warmbad' in Namibia for example (also known as 'Bela Bela', meaning the 'boiling place') was known to local tribes and was established as a bathing facility by white settlers in the late 1800s and soon became renowned for its beneficial waters, attracting many international visitors seeking relief from rheumatism and arthritis (Limpopo Happenings, n.d.).

Marketing today

In the 21st century, the health and wellness spa tourism has become an industry that many groups, communities and Governments believe can be used to enhance local economic opportunity, although it is recognised that this will be largely through the activities of private operators and investors (Hall, 2003). The result of this belief is often 'unbridled boosterism' by communities and governments; in marketing terms this translates as concentrating solely on the promotion of tourism to the exclusion of its many social, economic and environmental consequences, or indeed to other equally important aspects of marketing such as product protection and development (McCool & Moisey, 2001: 6). The difficulty with this situation is that private industry is concerned with far more than simple promotion when it is developing or operating a particular facility, and in any event marketing pitches by local or regional governments tend to assume too much of an obvious similarity or generality among facilities for individual firms to benefit greatly from them. Differentiation of facilities and attractions is the key to marketing for individual businesses, so while they may appreciate a generous level of promotional support they certainly do not want control of the marketing of their business exercised solely through state or local promotional budgets. In addition, the fact that the health and wellness spa business, in line with many other forms of tourism (Cooper & Erfurt, 2006), is primarily a referral-based business, with word of mouth and/or medical referrals being among the most common sources of new clients, means that more traditional methods of marketing and promotion may not be particularly useful.

Marketing models

Service industry marketing models covering tourism and hospitality are covered in depth in a number of publications by for example Kotler *et al.* (1999a), Witt and Moutinho (1995) and Zeithaml and Bitner (2000). All authors note several distinguishing features of the tourism and hospitality industry that separate it from other industries – product intangibility, product variability, product and consumption place coincidence and the often perishable nature of its products (Table 8.2). Marketing strategies for tourism and hospitality that recognise and use these differences are in essence both integral and complementary to the major task of positioning the tourism product in the marketplace. Strategies that overcome intangibility and variability are integral to positioning because they affect the definition of the product, and complementary because they mean that service providers in the tourism and hospitality industry must interact with clients to create superior value up to and *during* the point of sale moment (Kotler *et al.*, 1999: 44), rather than just passing on something that has stood on a shelf waiting for a buyer. Strategies that enhance producer and consumer interaction and control the relationship between capacity and demand are critical for customer satisfaction and the viability of the particular business involved. Even the physical place markers as found in *Geotourism* (e.g. hot springs) are dependent for their use by visitors on the flexible provision and acceptance of information, and thus remain as potential attractions until recognised and made tangible in the minds of the consumer.

Zeithaml and Bitner (2000) note that because of these basic differences, managers and marketers of services such as hot springs health tourism face some very

Table 8.2 Differences between goods and services

Goods	Services	Implications
Tangible product	Intangible product	Uncertainty as to eventual outcome of purchase, especially if inexperienced consumer; buyers look for tangible evidence from first impressions and/or word of mouth references (which can include guide books) rather than the product itself
Standardised product	Variable product	Quality depends on who provides service at the time of exchange (skills and performance consistency requires training); fluctuating demand; difficult to be sure that the service delivered matched what was planned and promoted; variability is a major source of disappointment and dissatisfaction with tourism product
Production and consumption are separate	Production and consumption occur at the same time	Producer and consumer must be present in the same place before transactions can take place; customers are also part of the product, and 'problem' customers cannot easily be segregated from others; customers must try to understand the terms of the service delivery system wherever they are in the world; hospitality managers must manage *both* their customers *and* their employees and mass production is difficult
Non-perishable product (in the sense of being a tangible product)	Perishable product	Services cannot be stored, returned or resold. Unsold hotel rooms in one period for example cannot be sold in the following: capacity and demand must be very closely managed if services are to maximise revenue and strong recovery procedures need to be in place for all eventualities

Source: After Zeithaml and Bitner (2000: 12) and Kotler *et al.* (1999b: 42–44).

real challenges, and must answer the following questions when designing marketing campaigns:

- How can service quality be defined and improved when the benefits of the product are intangible and often non-standard (health products and the use of hot springs vary between establishments *and* according to tradition)?
- How can new services be designed and tested effectively when the service is essentially an intangible product until consumed?
- How can a service firm be sure it is communicating a consistent and relevant image when the parts of the marketing mix that appeal to customers can vary by both individual product and customer?
- How does the service firm accommodate fluctuating demand when capacity is fixed and the service is perishable (accommodation)?

- How can a service firm best select and motivate employees who, because the service is delivered in real time in conjunction with the client, become a critical part of the product itself?
- How should prices be set when these may be inextricably bound up with perceptions of quality?
- How does the service firm communicate quality and value to consumers when the offering itself is intangible (e.g. the 'therapeutic value' of hot springs)?
- How can the service firm ensure the delivery of consistently high-quality service when both its employees *and* its customers can affect the service outcomes? (Zeithaml & Bitner, 2000: 14–15)

Various models of marketing behaviour have been developed in order to provide some framework for addressing these questions and making management and marketing decisions in service industries like tourism. They include the standard marketing mix (Product, Place, Promotion, Price) model, which, in the case of services (Zeithaml & Bitner, 2000), has added to it *People* (human resource development and customer education/training), *Physical Evidence* (tangibility enhancement) and *Process* (involvement of customers and control of activities) (Table 8.3). This is considered necessary because all of the human actors participating in the delivery of a service provide clues to the customer regarding the nature and likely quality of the service itself (as does customer experience of similar situations); evidence of tangibility can be enhanced by facility design, providing information on equipment and resources used, effective signage and literature (including the coffee-table book and magazines) and references (word-of-mouth) and guarantees; and customising/standardising the flow of activities in conjunction with the client can build trust in the services provided (Zeithaml & Bitner, 2000: 14–15).

All who play a part in the delivery of services to tourists have the potential to influence a buyer's decision-making – owners, employees *and* customers – with respect to the service desired, as does the facility itself and the services offered. In fact in many cases the provider is the service. But perhaps more importantly, the fact that the growing body of literature on tourist behaviour shows that buying services is perceived to be riskier than buying goods because of the people factor has implications for marketing (Berger & Dibattista, 1993; Dorsch *et al.*, 2000; March & Woodside, 2005; Mintzberg & Walters, 1982; Tversky *et al.*, 1988; Young, 1981; Zeithaml, 1981). Risk perception and contingency planning are important aspects of this and therefore should also be added to the marketing mix model (Table 8.3). The result is that actual decision-making behaviour in the context of service industries like tourism is anticipatory and limited, with reluctance to make decisions from afar because of complexity, with contingency planning undertaken in case decisions made are proven to be problematic, with often a preference for *unplanned* travel where perceived risk is high, and with the influence of product information being less clear-cut than for other consumption behaviours.

From a marketing strategy point of view, health and wellness spa industry firms should therefore seek to insert their product offerings as integral parts of the *total* visitor experience to a destination. The way to do this is to seek to have health and

Table 8.3 The modified marketing mix model for tourism services

Product	Place	Promotion	Price	People	Physical evidence	Process
Features of the product	Marketing channel	Promotional tools and outcomes	Flexibility	Employees	Facility design	Flow of activities
Quality	Exposure	Salespeople	Price level	Customers	Equipment levels	Customer involvement in design and implementation of activities
Accessories	Intermediaries	Sales promotion	Terms	Perception of risk	Signage on site	–
Packaging	Outlets	Advertising	Differentiation	Contingency planning	Employee dress code	–
Warranties	Transportation	Publicity	Discounts	–	Other tangibles	–
Branding and product information	Storage	–	Allowances	–	–	–
Product lines	Managing channels	–	–	–	–	–

Source: After Zeithaml and Bitner (2000).

wellness spa tourism included as a mainstream offering wherever possible, and on the well-known paths taken by tourists, or to suggest new paths to explore that include the opportunity to experience health and wellness spa products or services upfront rather than to seek to add them to visitor plans after they have arrived at a destination. Also, destination marketing managers should distribute such information well in advance of known visitors arriving, but to the specific market segments that they seek to attract. It is critical, too, not to rely on the assumed positive influence of experience on decision making and risk aversion as this relationship does not appear to be as direct as first thought in the context of tourism (Cooper & Erfurt, 2006; March & Woodside, 2005: 257). Experienced tourists do not rely on visitor information centres, travel agents or guide books any less often than inexperienced ones, and may be no less risk-averse: merely more experienced at understanding the likely effect of the various messages offered and basing at least their initial travel decisions on them.

Bitner (1995) explicitly includes internal and interactive marketing along with external marketing in the *Service Marketing Triangle Model* (Figure 8.1). This model recognises that the service firm must effectively train and motivate its customer-contact employees and their support staff to provide the maximum level of customer satisfaction in order to maximise its sales opportunities (Internal Marketing), and that perceived service quality depends greatly on the nature of buyer–seller relations at point-of-sale (Interactive Marketing). Standard marketing tools may be used in the *external* marketing of the tourism product in the same way as for goods (advertising, special promotions and sales, and differential pricing), but its marketing as a service also requires emphasis on the intangible and the personal (using relationship marketing; Figure 8.2) to make a lasting impression on consumers.

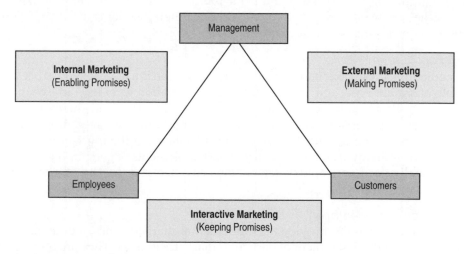

Figure 8.1 Services marketing triangle
Source: After Bitner (1995).

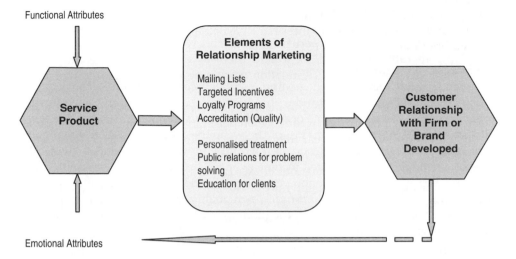

Functional Attributes

Service Product

Elements of Relationship Marketing

Mailing Lists
Targeted Incentives
Loyalty Programs
Accreditation (Quality)

Personalised treatment
Public relations for problem solving
Education for clients

Customer Relationship with Firm or Brand Developed

Emotional Attributes

Figure 8.2 Relationship marketing
Source: After Laws (2004).

Market segmentation

Market segmentation provides a means for all businesses to define their target markets. A market segment is a group of clients who share a set of common characteristics that distinguish them from other customers. This analysis is then used to determine market potential – the total demand for a product in a given environment. Segments can vary according to geographic location, demographics and psycho-graphics (psychological and behavioural states), and different marketing approaches are usually required to reach each of them (Kotler *et al.*, 1999a). Four generic segmentation strategies are as follows.

Geographic segmentation

Segmenting the market based on geographic location is usually effective because people of similar type, age, income, tastes and education level tend to live in the same place. People often choose to live among their peers, and therefore if the geographic characteristics of a particular neighbourhood, city, region or country can be defined there is a greater chance of understanding the tourism needs and wants of the individuals inhabiting that area. The elements of geographic segmentation usually used are country, region, city, city size and density of population (Kotler, 1999a: 148).

Demographic segmentation

Demographic profiles provide the fundamental characteristics of potential customers used for the assessment of particular market segments. They are often used as surrogates for direct measurements and indicate the likelihood of consumption of a particular product. The elements of demographic segmentation are usually age, gender, family size and status, income, education and occupation, religion or culture, and social class. Each of these has a particular relationship with purchasing behaviour (Kotler, 1999a: 149–151).

Psychographic segmentation

Psychographic segmentation attempts to create a complete profile of an actual or potential market's values, attitudes, product purchase behaviours and lifestyle preferences (Kotler, 1999a: 151). For example, in the case of health and wellness spa tourism, market information on 'Visitors between the ages of 35 and 45 with income over $50,000' to a particular destination would be refined to 'Clients between the ages of 35 and 45 with combined income over $50,000 who purchase health products and beauty magazines, and organic food'. The elements of psychographic segmentation are lifestyle and attitudes, personality, purchase habits – what and how they buy, the benefits sought, the usage rate of and loyalty to branded products, and price sensitivity.

Lifestyle segmentation

In the tourism field, market segmentation is particularly important in organising heterogeneous populations into more homogeneous subpopulations or segments in order to better understand, explain and influence consumption behaviour (Kotler *et al.*, 1999b). As we have seen in earlier chapters, one such segmentation is the foundation of the health and wellness spa industry: the quest for a healthy lifestyle. Lifestyle segmentation is a combination of consumer activities, interests, attitudes and opinions, demographics, and branding (Wilkie, 1986), where branding is often used to communicate self-image and values to others by particular consumers (e.g. owning a Porsche; Helman & De Chernatony, 1999). As Hall (2003: 273) notes, since the 1980s lifestyle has become much more important to many in the developed world. Increasingly this includes health tourism overall, and body image in particular. The concomitant rise in medical tourism and in health and wellness spa tourism can be seen as a direct result of this trend, and an important reason for lifestyle segmentation based upon it.

Goeldner and Ritchie (2003) recognise five specific market segments within the health tourism market:

(1) outdoor (sun and fun) activities;
(2) adventure and sport activities (healthy but health is not the central concern);
(3) travel for health (cruise or environment/climate change primarily);
(4) travel to spa resorts and to venues for other health activities; and
(5) travel for medical treatment.

Segments 3–5 are directly related to health and wellness based on natural hot and mineral springs, the subject of this book. Health and wellness spa tourism is a component of health tourism that usually incorporates the provision of mineral waters designed to assist in overcoming various medical conditions, as well as an increasing range of fitness and cosmetic (body image) add-ons resulting from a significant psychographic shift towards healthy lifestyles (see Chapter 2). On the basis of this, and the demographic changes discussed in Chapter 6, the major market segment for health and wellness spa tourism is the rapidly ageing 'baby-boomer' population that is seeking to retain good health and fitness for as long as possible. In close harmony with this trend, but which is also a rapidly growing market segment for health and wellness spa tourism in its own right, is the *general* acceptance of the importance of well-being among disparate human populations. This market segment includes people as much interested in spa-related beauty therapies, massage, detoxification, sports and exercise, and relaxation techniques as in thermal bathing or medical treatments, and it includes *all* age groups (Goodrich & Goodrich, 1987; Hall, 2003).

Modern forms of marketing

An extremely important part of interactive marketing to these health and wellness spa market segments is the need for believable information on the largely intangible nature of the product (solving health problems and the fulfilment of personal dreams), which will make a lasting impression on consumers. This need has seen the rise in recent years of the consumer-oriented high-quality Spa Magazine (in reality extravagantly produced travel magazines) and their close companion the coffee-table book, created by professional marketing strategists who know exactly how to sell an intangible product. Eye-catching illustrations dominate in most publications to create maximum attention to the intended message. Images representing health and beauty are combined with natural backgrounds to create the impression of an overall synergy between nature and the health and wellness seeking consumer. Text is often used only sparingly and only to reinforce the message of 'time out' at particular destinations. A lot is deliberately left to the imagination through expert manipulation of the senses of the reader (Figure 8.3).

Magazines like *AsiaSpa*, *SpaAsia*, *Spa Finder* and *Spa Life* are intended to be read in a relaxed state of mind to create a connection between the reader as potential customer and the industry by showcasing the best the market has to offer, to give the reader something to look forward to, and to suggest that even the most luxuriously appointed destinations are affordable for everyone who desires to use them (Figure 8.4). Supplementary advertising is directly aimed at customers who are in the know when it comes to top brand names like Rolex, Hyatt, Christofle, Rolls Royce, Ritz-Carlton and Veuve Clicquot. Easily recognisable is the use of style and ambience through which the reader is drawn to absorb every page offered in a way they cannot or should not resist. Photos usually depict a client under treatment, colours are pastel shades and soothing, and a touch of relaxation escapes from the page to embrace the reader with an invitation to step closer in a virtual sense. The intention is that a particular treatment package will be found by *many* readers, thus allowing them to benefit from what spa resorts are only too willing to share with affluent customers.

In another very transparent action the persons pictured are usually female, young, pretty and perfectly shaped, with immaculate skin and healthy hair, and generally with closed eyes, thus transmitting a feeling of total relaxation, bliss and well-being. The strong overall impression is that the treatment and the surroundings pictured will have the same effect on the reader and that the outcome will be

Figure 8.3 Coffee-table media blitz
Source: Photograph courtesy of P. Erfurt-Cooper.

astonishing. The effect of these attempts at visual persuasion is to imply without many words the health tourism possibilities and gently motivate the reader to decide how much they owe it to themselves to become involved in this activity. Quite often young couples are also featured in states of utter relaxation enjoying shared treatment Asian style in order to deepen and enhance the feeling of togetherness on their honeymoon or on other special occasions. This mind–body–environment–wellness connection is one of the goals of health and wellness spa tourism. As a result, apart from soothing water features and depictions of the physical well-being of individual clients, the relaxing tone in many of these magazine articles is also set by decorative architecture and a backdrop of lush vegetation, along with stylish and exquisite furnishings including both opulence and minimalism. The effect is in most cases stunning and very effective in its appeal. At least this is the philosophy of the 'Earth Sanctuary Day Spa' and many similar venues (see AsiaSpa, November/December 2005).

Some examples of the catchphrases used in spa magazines that are designed to create a surrogate for interactive marketing can be seen in Box 8.1.

Figure 8.4 Health, wellness and spa magazines including special issues for men
Source: Photograph courtesy of P. Erfurt-Cooper.

Box 8.1 Spa magazine slogans

'Find the new paradise within Shangri-La' (www.shangri-la.com/spa in *Asia Spa*, 2005).
'Immerse in tranquillity' (www.jwmarriottphuket.com in *Asia Spa*, 2005).
'Nature and nurture – a little bit of paradise' (www.trisara.com in *Asia Spa*, 2005).
'Ancient therapies, modern comforts' (www.sarojin.com in *Asia Spa*, 2005).
'Medispa – destinations that transform lives' (Front page *Spa Asia*, 2005).
'Spa on the Rocks – the ocean's ultimate treasure' (www.ritzcarlton.com/resorts/bali/spa in *Spa Asia*, 2005).
'Natural indulgence for your well-being' (Raffles Amrita Spa in *Spa Asia*, 2005).
'Spa experience unrivalled in China – cherishing life's beautiful moments' (Mandara Spa in *Spa Asia*, 2005).
'Sensual garden at the gates of heaven' (www.devaranaspa.com in *Spa Asia*, 2005).
'Stretch your mind, body and spirit' (www.destinationspas.com in *Spa Finder*, 2006).

Quite often, spa marketing promotions use wordplays in their advertising, for example 'Scents and Sensibility' (Spa Finder, 2006: 76), 'Wrapsody' (Spa Finder, 2006: 31) and 'Ageing Gorgeously' (Spa Life, 2006: 1). Flowers and herbs displayed in a tasteful fashion combined with a natural hot spring pool in a picture are another means of getting a holistic medicine message across. Natural treatment ingredients are presented like delicious meals with pleasing colours and just the right amount of information to get the attention of the reader. Space, dimension and distance in the illustrations are used to attract clients from closed-in urban environments to 'spas with a view'.

In its marketing, the health and wellness spa industry thus relies heavily on visual communications designed to reach as many potential target groups as possible. The quality of the information could be described as generally useful, persuasive and attractive in its format, and well designed to address the assumed needs and wants of a wide range of people from different social and/or cultural backgrounds. On the other hand, it is also highly manipulative and highly targeted. In addition, the methods used in marketing hot spring spas and spas without hot springs are different. Hot spring spas offer a truly natural product, generally closely reliant on the natural environment. Spas without hot springs have much more competition and therefore have to make a greater effort to convince the customer to choose their particular destination. Also, hot spring spas may be well known because they have a long established reputation and history, a situation that is beneficial in saving advertising and promotional costs (Reeves, 1961).

Presentation of the product: Summary

The tourism product 'Health and Wellness' is thus packaged and marketed in different forms depending on the source of particular wellness treatments and their physical characteristics (including hot springs), the surrounding natural and social environments, cultural aspects, customer demand and segmentation, customer–firm interactivity, ease of access and the on-site availability of technologies and infrastructure. Of course, what was of critical importance 100 years or even 25 years ago does not necessarily provide the same draw card in the new millennium. In France, for example, in the year 1921 the National Tourism Office offered to its health and wellness spa customers certain attractions in addition to its health spas with curative waters (Office National du Tourisme, 1921; Weisz, 2001). These were as follows (Box 8.2):

Box 8.2 Attractions for visitors to French spas in 1921

Lack of epidemics, Clean drinking water.
Incinerators, Public health office.
Electric lighting, Disinfection service.
Streets tarred and watered, Bureau of Hygiene.
Effective drainage system.

The French market had already by this time made provision for associated entertainments like casinos, theatres, concerts, golf clubs, tennis and horse racing, but must have felt the need to point out how protective of social health the advanced spa towns were compared to other holiday destinations in that country. While most of these concerns no longer appear on the public agenda, risk in relation to water quality and the therapies offered remains. An additional consideration is that changes in public health system funding of wellness treatments for users have resulted in modifications to the pricing and availability of products in France and Germany in particular.

In the 21st century, while the message no longer needs to be about social disease and related health factors when persuading visitors to consider the use of such facilities, health and wellness spa literature and information are everywhere. In fact, there is *so* much that it is becoming increasingly difficult for the consumer to judge the quality of the presented information, let alone make an educated decision in relation to the various tempting propositions. For the industry on the other hand though, helping a potential customer to find what he or she is looking for is equally difficult, because many people new to the health and wellness spa scene do not know what might suit them and what they should look for. A basic vocabulary explaining health and wellness spa terminology can help a lot and this has been recognised by spa providers and organisations in the form of guide books and glossaries relating to spas and their use that can be found on the internet by simply typing the keywords 'spa glossary', and in most souvenir shops and tourism information centres. Another easy way is searching the internet by simply typing the keywords 'spa glossary' and the result is an overwhelming fountain of information on the nature of treatments, on the best health and wellness spa environments, and on the imputed health benefits from within the spa industry for the potential traveller, although there is little critical analysis of this information (Bennett *et al.*, 2004; Goodrich & Goodrich, 1987).

Key marketing trends for 2008 and beyond

The health and wellness spa industry worldwide is well served with industry associations that provide members with support materials, new entrants with planning, development and marketing information, and commission marketing and other reports for the industry (and the magazines mentioned above). Brand marketing agencies also regularly publish their predictions of key consumer behaviour trends for the next year [e.g. SpaTrade, n.d.(a–b)]. Table 8.4 is a compilation of suggested market trends for 2008 from many such sources, and what is clear from this is that the ever-expanding numbers of health and wellness spa facilities increasingly need an action plan that makes sense to the company and its employees on the firm's side of the marketing equation, and accurately tracks what consumers really feel, really want and really do with their money on the client side. In the face of the increased lack of differentiation among spas, only innovation and an increased level of loyalty will actively guarantee a positive bottom line and increased profitability in 2008 and beyond.

Table 8.4 Top marketing trends for 2008 and beyond

Trend	Implications
An ongoing emphasis on engagement	Engagement means getting and keeping the attention of prospects and clients – interactive marketing. Innovation and loyalty will matter even more than they do today
More reliance on consumer-generated content	Consumer-generated content will awaken marketers to emerging values or trends, so marketers will be paying more attention than they traditionally have to these messages
Technology and engagement to meet consumer expectations	Firms are barely keeping up with customer expectations. Smart marketers will take advantage of unfulfilled expectations via such values as 'convenience' and 'customisation'. More marketers will rely upon websites and high-tech capabilities to accommodate these values and differentiate themselves from the competition
Fusion of entertainment and wellness product	Astute marketers will leverage plugging-in headline acts as a method for customising entertainment and selling products
Time to go green	A 'green' plan is no longer a luxury for most spa and wellness firms, customers want a sustainable future
Increasing potential of web sites, blogs, the digital world of games and streaming video	Interactive marketing, gaming and attempts to meet or exceed customer expectations will fuse and be most observed online and digitally. Promotion, training and education can be embedded in 'spa and wellness' games for particular clients. The digital world including Reader Subscriber Services (RSS) feeds, mash-ups and virtual worlds will also accelerate consumer control. Web2 will allow the creation of 'communities of ones'
Integrated media in the outdoors	Radio Frequency Identification (RFID)-activated billboards with personalised messages, selective marketing through 'narrowcasting' video networks are all now possible. 'Outdoor' advertising has been reinvented as a technology-rich means of engaging, entertaining and educating commuters. Mobile marketing will deliver highly personalised, and useful, information when and where needed
Join the club	Marketers will capitalise on the growing appeal of virtual social networks to expand their clientele
From behavioural to contextual marketing	Marketers will add behavioural targeting to their contextual search efforts
Marketing as a service	Marketing as service will transform customers into brand evangelists. Marketers who deliver real value to customers and prospects alike through genuine dialogue will be the most effective. This approach is most suited to the spa and wellness industry given the intangible nature of its product of 'wellness'
Market to men and youth segments	Men as a group and the young in general are increasingly realising that there is benefit in health and wellness treatments as preventive medicine

Source: Authors, based on material from Spa Knowledge (2008).

The need to focus on integrated marketing approaches is not new, but what will be important in the immediate future is that personalised experiences will move to the top of the priorities list, becoming the driving force of marketing communications. Events and other personalised initiatives were once treated as below-the-line afterthoughts (Neisser, 2007), but marketers increasingly realise that interactive, personalised brand experiences can be far more effective than arms length advertising and should be the starting point of a conversation with clients.

Management of Health and Wellness Spa Facilities

Two primary functions have been identified for service sector managers in this discussion (Laws, 2006): one is concerned with designing, developing and resourcing an appropriate delivery system for the particular service that also defines the parameters for its marketing in accordance with the above principles, and the other is concerned with human resource development and the creation of an organisational culture that empowers staff to operate in a fully interactive sense with customers and rewards them for contributing to customer satisfaction. Both of these functions underpin the health and wellness spa industry as they do for other service industries; determining how a facility is to be developed, how it is to be operated and how it is to be marketed – the major parameters of each of these will now be considered in turn.

Planning, feasibility and research

Making a decision to build a health and wellness spa facility may involve a substantial capital investment in a business that has unique nuances ranging from hot springs bathing through medical tourism to individual beauty treatments, and is often now associated with other facilities, such as hotel style accommodation and sports and recreation outlets. Indeed, in the early 21st century, health and wellness spa facilities are fast becoming a requirement in five-star hotel properties and are considered an advantage in most four- and even three-star properties (Singer, 2005). As a spa becomes a must-have facility of the 21st century, it has also become much more important for developers to make sure that it

- complements the intentions of the total project in style and ambiance if it is part of a larger development;
- will be or is operationally sound and of high quality (including provision for risk management);
- does or will meet the expectations of the target market;
- does or will provide an edge for destination marketing; and
- does not exceed the financial parameters set by the project for construction and operation.

Market research will in turn be needed to evaluate the opportunities, refine the project objectives, determine potential customer bases, determine demand and revenue potential and calculate the likely return on investment.

Operations management

Once the development, operational and marketing parameters have been set, and the facility has been built and has commenced operation, the quality of ongoing operations management is critical for a successful enterprise. A customer-focused company that delivers on service quality and has backup systems in place should that quality start to decline will more often than not meet customer expectations and thus maintain its financial health (Pegg & Suh, 2006). Management should, in this situation, develop the following elements:

- systems, processes and procedures that deliver and provide feedback on organisational goals;
- marketing and planning functions that can discover what customers want and develop these into strategic marketing plans;
- continuous improvement strategies like Total Quality Management;
- a service recovery system where service problems are quickly identified and effectively solved, with resulting insights into better operation passed on in the form of in-house training for staff as a core management tool (Pegg & Suh, 2006; Young, 1995); and
- effective technology support and human resource training programmes.

In the service industries as a whole and in health and wellness facilities especially, management requires a dual focus – on the technology employed and on the human interactions required to deliver satisfactory experiences to clients (Laws, 2006). As Laws notes, while few customers may be able to judge the technical quality of the service experience, they certainly do make assessments of the skills and attitudes of staff. This means that minimising employee discretion and judgement in health and wellness spa facilities as is normal in manufacturing industry is not likely to be a useful strategy for management to adopt. In fact the challenge of ensuring that the customer receives what is being demanded and paid for must be shouldered by all staff; management's task in this situation is then to ensure consistency in the product while also recognising the individual needs and concerns of both staff and customers. If gaps in performance occur at any point in the firm–customer relationship, they must be filled as quickly as possible. These can arise through not knowing what customers expect, by not selecting the right service design and standards, by not delivering to acceptable service standards and/or by not matching performance to promises (Laws, 2004: 481). And they can occur whether the facility is a Day Spa, a Medical Spa, a Spa Resort, an *Onsen* or other hot springs, or a hot spring-based Theme Park.

Laws (2006) emphasises that a frequent theme in the service management literature is the centrality of interactions between staff and clients in the service experience. Management therefore has to *orchestrate* those encounters (George & Kelly, 1983) to ensure that acceptable service standards are delivered. And this must be both ways, because supportive client behaviour has been shown to correlate highly with job satisfaction and performance on the part of the service worker. Effective relationship marketing and service recovery programmes can

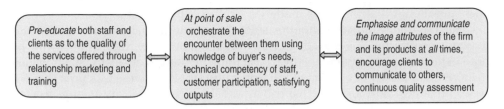

Figure 8.5 Management of the service experience
Source: After Laws (2006).

assist at this point, because they are as much based on getting-to-know the firm as they are its clients. So the steps in managing the service experience in the health and wellness spa industry may be characterised as in Figure 8.5.

Corporate social responsibility

Corporate social responsibility (CSR) is a term increasingly used in the business sector (McWilliams, 2001; Werther & Chandler, 2006; Williams *et al.*, 2007) to describe the necessary forms of ethical business behaviour that provide a framework for the above management–staff–client relationships and thus effective relationship marketing. While there is no commonly accepted definition of CSR (Dwyer *et al.*, 2007), it involves firms addressing social and personal concerns within its host community as well as those surrounding its corporate objectives with a range of stakeholders. These concerns may range from the intra-firm environment of staff and management, through the client relationship, suppliers and competitors, to the response of the general community and the impact of the firm's physical/cultural environment. This approach to the management of the firm and its environment integrates economic, social (including legal) and environmental factors into the operational frameworks the firm uses to provide its services to clients and to maintain itself in a healthy condition. Because the sites of tourism production and consumption are generally coincident, CSR is of critical importance to tourism and hospitality businesses, especially in relation to community stakeholders and the social and cultural constructs they use to evaluate the acceptability of tourism. As Cunningham *et al.* (2003) note, a tourism business is often in the position of needing a 'social license to operate' if it is to be able to take full advantage of the host community environment. And, given the importance of 'word of mouth' communication in tourism decision making, such reputational capital is of paramount concern to operators, especially if they are selling intangibles such as 'wellness' (Jackson, 1994 as cited in Williams *et al.*, 2006: 134).

The often strong interdependence between tourism businesses and their host communities means that the implementation of CSR strategies (including triple bottom line accounting) is a very useful tool for managers to influence the service relationship with potential clients favourably. Conversely, poorly conceived and managed CSR can lead to the firm losing its social license to operate from consumers (thus facing decreasing patronage of its services), and even seeing its relationship with local government and other businesses adversely affected. Management and operational control can be made very difficult by covert pressures from the external environment in this situation since the long-term viability of any business depends on effectively integrating economic, social and environmental objectives both external and internal to the firm. The implementation of clear CSR strategies is therefore a means of adopting clear and transparent business practices that are based on ethical values, and delivering sustainable value to society at large, as well as to the client, for the long-term benefit of both (WTTC, 2002).

Benchmarking in the health and wellness spa industry

Service quality may also be enhanced by the firm undertaking internal and external benchmarking as an indispensable adjunct to CSR. As Dwyer *et al.* (2007: 165) note, in view of the saying 'What isn't measured, isn't managed', service industry firms such as health and wellness spa tourism enterprises must endeavour to quantify the social and environmental impacts as well as the economic impacts of their activities. The SERVQUAL model of Parasuraman *et al.* (1985, 1994) was one of the early attempts to provide benchmarking of reliability of service, competence and attitude of staff, the tangible aspects of the facility itself, and the care taken to fulfil customer needs, and may be profitably used in the tourism and hospitality context today. Pearce and Benckendorff (2006) suggest that benchmarking may in fact take two forms: (a) internal benchmarking, where satisfaction scores as well as patronage and financial results are retained by an organisation and compared over time; and (b) external benchmarking, where the satisfaction-based performance of competitors as much as their financial and other operational performance constitutes the frame of reference for the firm. In the latter case, the aim of the individual health and wellness spa business should be to establish a customer satisfaction value that exceeds that of competitors.

In terms of the natural environment and the business environment of health and wellness spa businesses, there exist well-tried and supported external benchmarking methodologies such as the International Standards Organisation (ISO) range of performance measures and those administered by such organisations as *Green Globe* for firms in the ecotourism industry (Cooper & Erfurt, 2002). Each of these systems provide a firm with an externally verified set of performance benchmarks that may be used by management to market the firm's services to both internal and external clients as well as to measure the quality and performance of their business. In a similar fashion, the wellness side of the health and wellness spa tourism industry can draw upon many different benchmarking schemes in relation to the quality of products used in its facilities, to the mineralisation specifics in relation to its use of hot and cold mineral springs, to the firm's performance against local market averages, and in relation to the design and environment of the facilities themselves (Table 8.5). In addition, a particular advantage of externalising the benchmarking itself lies in the way that users assess the claims made by a firm. Imputed reliability is gained from external benchmarking and is known to be a powerful tool in marketing, but at the very least such benchmarking allows managers to better understand the 'trade-offs' that may need to be made in operational, human resource management and investment terms for service quality to be enhanced.

Table 8.5 Industry profile benchmarks

Spa profile benchmarks	
Benchmarks	*Notes*
Number of competing facilities	Count in the local market
Type	Main type for facility (e.g. hot spring, day spa, resort, medical, combination)
Location	Urban, rural, regional, other specific to the market
Size of facilities	Total area, breakdown of indoor area, etc.
Treatment facilities	Total number and breakdown of treatment rooms, occupancy capability, purpose of use
Infrastructure facilities	Availability of changing, relaxation, other support facilities
Treatments and services	Therapies, hot/mineral pools, consultations, programmes, classes, etc. available
Prices	Starting and incentive price structures
Business structure	Ownership, operational, marketing and Human Resource Management (HRM) structures
Business performance	Revenue, expenses, visitor numbers and types, repeat visitation, treatment choices, human resources. All expressed as ratios to facilitate comparisons
Communication of goals and standards to staff and clients	Use of media, suppliers, consultants and training to enhance firm image internally and externally, control costs, highlight areas needing improvement, improve relations with financial partners and government, and develop business plans
Trends	Knowledge of current industry trends

Source: Modified from Intelligent Spas Ltd (2008).

Human resource management in the spa and wellness industry

No universally accepted method has been developed for merging economic, social and environmental factors into a single measure of service quality and sustainability (Dwyer *et al.*, 2007). Nevertheless, parts of this integration have been achieved within many service firms over long years of industrial relations. The service firm imperative of close client–staff–management relations has borne fruit in recent years in the health and wellness spa industry. Research and company experience has identified and provided solutions for many of the critical inhibitors to service standards delivery, including deficiencies in human resource policies. The main problems for human resource management in the health and wellness spa industry are employees who do not clearly understand the roles they are to play in the company, employees who see conflict between clients and company management as being 'normal', management hiring the wrong employees for the demands of close client–staff interaction, the deployment of inadequate technology in the support of staff, inadequate recognition and reward of staff effort, and a lack of empowerment and teamwork in the workplace (Laws, 2004: 486).

Deficiencies in human resource management policies contribute a great deal to these problems and must be addressed across all management functions in the organisation, but in the case of tourism there exists another potential area of problems with respect to human resource management, and that is in the activities of intermediary firms and other service providers. The service delivery process is complicated by the existence of outside parties who may have other goals and responsibilities than ensuring service quality to the tourism firm's clients. If a health and wellness spa resort for example cannot procure sufficient supplies of wellness products, or receives already dissatisfied customers from a travel firm, its service quality–client relationship task may even be beyond the best trained and empathetic of its own staff. Equally, the customers themselves may simply be unwilling to engage in the way desired by management with staff, regardless of staff quality or the firm's service standards.

Another concern of human resource managers is the need to synchronise demand for service with the supply of labour. As a result of frequent demand fluctuations, firms in the tourism industry must rely on multi-skilling of employees and maintaining seasonal variations in the size of their employee pool, or a combination of these with active demand management (price changes, promotional campaigns, incentives, alternative services, etc.). The key task in this situation, apart from the need to ensure adequate trained labour supply at all times, is to maintain and if possible increase employee's levels of commitment to the organisation. This in turn requires management to commit to staff through retraining exercises, better equipment and feedback about the real situation the firm finds itself in. Commitment to the client also requires commitment to staff in good times and in bad. Again, firms that demonstrate social responsibility to their employees are much more likely to become an employer of choice and thus secure an economic and social advantage over others in the same industry (Sagawa & Segal, 2001; Weiser & Zadak, 2000).

Risk management in the health and wellness spa industry

Operational management in the health and wllness spa industry faces several broad areas of risk, of which human resource management problems are but one manifestation. The nature of extreme environments, which is basically what the geothermal core of the health and wellness spa industry is sourced from, makes them an object both of interest and of fear, and is the first area of concern discussed in this section. The increasing interest of tourists in new forms of extreme tourism has bought some new clients to the industry despite the possible hazards of such environments. The task of hazard and risk management for the health and wellness spa industry in active volcanic environments like Beppu, Japan or Rotorua, New Zealand is extremely challenging due to the varying degrees of potential danger from different types of hazards (Erfurt-Cooper *et al.*, 2008). Also, remoteness, difficult terrain and adverse climate conditions often present additional complications in an emergency (Buckley, 2007).

Health and safety issues play a major role in the health and wellness spa tourism industry based on *geothermalism* (Erfurt-Cooper, 2008). Several potential dangers that can cause serious problems need to be considered:

- water quality (minerals and/or organism contamination);
- unexpected eruption and/or heat changes in water supplies (usually only in natural surroundings because built facilities generally contain heat regulators);
- toxic fumes, gas emissions; and
- earthquakes.

The valid question is whether visitors in volcanic environments seek enough information about individual destinations from available sources like travel agents, guidebooks and the internet. Virtual reality is nowadays a valuable tool for travel planning and the internet offers many sources to assist closer research of the planned destinations including webcams, videos and computer simulations. Cyber visits to extreme landscapes and hazardous areas may lack the actual risk, but can help to understand the potential difficulties or even dangers that can be encountered in the real world. The spa tourist needs to know in advance how to avoid dangerous situations and how best to prevent accidents, as well as who is in charge and/or responsible. Communication can be a problem in remote areas at natural springs with potentially dire consequences. Also guidelines and instructions for emergencies may not be available everywhere or not in multiple languages.

To reduce the risk factor it is essential to raise special awareness about the imminent danger of geothermal environments. Marketing strategies for spa visits in areas of geothermal activity should not be based on geology, climate and adventure alone, but also include sufficient advice on how to cope with extreme events in difficult situations (Erfurt-Cooper, 2008). This may not always be the case and the question remains whether tourism should be encouraged at all close to active geothermal areas. Do the economic benefits from such tourism outweigh the potential risks? Several other concerns are raised by the following questions:

(1) Are visits to currently and potentially active geothermal areas a disaster waiting to happen?
(2) Guidelines and instructions for emergencies – is every tourist informed about rescue services and how to contact them?
(3) Are visitors to geothermal environments seeking enough information about the characteristics of individual destinations from available sources like the internet and guidebooks?
(4) Language barriers with respect to signage, announcements and warnings – do these reach every visitor or tourist?
(5) Should there be international guidelines about safety in such areas accessible in all languages and available in advance?

(6) *Electronic communication barriers*: Mobile phone reception is essential in remote areas and should be one of the priorities in hazard mitigation for tourism in extreme environments.

(7) What and how much is done to prevent accidents given these considerations? (Erfurt-Cooper, 2008).

The task of hazard and risk management in geothermal environments such as extreme temperature hot springs is thus extremely challenging. Varying degrees of potential danger from geothermal as well as seismic events generate different types of hazards, while remoteness, difficult terrain, adverse climate conditions and lack of reliable communication services can present additional complications in an emergency where the health and wellness spa site is within a natural setting. This may be illustrated by what happened during an earthquake in Japan on 14 June 2008. That earthquake caused a severe landslide that destroyed a hot spring resort in the *Miyagi Prefecture* and killed 12 people. Over 350 people were injured during the event, while the hot spring resort was inundated by torrents of mud and rocks, which completely destroyed the building (Japan Today, 2008; Kurakowa, 2008; Wikipedia, 2008). Other potential dangers are related to hydrogen sulphide, a gas not uncommon in hot spring or volcanic environments, which can cause fatal poisoning in a matter of moments in extreme cases.

In the case of more developed environments, adequate signage is needed to ensure that tourists do not stray into areas that are dangerous while enjoying the benefits of geothermal activity. The occasional severe seismic activity associated with such environments can intensify and worsen the risk situation for the tourist as well as for rescue crews. It appears to be general practice that tour operators require all participants to sign an assumption of responsibility before joining any tour incorporating extreme forms of geothermal activity as well as the use of hot springs (e.g. Volcano Discovery Tours), and advise that participants should bear in mind that an active volcano can be hazardous; whether this level of warning and care is legally defensible in the aftermath of an actual emergency remains to be seen (Erfurt-Cooper, 2008; Figure 8.6).

The second area of risk lies in the operation and wellness management procedures of the health and wellness spa industry itself. An increasingly important factor in the environment of this form of tourism is the health *hazards* associated with the use of hot springs in health and wellness spa facilities. These include those normally associated with swimming pools, but in addition include others resulting from the use of hot and mineralised water (Chapter 6; Figure 8.6). The high turnover rate of users in many spas and whirlpools also poses an infection risk, involving both microorganisms from the bathers and those present in the water where natural hot spas may contain a species of amoeba that can cause amoebic meningitis (Chapter 6; Barnett *et al.*, 1996; Madigan & Martinko, 2005; WHO, 2003). These infections are difficult to control and require frequent monitoring of the pH (degree of acidity/alkalinity) of the water, and its disinfection and filtration. Also, water quality treatment itself may also present chemical hazards unless the chemical disinfection is well managed. There is also a risk of accidents

Figure 8.6 Risk factor in hot springs tourism
Source: Photograph courtesy of P. Erfurt-Cooper.

around spas due to slips, trips and falls, and bathers may also pick up fungal and other infections from wet surfaces and other bathers (Chapter 6).

Summary

The health and wellness spa industry has worked to create a symbiotic relationship between its products and the desires of its clients for many years. It has used marketing to define the core essence of what the business is about and to effectively communicate its advantages to the most profitable opportunities currently available. This chapter has outlined how the health and wellness spa industry has marketed itself to tourists using the close associations of wellness with hot and mineral springs, nature, and with personalised service. It also discussed the influence of the industry's management and human resource development in this context. Marketing in the health and wellness spa industry has been shown to involve appealing to the hearts and minds of the baby boomer (and younger generations) in relation to their physical and mental well-being. A mixture of messages and message types have been used, from word of mouth through travel guidebooks, to their culmination in internet and print-based 'glossy' images of ideal spa types and of wellness outcomes. Spa magazines, internet and/or print based, informing the reader of everything luxurious and beneficial for their health and well-being that is available are now very common, as are coffee-table books about 'The 100 Best Spas of the World' or equivalent market-conditioning subject matter.

On the management side, the creation of an organisational culture that empowers staff to operate in a fully interactive sense with customers and rewards them for contributing to customer satisfaction has been of paramount importance in the development of the health and wellness spa industry (Donovan & Sammler, 1994; Intelligent Spas, 2008). The ability to sell the products offered and reassure clients as to the risks involved depends to a very great degree on the personal relationships between staff and clients, as this discussion showed. While a few customers may be able to judge the technical quality of the experience in an absolute sense, they certainly do make assessments of the skills and attitudes of staff. This means that the management challenge of ensuring that the customer receives what is being demanded and paid for must be shouldered by all staff; management's task in this situation is then to ensure consistency in the product while also recognising the individual needs and concerns of both staff and customers.

Chapter 9
Case Studies from the Contemporary World

PATRICIA ERFURT-COOPER and MALCOLM COOPER

Introduction

We have shown in earlier chapters that the contemporary world of health and wellness spa tourism based on geothermal resources is at once both complex and simple. Complex because there are a very wide and growing range of situations where geothermally derived resources impact on health and wellness spa tourism and simple because the major component of these resources (natural hot and/or mineral spring water) is relatively easy to understand in terms of its use. In an attempt to synthesise both of these dimensions this chapter presents selected case studies of variations in the availability of the hot springs resource, of differences in use, of different types of spa and of the major variables affecting use of these resources. The chapter is also designed to provide *additional* illustrations of the material discussed in earlier chapters.

The types of hot and mineral springs used for health and wellness spas as well as other purposes within the thermal spring tourism sector, and the variables that impact upon their use can be summarised as in Table 9.1. These range from undeveloped natural hot and mineral springs over developed facilities to extreme environments where the hot springs cannot be directly used but are often very effective visual tourist attractions. In the undeveloped natural situation there is usually no infrastructure but the hot spring resource is available to hikers and other nature tourists if they can be accessed. In the developed natural spring situation there are different degrees of development ranging from primitive changing facilities to one

Table 9.1 The different types of hot springs used for tourism. This table analyses a number of variables related to the different types of thermal resources and their locations

Variables determining use	Different types of hot spring environments					
	Undeveloped 'wild' hot springs	Developed natural hot springs	Redeveloped hot spring destinations	Medical use of hot springs	Hot spring aqua parks	Extreme hot springs as visual attractions
Ease of access	Depends on significance for tourism	•	•	•	•	Depends on significance for tourism
Availability (some examples are described in more detail in Chapter 9)	e.g. Antarctica, Australia, Greenland, Iceland, Japan, Russia, Mongolia, New Zealand, North and South America	Worldwide, e.g. Alaska, China, France, Greece, Iceland, Japan, Jordan, Taiwan, Russia	e.g. Japan, New Zealand, England, Switzerland, Germany, France	Worldwide	e.g. Brazil, Germany, Hungary, Japan, Sweden, Uruguay	e.g. Iceland, New Zealand, Japan, North America, Thailand
Scenic value	•	•	•	/	/	•
Uniqueness	•	/	•	e.g. Kangal, Turkey	/	•
Comfort	Lack of facilities	•	•	•	/	/
Temperature (suitable for direct use)	To be used with extreme caution	•	•	•	•	Can be cooled down for use e.g. Kusatsu, Japan

Mineral content	•	•	•	•	•	•
Therapeutic value	Depends on water quality	•	•	•	Depends on facilities available	Possible if temperature is lowered and/or beneficial minerals are extracted
Medical use	Not officially recognised	Depends on facilities available	•	•	Depends on facilities available	
Popular destination	•	•	•	•	•	•
Entrance fee	Possible if within a National Park	•	•	•	•	Depends on state of facilities
Curative properties	Possibly, depending on water quality	Depending on water quality	•	•	/	/
Cultural use	•	•	•	/	Possible – great number of people	•
Hygienic concerns	•	Rarely	/	/	/	/
Potential risk	•	Rare, unless danger of toxic gas emissions (H_2S)	/	/	/	Yes, due to extreme temperature

(Continued)

Table 9.1 *Continued*

Variables determining use	Different types of hot spring environments					
	Undeveloped 'wild' hot springs	*Developed natural hot springs*	*Redeveloped hot spring destinations*	*Medical use of hot springs*	*Hot spring aqua parks*	*Extreme hot springs as visual attractions*
Marketing	If located in National Parks	•	•	•	•	Depends on significance for tourism
Word of mouth	•	•	•	•	•	•
Management	Yes, if in National Parks or on private property	•	•	•	•	Depends on significance for tourism
Technology	/	•	•	•	•	Depends on significance for tourism and energy

• Indicates or confirms existence.
/ Indicates either not available, not applicable or not important.
Source: The authors.

where the hot mineral spring is an integrated secondary feature of a luxury resort used to attract visitors. Hot springs may also be used directly to supply health facilities such as hospitals (e.g. Queen Elizabeth Hospital, Rotorua; this chapter) and spa and wellness facilities with thermal water use for hydrotherapy and balneology (e.g. Peninsula Hot Springs, Melbourne; this chapter). Aquatic entertainment centres (e.g. Spa Hawaiians, Japan and Tatralandia, Slovakia; this chapter), which are popular in countries with an abundance of natural hot and mineral springs also benefit from geothermal water resources. Extreme hot springs (e.g. geysers and boiling ponds such as Beppu's *Jigoku*, Japan; this chapter) are visual tourist attractions but are often in or close to the same location as hot springs being used for health and wellness tourism, and thus give added value in the form of geotourism to the spa and wellness industry.

A growing trend in the health and wellness spa industry is that of medical tourism. We illustrate its increasing importance with case studies from both Europe and Asia with the main focus on facilities using hot and mineral spring water as part of their treatment sequence.

This chapter adds important information not covered in Chapters 2 and 3 in order to give a contemporary picture of the various types of usage of hot and mineral spring resources on a global scale that was covered in the earlier chapters from a historical or wellness perspective. The focus of the present discussion is on the actual practice of health and wellness spa tourism based on hot and mineral springs, but illustrated in a series of case studies that are intended to be used as a summary form of the material presented in earlier chapters, as well as a basis for cross-country and cross-case analysis. This allows for comment on the broad issues facing the worldwide spa and wellness industry as a whole, and the identification of comparative differences where these occur between contemporary types of use.

Europe

Northern and Western Europe

Thermal spas in Europe are generally considered as a valuable contribution to the health system, which is evident where the cost for treatments and accommodation is subsidised by the individual governments (Marktl, 2000). In countries such as Germany, where a number of traditional spa towns date back to the Roman presence around 2000 years ago, the increased interest in health and wellness in recent times has encouraged new developments as well as refurbishments of existing spas. Over the centuries European spa destinations relying on a supply of geothermal spring water have come and gone and today many new establishments offering a wide range of health and welfare treatments are found along with the more traditional survivors. Cities such as Aachen, Wiesbaden and Baden Baden are only a few of the well-known names of German hot spring destinations; many other European locations offer thermal treatments and cures for a variety of health complaints as well as for relaxation and rejuvenation. These are known as 'healing spas' and as such are recognised by government and whose information is made available to the public through special guidebooks like the *Conradi-Bäderlexikon* (Größchen, 1998).

Overall there are 142 thermal spa destinations in Germany; with another 38 offering thermal water cures in combination with related treatments, such as peloids, mud and brine. Guidebooks such as the above-mentioned Bäderlexikon only consider spa destinations where medical treatment under the supervision of highly qualified professionals is available (Größchen, 1998). Doctors specialised in 'Kurmedizin' are seen as highly competent professionals who work with the patient and recommend appropriate changes for individual lifestyles (Freisleben-Teutscher, 2004). The German model of the 'Kur' has a reputation as a sustainable improvement for the health and well-being of patients who have taken the necessary time for their rehabilitation (Marktl, 2000).

According to the European Spa Industry Association (2006) the development of the spa industry originated in peoples' interest in hot and mineral springs from ancient times. This tradition has survived with Germany as an important example for the use of natural resources such as geothermal springs as a contribution for medical care. Curative resources are springs with medicinal water for therapeutic use, both internally and externally. One of the most famous German health and wellness spa destinations is the prestigious city of Baden Baden with its history as a hot spring spa dating back at least to Roman times (see Figure 9.1). Today Baden-Baden is still considered as a top destination for balneological treatment and cures as well as a meeting place for the *haute volée* (Chapter 7). The health and wellness spa facilities are supplied with thermal waters from several hot and mineral springs with temperatures ranging from 52 to 67°C (130–153°F). Originally developed by the Romans as *Aquae Aureliae* the city of Baden Baden over the centuries has relied on its natural hot and mineral springs and to this day these springs still play a great role in the city's spa industry.

Today health and wellness spa activities are dominated by two major thermal facilities with the *Friedrichsbad* the traditional establishment, which has served relaxation and healing for more than a century (Sanner, 2000). The newer *Caracallabad* in the city centre opened in the year 1985 and features several indoor pools with temperatures ranging between 30 and 38°C (86–100°F). Public drinking fountains, hotels and hospitals also benefit from the thermal water supply. Healing effects from thermal treatments are applied for a diversity of disorders such as arthritis, rheumatism, circulatory disorders, chronic bronchitis, sinus problems and obesity (Carasana Bäderbetriebe GmbH, n.d.).

It is difficult to find statistics containing reliable visitor numbers for thermal health and wellness spas for most countries (see Chapter 7). The only visitor numbers available usually combine all health and wellness facilities, and are not separated according to thermal spring destinations. However, some figures were obtained from the German Association for Health Spas (Deutscher Heilbäderverband, 2007) for this case study and are listed in Table 9.2, although the overall numbers also include health spas offering thermal mud treatments as their major therapies. It is noticeable that there was an initial increase between 1999 and 2000, when the German medical benefits system re-included hot and mineral

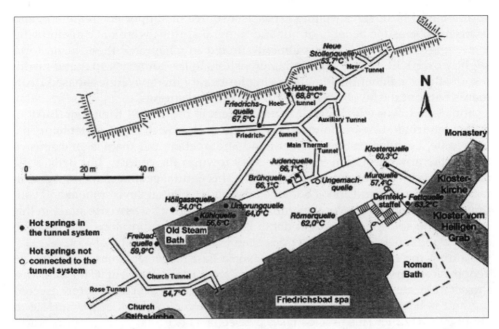

Figure 9.1 This location map shows the extensive development around the original hot spring sources of Baden Baden. The catchment works and tunnels were built between 1868 and 1902
Source: After Sanner (2000).

Table 9.2 Visitor numbers to health facilities in Germany offering thermalism as well as mud therapies

Arrivals	Thermal and mineral spring spas
1999	5,700,857
2000	6,099,605
2001	6,234,372
2002	6,129,399
2003	6,109,789
2004	6,203,661
2005	6,240,972
2006	6,476,794
Total increase 1999–2006	+775,937
Increase 1999–2006 in %	+13.61

Source: Deutscher Heilbäderverband (2007).

spring-based health and wellness spas as a source of supported treatment, and again in 2006 as the benefits of hot and mineral springs were once again being increasingly accepted by the public. As noted in Chapter 7 these visits form slightly over half of the total number of visitors to the country's spas and health resorts; the remainder presumably being for beauty therapy/fitness-based treatments without the involvement of hot and mineral springs.

Some spa towns with familiar names remain in the United Kingdom (Buxton, Bath, Llandrindod Wells, Holywell (Treffynnon), Droitwich Spa, Cheltenham Spa, Harrogate, Leamington Spa, Malvern and Strathpeffer) and there is an extensive beauty therapy orientation in almost every town in the country, but Bath is the only place with genuine hot springs (three). This natural geothermal resource is in fact unique for England and is both the reason for its initial development and continuous redevelopment over the centuries, and for its choice as a case study in this chapter. The springs originate at depth in carboniferous limestone and produce some 1.3 million litres of water per day at an average temperature of 45°C or 133°F (80% from the King's Spring – Bath & North East Somerset Council, 2002). The geophysical surveys carried out for their latest redevelopment (The Bath Spa Project) indicate that surface water descends to a depth of over 3 km before ascending and is heated to around 70°C (158°F) before cooling back at the surface to about 50°C (122°F). This process takes between 6 and 10,000 years (Bath & North East Somerset Council, 2002: 6–7).

The geothermal, historical and cultural ambience of Bath makes *Bath Spa* one of the major tourist attractions of the European region (Figure 9.2). As we noted in Chapter 3 there is archaeological evidence that occupation based around the hot springs on which the city is built began at least 3000 years ago. Coins thrown by the later Celts into the water, probably as offerings to their God Sul were found during excavations of the King's Bath. In 43 AD the Romans started the development of 'Aquae Sulis' as a sanctuary of rest and relaxation, not for a garrison like most Roman towns, and in 70 AD built a reservoir around the hot springs, a sophisticated series of baths, and a temple, dedicated to the goddess Sulis Minerva. As a religious shrine and bathing complex, Aquae Sulis attracted visitors from across Britain and Europe – foreshadowing Bath's status as a tourist destination (White, 2000). The Romans also used the Cross and Hetling springs. With the Roman military withdrawal from Britain, the baths and temple of Aquae Sulis fell gradually into ruin until the 11th century when the King's Bath was built over the temple precinct and spring, as part of an infirmary. In other words, the reputation of the springs was not lost during the intervening period.

Used between the 12th and 18th centuries as the basis for St. John's Hospital and the later Royal Mineral Water Hospital the springs largely catered for wealthy patrons (Queen Elizabeth I and other aristocrats), military rehabilitation or church-based alms giving initially. The springs continued in low-level use until their dramatic revival during the 18–19th centuries as a premier spa resort. These developments created the World Heritage City we see today, which attracts over 3.6 million tourists per year (Simons, n.d.). In the 1790s the Great Pump Room was built, along with extensive high-quality urban apartments throughout the city, the

Figure 9.2 Entrance to the old Roman Baths of Bath
Source: Photograph courtesy of P. Erfurt-Cooper.

King's bath was excavated in 1880 and water therapy treatments such as a Schnee Bath installed (White, 2000: 13). In the 1900s Bath spa water was bottled and sold as *Sulis Water*, promising relief from rheumatism, gout, lumbago, sciatica and neuritis. Following the First World War thousands of wounded soldiers rehabilitated in spa towns such as Bath. And in 1948, following the establishment of the National Health Service (NHS), the health authorities of Bath made arrangements to provide water-cure treatments on prescription.

However, despite the spa being the site for Roman Revival parties in the 1960s and 1970s, when the Great Bath was the setting for events that mirrored the revelry of earlier spa culture, the spa as an active health and wellness tourism attraction was to have a short life. In 1976 withdrawal of NHS funding for spa treatments and public health concerns (Chapter 6) resulted in the closure of the Spa Medical Facility (White, 2000: 13). This did not however stop the city becoming one of the United Kingdom's leading tourist attractions based on the built environment that had been created up to the 19th century around the Roman great bath. As a result, in the period 1983–1985 new wells beneath the King's and Cross Springs were drilled to establish a new supply of uncontaminated geothermal spring water for a planned new development known as the *Bath Spa Project*, finally agreed to in 1997 (Bath & North East Somerset Council, 2002: 10–11). This project made it possible to reopen the hot springs in 2006 for public use again after 28 years of closure and over 2000 years of history (see White (2000) for a description of this project).

In common with many new health and wellness spa tourism facilities the restored baths feature a medical treatment centre providing preventative medicines and therapies such as massage, physiotherapy, hydrotherapy and acupuncture, a research and interpretive centre, alternative energy generation from the hot spring resource (dependent on proving the reliability over time of the resource), and special bathing rights for the residents of the city (White, 2000: 14). Today, *Thermae Bath Spa* is a day spa attracting some 950,000 visitors and offering bathing in natural mineral-rich waters and a range of therapeutic spa treatments, as it did when a spa was first opened on this site 2000 years ago. The chemical composition of the waters includes 42 minerals and trace elements, the most important being:

- calcium (358 mg/l);
- sulphate (1015 mg/l);
- chloride (340 mg/l);
- bicarbonate (193 mg/l);
- magnesium (57 mg/l);
- silica (42 mg/l); and
- iron (0.6 mg/l).

In 2002, before Thermae Bath Spa opened, the English Tourism Council launched *Health Benefits*, a 2002 report analysing the nature and potential of the United Kingdom's health tourism market (Simons, n.d.). The data revealed by this survey suggested a total health and wellness market of some 38 million trips in the early 21st century, where sports-related leisure and recreation contributes 31 million and health and fitness a mere 7 million trips (by 1.2 million spa goers), many of which are to overseas destinations. Nevertheless, there are already over 13,000 residential and 7000 non-residential spa and sports facilities in the United Kingdom, and spa tourism is already worth over 1.4 billion pounds (Simons, n.d.: 24). The ISPA Global Spa Study published in 2007 suggests that the health and wellness spa industry in the United Kingdom has grown significantly since 2002, with 6.7 million spa goers a year now being counted, and has a great future as a reason for a short break holiday as well as for day spa therapies like facials and massage (ISPA, 2007).

France is one of the European countries where the use of natural hot and mineral springs is still an important part of annual health and wellness spa resort holidays and *thermalisme* is funded at least in part by the National Health Care System. Table 9.3 shows how developed French spa resorts were in the 1920s (of note are the number of doctors and the entertainment facilities available to the health and wellness tourists of nearly 100 years ago), and updates these to the present as an illustration of this point. Current internet sites claim that there is 'no equal to a real French spa' and that French mineral water is impossible to copy (French Health Spas, n.d.). The *Thermes de la Bourboule* for example are said to offer a pollution-free environment beneficial for the respiratory healing system

Table 9.3 This table demonstrates how advanced the French thermalism system was in the year 1921

1921	Spring type	Temperature	Main minerals	Flow rate	Annual visitor numbers	Season	Health applications	Medical personnel	Clinical indications	Amusement entertainment
Aix les Bains *Aquae Gratianae*	Two thermal springs	43–45°C	Sulphur, calcium, silica	4 million litres p/d	40,000 in 1921	April to November *All year in recent times*	*Therapeutic facilities are state run today*	23 doctors	Rheumatism, neuralgia, syphilis, war wounds	Two casinos, theatre, concerts, golf and tennis, boating, sailing, fishing, winter sports
Biarritz	Saline cold springs	13.9°C	Sodium chloride, iodine and bromide salts	1 million litres p/d	40,000 in 1921	All year	Salt baths	19 doctors	Tuberculosis, scrofula, anaemia, women's diseases	Two casinos, concerts, theatre, tennis, golf, races, fox hunting, bull fights, car hire
La Bourboule	Two warm alkaline springs	46–56°C	Sodium chloride, arsenic	1 million litres p/d	20,000 in 1921	15 May–15 October		19 doctors	Skin diseases, respiratory symptoms, diabetes	Casino, parks, tennis courts, concerts, young people's club, open air theatre
Dax	Hot springs and vegeto mineral mud	64°C constant	Mixed sulphates rich in oligo elements	5 million litres p/d	10,000–12,000 p/a	All year	Baths, inhalation	*Nurses, spa carers, physiotherapists, masseurs, beauticians*	Rheumatism, respiratory symptoms	Casinos, concerts, theatre, cinema, racing, bull fights, tennis, fishing, football and basketball matches

(Continued)

Table 9.3 *Continued*

1921	Spring type	Temperature	Main minerals	Flow rate	Annual visitor numbers	Season	Health applications	Medical personnel	Clinical indications	Amusement entertainment
Evian	Cold alkaline spring	10.5°C	Bicarbonate, magnesium, sulphur, calcium		15,000 p/a			16 doctors + 3 dentists	Gout, diabetes, metabolic and kidney ailments, plethoric gourmands	Casino, concerts, theatre, golf, tennis, pigeon shooting, boating, fishing
Plombieres les Bains	Two alkaline springs, clear and odourless	13–74°C	Sodium silicate, magnesium, sulphur	750,000 litres p/d		15 May–1 October	Baths, vapour baths, douches	11 doctors	Rheumatism, arthritis, gastrointestinal, nervous system	Casino, concerts, theatre, balls, pigeon shooting, parks and waterfalls
Vichy	Fourteen warm springs	15–42°C	Sodium bicarbonate	675,000 litres p/d	108,963 visitors during 1913 season	15 April–15 October	Bathing, drinking, vapour baths, hot baths, showers	More than 100, including specialists *Therapeutic facilities are state run today*	Liver, intestinal, diabetes, gout, malaria	Casino with theatre, cinema, concerts, races, golf, tennis, parks with fine trees
Bagnoles	Hot springs, slightly acidic 'Healing Springs'	41.5°C	Calcium, iron, potassium sodium, lithium, magnesium, sulphur	912,000 litres p/d		20 May–1 October	Balneotherapy, baths, therapeutic waters for respiratory and rheumatic symptoms, lymphoedema	Eight doctors	Sluggishness of the venous system, depression, arthritis, rheumatism, eczema, malaria	Casino, theatre, concerts, teas, lectures, tennis club, climate and food products, healthy and hygienic recreation

1921	Spring type	Temperature	Main minerals	Flow rate	Annual visitor numbers	Season	Health applications	Medical personnel	Clinical indications	Amusement entertainment
Lamalou	Warm, volcanic 'health giving springs'	25–50°C	Bicarbonate of soda, iron, magnesium, contains carbonated gas			Easter–15 November	Balneotherapy, baths, thermal bathing pools	Nine doctors	Nervous system, rheumatism, anaemia	Casino, theatre, concerts, cinemas, excursions, 'picturesque environs', archaeological curiosities, shooting, fishing
Hammam R'Irha *Aquae Calidae* (Algeria)	Hot sulphide springs	34–72°C	Calcium, sulphur, chloride			1 December–31 March			Arthritis, gout, rheumatism, wounds, neuralgia	Parks and forest, tennis, croquet, shooting, skating rink, cinema, motor excursions, Arab fêtes
Hammam Meskoutine (Algeria)	Hot springs	40–95°C	Bicarbonates, sulphates, sodium chloride			15 December–15 June	Baths, douches		Rheumatism, dermatosis, paralysis, malaria, sedative effect	

Note: The text in bold italics refers to facilities offered today.
Source: Office National du Tourisme (1921) and modified by the author.

and to have a reputation for anti-stress treatments. At *Aix les Thermes* sulphurous steam vents are used for healing therapies and at 77°C (170.6°F) are known as the warmest thermal springs of the Pyrenees. All these thermal springs are officially registered for medical treatments such as rheumatism, trauma, stress, injuries and respiratory problems (French Health Spas, n.d.) and there are numerous springs throughout the country.

The French health and wellness spas are very versatile and encourage visitors to take charge of a healthier lifestyle under the guidance of spa professionals, in addition to thermal-based medical treatment by qualified medical staff. *Aix-en-Provence* for example is known as the city of 100 fountains with geothermal springs, which have largely contributed to its existence (Laushway, 1996). The Pellegrini Thermal Baths in *Aix-les-Bains*, which are hosted in a 19th century historical building, underwent redevelopment in the late 1990s including adding an additional thermal pool and the latest treatment technology. Thermal therapy is in fact offered in a variety of locations at Aix-les-Bains and the city's new *Thermal Therapy* concept welcomes guests for water cures (Lund, 2000c). The benefits of thermal water can be enjoyed throughout the year and Aix-les-Bains has facilities and treatments for everyone in a unique environment; offering a variety of cures including mud therapy (clay soaked in natural thermal water) with therapeutic properties resulting in a soothing and relaxing effect for users (Les Thermes Nationaux d'Aix-les-Bains, n.d.).

ISPA (2007) puts the number of spa goers in France at 6.3 million, although these figures do not appear to include participation by foreign clients at French spa resorts. Sauna and steam baths are the preferred modalities in France as they are in Germany and Japan, and attract tourists from these markets as well as from Italy (17.8 million spa goers), Spain (6.1 million spa goers) and Austria (2.9 million; ISPA, 2007).

Central and Eastern Europe and Russia

The countries of Central and Eastern Europe are popular for their health and wellness spa destinations that offer good quality services for a lesser price than their western European counterparts (Lund, 2000a, 2002). Large numbers of West Europeans have visited countries such as Bulgaria, Romania, Slovakia, Slovenia, Hungary and the Czech Republic for health purposes for many years, because they get more of their desired treatment for less money. The health and wellness trend has merely reinforced this because most of these countries had already a sound thermal resource base (Lund & Freestone, 2001), which they could expand to cater for the increased demand from health and wellness seeking visitors.

In addition to their thermal spa resorts and health spas some countries such as Poland and Slovakia have invested in the development of large aquatic theme parks fed by natural geothermal water, which attract families as well. For example the thermal mineral water that supplies the relaxation pools of *Tatralandia* (Slovakia) is described as special in comparison to other facilities so forms a useful case study for this book. Its uniqueness apparently stems from ancient seawater intrusion that adds to the unusual composition of the mineral water

(Tatralandia Aquapark, 2006). The therapeutic effect of this water is said to be beneficial for locomotive and respiratory organs and considered an added plus for people using the natural thermal water pools. Aqua Park Tatralandia is also advertised as the biggest thermal water resort offering fun and relaxation not just in Slovakia, where it is located, but also in neighbouring countries such as the Czech Republic and Poland. Tatralandia is promoted as the perfect thermal paradise, open all year round, with nine pools in the complex for relaxation and swimming, together with various water-based attractions such as the 'volcano', the 'rocket' and the 'snake', all of them ending in the warm water of a thermal pool. A pleasant water temperature between 26 and 38°C (78.8–100.4°F) is maintained and there are many other attractions including geysers, water streams, water beds, water swings and children's slides that offer entertainment for every generation (Tatralandia Aquapark, 2006).

There are 44 recognised spa resorts in the Czech Republic (The Prague Post, 10 October 2006), the majority of which have been integrated into the national health care system as providers of medical treatments for Czechs that are fully covered by health insurance. Clients are also received from other European countries, including Russia, and this has become more important in the past two years as the Czech Government has tried to reduce the cost of medical services at the national level. In April 2006 the Health Minister sought to cut benefits for spa visits by 50%, and because of this doctors have become increasingly reluctant to prescribe treatment from this source for medical conditions (The Prague Post, 10 October 2006). One such spa, *Lazne Darkov* (Ostrava Region) that treats musculoskeletal, neurological and skin diseases, has sought to attract Russian clients based on the European tradition we described in Chapter 3. This spa can accommodate 1000 clients at any one time and until 2006 was turning clients away, but is now overshadowed by more well-known spas like Karlovy Vary that are more able to attract Western visitors to counter the downturn in Czech clients.

The health and welfare spa industry in the Czech Republic contributed some 4.6% of all trips in 2007 (Czech Tourism, 2008) and 4% of total revenue from tourism (186 billion CZK). The value of the industry based on the Czech hot springs in 2007 was therefore approximately USD440 million at current exchange rates.

The *Kamchatka Peninsula* in eastern Russia (bordering on China and also close to Japan) has appeared over recent years in advertising campaigns for nature-based tourism with a very interesting tourism industry emerging in this remote wilderness. Tourists can participate in ecotourism, geotourism and hunting tourism; all of them often combined with the use of natural hot springs. Responsible for the abundance of hot springs on the peninsula are the numerous active volcanoes of the Kamchatka, and many visitors are geotourists interested in the active volcanic environments or hunters who are after large game trophies (Buckley, 2006) and are not there for health and wellness tourism per se. However, after a day of volcano viewing or hunting the hot springs are appreciated by many travellers, either for a relaxing soak after a long day trekking and hiking or as a visual attraction such as the 'Valley of the Geysers'. Although it cannot be determined exactly when and by whom these natural hot springs were used in the past, as the population figures are extremely low in this part of the world, they are well known and anybody who comes across warm water in a cold climate is likely to make use of it.

Health and wellness spa tourism can in fact be found in various parts of Russia – in Moscow, in the Caucasus, in the Altai and the Urals, or on the Black Sea as well as in Kamchatka. Modern Russian life style emphasises healthy living; therefore, spas are more and more in demand. One such popular Russian spa area is Stavropolsky Krai in the Caucasus. There are four major resorts there – *Kislovodsk, Pyatigorsk, Essentuki and Zheleznovodsk*. These have a combined population of only some 130,000 residents but the resorts manage to attract some 440,000 tourists annually. Pyatigorsk is one of the oldest resorts in Russia, located 510–630 m above sea level in a valley of the river Podkumok. The area has more than 50 various mineral sources, including radonic earths and carbonic waters, and lies 180 km from Stavropol, 680 km from Rostov on Don and 1800 km from Moscow. Tourists go to this location to cure heart disease, to drink mineral waters or to stroll in local parks, and most are middle-aged, upper middle-class Russians who stay for three weeks (Tourism Review, August 2008).

Despite the long tradition of state-sponsored health and wellness tourism based on hot and mineral springs water as an important part of the medical system, most Russian health and wellness centres in the 21st century now follow the American wellness model of 'beauty therapy'. The majority of spas are located in Moscow, where there are approximately 3500 beauty salons, with hotels such as the Marriott and Hilton chains strongly represented, and the whole Russian beauty salon market is worth over US$2 billion per year. Russians now understand spas as expensive and elite, whereas once they were essentially free and concentrated on water therapy, and the majority of clients are female. Only some 23% of spa visitors are male (Tourism Review, August 2008).

The Mediterranean and Middle East

Many of the Mediterranean countries have an abundance of natural hot and mineral springs, which are used as tourist attractions, health and wellness spa and bathing facilities. This is especially true of countries with a volcanic past like Greece that have several areas with geothermal resources. Apart from interesting landscapes and natural scenic beauty, Greece has also one of the longest recorded histories of natural hot spring use: the country appears to have had a nearly unbroken line of thermal water use from at least 2500 years ago right to the present (Altman, 2002; Fytikas *et al.*, 1999; Katsambas & Antoniou, 1996; Melillo, 1995). Many places of thermal attraction in Greece are listed on the internet, but some of the more well-known destinations like Loutraki or Edipsos have also been described in the health and wellness spa literature due to their use traditions and reputation for therapeutical benefits (see Chapters 2 and 3).

Natural hot and mineral springs are found in many locations; however, the composition of the individual thermal springs varies according to temperature and the presence of mineral components. Because of these minerals the hot springs are used for therapeutic treatment such as balneology, hydrotherapy or thermalism. The thermal springs of *Kaifa, Kyllini* and *Langada* have been directly connected with tectonic activity and other springs of Methana, Milos, Lesbos, Samothrace and Limnos are related to volcanic activity. Most springs are used because of their therapeutical value in the treatment of arthritis and rheumatic diseases and can be applied internally as well as externally. The category of tourist infrastructure in Greece also includes 16 thermal treatment centres with natural mineral springs, in which 1.4 million therapeutic treatments (baths, etc.) annually are offered to approximately 100,000 individual wellness tourists; as well as thermal treatment facilities at 40 springs of local importance. Additional thermal health and wellness centres are under construction (Greek National Tourism Organisation, n.d.).

Turkey also has a long tradition of hot spring use for health and wellness and with approximately 1300–1500 natural hot springs (numbers differ depending on information sources) thermal bathing is an old and important Turkish tradition, and even today every city or town in Turkey has several public baths, warmed either by hot springs or by central heating (Özgüler & Kasap, 1999). One of the more unusual hot springs were first noticed by local inhabitants of the city of *Kangal* in the early 19th century when a shepherd with a foot injury healed his wound in the thermal waters of the local spring. Following this rather miraculous healing more people took an interest in the location and started to construct primitive pools and simple buildings (Blue World Travel, 2006; Kangal Hot Springs, n.d.) because the springs of Kangal are said to have no equal in the world for the treatment of *psoriasis*. Small fish inhabiting the hot springs assist in a remarkable relief from this severe skin disorder by removing the dead skin and thus encouraging the growth of new healthy skin (Health Spa Guru, 2008; Wave, 1999). These thermal springs are today highly sought after by psoriasis sufferers from all over the world; countries such as China, Korea and Japan have adopted the 'fish cure' as a successful healing component for skin conditions in their own facilities that have conditions similar to Kangal (Life in the Fast Lane, 2007). A growing interest in this particular spa treatment type is developing also in North America and Europe (Anastasion, 2008; Buzzle.Com, 2007; Canadian Spa Imports, n.d.; Health Spa Guru, 2008; Life in the Fast Lane, 2007; Mossman, 2007; Nedelcu, 2008; Pescovitz, 2008).

Tourism is a key contributor to the Turkish economy, generating over USD18 billion from approximately 23 million international visitors in 2007, and an unknown dollar amount from domestic tourists (Turkstat, 2008). Visitor arrivals have soared from 6.6 million in 1994, largely due to Turkey's popularity as a low-cost holiday destination with the added benefit of some of the world's most attractive hot springs mineral formations (at Pammukkale), and the more than 1300 hot springs noted above. Tourism accounts for around 5% of GDP and 3% of employment and represents a crucial source of foreign currency for Turkey (Tourism Statistics Bulletins, 2006).

Jordan is attracting health and wellness tourists mainly due to its proximity to the Dead Sea and its natural thermal springs, which have been used since ancient times (see Chapter 3). The official website of Jordan recommends, among other worthwhile attractions, the therapeutic hot springs of *Hammamat Ma'een* as an important tourist destination, and gives directions on how to get there and a description of the facilities available (The Hashemite Kingdom of Jordan, n.d.). The hot springs and baths of Hammamat Ma'een have been enjoyed for therapeutic and leisure pursuits for thousands of years and today they supply a commercial resort area with one of the main public attractions a large spring-fed waterfall, and a number of smaller springs within the private resort area (Harahsheh, 2002; The Hashemite Kingdom of Jordan, n.d.). The same hot springs, healing waters, thermal waterfalls and mineral salts of the Dead Sea are promoted on several other websites in various languages in order to attract international visitors. The natural thermal springs and baths of Jordan also offer thermal treatments that create a feeling of well-being and wholeness. Some such as *Zarqa' Ma'in* (*Zara*), *Afra* and *Al-Himma* offer historic architecture as additional attractions to the thermal baths (Baptism Land, 2000).

Tourism in Jordan is increasing year by year, and has now reached nearly 2 million. There are no accurate statistics collected on health and wellness tourism, but the Ministry of Tourism estimates that about 7% of all visitors make use of these geothermal resources, mostly Arabs. The Ministry has made strong efforts to increase the number of classified hotels offering a higher standard of accommodation and upgrading the infrastructure associated with the hot springs through tax and customs exemptions during construction. It is hoped that this will increase the length of stay in the country by tourists, which is currently around four days, whereas it is 18 and eight days in the adjacent resorts of Israel and Egypt, respectively (The Hashemite Kingdom of Jordan, n.d.).

Research by Salameh Harahsheh in 2002 revealed that the majority of health and wellness tourists to Jordan's spas and health resorts were men, of 50+ years old, and who stayed in spa hotels or chalets between 21 and 30 days, had an income level of €1000–3000 per month, spent between €141 and €220 per day and came (non-Jordanians) from the EU countries, mainly Germany and Austria (Harahsheh, 2002). This research also revealed that 20 health and wellness sites around Jordan, including those of the Dead Sea area, have been identified and classified according to their technical and economic feasibility for future development by the Government. Nevertheless health and welfare tourists to Jordan suffer from some problems during their stay in the country at the time of writing. The main ones include lack of public transportation, a low level of cleanliness at facilities, accessibility (road quality) problems, limited accommodation (and its unavailability at some sites), treatment services not available at many sites, prices very high in comparison with the level of services rendered, few entertainment programmes and alternative activities, and communication facilities not being available at some sites as yet.

Africa

A number of African countries have volcanic areas and natural hot springs, which are used by the local population wherever these springs are accessible. These range from Tunisia in the North to Namibia in the South. Given the political situation in many African countries, relatively little development on a commercial scale for health and wellness tourism has so far been exercised. And the countries with a known tradition of hot spring use do not have much to offer in the sense of reliable records, which could indicate the historical evolution of thermalism in Africa. The following paragraphs give some brief examples of what is commonly known about African natural hot and mineral springs and what is available for the tourist.

In Namibia, not far from the capital Windhoek, are two hot spring spas, *Gross Barmen Thermal Baths* and the *Reho Spa*, both said to relieve rheumatism [Namibia Tourism, n.d.(a)]. Another trendy hot spring destination in Namibia is the *Ai-Ais Hot Springs Resort* situated at the southern end of the Fish River Canyon and popular with hikers who can soothe their bodies in the lukewarm sulphurous spring water [Namibia Tourism, n.d.(b); Ai-Ais Hot Springs Resort, n.d.(a); Ai-Ais Hot Springs Resort, n.d.(b)]. The town of *Warmbad* (also known as Warmbaths) in Namibia was known by the local tribes as 'Bela Bela' meaning the 'boiling place', which indicates earlier use by local communities without giving a precise timeline (Warmbaths, n.d.). Established as a bathing facility by white settlers in the late 1800s, Warmbad soon became locally renowned for its beneficial waters and attracted visitors mainly seeking relief from rheumatism and arthritis (Warmbaths, n.d.). The relatively close proximity of the Warmbad resort and other related facilities to Johannesburg airport attracts international visitors as well as domestic tourists (Warmbaths, n.d.), even though the name 'Warmbad' changed to Bela Bela in the year 2002 (History of Warmbaths, n.d.).

Namibia attracted 928,912 tourists in 2007, up 11% on 2006 and comprised of 61% male and 39% female visitors staying an average of 19 days [Namibia Tourism, n.d.(a)]. Their age distribution reveals a pronounced concentration in the 20–49 age group (66%), with a secondary concentration 50+ (22.5%), while their distribution across the year is even except for lower numbers in January and February. Nearly 700,000 visitors were from adjacent countries (73% of all visitors came by road), while 195,000 came from Europe (largest number 80,500 from Germany), and 44,200 from the rest of the world including 19,300 from the United States [Namibia Tourism n.d.(c)]. No actual statistics are available for hot springs use, or indeed any other particular tourist attraction, but it may be assumed that given the visitor profile and the information from the local spa resorts revealed above, numbers of these tourists and VFR travellers do use the baths.

In Tunisia geothermal resources in the form of hot springs have been used for Balneology for centuries (Ben Mohamed, 2003). Tunisia's *hammams* (also called thermal stations) are not only for bathing or undergoing curative treatments (including mud baths), but are also for fun, recreation, exercise (including mud baths) as well as for many other reasons. Hammams are spread all over the country, especially in the south and in the Arabic language the world *'Hami'* means hot. In the south of Tunisia are two areas called *hamma* (Gabes and Tozeur regions) because of their association with natural hot and mineral springs; with 10 traditional small thermal baths also in the Kebili area. Hammans such as the *Steftimi* baths have two pools each for men and women, sitting rooms, dressing rooms and a prayer room (Ben Mohamed, 2003).

In the year 1975 the Tunisian Office for Thermalism (*Office du Thermalisme*) was established and located in the capital Tunis. This office works in cooperation with the state-run Tourism Organisation (Nouira, 1975) to promote and supervise the geothermal resource. The hot spring sector these days is privatised with over 80 thermal spring locations in Tunisia, which attract approximately 2.5 million visitors annually seeking various treatments. The *Hammam Sidi Abdelkader* alone is said to receive over one million visitors each year (Office du Thermalisme, n.d.). About 20 traditional Hammams across the territory from north to south also receive 2.5 million bathers annually. El Hamma of Gabes with its three traditional centres receives more than one million visitors annually. More thermal baths are established every year, indicating the importance of this tourism sector (Office du Thermalisme, 2003).

Asia

Many Asian and central Asian countries use natural hot and mineral springs for various purposes. In recent times not only the locals are benefiting from the thermal waters; increasingly international visitors discover unique regions and are exploring them, especially if they are interested in nature-based and hot spring tourism. A number of Asian countries are dominated by active volcanoes, which means there are also numbers of natural hot and mineral springs in many locations. Not all of these are developed for hot spring bathing or medical thermal treatment, but the majority of these natural resources are in fact used as tourist attractions in individual countries. Most of the original hot spring users are the local residents; but the growing numbers of travellers to remote and exotic destinations is responsible for spreading the word of must-see places among other travellers. Today it is relatively easy to find information about hot spring locations in areas that were under-reported in the past, but are now promoted on the internet and discussed in travellers' blog sites, such as in Mongolia.

East Asia

Mongolia is one of these rather recent additions to the list of countries who are promoting natural resources like geothermal springs and unique geosites in order to attract international visitors for health and wellness spa tourism and other associated forms of tourism. At present there are about 43 hot springs in Mongolia, which are used for various purposes, including several sanatoriums and health resorts (Mongolia Investors Forum, 2006). Most hot spring destinations are located in the mountains at nearly 2000 m above sea level and some are accessible with 4WD vehicles only. Historical records are scarce, at least outside Mongolia, but there is some indication that one of the mineral spring areas (*Aurag City*) is connected to Chingis Khaan (Mongolia Web News, 2007b). Several hot spring sanatoriums and health resorts are listed in Mongolian travel guides, which point out that the thermal waters are believed to cure many 'aches and diseases' (Mongolia

Web News, 2007a). Hot springs also seem to be major destinations on organised tours through Mongolia (e.g. Tsenkher Hot Springs) and 'traditional treatment methods' indicate the age-old use of thermal waters for medicinal purposes (Tsenkher Hot Springs, n.d.).

Over the last few years additional information has emerged on the internet from tour operators and tourism-oriented websites for travellers interested in the diversity of tourist attractions Mongolia has to offer. This includes not just mountains and deserts, and culture, but also hot springs and their use for health and wellness tourism. Accordingly, the Government of Mongolia has recognised tourism as a priority sector with a great potential to contribute to socio-economic development of the country (Ministry of Road, Transport and Tourism Mongolia, 2006).

Japan is a country that is extremely proud of its active natural hot spring (*Onsen* 温泉;) culture and the many geothermal springs all over the country; of which the majority are used for the Japanese people's favourite pastime – hot water bathing (Clark, 1999). Traditional bathhouses (*Sento, Furo*) are still frequented regularly as a means of socialising with friends, family and neighbours, while soaking in the hot water and relaxing, however, these establishments do not necessarily offer genuine hot spring water, but may use artificially heated tap water. Even so, these facilities are used by many Japanese on a regular basis and people can be seen wandering between their homes and their local bath house in the early evenings with their bathing paraphernalia in a small basket. It is not uncommon for whole families to share an *Onsen* bath, from very young to very old family members (personal observation). During the cooler seasons, especially in the northern parts of Japan, a long soak in a hot bath helps to keep warm, as many houses and apartments do not have central heating. Houses with connections to local hot spring water supply (where available) are highly sought after and although the extra cost can be considerable, the benefits offset this by providing genuine hot spring water 'on tap' as well as saving the cost of heating (personal experience).

Part of the Japanese domestic travel pattern is the 'collection' (experience) of as many different *Onsen* sites as possible, with large tour buses constantly arriving at the popular *Onsen* destinations and helping to carry over 150 million visitors to these each year (Table 9.4). Preferred for accommodation are the traditional Japanese inns called *Ryokan*, which use their *Onsen* as the main attraction combined with beautiful Japanese garden settings, regional culinary specialties, local attractions and unique landscapes. This integration of hot springs with the natural environment draws visitors from the corporate sector (collective getaways for social bonding) to families and couples of all ages. The close bond of many Japanese with their treasured thermal springs has however made them very critical when it comes to the potential addition of unwanted chemical substances to the natural hot spring water (Chapter 6). Nevertheless, there are vast differences among the many hot springs of the country, which means that they can vary in colour from clear or milky over blue and green to brown or even nearly black, a situation that is directly related to the mineral content of the spring (Biddle, 2001).

Table 9.4 Use of Japanese hot springs by prefecture, 1998–2005

Prefecture	1998	2000	2004	2005
Hokkaido	16,672,271	14,747,469	13,673,989	14,288,625
Aomori	1,813,377	1,867,734	1,906,229	1,771,060
Iwate	3,374,891	3,430,093	2,640,879	2,656,189
Miyagi	3,336,463	3,020,195	3,092,964	3,374,637
Akita	2,588,467	2,772,071	2,823,211	2,771,174
Yamagata	4,769,089	4,513,143	4,237,515	3,947,504
Fukushima	6,208,028	7,514,749	6,272,245	6,253,964
Ibaraki	565,265	615,763	1,394,278	727,358
Tochigi	8,401,787	7,665,321	6,827,274	6,732,735
Gunma	7,464,352	7,418,184	6,703,286	6,820,062
Saitama	136,270	350,538	313,925	390,741
Chiba	1,326,958	1,466,344	1,946,805	2,318,857
Tokyo	251,046	173,998	205,230	221,057
Kanagawa	6,478,756	6,160,111	6,077,129	5,961,606
Niigata	5,876,842	6,114,971	4,674,371	5,093,743
Toyama	1,402,387	1,671,793	1,520,123	1,498,594
Ishikawa	4,741,178	4,731,476	4,155,579	3,833,843
Fukui	1,674,061	1,359,458	1,296,409	1,241,920
Yamanashi	2,932,317	2,953,362	4,081,016	4,092,550
Nagano	10,149,303	10,304,344	9,988,594	9,964,165
Gifu	4,592,319	4,428,346	4,143,268	3,634,321
Shizuoka	11,481,307	11,044,942	12,395,482	12,486,502
Aichi	954,586	1,498,223	1,874,496	1,847,515
Mie	1,954,068	1,801,791	3,036,952	3,963,208
Shiga	954,710	1,031,153	1,084,390	1,136,445
Kyoto	906,564	1,419,572	1,414,199	1,091,031
Osaka	400,111	907,033	905,327	918,268
Hyogo	3,893,516	3,473,937	3,781,871	4,248,442
Nara	461,987	412,421	462,067	440,864

(*Continued*)

Table 9.4 *Continued*

Prefecture	1998	2000	2004	2005
Wakayama	4,169,348	4,073,028	3,743,492	3,641,382
Tottori	1,724,540	1,640,253	1,542,460	1,449,648
Shimane	1,278,844	1,269,646	1,175,422	1,085,337
Okayama	1,150,206	1,256,447	1,261,442	1,150,147
Hiroshima	563,992	574,028	650,518	669,603
Yamaguchi	2,076,631	1,994,187	2,192,505	2,161,455
Tokushima	249,886	286,242	453,190	523,863
Kagawa	1,114,070	852,541	974,839	880,495
Ehime	1,736,482	1,696,599	1,737,506	1,719,635
Kochi	398,590	592,179	471,995	501,422
Fukuoka	821,396	1,007,346	812,955	877,878
Saga	1,377,282	1,307,186	981,082	1,107,118
Nagasaki	2,883,988	2,973,241	2,217,963	2,325,045
Kumamoto	4,146,508	3,777,658	3,715,798	3,631,277
Oita (mainly Beppu City)	**8,267,125**	**10,131,485**	**11,141,122**	**11,113,174**
Miyazaki	540,397	835,922	953,990	986,806
Kagoshima	4,130,880	3,498,813	3,399,942	3,160,473
Okinawa	425,518	491,414	618,075	634,688
Total	**152,817,959**	**153,126,750**	**150,973,399**	**151,346,426**

Source: Beppu City Council (2007).

Many *Onsen* destinations have cultivated a reputation for a particular type of water, knowing that the true *Onsen* connoisseur expects nothing but the genuine product (see Chapter 6). The recycling or circulating of thermal water is also frowned upon, as it indicates that chemicals have been added to satisfy certain hygienic requirements. This also means that the water may have been artificially heated and possibly tap water has been added as well. These types of *Onsen* are quickly blacklisted once they become known for disreputable conduct such as falsely advertising genuine hot spring water. There have been a few dishonest *Onsen* providers in the recent past, which dominated the Japanese media for a considerable time (Chapter 6). Public apologies are only one of the more minor sanctions applied in such cases; because many *Onsen* have been managed by the same family for centuries it becomes a matter of honour to cater for the expectations of the customer by supplying genuine hot spring water. This explains why the Japanese are particularly sensitive about their hot springs; they do not take kindly to the addition of chemicals, colouring agents, or recycled and artificially heated water and especially they do not appreciate being lied to about the water quality.

Adding to the benefits of relaxation and keeping warm the Japanese do also use their *Onsen* for healing purposes. It is widely believed and expected that different hot springs have different curative effects and Japanese doctors recommend the use of natural thermal water as beneficial for everybody in order to maintain or regain good health and well-being. Various health problems, including arthritis, rheumatism, circulatory and nervous disorders and trauma to name only a few, are treated with balneotherapy using natural hot spring water (Agashi & Ohtsuka, 1998). The popularity of thermal spas for both bathing and balneotherapy has turned hot spring locations such as Beppu City into one of the most prominent tourism destinations of Japan.

The City of Beppu

Beppu City is located on the east coast of Kyushu Island in Oita Prefecture and attracts annually more than 11 million tourists, mainly domestic. The core reason for their visit is the more than 2600 natural hot springs in and around Beppu delivering a volume of hot mineral water second only to Yellowstone National Park in the USA (Lund, 2002). Traditional bathhouses such as *Takegawara Onsen* (see Figure 4.7) offer sand baths and regular *Onsen* baths with nostalgic ambience and are a definite tourist attraction from the outside as well as inside because of the time-honoured Japanese architecture. On the other side of the scale are some natural *Onsen* like the *Hebinyu Onsen*, which is hidden away in the forested hills of Beppu on a narrow old supply road leading to the hot spring site. Despite the hidden location this is a very popular *Onsen* and is frequented by people at all seasons. Also, on *Kitahama* beach at Beppu is a sand bath, which has been used by locals for centuries and is a great attraction for visitors from other prefectures as well as from overseas. However, the majority of Beppu's hot springs are utilised for *Onsen* facilities within the hotel industry, or within local community or private baths, with the *Suginoi* Hotel taking advantage of the abundance of hot spring water to run their own geothermal power station in addition to supplying a large variety of themed hot spring baths and an aquatic entertainment centre (Chapter 7). The city of Beppu even has special view points where the steam rising from many vents can be observed (Figure 9.3).

Apart from creating many bathing facilities Beppu's hot spring tourism resource can be viewed in several *Jigoku* (Japanese for hell) as mentioned in Chapter 4 in conjunction with their cultural value. A group of 10 Jigoku with geothermal manifestations such as bubbling mud pools, boiling crater lakes in different colours, hissing steam vents and the odd geyser attract vast numbers of 'hot spring' tourists, who enjoy the unique sights while they have a foot spa and consume eggs (*Onsen tamago*), vegetables and dumplings boiled in steam, but do not bathe. The tour of the Beppu hells (*Jigoku Meguri*) is one of the most popular tourist

Figure 9.3 Beppu's active steam vents are synonymous for thousands of individual thermal springs which supply the town with an abundance of *Onsen* facilities
Source: Photograph courtesy of P. Erfurt-Cooper.

attractions of the city and as with many locations throughout Japan; repeat visits during different seasons are encouraged.

The Beppu Hydrothermal field based on the Tsurumidake-Garandake volcanic complex contains three types of thermal water: the high-temperature Jigoku water is basically of the sodium chloride type (150°C–300°F), the *Onsen* are mainly of a lower temperature bicarbonate type, and there is a sulphate type used mainly for the precipitation of sulphur and sulphates used in making mineral bath additives (Yusa & Ohsawa, 2000: 3006). This water has been estimated to be around 50,000 years old once it reaches the discharge areas in the city (Yusa & Ohsawa, 2000: 3006). The main uses of *Onsen* water other than for simple bathing are for the treatment of rheumatism and neuralgia (virtually all of the main *Onsen*), diabetes and 'female disorder' (not further defined – Beppu City Office, personal communication), with various skin diseases, gastroenteric disorder and 'weak body' also treated, as is common for bicarbonate springs around the world (see Chapter 2). It is likely that the potential for medical treatments will be more fully realised in the near future as the City Council has asked *Onsen* owners to explore this avenue.

The use of natural hot and mineral springs for health and well-being in China has a long tradition. The Chinese can provide written evidence (Schafer, 1956) that for thousands of years they have utilised thermal springs for multiple purposes including the use for therapeutical benefits as well as enjoying the pleasure of a hot spring bath during the cooler seasons. The *Yunnan* province for example has many hot springs and most of them have been known to the local residents who used the thermal waters for healing purposes or simply as a source of hot water (Šilar, 1968). In the Lintong District 30 km east of *Xian* the Huaqing Hot Springs were a preferred destination of the emperors of China [Huaqing, n.d.(c)] and the rediscovered ruins have been restored and redeveloped and are a major tourist attraction with the opportunity to take a thermal bath in the imitation Guifei pool in the new Huaqing Hot Spring development.

The Huaqing thermal pool with its natural springs today is a well-promoted destination, based on the fact that it is the place where emperors built their palaces as health and wellness resorts. Since ancient times, it has been a famous bathing and tourist destination with the design of the palace including the natural thermal waters to supply several hot pools inside the palace compound for members of the imperial court [Huaqing, n.d.(c)] and the Guifei or Hibiscus pool (built between 712 and 756 AD) has been restored and is now open for public viewing (since October 1990) along with a reproduction of the original fountainhead with a museum built on the remains of the Tang dynasty facilities. The hot springs can be used for a therapeutic bathing to treat a variety of diseases such as rheumatism, skin problems and arthritis (China Travel Experience, n.d.; Travel China Guide, 2008). In the year 2005 the Huaqing pool underwent extensions to add a lake to the Lotus Park [Huaqing, n.d.(c)].

Other hot and mineral springs of note in mainland China include *Guantang Thermal Spring* on Hainan Island and Zhuhai. In 1994, the China National Mineral Resource Storage Committee verified and approved thermal springs in the Guantang area of Hainan Island (Qionghai Tourist Guide, 2006). The verification noted that the Guantang thermal field spreads over on the south bank of the Wanquan River and is 9 km long, 1–1.7 km wide and covers 13 square kilometres. On the geothermal field 2.5 square kilometres in total are occupied by thermal springs. The characteristics of the hot spring are: the thermal water is between 52.5° and 74° (126–165°F), the daily flow amount is up to 10,700 ton and the hot water is rich in different minerals such as strontium, bromine (0.18–1.07 mg/1), iodine and lithium (0.0632–0.45 mg/1). Therefore, this spring complex may be used for medical treatment purposes, in line with the national standard *GB11615-89 Terrestrial Heat Resource Geographic Inspection Regulation* (http://www.wanquan-river.org/en/tguantang.html). In recent years an open-air indoor thermal spring swimming pool (2700 m^3) has been built in the Guantang Thermal Spring Recreation Center and is the largest in China.

Zhuhai City, located in the south of Guangdong Province on the west bank of the Pearl River facing Shenzhen and Hong Kong and bordering Macau, is 140 km from Guangzhou. Development of the *Zhuhai Marine Hot Springs Project* by China Travel Service (HK) Ltd and investment in other hot and mineral springs in this area to a total of 1–2 billion Yuan (USD121–242 million) are the cornerstone of an attempt by the city to build a high-status, elegantly designed tourist city (Zhuhai Daily, 20 February 2005). As a result, the area is recording rises of more than 35% in the number of visitors to the hot springs each year (to 3.5 million in 2004; Zhuhai Daily, 20 February 2005). Located in Pingsha Town, Jinwan District, *Zhuhai Hot Spring* is about 60 km away from the urban area of Zhuhai. It is a high-temperature ocean hot spring that can reach 83°C (181.4°F) and contains a large variety of minerals that are beneficial to health such as potassium, sodium, calcium, silicate and chlorine. Located in the village of Doumen, the *Imperial Hot Spring* is the first Japanese-style open-air hot spring complex in China. There are over 20 kinds of hot springs in this location and these are offered in garden-like lounges with independent indoor *Onsen* for guests. In addition, there are large sauna rooms and standard massage rooms and a four-star resort hotel. Located in the Lanpu area of the city, by the west side of New Yuan Ming Palace, *Chinese Medicine Valley* is divided into several areas with different functions. Here hydrotherapy and Chinese traditional medicated bathing and dining are offered in a distinctive Tang Dynasty palace style (Zhuhai Hot Springs, 2003).

Research by the Intelligent Spas Company of Singapore indicates that the health and wellness spa industry is growing quickly in China and the Hong Kong SAR (Intelligent Spas, 2008b). The total number of purpose-built health and wellness spas reached 190 in 2007, with the industry forecast to grow by 20% between 2008 and 2010. These spas attracted more than 2 million visitors as day spas (64%) and destination spas (36%), and contributed 6000 jobs and USD186 million in revenue. Although only a minor part of the enormous Chinese tourism industry (22 million international tourists and 1212 million domestic tourists in 2006 – Ministry of Public Security, 2007) to date, these and other locations form part of the long history of hot springs use in this country and are a firm basis for the continued development of its health and wellness spa industry.

Central Asia

The Central Asian Republics of the former Soviet Union, and Afghanistan and Iran make up this group of nations. In this section we have chosen to discuss the hot springs of the Islamic Republic of Iran that were the subject of a study and report in 2005 by the *Forum on Thermalism of Japan* for the Iran Culture, Heritage and Tourism Organisation, Tehran (permission to use this data was obtained from Mr Hamid Amini, Ministry of Culture and Tourism, September 2008).

Hot springs are utilised for tourist purposes and are found throughout Iran in upland areas. The 23 major locations studied in 2005 are given in Table 9.5. Most of the hot spring waters are collected in either the Elburz or Zagros Mountains (average elevation 1570 m) and derive from pressure gradients in the underlying rock strata. Many are small, often un-commercialised natural springs, but most have some form of built facility associated with the spring waters, some have histories spanning thousands of years and seven are major spa resort complexes dating from the end of the previous regime or earlier. A very small number of visitors actually use these resources (except for those at *Arshia* and *Geno*), but local people certainly do, and there is therefore significant room for expansion as international and domestic tourism becomes established in Iran once more.

South Asia

The South Asian subcontinent has large areas scattered with natural thermal springs; many of them at the foothills of the Himalaya Mountain range in the

Table 9.5 Characteristics of major hot springs in Iran, 2005

Hot springs in Iran

Spring	Location	Description	Temperature, pH, flow rate	Visitor numbers	Use
Arshia	Qazvin City	Segregated pools/changing rooms; 20 staff in summer, 10 in winter; massage services	50.5°C (122.9°F); pH 7.0; 180 l/min flow	1000/day winter; 2000/day summer	Rheumatism Neuralgia Circulation
Vantagh	Zanjyan City	Concrete pool, no buildings	40°C (104°F); pH 8.5; 200 l/min	Summer campers only	Bathing
Boston Abad	Bostan City	Several segregated pools; local government operated; 17 staff; new buildings	31.1°C (87.98°F); pH 7.0	60/day winter; 700/day summer (500 international)	Rheumatism Arthritis Neuralgia
Garmish	Sarein City	12 hot springs, *aquacure* complex; open 24 h summer	44°C (111.2°F); pH 6.2; 840 l/min	50–200/day winter; 1000/day summer	Circulation
Besh Bagjilar	Sarein City	Rebuilt 1995, owned public, operated private sector	36°C (96.8°F); pH 6.3; 600 l/min	Women 1.5 × men	Circulation Myalgia
General	Sarein City	Built by Russians after WWII; owned public, operated private sector; 6 staff	42.3°C (108.14°F); pH 6.2; 1200 l/min	100/day winter; 500/day summer	Circulation Myalgia
Semnan 1	Semnan City	Two hot springs; no fee; lodge accommodation	34.3°C (93.74°F); pH 7.2	N/A	Rheumatism
Semnan 2			24.8°C (76.64°F); pH 7.4; 140 l/min		Skin disease Neuralgia
Dehloran	Ahwaz City	4 hot springs with 1800 years of use; 3 staff; massage available (1USD/10 min)	38.5°C (1–1.3°F); pH 7.0; 1000 l/min	40–70/day winter 20–50/day summer Mainly male	Body warming Skin disease

		Facilities	Temperature; pH; flow	Flow	Indications
Gonabad (Ferdoos)	Dasht Kawir	1 thermal and 6 private baths; 70 staff; accommodation; mosque; restaurant, shops	44.3°C (111.74°F); pH 6.3; 100 l/min	N/A	Arthritis
Ziyarat-1	Golestan City Park	No spa facilities; used for drinking (piped to houses)	24.4°C (75.92°F); pH 7.5; 30 l/min	300/day to park	Drinking
Ziyarat-2	Gorgon	1 thermal pool, separate changing rooms; 50 y/s old	30.7°C (87.26°F); pH 7.5; 300 l/min	200/day summer	Skin diseases
Mahalat	Bam City	1300 years history; 30-year-old tourist spa complex; pools, private baths; 40 twin rooms; 5 springs; 20 staff	46.3°C (115.34°F); pH 7.1; 30 l/min	300/day summer; 10/day winter	Skin diseases Arthritis
Cham Galle	Yadz City	Covered by mudbrick dome 170 years ago; 1.5 m diameter pool; 2 lodges	26.5°C (79.7°F); pH 6.3	50/day summer	Arthritis Neuralgia Circulation
Siraj	Kerman City	8 m × 3 m pool beside the road; free; no buildings	46°C (114.8°F); pH 6.9; 100 l/min	500 total in spring only	Bathing
Bazman-1	Bam (4 h)	10 m × 10 m pool only	35.1°C (95.18°F); pH 7.96; 30 l/min	50/day	Bathing
Bazman-2	Iranshahr City	10 m diameter, 30 cm deep; NaCl spring	43.7°C (110.66°F); pH 8.4; 50 l/min	60/day	Arthritis Neuralgia Circulation
Dasht-E Azam	Bandar Abbas	3000 years history; spa facilities built 25 years ago; 2 staff; 2 pools 4 m × 3 m × 1.5 m deep, segregated; 4 lodges	41°C (105.8°F); pH 6.1; 55 l/min; High salinity (NaCl)	300/day	Arthritis Neuralgia Circulation Rheumatism
Geno	Bandar Abbas	6 springs; 1000 year history; hydrotherapy and tourist complex; mosque; hotel, restaurant; 30 staff	39.6°C (103.28°F); pH 6.55; 55 l/min; High salinity (NaCl)	3000–4000/day all seasons	Arthritis Rheumatism Neuralgia

Source: Forum on Thermalism of Japan.

north of India. The village of *Manikaran* on the banks of the Parbati River in the Kullu district of *Himachal Pradesh* State is for example investigating new ways of utilising the local geothermal resources for commercial spa purposes because presently the natural thermal springs are only used for ad hoc therapeutic purposes and for recreation (Chandrasekharam *et al.*, 2005) on a small scale. Similarly, in Pakistan research is being carried out on the fairly large number of hot springs in different parts of the country resulting from Quaternary volcanism (Zaigham, 2005). It is likely that the latter may have had significance to the Indus Valley Civilisation, given its considerable use of water as a community and perhaps religious resource (see Chapters 3 and 4).

Summary tourism data for the countries with geothermal resources for tourism on the South Asian subcontinent were for India in 2006, 4.5 million international visitors and 430 million domestic tourists; however, for Pakistan the totals were 898 thousand international visitors and 44.5 million domestic tourists in 2007 (CIA Factbook, 2008; UNWTO, 2008; World Bank, 2007; WTTC, 2008). Afghanistan is omitted as its tourism trade is basically non-existent at the time of writing due to war, and Bangladesh, Nepal and Bhutan do not contribute to this form of tourism. These data are indications only as consistent estimates of even basic tourism flows are difficult to obtain let alone hot springs use, data are missing and/or controlled by sources who charge considerable sums for data of unknown quality, and most are continuously and retrospectively modified as new information comes to light. The available data do however show that the South Asian subcontinent's attractiveness for international tourism (% of international visitor numbers) is very low compared with its proportion of the world's total population (0.1% and 22.7%, respectively); compared with China at 3% and 19.7%, or France with 8.3% and 1.1%, and we may expect that this is true of health and wellness-based tourism. Nevertheless, employment in the overall tourism industry is important at 15.5 million, and there are significant flows of both domestic and international tourists (but based mainly on river and cultural tourism) to particular sites in the region. International visitors are mainly from the Asia Pacific region or are intraregional to South Asia, although significant flows originate in Europe, mainly from countries like Germany and the United Kingdom. Domestic tourism is very large in India and Pakistan, made up primarily of religious pilgrims (based on water), and this latter pattern may be the case with Bangladesh but figures are not available at the time of writing for this or for health and wellness tourism.

Nevertheless, in India there is a growing *medical* health and wellness tourism market, with some minor use of spa facilities as adjuncts to medical treatments. The increasing number of patients travelling abroad from the United States and United Kingdom for example for specialised treatment and surgery is a key part of this market. In 2006 over 50,000 US citizens travelled abroad for the purpose of treatment. They went to India for spinal fusion at the cost of $5500 as against $62,000 in the United States or they went to Thailand for heart bypass surgery at the cost of $11,000 as against $130,000 in the United States (Globe Health Tours News, 2008). India's rich cultural history also affords many holistic forms of adjunct treatments such as ayurveda, yoga, siddha, unanni and other ancient treatment modules. South India, especially Kerala, has many ayurvedic medical spa resorts and meditation centres where Western medical tourists pay for health packages that include de-stressing, body toning, weight loss and healing of aches and pains like sinusitis and backaches. These treatments last for a period of 3–21 days and mostly involve herbal remedies with some minor medical treatments added. Costs in these centres are reasonable and the focus is on the healing of the body, mind and spirit. Such rejuvenation centres offer additional facilities like airport pick-up/drop, accommodation and food for their clients.

South East Asia

In South East Asia the Taiwanese consider hot springs as one of the most precious gifts that Earth has bestowed upon them (Lee & King, 2008). They call them 'the hot tears of the Earth' and it is very likely that people have used hot springs since ancient times for their rejuvenating and therapeutic properties. More than 130 hot springs have been discovered in Taiwan with the highest concentration found in the volcanic north [Taiwan Government Information Office, n.d.(a)]. Hot springs in Taiwan were first mentioned in a manuscript (*Beihai Jiyou*) in 1697 AD, but not developed until the Beitou hot springs were discovered in 1893–1894. During the Japanese colonial period they brought with them their own hot spring (*Onsen*) culture and built many hot spring spas that greatly influenced the Taiwanese thermal development [Taiwan Government Information Office, n.d.(a)]. But according to the Taiwanese Hot Spring Association the Japanese failed to realise the full extent of Taiwan's hot spring resources until after the war. However, they conducted significant research on hot springs while Taiwan was a part of the Japanese empire and this research data proved quite valuable for the later development of Taiwan's hot spring industry. Soon after 1945 the relatively short lived hot spring way of life went into decline with the remaining facilities either falling into disrepair or supported a red-light district (Taipei Journal, 2002). Not until the year 1999 did the authorities consider promoting Taiwan's hot springs again to provide health and wellness spa destinations for the tourism industry [Taiwan Government Information Office, n.d.(a); Taiwan Government Information Office, n.d.(b)].

Wulai is one of the northern hot spring centres along with Peitou and Yangmingshan, and when the wellness boom arrived in Taiwan these hot spring areas took this as a sign to start developing their natural resources without great delay. Wulai is said to have been settled centuries ago by the Atayal who were possibly the first people to have used the hot springs, as they gave it the name Wulai after *Kirofu-Ulai*, which apparently means 'hot and poisonous' [Taiwan Government Information Office, n.d.(c)]. In recent years Taiwanese hot spring resorts have increased in popularity and use their natural environment, local culture and history as well as the medical benefits to attract health and wellness tourists to the many hot spring spas that have been established.

But there is a question mark hanging over the use of at least one of the most popular hot springs sites, which illustrates the risk inherent in the use of such resources for health and wellness tourism: how safe is Taroko National Park's

Wunshan Hot Spring? (Taiwan News, 27 August 2007). Based on an assessment by the Chinese Institute of Environmental Engineering the grotto of the Wunshan Hot Spring area has a high probability of disastrous rockslides, which means massive rockslides may occur suddenly with a direct impact on the area. Therefore, without proper protection measures, it is a very dangerous place for tourists. This assessment analysed the Wuhan area and found that four sections should be designated 'dangerous', five sections 'unstable' and four sections 'stable'. Of these sections, the cliff above the hot spring itself is quartz-mica schist, which was given the highest danger rating. As for sections that are dangerous or unstable, the study urged that protection measures should focus on tourist safety and moreover that safety facilities should *effectively* protect tourists while allowing a clear view of scenery and not harming the ecology (Taiwan News, 27 August 2007). Under such circumstances, it is obvious that the National Park Headquarters could face a very difficult task in the management of tourist safety.

Taiwan attracted some 3.7 million international tourists in 2007, who spent over USD5.2 billion and stayed an average of 6.5 days in the country; and the major groupings were 44% for pleasure, 25% on Business and 11% to visit friends and relatives (96 年來臺旅客目的統計, 2008; Lee & King, 2008). Data from the same source show the total number of visitors to the principal scenic spots in Taiwan at 149Mn in 2007 (96 年臺閩地區主要觀光遊憩區遊客人次月別統計, 2008), with the listed hot springs in this group attracting 3,733,450 visitors (2.5%). While as yet small, this sector of tourism is experiencing a development boom fuelled by both domestic and international tourists, especially from Japan [Taiwan Government Information Office, n.d.(a)].

Hot springs in Thailand on the other hand are generally used to cook vegetables such as bamboo shoots and eggs, but may also be used for recreational and therapeutical bathing. It is this possibility that has been recognised recently by both the private sector as well as local communities, who are now promoting natural hot springs for health and wellness spa tourism (Raksaskulwong, 2000). New developments using hot springs are gaining in popularity and it is also now recognised that hot springs with extreme temperatures can also be used as visual attractions.

From *Sankampaeng* in the north to the *Ranong Hot Springs* and *Raksawarin Park Arboretum* in the south, Thailand has a number of springs available to visitors. Some are basic in their approach (simply pools of hot water), others have been turned into spas and health centres. Ranong's chief attractions include its hot springs and the Raksawarin Park Arboretum. Situated 2 km east of Ranong town, mineral water coming from the springs maintains a year-round temperature of 65°C (149°F). The waters have proven healing qualities and are often prescribed by local doctors as a form of treatment for rheumatism and similar physical problems (Thailand Travel Information, 2008). There are three main spring pools: the Father Pool, the Mother Pool and the Child Pool. The water from each of these springs is considered so pure that it was used during important ceremonies to celebrate the 60th Birthday of King Bhumibhol.

Located in Raksawarin Forest Park, Raksawarin Park Arboretum is a private health resort offering full health facilities and a range of package holidays. This location is the only Thai resort given permission to draw hot spring water for commercial purposes and is maintained by local authorities. The surroundings are suitable for picnics or for just relaxing. The spring water can also be experienced at Tapo Tharam Temple, a short distance from the resort. The temple provides free showers with hot and cold spring water although a donation is suggested (Thailand Travel Information, 2008).

The Thai medical profession is probably one of the most advanced in the Asia Pacific region, as successive governments have invested in ensuring that their education and training is at least parallel to that offered elsewhere. Thailand's hospitals and clinics are in fact world class (ISO 9001 accreditation). All this expertise and proficiency means that Thailand's hospitals are a secure option for those seeking low-cost medical treatment, and yoga, meditation, reiki and pranic healing are now becoming increasingly mainstream in Thailand. Herbal medicine and natural healing coupled with the highest standards of Western medicine and the availability of hot springs have meant that over the last few years Thailand has become the ideal place for a visitor to explore alternative approaches to the medicine available in their home countries (Travel Guide, 2008). ISPA (2008b) research shows that there are at the time of writing at least 585 health and wellness spas in Thailand, generating USD263 million from 3.6 million visitors and employing 11,240 people.

The Pacific

The other island nations of the Asia Pacific region do not seem to have a *tradition* of hot spring use in the sense of Japan, China, Taiwan, North and South America, New Zealand or European countries. However, the Fijian Islands for example have natural hot springs that are used by the locals for steaming vegetables (Savusavu Tourism Association, n.d.) and have hotels named after them (Hot Springs Hotel, 2008), but they are not utilised for health and wellness spas. The Philippines on the other hand include their geothermal springs, including the famous *Hidden Valley Springs* (Laguna Hotspring Resort Philippines, n.d.; Tanko, 1999; WOW Philippines, n.d.), when promoting the attractions of individual regions of their islands. They may not be highly developed as yet but that seems to add to the attraction of a quiet natural environment without great crowds of people (Fabulous Philippines, 2008). Nevertheless, the Philippines does have thermal activity consisting of active volcanoes and hot springs. *Maquinit Hot Springs*, located on a scenic beach in Palawan, Luzon, is the premium hot spring in the Philippines, while thermal exploration following the 1991 eruption indicated that *Mt. Pinatubo* hosted a hydrothermal system that today manifests hot springs at varying degrees of temperature. Some of these are the thermal springs along the *Sacobia River* in Sitio Puning where temperatures range from 40°C to 70°C (104–158°F). Scientific testing indicates a neutral 7.5 pH level and zero coliforms for these hot springs – all attesting to the quality of the water. Cold mineral springs may also be found in close proximity to the hot ones.

The hot springs and their associated landscapes have been adopted by the Philippines Department of Tourism for the purpose of building a better quality of life for local people affected by eruptions of Mt Pinatubo through travel and tourism. The *Kabuhayan sa Turismo* Ecotourism Program is designed to create jobs and livelihood for the more than 400 indigenous households whose economic well-being was drastically compromised following the volcanic eruptions of 1991 (Department of Tourism, Philippines, 2007). Basic income from the program comes in the form of contributions from local and foreign visitors through conservation fees, guide fees and payment for services such as hot springs use, the use of 4 × 4 vehicles or for the sale of souvenir items. For example, as part of this project the Puning hot springs location along the Sacobia River incorporates a restaurant, volcanic sand pool, bar, five hot spring pools, one plain bathing pool, mud pack treatment rooms, a mini store, cottages, and restrooms (Department of Tourism, Philippines, 2007).

Through focused marketing and the carving out of new niches such as the combination of hot springs and health and wellness, 3 million foreign tourists visited the Philippines in 2007, a rise of almost 20% on the year before. This has continued the reversal of the decline in arrivals that lasted from 1997 to 2003. The country is now on its way to reaching the government's goal of five million visitors by 2010. In 2007 domestic (16.8 million) and international tourists contributed nearly USD5 billion to the Philippine economy, 40% more than in 2006 (Department of Tourism, Philippines, 2008). A shift in strategy from concentrating on Western markets to paying more attention to Asia Pacific markets has yielded dividends in the international sphere. As a result there has been a sharp growth in visitors from South Korea and China, with South Korea in 2007 overtaking the US as the top market. The other top markets included Japan at number three, followed by China, Australia, Taiwan, Hong Kong, Singapore, Canada and the UK. Noticeably mainland Chinese arrivals rose 18% in 2007 over 2006, with Scandinavian and Indian visitors also showing double-digit gains.

Indonesia is a highly volcanic archipelago and, as is noted on *Wikipedia* and in most guidebooks, must consequently have hot springs (*air panas*) in many locations; but in fact few are developed or used to support tourism (Wikitravel, 2008). The Island of Bali is the most popular hot spring destination in the archipelago, but many of the springs found there are considered holy and have been developed into temples, where the locals come to bathe (fully clothed) but foreigners are generally not welcome. A few, however, have been developed and are open to all, such as *Air Banjar* near Lovina Beach where stone mouth carvings allow hot water to pass between pools which are set among a lush tropical garden. Another set are near Bandung's (Central Java) *Tangkuban Perahu* Volcano and include *Ciater Hot Spring*, which is a park with small pools in which visitors can sit or swim, and the *Sari Ater Hot Spring Resort* among other thermal resources. Warm mineral water pools are the attraction, said to be good for healing skin problems as the water contains iodine and sulphur. The resort provides visitors with a bar, restaurants, tennis courts and cottage-style hotels.

New Zealand has traditionally used the thermal resources widely available throughout the North Island and to a lesser degree in the South Island for tourism promotion, tourist use (including medical tourism in Rotorua) and for domestic energy sources (Jackson, 2003; McClure, 2004; Rockel, 1986; Young, 1998). A large part of tourism promotion includes marketing geothermal waters either for bathing, beauty and relaxation or when these are extreme hot springs, as visual attractions, and New Zealand does not appear to have suffered as much as some other countries from a decline in the use of thermal facilities related to medical health benefits changes (Chapter 2). Many thermal resorts have been modernised to keep up with health and safety expectations and expanded to attract more visitors, and due to the fact that the tourist in New Zealand is constrained to indulge mainly in nature/culture-based tourist activities, visits to thermal spas and geo parks with geysers and bubbling mud pools are definite must-see and must-do items on the agenda. The trend to natural environments for thermal spa facilities in New Zealand also extends to the design of outdoor hot spring pools, which are created to blend in with the landscape; especially in facilities developed with an *Onsen* theme in mind as at *Maruia Springs Resort* in the South Island, owned and operated by Japanese investors (see Figure 9.4).

The premier geothermal resort city of *Rotorua* is our case study. The New Zealand Ministry of Tourism estimates that there were 2.9 million visitor arrivals to Rotorua in 2007, a city of some 70,000, comprised of 1.5 million overnight

Figure 9.4 Maruia Springs Resort, South Island, New Zealand is built in the style of a Japanese *Onsen* resort, with bathhouses separate for men and women, but also with private pools for individual use
Source: Photograph courtesy of P. Erfurt-Cooper.

visitors (at an average stay of 2.3 nights) and 1.4 million day visitors, who collectively are estimated to have spent some NZ484 million during their stay in Rotorua.
This level of impact means that tourism contributes around 12% of economic activity and is third after forestry (16%) and manufacturing (14%). The industry provides an estimated 7000+ full-time equivalent jobs in the Rotorua district, which is
equivalent to 25% of the city's total workforce and ranks the tourism industry as
the largest employer. Direct employment in the tourism industry accounts for
approximately 20% of the total district workforce, and a further 5% of the total
workforce are indirectly employed in the tourism industry by virtue of having jobs
that are dependent on it. It is unlikely that businesses servicing the tourism industry, such as food wholesalers, would exist in Rotorua if the tourism industry was
not present (APR Consultants, 2004: 42).

Tourism has been a major focus of the Rotorua community since the 1830s
when the first Europeans arrived in Rotorua and Maori recognised the economic
opportunities from hosting these European visitors in their homes, guiding
them around the natural (mainly geothermal) attractions and entertaining them
with cultural performances. In 1908 the New Zealand government celebrated
its first major tourism investment with the opening of the Tudor-style Bath
House in Rotorua (Chapter 3 and Figure 4.8). Known as the *Great South Seas Spa*,
this building was administered by the Department of Tourist and Health Resorts
until 1947 when all spa treatments were transferred to the Queen Elizabeth
Hospital as part of treatment for returning WWII soldiers. Today it has been
restored and houses Rotorua's Art and History Museum, with exhibits detailing
its central role in the area's health and wellness spa history. Thus, geothermal
attractions and associated experiences have been and are an important part of
the Rotorua tourism industry, with 45.5% of all visitors at the present day making use of the thermal pools in the district and at least 30% using purpose-built
health and wellness spas. However, the range of tourism products has been
greatly increased in recent years to include further dimensions of Maori culture
and history (*Tamaki Maori Village*), ecological and agriculture-related tourism,
lake and helicopter tours, and more recently adventure products such as the
luge, white-water rafting, parachuting, volcano helicopter rides and bungy-
jumping ventures.

Australia is a land of contrast, not just when it comes to extreme landscape features and climate conditions, but also in its contrasts to other regions of the world
where similar natural resources are used by humans. As a nation with a slightly
casual attitude the use of thermal springs is not regulated by strict legislation nor
even especially important enough to be recognised as a valuable resource, especially not in the central and northern parts of the country. Although there are many
natural hot springs in Australia, due to the vastness of the country and the generally undeveloped nature of areas outside the cities most of them are only reached
after days of driving through the outback, and usually there are no facilities such
as showers and change rooms available. These hot springs are for the very determined who do not mind driving long distances and camping in the desert or at
one of the isolated campsites near small settlements.

Figure 9.5 Thermal springs in Katherine, Northern Territory, Australia
Source: Photograph courtesy of P. Erfurt-Cooper.

The thermal pools of *Mataranka* (Northern Territory) for example are located in the Northern rainforest belt 100 km south of Katherine and are relatively underdeveloped. They have over the years been made accessible via a raised boardwalk and a paved area around the main bathing area, but there are few other facilities. There always seem to be people in the pool however, and it is a very casual event – a far cry from the elegant thermal spa baths in European countries, but nevertheless frequented by many visitors from other continents, who are passing through the area (personal observation and communication). The town of Katherine not far from Mataranka also has natural thermal springs, popular with the locals, but if visitors persist in trying to locate them they are worth seeing and experiencing. Again, these geothermal resources have no comparison to spa facilities elsewhere, but the unique natural setting adds to the distinctiveness of the thermal stream and the atmosphere. Children love the thermal water and indulge in making mud packs, which they put on their skin because they like the feeling (personal observation, see Figure 9.5).

Peninsula Hot Springs Resort

On the Mornington Peninsula southwest of Melbourne in the State of Victoria, Mr Charles Davidson, founder of the *Peninsula Hot Springs Resort*, was inspired and motivated by the pleasures of *Onsen* bathing while in Japan during 1992. From this time he and his brother Richard were determined to open similar hot spring facilities in Australia (Svart, 2006). After eight stressful years of 'perseverance and determination' while drilling for natural hot water and building the Peninsula Hot Springs Centre it finally opened on 28 June 2005 (Figure 9.6), and is the only genuine hot spring spa in Victoria (Webb, 2005). The Mornington Peninsula has been accredited by UNESCO as the world's first 'Urban Biosphere' and the education on the possibilities of a sustainable future with geothermal is according to Davidson (2003) more than a responsible activity; it is a community expectation. Information published on the internet by Peninsula Hot Springs (n.d.) explains that their mineral water is so pure that it was officially classified as suitable for drinking as well as bathing (Table 9.6).

The facilities are located on 17 hectares of revegetated farmland located in the Cups region near Rye Ocean Beach approximately 2 hr drive southwest from Melbourne. Stage one comprises a multi-purpose building housing change rooms, cafeteria and offices, with associated wellness spa building offering Maori, Japanese, Thai, Indian and Arabic health treatments as a *Day Spa*. The pools are open air apart from one indoor thermal basin and range in temperature from 30°C to 42°C (86–107.6°F), derived from a Bicarbonate spring delivering water to the surface at 50°C (122°F) from 637 m depth by natural pressure. The Centre employs a staff of 85 to service approximately 100,000 visitors at present, with a projected final development clientele of 500,000 and 105 employees within three years (Charles Davidson, personal communication, 10 August 2008). The owners previously operated a cold water bathing facility, the *Mizu* Spa not far from the new Peninsula Hot Spring.

In the hot spring baths, the water runs direct from the source to the pool. It enters each pool at one end and flows in a continual stream to the other end and out to the ocean in Bass Strait. There is no re-circulation and the total volume of water in each pool is replaced at least every 4 hrs. Overnight all pools are emptied, cleaned, sterilised and refilled. The geothermal water contains a total of 3836 ppm (parts per million) of dissolved minerals (Table 9.6). The primary mineral groups include bicarbonate, magnesium, potassium and sodium with good levels of calcium, boron, selenium, as well as several key trace minerals, also present in the water. The sulphur content of the natural hot spring gives the water a distinctive smell.

(1) Health benefits

The water is classified as a 'Sodium Chloride Bicarbonate Spring' (Na-Cl.HCO$_3$). According to the Japanese Environmental Agency, the therapeutic benefits of bathing in this type of thermal mineral spring are said to include the alleviation of neuralgia, bruising, breaks, articular rheumatism, stiffness of the shoulders, skin diseases, recovery from fatigue and muscular complaints. It also assists fertility.

(2) Stage Two

Stage two will include an increased capacity for 'social' public bathing parallel with the private day spa 'sanctuary' experience. Ultimately the complex will include simulated river cascades, pools, 126 accommodation units and healing centres, and will be layered from noisy to quiet areas so that both wellness clients and social bathers gain maximum benefits. Children will be admitted for the first

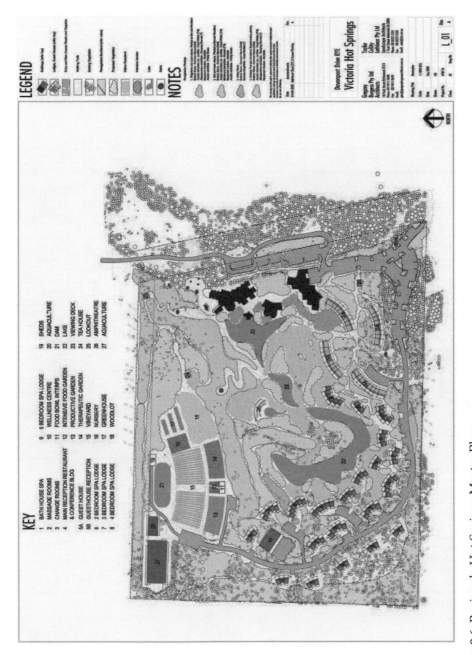

Figure 9.6 Peninsula Hot Springs Master Plan
Source: Charles Davidson (2008).

Table 9.6 Analytical results for Peninsula Hot Springs geothermal water

Analytical category	Unit	Amount
pH value	pH units	6.82
Total dissolved solids (TDS)	mg/l	3836
Total hardness as CaCO$_3$	mg/l	705
Langelier index	mg/l	0.34
Calcium	mg/l	116
Bicarbonate	mg/l	1163
Magnesium	mg/l	90
Sodium	mg/l	868
Potassium	mg/l	64
Alkalinity as CaCO$_3$	mg/l	714
Sulphate	mg/l	20
Chloride	mg/l	1432
Iron	mg/l	<0.1
Fluoride	mg/l	0.73
Lithium	mg/l	0.15
Silica (as SiO$_2$)	mg/l	23
Manganese filtered	mg/l	0.08
Ammonia as NH$_3$	mg/l	2.7
Nitrate as N	mg/l	0.03
Zinc	mg/l	0.038
Rubidium	µg/l	0.14
Tellurium	µg/l	0.238
Selenium	µg/l	71
Total cations	me/l	49.22
Total anions	me/l	44.32
Actual (anion/cation) difference	me/l	4.9

Source: Peninsula Hot Springs (n.d.)

time once Stage Two is built at the end of 2008. Among the interesting design features of the new public bathing area are aspects that enhance the idea of 'the spa
as a social hub' borrowed from the Roman, Japanese and many other cultures' use
of hot springs bathing as a forum for a swap of ideas, friendly banter and a place

to relax with friends (Charles Davidson, personal communication). There will be dedicated family bathing pools for young children to share relaxing time with their parents, while wellness clients will be able to take advantage of a mid-level foyer that is very much designed as a 'casual' relaxation area with a new range of treatments that do not require the full Day Spa experience, including neck and shoulder massages, foot massages and the like. This area will very much be a place encouraging the social element of a hot springs experience.

(3)   Stage Three

The total site is 17 hectares (42 acres) and will be home to accommodation, and a Wellness (Health and Well-being) Centre that will offer health services and a European and Asian mix of styles where one 'takes the healing waters' in a 'natural setting'. Health programmes will see visitors staying for extended periods from a few days to a few weeks in length (Davidson, 2003). Walking tracks around the property will lead people to lakeside and hilltop relaxation areas. There will be private lodges for couples, friends and groups of up to 14 as well as guest houses with double rooms and a capacity of 30. The lodges will include their own gardens and private outdoor hot spring landscaped baths, lounges with open fires and couches. Ecologically sustainable programmes including the hydronic heating of buildings, green houses and the heating of the waters of the fish farm will provide a living example of what is possible with geothermal waters (Davidson, 2003). The Peninsula Hot Springs Centre is a development that has grown from the environment and one with a will to respect, learn from and share with the environment (Davidson, 2003) and guests will ultimately come for short luxurious getaway stays and for weeklong wellness programmes (Figure 9.6).

The hot and mineral springs of the Mornington Peninsula are not the only popular spa destinations in Australia; the spa town of *Moree* in northern New South Wales attracts many visitors every year who come to these natural hot spring pools for their therapeutic benefits. Residents with a European background from the greater Sydney area use the Moree thermal pools as domestic tourists to maintain their health and well-being for example, because they remember this from their home countries (personal observation). The pools are also known for their healing power and around 300,000 visitors annually indicate the popularity of the natural thermal springs (Moree Plains Shire Council, 2004).

The Americas

United States and Canada

The United States has vast numbers of hot springs (Lund, 2000b; NGDC, 2007) that are appreciated alike by connoisseurs of thermal bathing, local people with a preference for natural environments and many tourists who place some kind of geothermal manifestation on their trip agenda. Thermal spas and resorts today are important for health and wellness, but are not exclusively reliant on geothermal resources. If natural hot springs are available at a resort or spa they are an added bonus, but often the reproductions of natural landscape features offer water facilities that look natural but are chemically treated and artificially heated. This is quite common worldwide as the consumer decides on visitation by consulting promotional websites, brochures or guide books not generally through personal experience; if they like what they see and if they are not determined to seek thermal treatments using *authentic* natural hot and mineral springs, they will make decisions based on the advertising appeal of the attractions, not on the actual state of water elements. The health and wellness spa literature offers a variety of general literature about spa-related destinations within the United States, with many of the natural hot spring areas being covered in guide books of individual regions. Health and wellness spas with thermal facilities on the other hand are often less noticeable because of the greater fixation of American consumers on cosmetic and fitness results rather than therapeutic value and recovery from illness, although they are generally included in books about (a) particular areas, (b) hotels, resorts and spas, (c) historical architecture or (d) special interest destinations. This is in direct contrast to countries, especially in Europe, where thermal spas are much more visible, enjoy quite a prestigious reputation and are largely accepted as medical facilities.

The US National Geophysical Data Center lists 1661 hot springs as at August 2007 (NGDC, 2007), along with their location, 'popular' or US Geological service spring name, surface temperature and descriptions (if any) in USGS Professional Papers/Circulars. This data source is very comprehensive, and in correlation with the coffee-table or general descriptions mentioned earlier (Chapters 2 and 8) it means that background knowledge of hot spring resources is comprehensive in the United States. Nevertheless, official tourism statistics do not often differentiate health and wellness tourism based on hot and mineral springs from other forms and it is left to industry sources to estimate the size and characteristics of this segment of the tourism market. The United States received 56 million international visitors from 213 countries during 2007, up 10% from 2006 (US Department of Commerce, 2008). Domestic tourists contributed some 593 billion dollars to the economy, and the total of inbound/outbound and domestic tourism supported 8.5 million jobs in 2006 (Mattingly & Griffith, 2008). Within this, data from the ISPA Consumer Trends Report (Barry, 2008) show that 32 million US tourists had been to a spa in 2006, but that only slightly more than 10% treated spas as part of a wider *health and wellness lifestyle* rather than as an indulgent habit. The most popular spa services in the United States are as a result day spa-based massage and similar 'beauty therapy' treatments, with hydrotherapy treatments at mineral springs spas used by only 13% of visitors (4.2 million), and medical spas by 12% (3.9 million). It is therefore apparent that the US health and wellness spa market does not use the country's available hot and mineral springs resources in the (bathing, medical) way that the Japanese and European markets do, although this pattern varies by location and the more famous hot springs mentioned earlier in this book are experiencing a revival in use based upon these alternatives.

The Banff and Jasper National Parks in Alberta and the Kootenay National Park in British Columbia, *Canada* all have natural thermal springs, which have been used for bathing and relaxing by visitors since their discovery by Europeans between the mid 19th century and the early 20th century. National Parks in Canada attract many visitors and if there are associated hot springs they are among the greatest attractions the parks have to offer. Some hot springs such as the *Radium Hot Springs* (Kootenay National Park) and the *Upper Hot Springs* (Banff National Park) are open all year, but the *Miette Hot Springs* (Jasper National Park) are seasonal and only open from spring to autumn (Parks Canada, 2008). Interestingly though Canadian spa-goers appear to favour off-shore experiences as only 45% visited Canadian spa resorts in 2006 (68% of US spa-goers used domestic spas), compared with 39% who went to Mexico/Caribbean spas, 30% who favoured US spas, 24% who went to Europe for this experience and 12% who travelled to Asia (Barry, 2008). This may reflect a wider spa-type use pattern by Canadian health and wellness tourists than their US colleagues given the very different European and Asian wellness and bathing traditions.

In 2007 Canada attracted some 17.8 million overnight trips from international tourism markets, of which 76.5% came from the United States and Mexico. Domestic tourists totalled approximately 81 million. The total demand in the economy from tourism was CAN70.8 billion, made up of 54.6 billion from domestic travel and 16.2 billion from international visitors, and employment in the sector totalled 653,000 (Canadian Tourist Commission, 2008). Within this pattern of total tourism demand the Canadian health and wellness spa industry generated just over 1 billion in revenues from 14 million visits to some 2300 locations (not all hot or mineral springs based). Day spas account for 75% of the facilities available, and are mainly concentrated in the cities of Ontario, British Columbia and Quebec, indicating an industry profile similar to that of the United States. The industry in Canada employed around 26,000 as at March 2006 (Association Resource Centre, 2006).

This research by the Association Resource Centre has also identified the proportion of Canadian spa facilities dependent on tourism, an important statistic in our efforts to analyse this US beauty therapy-based tradition in relation to the others that show more a direct relationship with hot and mineral springs. In the Canadian version no more than 33% of all spas qualify as being tourism oriented (Association Resource Centre, 2006: ii–iii). Canadian 'spas' rely on tourists for only 29% of visits and 25% of revenues, and direct only 20% of their marketing efforts towards them. Thus, while resort/hotel spas certainly understand the importance of tourists in the Canadian as in any market, there is great untapped potential for 'beauty therapy' based spa traditions to tap into the wider tourism market.

Central America

Many countries in Central America use their geothermal springs for health and wellness spas and combine this with the overall trend to visit their countries to see unique natural environments. *Cuba* offers thermal tourism for people interested to try natural ways of gaining better health away from home, with developments over the last 10 years of existing thermal spas to ensure that tourists have a healthy experience (Sainsbury, 2006: 214). Specialised clinics and comfortable hospitals equipped with sophisticated technology and operated by highly skilled staff have

also successfully introduced health-oriented tourism in Cuba, which is also promoted as a quiet and safe place to take time out (Ministry of Foreign Affairs of the
Republic of Cuba, 2005). Natural resources are a fantastic draw card for many
countries that have missed out on tourism so far. Discovering the value of geothermal springs has been the foundation for economic success in some areas otherwise
deprived of tourist attractions.

St. Lucia belongs to a group of islands forming the volcanic island arc of the
Lesser Antilles in the Caribbean. Natural hot springs have been used in the past by
the local population and the first thermal baths were built by King Louis XVI (St.
Lucia, 2007) who noticed the similarity of the mineral content to the thermal waters
of Germany and France (Dabrowska, 2004). Some of the original baths have been
re-established under private ownership and a further large restoration project is
planned to preserve the historical value of these ancient thermal baths (St. Lucia,
2007). At this point in time it is mainly the local residents who use the natural hot
springs pools and the small waterfall within them. The water has high iron oxide
content and has a reputation of being beneficial in the treatment of eczema, rheumatism, arthritis, gout and sunburn while the mud on the bottom of the pool is
used for therapeutic mud treatments because its rich zinc, iron and sulphur contents. The redeveloped baths are more modern with water temperatures higher
than the natural hot springs used by the locals; however, the colour of the water is
almost black and may stain clothes and other materials (Register, 2008b).

South America

South American countries are blessed with natural hot springs as a result of the
continent's highly volcanic topography related to the Pacific 'Ring of Fire'
(Rosenberg, 2007). Numerous active and dormant volcanoes are scattered over
several countries, mainly bordering the Andes mountain chain. Most of the natural hot and mineral springs are popular with the locals, but in recent times more
international visitors are discovering the attractions of thermal bathing.

Many regions of *Argentina* are abundant with thermal springs which surface naturally along the *Cordillera de los Andes*. Thermal spas exist or are developing also in
non-volcanic areas such as *Entre Ríos*, *Buenos Aires* and the *Chaco* (Leitner, 2001: 27).
However, access to a large number of hot springs in Argentina is seasonal and some
can only be reached by 4WD vehicles. Others can only be reached via hiking trails or
climbing mountain sides and are located in as yet unspoilt natural settings or else on
private properties with no public access. In the *Catamarca* province for example are
hundreds of hot springs, most of them with therapeutic properties but with very few
tourist facilities. Several thermal springs have names which indicate a patron saint
(*Aguaditas de San José*, *Aguas de Dionisio*) and thus suggest a history of either cultural/
religious use or therapeutic use by members of a religious order (see Chapter 3).

Uruguay has also rich thermal water resources and has subsequently developed
thermal aquatic centres with their main purpose being to cater for leisure and recreational tourism. The *Parque Acuático Acuamanía* in Salto, which is fed by natural
hot spring water, is an example for aquatic entertainment for the whole family.

However, the health tourism side is catered for as well as the thermal facilities employ qualified medical staff who are trained to apply preventive as well as curative balneological treatment as well as hydrotherapy (Salto Uruguay, n.d.). The successful spa industry in Uruguay has also led to the proposal of similar developments on the Argentinean side of the Uruguay River. After successful drilling for thermal water the first thermal spa in the northeast of Argentina was opened in 1997. Other thermal wells were drilled and more are planned on both sides of the Uruguay River (Pesce, 2002).

The joint thermal resource lies within what is known as the *Guarani Aquifer System*, discovered and mapped some 60 years ago during oil exploration programmes (Pesce, 2002: 22), but during the last six years the commercial exploitation of thermal (30–50°C/86–122°F) aquifers along the Argentine and Uruguayan sides of the Uruguay River has grown significantly. The establishment of therapeutic and recreational facilities such as *Chajarí, Federación, Concordia, Villa Elisa* and *Colón* in Argentina, and *Arapey, Daymán, Guaviyú* and *Almirón* in Uruguay contributes considerably to the local economy through health and wellness spa tourism. The geothermal resources are low-temperature and are found in a volcanic-sedimentary basin. Three thermal aquifers with large potential (only with responsible management and a focus on resource sustainability) for direct geothermal applications have been identified, and the wells supplying spa water produce from different levels of the aquifer depending on location.

The lower aquifer is exploited at Almirón in Uruguay and at Villa Elisa in Argentina and is quite saline, while the middle and most important thermal aquifer is in Lower Triassic to Lower Jurassic sedimentary rocks and is of low salinity. The spas at Chajarí, Federación, Concordia, Arapey, Dayma and Guaviyú tap into this aquifer. The upper aquifer is located within sedimentary rock layers interspersed with thick basaltic flows, particularly toward the bottom. The spa at Colón extracts water from this low salinity water bearing unit. In the mid-1990s a number of investors, witnessing the successful spa industry in Uruguay, proposed similar developments on the Argentine side of the Uruguay River. This led to the drilling of the 1260-m-deep *Federación* well, which produced water at a temperature of 43°C (109.4°F) and the opening of the first thermal spa in Northeastern Argentina in January 1997, with others also drilled at *Concordia, Colón* and *Villa Elisa*. All the thermal wells on both sides of the Uruguay River are flowing artesian wells (Pesce, 2002: 27), and the opening up of the geothermal resource has since led to a very rapid increase in both visitor numbers and tourist facilities. The growth of economic activity is made obvious by the increase in the number of hotel beds in towns having spas, and a drop in local unemployment from 25% to 7%. For example, at Federación the number of hotel beds went from 182 in 1994 to 2150 in 2001 (Pesce, 2002: 28).

Like many other South American countries *Brazil* has numerous thermal spring areas which are used for health, wellness and leisure tourism as well as for geotourism. It is commonly understood that these hot springs were used long before the European invasions of the South American countries, but the first written references about thermal waters of the (region in the state of Goiás were made in 1545 AD in Spain [Chapter 3; Caldas Novas, n.d.(a)]. Today, the hot springs and the volcanic environment of Caldas Novas are one of the most important tourist attractions of the region, drawing increasing numbers of international visitors with more than 80 hotels (Rodrigues, n.d.). Eighty-six active wells are producing an average of 1200 m³ an hour at temperatures between 34 and 57°C (93.2 and 134.6°F). Other thermal establishments in Brazil are the *Rio Quente Resorts* (over 1 million tourists a year), the *Parques das Fontes* and the *Costão do Santinho Spa* in Florianopolis, European treatment methods are used (Brazil Spas, n.d.). Thermal mineral resorts also exist in all parts of the Brazilian State of Santa Catarina with *Gravatal, Tubarão, Santo Amaro da Imperatriz, Águas Mornas, Treze Tílias* and *Piratuba* as the most popular ones. *Balneário Camboriú* is the preferred destination for third age tourists due to its excellent infrastructure (Santa Catarina Brazil, n.d.).

Peru features over 500 locations where visitors can enjoy the benefits of thermal baths in the hot springs which are equated with good health due to their mineral content. Most hot springs in Peru appear to be ideal for easing aches and pains as well as being a place to relax for tourists. The Incas of Perú enjoyed the great number of hot springs scattered throughout Peruvian territory for medicinal purposes as far back as the 15th century (Prazak, n.d.). The recently refurbished thermal springs of *Aguas Calientes* (Machu Picchu Pueblo), also in Perú are believed to possess curative powers and offer several pools of varying size and temperature to the health seeking tourist (Hamre, n.d.).

Chile recognises 270 thermal sources, mainly concentrated in the central area along the *Liquiñe-Ofqui* Fault. These coincide with the most developed area of the country in terms of tourist facilities, having a high density of hotels and resorts as well as hot springs. Over 2.3 million international tourists visited Chile in 2006 and most stayed in the central region, which leads to the assumption that the hot springs were well-patronised, although accurate statistics do not exist. The main usage of these geothermal resources appears to be in form of energy generation, mineral waters to drink, thermal mud applications, bathing, sauna, with some medical tourism packages available (Turismo Chile, 2007).

The Arctic and Antarctic

The countries in the cooler regions on our planet are also not without natural hot springs; perhaps as a compensation for the sometimes quite unhospitable climate! It may come as a surprise for many people to learn that the Arctic and Antarctic regions of the world do have hot springs, with Iceland and Alaska often quoted as examples of the establishment of a successful tourism industry based on hot spring spa tourism for health and wellness.

Iceland and Greenland

Iceland's biggest draw card is its uniqueness as a creation of massive volcanic outpourings from the Mid-Atlantic Ridge, and in terms of attractions for hot spring visitors it is at the top of the list. But it is not for the fainthearted by any means; travelling to Iceland's many hot springs can mean a major adventure trip. To get to

Landmannalaugur for example, a main tourist destination in the south of Iceland the right form of transport (4WD) is essential, and drivers should preferably have some experience in off-road driving combined with the ability to judge the depth of fast-flowing rivers and streams which need crossing en route. Nevertheless, when arriving at Landmannalaugur, ostensibly in the 'middle of nowhere', the place can be crowded with tour busses, cars, tents and hikers – never mind the weather conditions. The lack of sophisticated and heated facilities directly next to the natural hot spring pools does not seem to be a serious deterrent; heated change rooms are within walking distance and entering this unique hot spring is a serious achievement for many visitors (personal observation).

Due to the abundance of Iceland's geothermal resources hot springs have been widely used for tourism, domestic and industrial purposes at least since the beginning of the 20th century (though see Chapter 3). Thermal swimming pools sourced from hot spring water have been constructed in just about every town for the benefit of the population as well as for visiting tourists. The most widely known geothermal attraction for human use is the popular *Blue Lagoon* on the Reykjanes Peninsula near Keflavik International Airport; an absolute 'must-see-and-do experience' on the Iceland tourist agenda (see Figure 2.1). However, these days this extraordinary hot spring 'Lagoon' is often too crowded to enjoy thoroughly, especially during the peak tourist season in summer. The Blue Lagoon was originally (and artificially) created from waste water pumped out by the Svartsengi power station, which was built in the year 1976. Following the increasing use of the warm waters of the 'lagoon' by the local population the first spa facilities were developed and subsequently needed to be extended because of their rapidly growing popularity with international as well as local users.

The Blue Lagoon's facilities are famous worldwide as one of Iceland's most unique and popular attractions where guests can enjoy bathing and relaxing in geothermal seawater, and obtain benefits from its positive effects for the skin at the same time. A visit to the spa is promoted as 'harmony between body, mind and spirit, and enables one to soak away the stresses of modern life … the spa's guests rekindle their relationship with nature, soak up the scenic beauty and enjoy breathing the clean, fresh air' (Blue Lagoon Iceland, n.d: Accessed November 2008). Sauna access with views over the lagoon, steam baths, a warm massaging waterfall and the famous white silica mud are essential parts of the Blue Lagoon experience. Special water spa treatments and massages, combined with fresh air and natural surroundings increase the well-being of the guests (Blue Lagoon Iceland, n.d.).

Another important part of the Blue Lagoon is the Health Clinic with special treatment for *psoriasis* sufferers based on bathing in the geothermal seawater and using its active ingredients such as minerals, silica and algae for their positive effects on the skin. This natural treatment is classed as unique in the world, has no side effects and is scientifically verified in cooperation with Icelandic Health Authorities as an effective complementary part together with other skin treatment options. The Icelandic Social Insurance Scheme recognises the benefits of thermal treatment at the Blue Lagoon and Icelandic patients have their treatment costs covered (Blue Lagoon Iceland, n.d.).

In the north-east of Iceland the *Mývatn Nature Baths* (Jarðböðin við Mývatn) are a must-go destination for connoisseurs of natural hot springs in a unique landscape. In a similar fashion to the original Blue Lagoon in the south-west of Iceland, the Mývatn Nature Baths are also using wastewater from a nearby geothermal power station. The popularity of the Blue Lagoon with international and domestic tourists was an encouraging factor when a similar facility near Lake Mývatn was proposed. The Mývatn Nature Baths presently consist of a large lagoon (5000 m²) of warm, soothing geothermal water, which is 'beneficial to skin and spirit alike', a natural steam bath, hotpots and relaxation areas and was officially opened in June 2004 (Mývatn Nature Baths, 2008).

The water supply for the lagoon, which is a manmade construction with a bottom of sand and gravel, comes directly from the National Power Company's bore hole in *Bjarnarflag* at a temperature of about 130°C (266°F). A heat exchanger cools the water down to a more acceptable temperature and it is then directed into a large holding basin beside the lagoon where it forms an impressive hot spring lake. From here the water is fed into the Nature Baths for people to enjoy at a pleasant temperature. Together, the lagoon and the holding basin contain approximately 3.5 million litres of water at temperatures between 36–40°C (96.8–104°F). Like the Blue Lagoon (Figure 2.1) the Mývatn Nature Baths contain large amounts of beneficial minerals with alkaline water which is classed as ideal for bathing (Figure 9.7). Due to the chemical composition of the water, no harmful bacteria and vegetation can thrive in the lagoon, which makes the addition disinfecting chemicals unnecessary (Nordic Adventure Travel, 2008).

The visitor numbers for the Mývatn Nature Baths are increasing every year and to date they are impressive when considering its location away from the main centres of population (Table 9.7). Since opening in June 2004 numbers have more than doubled, from 30,000 to 64,000 in 2007. The number of foreign visitors has

Figure 9.7 Mývatn Nature Baths – as yet not overrun by visitors, but its popularity is rising and it may only be a matter of time until it takes on similar dimensions as the Blue Lagoon near Keflavik
Source: Photograph courtesy of P. Erfurt-Cooper.

Table 9.7 Visitors to Mývatn Nature Bath, 2004–2008

Year	Total visitors	Foreign visitors
2004 (opened 30 June)	30,000	12,000
2005	51,500	20,400
2006	62,500	31,200
2007	64,000	37,200
2008 (to 13 July)	25,000	13,100

Source: Mývatn Nature Baths.

trebled in that time. Visitors to Iceland in fact usually have no reservations about travelling to as many places as they can because the distances are acceptable and the destinations extremely tempting; even if they can be also a physical challenge to reach. An excellent marketing strategy, tasteful brochures and websites in different languages and a word-of-mouth campaign by people who have been there and have enjoyed it are part of the success story of the Mývatn Nature Baths. The visitor numbers were kindly supplied by the manager of the Mývatn Nature Baths, Stefán Gunnarsson (email correspondence to the authors, July 2008) with permission to be used for this book. In addition to the existing facilities a new restaurant, the Magma Café, opened in June 2008 to offer visitors regional healthy cuisine with specialities like fresh Hot Spring Bread with smoked char – an absolute delicacy (personal experience – the authors).

The total number of tourists visiting Iceland is also increasing, with less than 150,000 visiting in 1990 but 485,000 by 2007 (Icelandic Tourism Board, 2008), plus an additional 60,000 on cruise ships. Tourism contributes about 5% of Gross National Product (GNP) (12% of foreign income) and employs some 7000 people. The Tourism Board's international visitor survey of July–October 2007 showed that 70% of visitors were influenced by the natural environment of Iceland in making their decision to visit, and 64.5% undertook health-related activities while in the Reykjavik area. While the latter percentage fell to 41% when outside the capital area, the places visited [Geysir (76%), Skaftafell (35%), Mývatn (30%), Landmannalaugur (25%), etc.]) indicate that the majority of these tourists would have come across at least one hot spring during their stay in other parts of Iceland. If they missed out on the Blue Lagoon they surely went to the geyser fields in *Haukadalur* instead to see *Strokkur* in action and hoped for the original *Geysir* to erupt one more time. These visual hot springs with their extreme temperatures are popular geotourism attractions and have enchanted many visitors over the centuries. The Tourism Board data show that there is a pattern of increasing visitor arrivals outside the summer months, which indicates that Iceland is also becoming a great destination to visit in winter when the hot springs really come into their own.

Even *Greenland* has thermal springs warm enough for tourists to take a bath in the middle of the wilderness, even if they are surrounded by icebergs floating in the sea nearby. However, the only ones warm enough to be used for bathing all year round are in the south east of Greenland on the island of *Uunartoq* (Greenland. com, n.d.). No spa development to attract tourists for health and wellness based on local resources is likely to take place therefore, and this is made more certain by the close vicinity of Iceland, where a considerable hot spring tourism industry is already in place. However, environmental concerns are probably playing a role as well in order to preserve the pristine nature of this environment.

Antarctica

Tourism in Antarctica appears to be increasing at a steady rate as more people have the inclination and the financial means to travel to the most remote places left in the world. In the years from 1999 to 2003 between 13,000 and 15,000 tourists made landings in Antarctica and during the season of 2003/2004 these visitor numbers increased by 45% to over 19,500 (Bastmeijer & Roura, 2004: 763). Deception Island is currently one of the most visited sites in Antarctica with tourists arriving with cruise ships (Deception Island, n.d.), who ferry their passengers in small boats to the special area of Pendulum Cove on Deception Island. Here hot springs are seeping out of the ground of the black volcanic sand on the beach and mix with the ice cold seawater. This creates a good deal of interest among the cruise ship passengers and many of them brave the freezing temperature of the arctic air to experience a dip in the thermal water. But it may be more the unusual environment of volcanic hot springs in the Antarctic than a quest for health and wellness through the experience of thermal bathing that makes this place one of the main attractions of a cruise through the southern oceans (Deception Island, n.d.).

Discussion

Many countries are popular holiday destinations not only due to their interesting landscapes and outstanding natural scenery but also due to their natural hot and mineral springs used as tourist attractions. Although natural thermal springs can be found worldwide, it is the mineral and water temperature composition of *individual* hot springs that makes them so attractive as destinations for health and wellness spa centres and resorts. Besides the trendy spa resorts the range of natural hot spring locations includes undeveloped natural hot and mineral springs, as well as extreme environments where the hot springs cannot be directly used but create very effective tourist attractions in a visual sense.

The types of hot and mineral springs used for health and wellness spas within the thermal spring tourism sector depend greatly on the presence of favourable mineral components and a suitable temperature range in order to be used for therapeutic treatment such as balneology, hydrotherapy or thermalism. Thermal springs may also be used directly to supply health facilities such as hospitals and spa and other wellness facilities with thermal water use for hydrotherapy and balneology. The renewed worldwide trend towards the use of natural hot and mineral springs as curative resources for therapeutic use, both internally and externally, is in fact based on community interest in these springs since ancient times. Aquatic entertainment centres are popular in countries with an abundance of natural hot and mineral springs as they also benefit from geothermal water resources.

Reliable statistics containing visitor numbers for geothermal health and wellness spas are however rather difficult to find, as they are usually combined with all health and wellness facilities. Although not separated according to thermal spring destinations, these springs are most certainly of local and regional importance as visitor attractions. Hot springs have been used for centuries and are still popular among native residents and visitors alike, because of their potential to create a feeling of well-being and wholeness, as well as a valuable resource for complementary medicine. Their special status as a renewable resource, if managed responsibly and in a sustainable manner, is a further important contribution to the tourism infrastructure.

While many countries have developed their own individual bathing cultures, they now share these with visitors from other parts of the world. Hot spring bathing is often included in package deals either including stays at luxury resorts or at the other end of the spectrum being included along with extreme sports in extreme environments (hiking, trekking and hunting tours) through pairing these with hot soaks in natural thermal springs to speed recovery from strenuous activities. In fact, the integration of hot springs combined with the natural environment now draws millions of visitors every year and their popularity for health and wellness has supported a lot of new developments such as health and wellness spa facilities.

Summary

The popularity of health and wellness holiday destinations in many countries is thus not only due to their interesting landscapes and natural scenic beauty, but is in part also due to the abundance of natural hot and mineral springs used as tourist attractions. Although these thermal springs can be found worldwide, it is the particular mineral composition of the *local* spring that makes a particular area so attractive as a health and wellness spa centre, resort, or simply as a nature-based experience. Besides the trendy spa resorts the range of natural hot and mineral spring locations includes undeveloped springs as well as extreme environments where the hot springs cannot be directly used but are often very effective visual tourist attractions.

The types of hot and mineral springs used for health and wellness spa tourism sector depend greatly on the presence of beneficial mineral components and a suitable temperature range in order to be used for therapeutic treatment such as balneology, hydrotherapy or thermalism. Thermal springs may also be used directly to supply health facilities such as hospitals and spa and wellness facilities with thermal water use for hydrotherapy and balneology. Our case studies have reinforced this book's message that the recently renewed trend towards the use of natural hot and mineral springs as curative resources for therapeutic use, both internally and externally, is in fact based on the enduring interest of human populations in hot and mineral springs since ancient times. While statistics containing reliable visitor numbers for thermal health and wellness spa tourism are rather difficult to find, as they are usually combined with all health and wellness facilities and not separated according to thermal spring destinations, the further message of this book and these case-studies is nevertheless that this industry is presently undergoing rapid expansion because the number of people actively looking for health and wellness is increasing worldwide.

Additionally, wherever there are thermal springs they are most certainly also of great *local* importance: be it for social and cultural reasons, for health and wellness purposes, or purely to attract tourists with their visual impact. Natural hot springs have been used not just for centuries, but for millennia and many of them remain popular among native residents and visitors alike, because they can create a sensation of feeling 'well' in body, mind and spirit. Hot springs are therefore important contributions to the tourism infrastructure, especially as they are generally now treated as a renewable resource under sustainable management. The case studies and examples used in this chapter confirm and demonstrate that hot and mineral spring bathing is more than just a part of the health and wellness spa industry. Package deals often include visits to hot spring destinations, but these may now be combined with adventure tourism or even extreme sports in extreme environments and hot springs are also an essential component of beauty spa therapies based on regional traditions and the combined medical and spa culture that is developing in the Asia Pacific region.

Countries all over the world have developed a diversity of bathing cultures, which they share with millions of visitors every year, who value and appreciate the benefits for health and wellness obtained from thermal treatments and applications such as balneology and hydrotherapy. Extreme hot spring phenomena are used as visual attractions in geothermally active environments and are generally integrated as a must-see destination on the trip agenda when visiting countries such as Iceland, Japan, New Zealand, China and the Americas. The popularity and attractiveness of hot and mineral spring spas for health, wellness, leisure and recreation, in combination with the natural environment, is thus reinforcing and supporting a tourism industry of worldwide significance.

Chapter 10
Conclusions

MALCOLM COOPER and PATRICIA ERFURT-COOPER

Introduction

The fact that natural hot and mineral springs are among the most significant assets for the practices that form the core of health and wellness spa tourism, coupled with their distribution across much of the earth's surface and their importance to many community groups both now and in the past, made it difficult to choose between geographic locations in presenting the material covered in this book. The main aim was to develop a framework to highlight the distinctively different attitudes towards the utilisation of geothermal resources found on a global basis, but within our main focus on the use of thermal springs for health, wellness and leisure. In doing this we tried to achieve a balanced global view without using a Euro-centric or US-centric approach to analyse this form of health tourism. These approaches are apparent in the sparse academic literature to date (though see Cohen & Bodecker, 2008; Lund, 2002; Smith & Kelly, 2006) but do not represent the total picture. Nevertheless, certain major hot spring-based health and wellness spa traditions do pick themselves: the Japanese *Onsen bathing* tradition, the Central-European and former USSR state-sponsored *community health* tradition, the German *Kur* tradition and the American *beauty therapy* tradition had to be covered because the different forms of health and wellness tourism associated with these are equally important, and each may be found to varying degrees using hot and mineral springs resources for tourism.

Like many other water bodies natural hot and cold mineral springs have become important locations for travel, cultural and religious tourism, geotourism, and in some cases extreme tourism, and other water-related activities that many people travel long distances to experience. However, natural hot and mineral springs are particularly iconic in tourism for the reasons outlined in the book. In addition, the forms of tourism based on the use of natural hot and mineral springs chosen as examples or case studies for this book provide a descriptive concept map (Moscardo *et al.*, 2006) of the main elements of health and wellness spa tourism that can be applied to most if not all other areas.

We noted in the introduction to the book that since the beginnings of recorded history (or at least as far back as we can be relatively confident about our sources) natural hot and mineral springs have played a critical role in health treatments for injured soldiers, for the leisured classes, then for a wider range of people and more recently based on the economic development of medical tourism. In ancient times thermal springs facilitated community health, were a reason for travel, and provided rewards and support for military occupation of an area. They were also instrumental in promoting tourism within ancient empires such as the Roman and Chinese, and were central to recreational opportunities wherever they occur.

Tourism and the use of natural hot and mineral springs

Several direct relationships between tourism and hot springs have been identified in this book. First, springs and their often associated geothermal phenomena provide a wealth of attractions and aesthetic appeal for tourists and provide a unique venue in which tourism can take place. In some parts of the world, the physical morphology of springs results in unique natural landscapes that draw visitors from all parts of the globe (e.g. Pamukkale in Turkey; Yellowstone National Park in Wyoming, USA). The second relationship of importance comes about through hot and mineral springs used as alternative health resources. As discussed in Chapter 2, during the late 20th century a new importance regarding fitness and well-being emerged worldwide and subsequently turned into a way of life embracing all age and income groups. This awareness of the importance of well-being was supported to a large degree by the predicted baby boomer 'middle age wellness explosion', which started to take hold in the fitness industry over a relatively short time period during the late 1980s and early 1990s. For many, this increased awareness of the need to actively maintain health and wellness encompassed preventative therapies based on visits of health and wellness resorts and spas. Finally, mineral spring water supports the massive bottled mineral water industry that forms another part of the wellness movement which, although bottled mineral water has always been available in European countries, is now a wellness attribute in most parts of the world. The raised awareness of the imputed health benefits of such waters have taken on the aura of an essential item for many consumers, even for those who do not otherwise utilise hot and mineral springs for any wellness purpose.

In summary, the use of hot and mineral springs is a complex phenomenon that has been noticeably influenced by many human activities, including settlement, tourism and recreation. The tourist use of the world's hot springs must be monitored and well managed to enable conservation of the natural and cultural wealth of these unique ecosystems for present and future generations. A distinction has to be made between tourism based on use of the hot water itself and the often associated wellness/beauty therapy treatments *that may or may not use these resources*. Nevertheless, while many important health and wellness spa tourism destinations are without geothermally based water sources and use artificially heated water as a substitute, many also imply that they have utilised such resources where available precisely because of the importance of this association.

Health and Wellness Tourism in Retrospect

As we have noted throughout this book the use of natural hot and mineral springs is an important but surprisingly neglected aspect of the study of the global health and wellness tourism industry. Yet geothermal systems form the basis for many of the bathing and other recreational activities provided by health and wellness spas, in addition to providing water to sustain the growth of the beauty therapy and 'wellness' industries that they are increasingly based on. Compared to the research attention that ocean cruising, ecotourism or adventure tourism have attracted recently, hot and mineral springs have apparently been of relatively minor interest to tourism academics (Hall, 2003; Smith & Kelly, 2006). However, the same cannot be said for reporters in the popular media, the many millions of enthusiastic spring users and the industry operators themselves who have all demonstrated considerable interest in the use and marketing of geothermal systems as indoor/outdoor recreation resources in recent years (Cohen & Bodecker, 2008). The aims of this book were to help redress this lack of academic attention through careful exploration of the background of and current issues relating to health and wellness spa tourism, to raise awareness of the role that hot and mineral springs play and have played throughout history in health and wellness tourism, and to identify areas that require further research in order that a more complete understanding of this form of tourism might be reached.

One of the main components of health and wellness spa tourism as it has developed in recent years is the natural feature of hot and mineral spring water, which is without a doubt one of the most popular of natural settings for rest and recreation. Even short periods in and near such waters have a beneficial effect on most people, which explains why hot-spring-based tourist destinations such as Japanese *Onsen* are so accepted worldwide. If hot water is not directly available in a natural state, man-made landscaping often includes fountains, ponds, swimming pools and artificial waterfalls designed to appeal to the tourists. One of the most unique hot spring settings of this type has been created by using the outflow from the geothermal power stations that supply the Blue Lagoon and the Mývatn Nature Baths in Iceland. The potential of a hot river or stream is even greater, largely due to the changing scenery and different natural settings along its banks as much as to the water itself (e.g. 'Kerosene' Creek near Rotorua, New Zealand).

But this is not the only attraction of geothermal springs: Chapter 4 showed that in many countries they have been equally important for their cultural and religious value. In this sense, the significance of water in culture is associated with two distinct environments – the physical and the spiritual. Both are of extreme importance to various cultures worldwide, although with regional differences. Often the physical and the spiritual overlapped and resulted in 'water worship', which attributes the source of the water to divine intervention. Hot springs have universally been seen as extraordinary and awe inspiring, mainly because people were not sure how to explain their occurrence. As a result, hot springs were considered a gift of the gods, and temples and shrines were erected in their vicinity (Lee, 2004). This lack of scientific knowledge did not however stop people from using thermal waters if they could access them without danger and if the temperature was acceptable.

In more modern times many government authorities have presented a medical view of the role of water in the body, but this is still essentially referring to the *culture* of water use in those particular countries: 'Water is an essential element in maintaining physical performance and intellectual capacity, helps fight against heat, hydrates the skin, enables the transportations of hydro-soluble vitamins and minerals, favours urinary waste elimination and facilitates kidney operation' (Thermalism Office Tunisia, n.d.). Water is described by Arvigo and Epstein (2003: 12) as having unique transformational power, especially when combined with prayer, and they reinforce the universal thought that water refreshes as well as calming and balancing body, mind and soul (Smith & Puczko, 2008).

Somewhere in the genesis of every civilisation therefore is the idea of water as being divine, life-giving, healing, cleansing and renewing. King (1966: 186) maintains that throughout history such water sources have been associated with religious observances, legends of gods and heroes and miraculous events. Nevertheless, the location of springs also often determined the location of human settlement by encouraging the development of townships nearby (Bullard, 2004).

Cross-cultural adaptation

Another very important feature of the use of hot and mineral springs can be found in the translocation of specific traditions relating to the use of water created in one part of the world to other cultures. When people migrate to other countries they often take along their customs and cultural traditions, including the use of water (Chapter 4). For many people the way they use water or have supported water-related traditions in their home country is the way they want to use them anywhere else too. This can be for hygienic, health or religious purposes (ablutions, purification rituals, baptism), or for decoration inside or outside their homes, or as part of the environment they live in. This does not just apply to permanent migrants, but to tourists as well. Lakes, rivers, streams, waterfalls, oceans or special bathing facilities fed by thermal spring water may therefore be preferred locations for living *and* holiday destinations. If no natural resources like local hot springs can be accessed nearby other facilities for wellness purposes may be a sauna in the backyard, a fitness room or a cold-water swimming pool.

Apart from the migration of people and tourists and their traditional customs moving with them, there have been several other methods through which certain types of health and wellness spa-related practice have found their way into other cultural environments. Their import or export on a more business-oriented scale includes the introduction of different ways to use and hot water and wellness treatments that can be adapted elsewhere, for instance in the Germany–Japan example below. It all depends on the congruence between the way a natural spring might be used and the traditions of the new host culture (Chapter 4). The following examples provide some insight into the variety of cross-cultural acceptance of bathing and wellness customs:

- Japanese *Onsen* bathing traditions – export of the concept to Australia, New Zealand, USA/Canada;
- *Hammams* or Turkish Baths can be found in Europe and elsewhere, for example in Hungary, England, USA, Germany;
- Finnish *Saunas* have been exported worldwide;
- Jewish *Mikvahs* were built wherever the need for this particular type of religious bath was required within Jewish communities (Germany, Poland, USA);
- German *Kurhaus* – the concept has been re-interpreted, modified and imported by the Japanese who call it *Kuahausu* and use it as a water activity and treatment centre for the whole family;
- Roman *Thermae* – the concept is used for example in Germany, England, and even as far away from Europe as Tasmania, Australia;
- Russian *Banias* have been exported to countries like the USA/Canada and Europe by Russian immigrants;
- Swedish Massage has been introduced to Asia, where it is used alongside Asian wellness treatments; and
- Asian spa and wellness treatments including traditional Chinese medicine (TCM) have been introduced to Europe and the Americas, where these are used together with traditional Western treatment methods.

The environments of health and wellness spa tourism

One of the main reasons for visiting hot spring environments formed by and close to *active volcanism* seems to be the desire to experience the scenic attraction of unique natural phenomena as much as for the hot spring experience; a situation that is plausibly demonstrated by the difficulties tourists are prepared to overcome when embarking on excursions to places like for example the Aleutians or Kamchatka. Curiosity and an educational aspect may be other important factors, as the more general form of tourism in the natural environment now defined as *Geotourism* is gaining momentum and becoming the current motivating impulse to visit destinations that include not only geological features but also a diversified ecology, and thus offer more than just sightseeing and photo opportunities as part of the trip agenda (Erfurt-Cooper, 2008).

Of central concern in using extreme geological phenomena as tourist attractions is their long-term sustainability, which requires responsible management of these renewable natural resources (Chapters 5 and 6). The high number of hot spring environments with distinctive and unique natural surroundings in many countries worldwide is of considerable economic value for the tourism industry and in some regions the *majority* of the revenue derived from tourism is directly related to hot spring tourism and Geotourism in active volcanic environments (Erfurt-Cooper, 2008; Lund & Freeston, 2001). National parks and world heritage sites contribute significantly to the attraction of areas with geothermal features. To attract visitors of different interest groups to these, tourism operators offer a diversity of tours including activities ranging from trekking, hiking, climbing, skiing on or around active volcanoes and hot springs to canoeing and fishing on crater lakes. This is combined with overnight accommodation with hot spring and other wellness/beauty therapy facilities for relaxing. In Iceland for example a day of hiking cross country usually ends with a soak in a hot spring or a hot tub fed by natural spring water. The same goes for New Zealand and Japan, where a hot spring bath is one of the main attractions of the day, whether it is after exercise on the ski slopes or a strenuous day trekking cross country or just leisurely shopping for souvenirs and visiting the local cafés.

As noted in Chapter 6, tourism based on health and wellness spa facilities is multi-dimensional, active and sophisticated. While there is an increasingly enhanced appreciation among tourists and local communities of the importance of the geological resources described in Chapters 2 and 5, especially those of thermal water resources as a framework for health and wellness, there is also recognition that behavioural factors and social environments together with new combinations of landscapes and facilities greatly impinge on the willingness of visitors to travel to a particular location or spa resort. Health and wellness spa tourism involves an individual in a personal assessment of his or her health and psychological status (and/or vanity) as much as it involves their providers' recognition and understanding of the physical, social, regulatory and business environments surrounding this activity. Equally, it involves communities and their governments in the creation of regulatory frameworks for the spa and wellness industry so that community health standards are not compromised.

Contribution of this Book

Health and wellness spa tourism has developed over the last century, but especially over the past 20 years as an almost essential adjunct to a healthy lifestyle for many people. The current size and economic importance of this type of tourism have very recently been explored for the Global Spa Summit 2008 (New York, May 2008) by SRI International (formerly Stanford Research Institute – Spa Business, 2008). The resulting data, while it concentrated on formal spas and thus did not pick up the informal and/or undeveloped health aspects of hot and mineral springs, or differentiate between those spas using thermal waters and those not, nevertheless provide the first attempt to quantify this growing sector of tourism. The data obtained through this research indicate that in 2007 spa-related hospitality and tourism contributed some USD106.5 billion to a total spa and lifestyle-associated health and wellness industry having a market size of some USD1353 billion (Chapter 7). On a worldwide basis SRI estimates that there are around

72,000 facilities employing about 1.2 million people offering services that 'promote wellness through the provision of therapeutic and other professional services aimed at renewing the body, mind and spirit' (Spa Business, 2008: 41).

Table 10.1 (developed further in Table 10.5) gives the *regional* breakdown of the global spa market as determined by this study, which shows its concentration in Europe, the Asia-Pacific (heavily influenced by Japan) and the USA/Canada. The top five countries in terms of market share are the United States (26%), Japan (12%), Germany (8%), France (5%) and Italy (5%). The UK, China, Spain, Canada and South Korea make up the next five, all with 3–4% of the global spa market. However, in terms of investment in facilities for the future the picture is different, with the Middle East and North Africa (MENA) countries and South America currently spending much more than other regions to develop new and existing facilities.

Given the considerable gaps relating to health and wellness spa tourism in the existing literature identified in the introduction, the purpose of this book was to describe and analyse the significance of the use of hot and mineral springs for health and wellness spa tourism. As a result, it provides an overview of the traditional and contemporary use of natural hot spring use for leisure, health and wellness activities with the intention of closing these gaps. One of its key objectives was to correct the common perception that wellness centres including thermal spas have their sole or major origin in Europe, namely in imperial Rome and its immediate antecedents. While the Roman Empire certainly contributed to the development of recreational health and wellness facilities and thermal bathhouses (*thermae*) in its constituent regions, most of the sites that were utilised near natural hot springs were already used from ancient times by local native inhabitants. The 'Rest of the World' enjoyed not just as many, but even more sites across a similar or longer span of history. This book clarifies the factual origins of hot spring use for health and wellness with examples from all continents and presents comprehensive support for the worldwide significance of natural hot springs for health and wellness spa tourism.

Table 10.1 The global spa market

Region	% of global spas	% of global revenue	% of global employment	Capital investment as a % of spa revenue
Europe	32	39	36	27
Asia-Pacific	30	24	30	32
North America	29	29	25	13
South America	8	1	7	64
MENA*	1	5	2	142
Africa	1	1	1	33

*Middle East and North Africa.
Source: Based on SRI International (2008); Spa Business (2008: 41–43).

The book also provides readers with an introduction to each region in which the use of hot and mineral springs for health and wellness tourism is important and their history. A summary of our findings is as follows:

(1) The majority of hot and mineral springs are located within active volcanic environments. Others can result from artesian groundwater heated deep in the earth and rising to the surface under pressure, sometimes in areas where they are least expected. Both settings are usually in a natural environment, although some areas may be heavily developed around them (e.g. Beppu City, Japan). The hot springs keep flowing from their original source, unless they are piped to other areas to supply more facilities.

(2) Historical use has resulted in another pattern where similarities can be observed that apply to a vast majority of hot springs worldwide. Religious connections are common, whether the springs are in Thailand, Japan, France, England or South America. If it is not religious tradition pertaining to the use of natural hot springs, then mythological and legendary events are often directly related to the discovery and use of a particular hot spring in a particular location. Springs, hot or cold, frequently and habitually carry the name of their patron saints, which alone makes for a significant pattern among hot springs worldwide. This fact lends strong support to the importance of these springs in relation to socio-cultural environments as well as the health and wellness sector and is a definite contribution towards establishing the significance of these resources for health and wellness spa tourism.

(3) A large percentage of all known hot and mineral spring destinations, locations or centres have been developed in stages over time. Some go back several thousand years, and were developed, went into decline, were rediscovered and subsequently redeveloped (e.g. Bath, England; Huaqing, China). This pattern of establishment, growth, decline and redevelopment applies to many hot springs worldwide and indicates their continuing significance.

(4) Another common denominator is the use of hot springs as a natural resource for domestic and commercial purposes other than or in conjunction with bathing. Many countries still use hot springs for washing, cooking and baking (Icelanders bake a delicious 'hot-spring-bread', Asian countries use boiling springs to cook eggs and vegetables), heating and geothermal energy production.

(5) Most hot springs are associated with curative powers and therapeutic value. In many cases or locations this is verified by testimonies of a great number of people, often in writing, and of course that so important for the tourism industry source of information word of mouth (WOM). Prospective new visitors place reliance on friends and/or relations stating that their health conditions have vastly improved depending on the treatment and care they received.

(6) Natural hot and mineral springs have a longstanding tradition, mainly in European countries, for being used by highly qualified medical professionals to treat a number of physical and mental conditions. These vary in severity and their treatment is designed to maximise the improvement of the patient or client under the most favourable conditions. The following table provides an overview of the most common disorders and conditions, which can be

treated successfully with thermalism (balneology, hydrotherapy, crenotherapy) involving the use of natural hot and mineral spring water. European countries have in the past carried out medical research in clinical trials, analysing balneological treatments, either in combination with other therapies or as individual treatment. The results strongly support the benefits of natural hot mineral-rich water for a large variety of health conditions (outlined in Table 10.2). These results, along with concern over prices for medical services in developed countries, underpin the current investment in medical tourism in many countries of Asia and the Middle East.

(7)   The systematic worldwide analysis of hot spring use provided in this book makes it clearly evident that hot spring use has similarities in many countries, although with regional and cultural variations and on the whole the general patterns of hot spring use differ only marginally. Variations are usually determined by access, water temperature and the development status of the surrounding area and of course individual local socio-cultural conditions.

(8)   It also appears that no culture can lay claim to being the first to use hot springs for domestic and therapeutic purposes. While it is a matter of availability and access to geothermal resources, not many cultures have kept reliable records from first use to be able to pass this information on to future generations. Table 10.3 gives examples of past and present hot spring use in selected countries. Considering that in countries like Japan even animals (e.g. snow monkeys) frequent hot springs it does not require much evidence or logic to be able to assert that humans would have used available geothermal resources as soon as they were discovered. When the temperature and availability was right for the purpose, be that washing, bathing or cooking and baking, it makes sense to assume that the use of particular hot springs must go back well before written historical records in most areas with geothermal resources.

Table 10.2 Examples of physical conditions that may improve through treatment with thermalism, although this may depend on the individual case

Health conditions treated with thermalism		
Arthritis	Metabolic disorders	Respiratory disorders
Central nervous system	Muscular problems	Rheumatism (various types)
Degenerative bone disease	Neuralgia	Sciatica
Digestive and nutritional disorders	Neurological and physical exhaustion	Skin problems: acne, eczema, dermatitis
Exhaustion	Orthopaedic disorders	Stress
Gastric, intestinal and renal problems	Post-injury problems and post operative traumas	Urologic disorders
Gynaecological diseases	Psoriasis	

Source: Compiled by P. Erfurt-Cooper.

Table 10.3 Examples of past and present hot springs use

Country	Number of hot spring locations currently known	First assumed users	Earliest recorded use	Under past Roman occupation	Used for tourism health and wellness, geotourism, ecotourism
Albania	3 hot spring areas	Local tribes	229–9 BC	Yes	Yes
Algeria	70 hot spring areas	Local tribes	1st century BC	Yes	Yes
America (North)	1702 hot springs in 23 states (Berry et al., 1980)	Native Indians	1700s	–	Yes
Antarctica	1 hot spring area (Deception Island)	Whalers	–	–	Yes
Argentina	119 hot spring areas	Local inhabitants	–	–	Yes
Australia	38 hot spring areas	Aborigines	1895	–	Yes
Austria	13 hot spring areas 18 hot springs in Baden alone	Local tribes	50 AD	Yes	Yes
Belgium	2 hot spring areas	Romans	14th century AD	Yes	Yes
Brazil	121 areas (86 Caldas Novas only)	Local inhabitants	1545	–	Yes
Bulgaria	97 areas – 520–800 springs (depending on the source)	Local tribes	5th century BC	Yes	Yes
Canada	110 hot spring areas 382 hot springs	Native Indians	1859	–	Yes
Chile	41+ hot spring areas 275 hot springs	Local inhabitants	–	–	Yes

Country	Hot spring areas	Users	Date		
China	88 hot spring areas 2509 hot springs e.g. 81 hot springs in Tengchong	Local inhabitants	Western Zhou Dynasty 1050–771 BC	–	Yes
Croatia and Slovenia	40 hot spring areas	Local inhabitants	1st century AD	Yes	Yes
England	1 hot spring area	Celtic tribes	43 AD by Romans	Yes	Yes
Ethiopia	11 hot spring areas 65 hot springs	Local tribes	–	–	Yes
Finland	1 hot spring	Local inhabitants	1700	–	Yes
France	124 hot spring areas	Local tribes and Romans	120 BC	Yes	Yes
France, Corsica	6 hot spring areas	Phoenicians, Etruscans, Greeks and Romans	238 BC and 400 AD	Yes	Yes
Germany	57 hot spring areas	Local tribes	1st century BC to 1st century AD	Yes	Yes
Greece	68 hot spring areas 750+ hot springs	Ancient Greek civilisations	5th–6th centuries BC	Yes	25% presently used for balneotherapy
Greenland	3 hot springs	Eskimos Missionaries	Icelandic Sagas (n.d.)	–	Yes
Honduras	56 hot spring areas 181 hot springs (125 springs >35°C)	Maya	1st century AD Spanish records	–	Yes
Hungary	34 hot spring areas 1000+ hot springs 100 in Budapest alone	Celtic and Dacian peoples	1st century BC Roman military	Yes	Yes

(Continued)

Table 10.3 *Continued*

Country	Number of hot spring locations currently known	First assumed users	Earliest recorded use	Under past Roman occupation	Used for tourism health and wellness, geotourism, ecotourism
Iceland	516+ hot spring areas	Local inhabitants	Icelandic Sagas (n.d.)	–	Yes
India	202 hot spring areas 320+ hot springs	Local inhabitants	Hindu Epics (n.d.)	–	Yes
Iran	17 hot spring areas 149 hot spring areas	Local inhabitants	–	–	Yes
Italy		Etruscans	Etruscan records Greek records	Yes	Yes
Israel	17	Local inhabitants	2nd century AD	Yes	Yes
Japan	5500+ hot spring areas 26,796 hot springs (in 2001)	Local inhabitants	631 AD (earlier records not reliable)	–	Yes
Jordan	7 hot spring areas 104 hot springs (55 near Dead Sea)	Native inhabitants, Bedouines	1st century BC	–	Yes
Kenya	3 hot spring areas 64 hot springs	Local inhabitants	–	–	Yes
Korea	17 hot spring areas 70 hot springs	Local inhabitants	Japanese Onsen developments	–	Yes
Mexico	131 hot spring areas	Aztecs	1541	–	Yes

Country	Hot springs	Peoples	Date		
Mongolia	43 hot springs	Local tribes, Nomads	–	–	Yes
New Zealand	67 hot spring areas 170+ hot springs	Māori	19th century Earlier oral transmissions	–	Yes
Pakistan	33 hot spring areas	Indus Valley Civilisations	–	–	Yes
Peru	72 hot spring areas 500+ hot springs	Incas	1550	–	Yes
Poland	7 hot spring areas	Local inhabitants	10th century AD	–	Yes
Portugal	34 hot spring areas	Local inhabitants Roman occupation	1st century BC to 1st century AD	Yes	Yes
Romania	20 hot spring areas	Local inhabitants Romans	106 AD (Romans)	Yes	Yes
Russia	140+ hot spring areas 64 hot spring areas in Kamchatka alone	Local inhabitants (Romans in Georgia)	5th century AD	Yes	Yes
Slovakia and Czech Republic	13 hot spring areas	Local inhabitants Romans	1113 AD 14th century AD	Yes	Yes
Spain	46 hot spring areas 300+ hot springs in Galicia alone	Local inhabitants Romans	1st century BC Roman occupation	Yes	Yes
Switzerland	18 hot spring areas 39 hot springs	Local inhabitants	58 BC (Romans)	Yes	Yes
Syria	5 hot spring areas	Semitic Empire?	64 BC (Romans)	Yes	Yes

(Continued)

Table 10.3 *Continued*

Country	Number of hot spring locations currently known	First assumed users	Earliest recorded use	Under past Roman occupation	Used for tourism health and wellness, geotourism, ecotourism
Taiwan	14 hot spring areas 130+ hot springs	Local inhabitants, Japanese influence	1697 during WWII Japanese *Onsen* developments	–	Yes
Tanzania	3 hot spring areas 30+ hot springs	Local tribes	–	–	Yes
Tajikistan	200+ hot springs	Local tribes	–	–	Yes
Thailand	27 hot spring areas 90+ hot springs	Local tribes	–	–	Yes
Tunisia	57 hot spring areas	Romans, local tribes	120 AD	Yes	Yes
Turkey	113 hot spring areas 1300–1500 hot springs depending on source (Anatolia alone has over 700 hot springs)	Hittite Empire and earlier local tribes	15–18th century BC	Yes	Yes
Uganda	26 hot spring areas 30 hot springs	Local tribes	–	–	Yes

Note: The numbers of hot spring areas and individual hot springs have been collected from a variety of sources and may not be completely accurate, but reflect the vast amount of hot springs worldwide. Examples of past and present hot spring use indicate the popularity of natural geothermal springs throughout history.
Source: Compiled by P. Erfurt-Cooper.

Risky environments

Importantly, the book also discusses in a number of contexts the risks associated with the use of hot spring water. These include those normally associated with keeping swimming pools clean and those resulting from the use of natural hot and mineralised water. The high temperatures in some types of spas may adversely affect some visitors, may exacerbate the effects of alcohol or drugs if present and may heighten the risk of drowning through the lack of transparency in coloured or turbid spa waters. Deaths from the mineral constituents of the water itself are rare, those that do occur in hot springs have been associated with a combination of high water temperature and the over-use of alcohol or drugs, or inadequate supervision of young children (Chapter 6).

The high turnover rate of users in many spas and whirlpools also poses an infection risk, involving both microorganisms from the bathers and those present in the water. The warm, usually nutrient-containing aerobic water provides an ideal environment for many pathogenic organisms (WHO, 2003). Infections resulting from these organisms can be difficult to control and guarding against them requires frequent monitoring of the pH (degree of acidity/alkalinity) of the water, and its disinfection and filtration. Water quality treatment itself may also present chemical hazards unless the chemical disinfection is well managed. There is also a risk of accidents around spas due to slips, trips and falls, and bathers may also pick up fungal and other infections from wet surfaces and other bathers.

Technologies and the built environment

The most common built environment in a health and wellness spa facility generally incorporates the following components (Luxury Spa Finder Magazine, 2006; McNeil & Ragins, 2005):

- wet treatment rooms (may be male, female and/or common);
- dry treatment rooms;
- baths and showers;
- laboratories;
- reception, relaxation and waiting areas;
- locker rooms;
- retail areas;
- administrative and associated service areas, and, if provided, these additions
- beauty salons;
- fitness areas;
- café and restaurant facilities; and
- accommodation.

These are also usually provided within a visual environment that increasingly incorporates the outdoors, makes use of colours and textures to create a sense of isolation (peace, security) from the outside world, and pays attention to the way in which the built environment can enhance the overall experience (Chapter 7). Larger health and wellness facilities can include conference rooms and health clinics (e.g. Blue Lagoon, Iceland).

More and more frequently the modern health and wellness spa facility is being used to promote medically sanctioned health treatments among visitors and locals. Travel packages that combine medical checkups and/or treatment with fun and relaxing activities are enjoying a steady growth in popularity. This has meant heavy investment in medical equipment, buildings and trained personnel in the health and wellness spa facilities of a number of countries in recent years, especially in Thailand and India. A typical package of this sort involves the traveller being given an extensive medical checkup and treatment at a hospital before enjoying a relaxing and therapeutic stay at a resort either with or without hot or mineral springs. This type of 'tour' or 'cure' was common in Europe and in the United States in the early days of the modern spa tradition before it suffered a decline due to the withdrawal of government support, is still common in Europe, and is now becoming more and more popular in Asia. The latter trend is also being supported by the much lower cost of quality medical treatment in Asian countries compared with that of Europe and North America.

Marketing

The marketing of these and other forms of treatment in the health and wellness spa industry currently involves appealing to the hearts and minds of the baby boomer as well as the younger generations in relation to their physical and mental well-being. Chapter 8 showed that a mixture of messages and message types is used; from WOM through travel guidebooks to internet and print-based 'glossy' images of ideal spa types and of wellness outcomes. Spa magazines and coffee table books about 'The 100 Best Spas of the World' or equivalent market-conditioning subject matter (Chapter 8), as well as the internet, are informing the reader of everything luxurious and beneficial for their health and well-being that is available. It is also noticeable that most of the glossy magazines and coffee table books emphasise *personal* luxury and well-being to sell their products; revealing the nature of the actual water sources (beyond temperatures) where these are used in treatment is not common for spas without access to natural hot springs. This may be because such details are not important once a decision has been made that hot or mineral waters are to be part of a particular experience, or it may be that some of the spas advertised are not in a position to offer genuine hot springs, but cleverly exploit unspecific mineral spring terminology to advertise their facilities (Chapters 2 and 6). Although some spas do not go into much detail about the water itself, most spas and resorts use natural water features such as rock pools and waterfalls to market to the customer the sought after natural environment associated with water therapy-based wellness. However, genuine hot spring spas nearly always offer details about the water and its contents among the basic information for visitors.

Management

The health and wellness spa industry has worked to create a symbiotic relationship between its products and the desires of its clients for many years. It has used marketing to define the core essence of what the business is about and to effectively communicate its advantages to the most profitable opportunities currently available. And in searching for effective management styles it has also evolved methods for securing, developing and keeping trained staff. Almost always the quality of the experience gained by the visitor to any particular facility depends very much on the existence of qualified and competent staff, rather than on the superiority of the décor or the sophistication of the equipment available. Human resource development in this industry, as in any other, therefore involves

- understanding of the role of the spa operative and manager;
- effective leadership;
- personal organisation;
- effective time management;
- financial awareness;
- recruitment of visually competent marketing and selling managers (much of the marketing of the industry is based on visually communicated health attributes – Chapter 8);
- generally recruiting the best operatives that can be found (and training them to an even higher level);
- effectively managing day to day performance;
- developing training and coaching skills;
- performance appraisals; and
- assisting staff to effectively manage client relationships.

Changes in national health systems have also had a major impact on the management of spas in Western Europe, the former socialist countries of Eastern Europe and the Americas (see e.g. Tourism Queensland, 2004 and Chapter 2). Health and Wellness Spa tourism has long been an important component of health care in a wide range of jurisdictions; from the countries of the former USSR, to Germany and France, Austria, Italy, Israel, New Zealand, and now India, Malaysia, Thailand, and a host of other countries interested in the recent boom in medical tourism (Hall, 2003). In many of the countries of eastern and western Europe the cost of domestic visitors to health spas has been in the past wholly or partly subsidised by the state as part of national health care delivery, while in other countries the lower relative cost of medical services has led to a rapid recent expansion of health tourism in part also based on the existence of hot and mineral spring resources.

The size of the spa industry and its economic value

Estimates vary but the overall pattern of visitors to facilities offered by the health and wellness spa industry worldwide indicates that this form of tourism is becoming increasingly popular. At the bathing end of the spectrum of treatments, in Japan some 150 million people visit *Onsen* facilities in any one year (see Chapters 7 and 8), while in both Europe and America there are over 30 million visits per year to facilities offering medically based health tourism (Smith & Jenner, 2000; Chapter 2). The overall trend of indulgence in a relaxing environment has turned into a global movement with a new emphasis in prevention of disease and maintenance of good health, and with high expectations regarding health improvements even if there are no major health problems. Not just the body is of concern; the mind and soul are also catered for in many spas where a holistic approach of creating harmony for those in need is used as well as the more traditional rehabilitative therapies.

We also noted in Chapter 2 that several demographic, economic and lifestyle trends are contributing to these patterns in the 21st century. The ageing of the 'baby boomer' populations, a new desire for fitness, changing travel expectations combining travel with fitness and health opportunities, and the high cost of health care in developed countries are all increasingly important factors in the development of the market for health and wellness spa tourism. The main focus appears to be on natural healing methods incorporating Asian and European treatments accompanied by the aesthetic appeal of Eastern lifestyle and culture. The newer medical spa treatments in developing countries based on quality medical care combined with spa treatments are offered at a much lower cost than in the developed economies. In the less medically specialised format, therapies of Asian origin (e.g. Ayurvedic massage and skin care, yoga, reflexology, natural hot spring baths, TCM, and other native cures and remedies) are often combined with European thermalism (including balneology, hydrotherapy, medicinal baths, peat and mud packs, Kneipp cure, Thalassotherapy, drinking of medicinal waters as well as sport and fitness facilities). In these ways nearly all such spas cater for health and wellness as well as beauty aspects, with special signature treatments often devised to make sure there are no missed economic opportunities.

In summary, it is estimated that there are well over 100 million active spa-goers worldwide (ISPA, 2007; Table 10.4), with the following characteristics:

- women continue to dominate health and wellness spa tourism. However, men account for more than 40% of spa-goers in Australia, Austria, Germany, Japan, Singapore, Spain and Thailand;
- baby boomers are one of the core markets for the wellness industry with a growing interest in new age remedies and alternative treatments;
- on average, spa-goers are in their upper 30s to early 40s;
- relaxation and relieving stress are universally cited as the primary reasons for visiting spas; and
- facials, sauna/steam baths and full-body massages are among the most popular treatments worldwide.

For many tourists the term 'spa' has thus become a household word and the health and wellness spa industry is now a leading leisure industry, generating some USD250 billion worldwide (ISPA, 2007; Osborne, 2006). At the moment this market is principally split between local users and health and wellness spa tourists, but the

Table 10.4 Recent estimates of the size of the spa industry in a representative selection of countries, including hot spring spas

Examples of visitor numbers to health and wellness spas (including hot spring spa destinations)		
Country	*Visitor numbers*	*Economic value*
Global		Over $250 billion
America (North)	111 million	USD9.4 billion
Austria	2.9 million	–
Australia	2.3 million	USD271 million
Cambodia	200,000	USD6 million
Canada	17 million (2006)	USD1.03 billion
China	2.0 million	–
England	6.7 million	–
France	6.3 million	–
Germany	6,476,794 visitors to thermal and mineral spring spas (2006)	USD3.8 billion
Iceland	500,000+ (estimate for 2007 including foreign and domestic visitors, possibly higher)	–
Iran	1,481,000 (2005)	–
Italy	17.8 million	–
Japan	150 million	USD5.7 billion
New Zealand	–	USD50 million
South Africa	1.1 million	USD46 million
Spain	6.1 million	–
Taiwan	3.7 million	–
Thailand	3.6 million	USD263 million
Tunisia	2.5 million	–
United Arab Emirates	2,305,000*	USD70 million total spa industry revenue
Vietnam	428,000	USD9 million

*Intelligent Spas, UAE Spa Benchmark Report 2005–2010 and other sources.

industry can expect to see niche products and markets evolve in the direction of greater market segmentation, along with diversifying corporate investment, new ways of delivering services and a further expansion of health and wellness spa-based advertising media (Chapter 8).

Gaps, Challenges and Future Research Directions

Despite the great progress made in tourism research recently, the fact that this book represents one of the very first endeavours to document *health and wellness spa tourism* means that the editors must acknowledge that their choices of subjects and geographical areas may be overtaken by new research in the short to medium term, particularly in the study of a range of destination issues for spa tourism under the broad umbrella of sustainability. In this context the limitations on improving the understanding of tourism policy in this area result from two main weaknesses:

- the beauty therapy approach to much of the literature results in restricted analytical approaches being applied to destination management issues in health and wellness spa tourism; and
- a lack of recognition of the interdependencies and complexities of health and wellness (including medical)-related tourism systems.

In particular, for effective health and wellness spa tourism development and governance this implies the following gaps and challenges:

(1) The advertising and marketing of hot spring spas must be aimed at a much broader group of people, *and be more informative than reliant on glossy pictures of young females*, including all generations (this is in fact now happening in brochures from New Zealand and Iceland).

(2) Hot spring spas do not always present a clinical environment solely with the intention of supplying balneological treatment, and should not imply that they do. This is particularly noticeable in countries like New Zealand, Japan, Iceland and Hungary, where apart from using thermal spring water for medical treatment, people can also enjoy a variety of thermal pools at different temperatures for swimming and aqua-fun and games (including water proof chess – Budapest). A change would make this form of environment more attractive to a wider range of potential visitors.

(3) The concept of wellness has a complex history and dating the exact onset of the revival in interest for personal well-being is not easy because of a division in opinions; several sources are suggesting that health and wellness spa holidays have in fact been around for hundreds if not thousands of years. In addition, almost every spa visitor or tourist has different expectations of the likely experience and/or outcome that they are seeking and/or will tolerate (Adams, 2003), and this makes for considerable confusion as to the precise nature of this form of tourism.

(4) We chose therefore to segment health and wellness tourism in this book (see Figure 1.1) in order to establish a range of likely definitions for closer analysis.

It is possible though that other segments could be equally as important, but only further research will establish this with any degree of certainty.

(5) The approach taken in this book in assessing the importance of health and wellness spa tourism was to adopt the definition proposed by Myers *et al.* (2005: 1) that wellness tourism is 'a way of life oriented toward optimal health and well-being in which the body, mind, and spirit are integrated by the individual to live more fully within the human and natural community'. As a result of the trend towards this way of life a new kind of spa travel has emerged worldwide in recent years, where the curative properties of mineral waters are successfully combined with other wellness treatments and therapies as well as with enjoyable holidays.

(6) In this book natural hot and mineral springs are included in health and wellness spa tourism as both a location *and* a major form of treatment for visitors. However, although there are various definitions of health and wellness spa tourism by different authors, not many refer directly to the use of hot springs. From the evidence we present it becomes obvious that hot and mineral springs fall into the category of natural resources which are often favoured and given preference if available – the challenge is to have their centrality to health and wellness spa tourism recognised.

(7) While there is a lot of scientific research being conducted in relation to hot springs and their use in (medical) thermalism and for a variety of purely wellness-related purposes, the field of hot spring and spa tourism is underreported as yet, especially in the tourism literature. Nevertheless, the term 'wellness' is in fact widely used in European and other tourism industry circles when assessing a tourist's likely behaviour in a market (Mueller & Kaufmann, n.d.). The principal problems regarding wellness as a tourism industry resource and attractor for tourists concern the expanding supply of facilities in a situation of *insufficiently researched demand* for such facilities. This situation impacts on the quality dimension of wellness services, which has increasingly become the decisive competitive factor in the market. For this reason quality management is now seen as playing an important role. Existing market research shows that the average three- to five-star hotel provides fairly comprehensive health and wellness facilities (Chapter 8), where they specialise in health information, individual care and a wide range of cultural and relaxation programmes. However, although the same hotel can host health (cure) guests and wellness guests simultaneously, these two segments have to be considered separately when deciding on appropriate marketing strategies. It is therefore assumed in the industry that wellness is pursued solely by 'healthy' people, the primary aim being prevention rather than cure, in comparison to health resort guests, who may seek rehabilitation and recovery from injury or illness. Nevertheless, some overlap cannot be excluded and needs to be researched.

(8) While health and wellness tourism is not new according to historical accounts of travelling for health purposes, the recent wellness movement has resulted in changes in lifestyle choices for an increasing number of people, no matter

whether this is actually based on natural hot springs or not. Several authors of academic papers have given valuable insights into the natural hot and mineral spa system in a variety of countries, some of which are quite unique by global standards. Bathing in hot and mineral springs and drinking mineral water sourced from natural springs is thus a critical part of a holistic approach to the multi-dimensional health and wellness concept.

Final Comments

This book has highlighted the opportunities that exist for developing health and wellness spa tourism in conjunction with hot and mineral springs. In particular, we were able to show that the benefits of hot and mineral springs include the following:

A Therapeutic Value: A very good way to relax in different and natural environments while bathing in hot and mineral water.

A Curative Value: Depending on the condition or illness and on the individual's 'personal biochemical makeup' (Clark, 1994: 132). Hot springs and their associated minerals have generally been found to be important for the treatment of skin conditions like psoriasis and diseases like rheumatism and arthritis (see Table 10.5).

An Associative Value: Especially mentally uplifting due to relaxation and the increased feeling of well-being of body, mind and spirit when associated with modern wellness/fitness therapies and medical procedures.

Finally, our research strongly supports the health value of geothermal springs worldwide as well as helping to clarify the importance of traditional and contemporary applications and treatments utilising these natural resources. This is especially true for the recent and rapidly developing trend towards the combination of medical treatment with balneology in those countries that have the hot and mineral spring resources as well as the hospital facilities needed to offer medical and surgical procedures for international clients. Many European countries have in the past carried out medical research through clinical trials of balneological treatments, either in combination with other therapies or as individual treatment, and those results underpin the current acknowledgment that the treatment with natural hot and mineral-rich water is beneficial in the recovery from major medical procedures and conditions. These results, along with concern over prices for medical services in developed countries, support the current investment in medical tourism in many countries of Asia and the Middle East. This in turn gives further support for the worldwide significance of natural hot and mineral springs for health and wellness spa tourism. As a final word the following table details representative examples of established natural hot and mineral spring destinations and is designed to emphasise the global significance of health and wellness spa tourism.

Table 10.5 The use of geothermal water for health and wellness treatments: Selected examples from a number of countries. The figures may vary according to source

Country	Hot spring or location	Used since	Water temperature (°C)	Water composition	Daily flow rate	Depth of the source	Therapeutic qualities	Visitor numbers
Argentina	Federación Thermal Spa	1997	41	Sodium bicarbonate Sodium chloride TDS 698 mg/l, pH 8.5	10.8 million l/d	1300 m (bore)	Digestive and respiratory systems, chronic rheumatism, vertebral arthrosis, locomotive apparatus, skin, relaxation	220,000 visitors in 2002
Australia	Moree Artesian Bore Baths	1895	41.6	Alkaline springs	13.5 million l/d	951 m (old bore), 868 m (new)	Rheumatism, arthritis, sciatica, analgesic and sedative effects, muscular problems	300,000 visitors p/a
Australia	Peninsula Hot Springs*	2005	38–43	Sulphur spring sodium, chloride, bicarbonate	4,752,000 l/d	637 m (bore)	Rheumatism, arthritis, central nervous system, orthopaedic and gynaecologic disorders, post-traumatic and post-operative	100,000+ visitors p/a

(Continued)

Table 10.5 Continued

Country	Hot spring or location	Used since	Water temperature (°C)	Water composition	Daily flow rate	Depth of the source	Therapeutic qualities	Visitor numbers
	Classified as true hot and mineral spring			TDS 3200 ppm, pH 6.8				
Austria	Baden (*Aquae*)	50 AD	36–47	Sulphur spring sodium-calcium chloride sulphate water	1 million l/d	3000 m (bore)	Rheumatic diseases, injuries, metabolic disorders, neurological, heart and cardio-vascular diseases	N/A
Belgium	Spa	14th century AD	32	High concentration of iron and sulphur	N/A	N/A	Rheumatism, arthritis, wellness, beauty centres	N/A
Brazil	Caldas Novas	1722	34–57	Alkaline springs	28.8 million l/d	Artesian bores	Aquatic centres at hotels, but also 'certified therapies' for blood pressure, kidney stones, digestion, rheumatism	300,000 during carnival 100,000 during high season

Canada	Fairmont Hot Springs	1869	32–39, varies by season	Sulphur springs TDS 559 ppm, pH 8.41	7.5 million l/d	Cluster of springs 130 m (bore)	Increase of metabolism, detox of lymphatic system, improvement of blood circulation	500,000 visitors p/a
China	Huaqing	Western Zhou Dynasty (1050–771 BC)	43	Spring water contains limes, sodium carbonate, sodium sulphate	2.7 million l/d	1750–2500 m	Therapeutic effects on the skin, dermatosis, rheumatism, arthritis, and muscular pain, relaxation	25,000 visitors a day in Golden Week 2007
England	Thermae Bath Spa and Roman Baths (Aquae Sulis)	2006 opening of new Thermae 863 BC (Legend) 43 AD (Romans)	43–49	High concentrations of sodium, calcium, chloride and sulphate	1,250,400 l/d	3 natural geothermal springs	Newly developed health and wellness spa complex and treatment centre	Thermae Bath Spa 150,000 visitors p/a Roman Baths 834,742 visitors (2008)
France	Aix-les-Bains	120 BC	43–45	Sulphur springs	4 million l/d	Natural geothermal spring	Rheumatism, neuralgia	40,000 (in 1921)

(Continued)

Table 10.5 *Continued*

Country	Hot spring or location	Used since	Water temperature (°C)	Water composition	Daily flow rate	Depth of the source	Therapeutic qualities	Visitor numbers
Germany	Bad Füssing	1938 (discovered during oil exploration)	56	Sulphur springs chloride, natrium, fluoride, hydrogen carbonate	2.4 million l/d	1000 m (bore)	Rheumatism, degenerative bone diseases	1.5 million day visitors (2007) 260,137 stay visitors (2007)
Germany	Aachen (Aquis Granum or Aquae Grannii)	100–39 BC Used by local tribes followed by the Romans	45–75	Sodium, sulphur, chloride, fluoride, natrium, hydrogen carbonate	3,500,000 l/d	Artesian Springs	Rheumatism, post-injury and, post-operative rehabilitation, gout, osteoporosis, infections and degenerative bone diseases	e.g. Carolus Thermal Baths 384,500 visitors (2007)
Greece	Edipsus (Aedipsos or Aidipsos) Thermae of Sulla Bath of Herakles	2nd xentury BC (mentioned by Plutarch 84 BC)	78–86	Sulphur springs pH 6.65	N/A	Natural geothermal springs	Arthritis, gout, rheumatism, neuralgia, sciatica, post-injury treatments Centre for hydro-therapy	N/A

			Temperature (°C)	Composition	Flow	Source	Benefits	Visitors
Hungary	Budapest (Aquincum)	Possibly since Neolithic Era (4000–2000 BC)	21–78	Calcium, magnesium, hydrogen carbonate, sulphate chloride, some radio-active waters	70–80 million l/d	118 springs and bores	Several medicinal baths within Budapest, proven medicinal properties, qualified medical assistance	1.6 million p/a
Iceland	Blue Lagoon	1981	40 (average)	Geothermal seawater sulphur and silica, pH 7.5, TDS 31,900 mg/kg, salt content 2.5%	21,600,000 l/d (6 million l replaced every 40 h)	2000 m	Clinic for psoriasis patients and other skin problems	100,000+ p/a
Iceland	Myvatn Nature Baths	2004	36–40	Contains a large amount of minerals, is alkaline and well suited for bathing	Geothermal water from a cooling and holding basin	Natural geothermal spring	Beneficial for health, skin, relaxation	64,000 (in 2007)
Israel	Hamat Gader	4th century AD (Health Resort since 1977)	20–42, varies by season	Sulphur springs Chloride, calcium, magnesium	12–16.8 million l/d	5 natural geothermal springs	Rheumatism, muscular problems, diseases of the joints and spine	N/A
Italy	Abano Terme Aquae Patavinae			Thermal waters containing bromide and iodide salts	86.4 million l/d	Natural geothermal springs plus	Treatments with thermal waters and thermal mud	N/A

(Continued)

Table 10.5 *Continued*

Country	Hot spring or location	Used since	Water temperature (°C)	Water composition	Daily flow rate	Depth of the source	Therapeutic qualities	Visitor numbers
		Used by Romans and was rebuilt during 12th century AD	65–87			230 wells, 300–700 m deep	Seborrheic dermatitis, acne, eczema, respiratory disorders	
Japan	Beppu (over 2200 active springs)	8th century AD	150 *underground then cooled*	Sodium-chloride-type water	50,143,680 l/d	Natural geothermal spring	Relaxation, health treatments according to mineral content – great variety of health benefits	12 million visitors p/a
Japan	Yumoto (Tochigi Prefecture)	Heian period (mentioned in ancient literature – 927 AD)	59.8	Sulphur spring contains sodium and chlorides	7,200,000– 11,520,000 l/d	Spring water rises from old Joban coal mining shaft	Neuralgia, female disorders, chronic dermatitis, eczema, diabetes, joint and muscle pain, health enhancement	Tochigi Prefecture 6.7 million visitors p/a

Country	Name	History	Temperature	Water type	Flow rate	Source	Benefits/uses	
Jordan	Wadi Afra Springs	73–4 BC (Herod the Great)	47–49	Alkaline springs Chloride, radioactive	38,880,000 l/d	Natural geothermal spring	Arthritis, rheumatism, muscular problems, gynaecological diseases, infertility	N/A
Korea	Icheon Hot Springs	1870s First spas developed under Japanese occupation	28–31	Sodium based, alkaline	N/A	Natural geothermal spring	Eye problems, relaxation, rejuvenation, blood circulation, arthritis, relaxation and rejuvenation	N/A
Mexico	Agua Hedionda (popular tourist attraction)	Legendary use by Montezuma I mid-1400s	26.6–27.7	Sulphur springs – slightly radioactive, pH 6.45**	65,404,800 l/d	Natural geothermal spring	Respiratory diseases, skin problems, stress	N/A
Namibia (South Africa)	Warmbaths (Bela Bela since 2002)	Around 1873	52	Sodium chloride	528,000 l/d (6 l/s)	Natural geothermal spring	Rheumatism, relaxation	N/A
New Zealand	Miranda Hot Springs (Hauraki Hot Springs)	Used by Ngati Paoa Maōri (n.d.)	33–57	Alkaline/saline pH 8.9, TDS 430 ppm***	720,000 l/d	Natural geothermal spring plus bore	Recreation, relaxation Largest thermal pool in the southern hemisphere	N/A

(Continued)

Table 10.5 *Continued*

Country	Hot spring or location	Used since	Water temperature (°C)	Water composition	Daily flow rate	Depth of the source	Therapeutic qualities	Visitor numbers
New Zealand	Polynesian Spa	Springs discovered 1878 Polynesian Spa since 1972	33–43	Acidic springs mineral content and water level change frequently	5 million l/d	Natural geothermal spring, water is cooled down by mixing with town water	Rheumatism, arthritis, muscular problems, soothing, relaxation, gout	1.62 million visitors to Rotorua's geothermal tourist facilities
India	Tattapani (Himachal Pradesh)	N/A	65–83	Alkaline and sulphur springs	90,000–1,530,000 l/d	2 natural geothermal springs	Rheumatism, skin problems	Under-developed
Peru (South America)	Cajamarca (Baths of the Inca)	Around 1550	65–87	Sodium, potassium, iron, calcium and strontium, silica and magnesium	N/A	Natural geothermal spring	Relaxation therapies, rheumatism, skin problems, nervous system	N/A
Portugal	Caldas da Rainha	1495	60	Sulphur springs	400,000 l/d	Natural geothermal spring	Rheumatism, arthritis, skin problems	N/A
Switzerland	Baden	58 BC	35–47	Sulphur springs	4,536,000 l/d	14 natural geothermal springs	Relaxation, Roman bathing rituals, hammam bathing, health and wellness	N/A

Taiwan (over 100 hot springs)	Beitou	1893 AD (1697 AD first records of use)	40–75	Sulphur springs	N/A	Natural geothermal spring	Heritage of Japanese *Onsen* culture, therapeutic effects for many diseases	3.7 million visitors in 2007
Turkey	Pamukkale (Hierapolis)	2nd century BC	36–38	Calcium–magnesium sulphate and bicarbonate waters TDS 2430mg/l, pH 6	34,560,000 l/d	Natural geothermal spring	Rheumatism, dermatologic and gynaecologic diseases, neuro-logical and physical exhaustion, digestive and nutrition disorders	Capacity for treatment of 600 people p/d
Turkey	Bursa (Çekirge Hot Springs)	Ottoman Empire	39–58	Calcium–magnesium and bicarbonate waters TDS 1164 mg/l, pH 7.2–6.6	432,000 l/d	Natural geothermal spring	Rheumatic diseases, hepatic and gall bladder, metabolic disorders, gynaecological, post-operative disorders	Capacity to treat 400–600 people p/d

(Continued)

Table 10.5 Continued

Country	Hot spring or location	Used since	Water temperature (°C)	Water composition	Daily flow rate	Depth of the source	Therapeutic qualities	Visitor numbers
Turkey	Yalova Hot Springs	6th century AD	57–60	Sodium chloride, calcium sulphates, fluoride waters TDS 1435 mg/l	1,296,000 l/d	Natural geothermal spring	Rheumatic diseases, digestive and metabolic problems, neurological and urological disorders, metabolic	Capacity to treat 2000 people p/d
United States	Thermopolis Wyoming	1896 – Treaty between Native Tribes and Federal Government	22–56	Bicarbonate, sulphide, chloride, sodium, TDS 2400 mg/l	10.4 million l/d	Cluster of natural geothermal springs	Chronic pain management, head and spinal injuries, bedsores, burns rehabilitation	N/A
Uruguay	Termas de Salto Grande (Thermal Spa Resorts)	Established in recent years	38–45	Bicarbonate sodium chloride	N/A	Well spring Depth 1295 m	Skin problems, relaxation, renal, gastric and intestinal conditions	N/A

*TAG (2006); Webb (2005); **National University of Mexico and ***Freeston (2005).

References

Aachen (n.d.) *Aquae Grannii*. On WWW at http://www.aachen.de/EN/ts/100_taking_a
_cure/100_99/index.html. Accessed 12.2.2006.

Aachen (2005) *Thermalquellen*. On WWW at http://www.koelnerbucht.de/regioinfo-
aachen.htm. Accessed 12.2.2006.

Aaland, M. (1998) *The Russian Bania – A Boisterous Bath in Leningrad, The Spreading Influence
of the Russian Steam Bath*. On WWW at http://www.cyberbohemia.com/Pages/
russianbania.htm. Accessed 10.12.2008.

Abels, D.J., Even-Paz, Z. and Efron, D. (1996) Bioclimatology at the Dead Sea in Israel.
Clinics in Dermatology 14 (6), 653–658.

Adams, T.B. (2003) The power of perceptions: Measuring wellness in a globally acceptable,
philosophically consistent way, *wellness management*. On WWW at http://www.hedir.org.
Accessed 12.2.2006.

Agishi, Y. and Ohtsuka, Y. (1998) Present features of balneotherapy in Japan. *Global
Environment Research* 2, 177–185.

Ai-Ais Hot Springs Resort [n.d.(a)] *Ai-Ais Hot Springs Resort*. On WWW at http://www.
tourism-africa.co.za/namibia-accommodation/ai-ais-hot-springs-resort.html. Accessed
17.6.2006.

Ai-Ais Hot Springs Resort [n.d.(b)] *Ai-Ais Hot Springs Resort – The Fish River Canyon Namibia*.
On WWW at http://www.namibian.org/travel/lodging/ai-ais.htm. Accessed 17.6.2006.

Allaby, A. and Allaby, M. (2003) *Oxford Dictionary of Earth Science*. Oxford: Oxford University
Press.

Alma-Tadema, Sir L. (1877) *The Balneator*. On WWW at http://www.fineart-china.com/
index.htm. Accessed 10.12.2008.

Altman, N. (2000) *Healing Springs: The Ultimate Guide to Taking the Waters – From Hidden
Springs to the World's Greatest Spas*. Rochester, Vermont: Healing Arts Press.

Altman, N. (2002) *Sacred Water: The Spiritual Source of Life*. New Jersey: Hidden Spring: An
Imprint of Paulist Press.

Altmuehlterme (2007) *Das Treuchtlinger Heilwasser*. On WWW at http://www.altmuehltherme.
de/4.0.html. Accessed 10.12.2008.

American Heritage® Stedman's Medical Dictionary (n.d.) *Wellness*. On WWW at http://
dictionary.reference.com/browse/wellness. Accessed 10.12.2008.

Anastasion, D. (2008) *Flesh-Eating Fish Perform 'Pedicures', National Psoriasis Online Forum*.
On WWW at http://www.psoriasis.org/forum/showthread.php?t=31655. Accessed
20.4.2008.

Anderson Stuart, T. (1920) *Helidon Spa: Australia's Wonderful Mineral Water*. Brisbane: Unknown publisher.

Andreassi, L. and Flori, L. (1996) Mineral water and Spas in Italy. *Clinics in Dermatology* 14 (6), 627–632.

Andreu, L., Kozak, M., Avci, N. and Cifter, N. (2005) Market segmentation by motivations to travel: British tourists visiting Turkey. *Journal of Travel and Tourism Marketing* 19 (1), 1–13.

Andreu, L., Bigne, E. and Cooper, C. (2000) Projected and perceived images of Spain as a tourist destination for British travelers. *Journal of Travel and Tourism Marketing* 9 (4), 47–67.

APR Consultants (2004) *Economic Impact of Tourism on the Rotorua District Economy* (Final Report). Prepared for Tourism Rotorua. Rotorua: APR Consultants, May.

Aquarius Roman Baths (2005) *Aquarius Roman Baths*. On WWW at http://www.romanbath.com.au/main.html. Accessed 10.12.2008.

Archaeological World (2006) *Hamat Gader – Roman Baths*. On WWW at http://www.archaeology-classic.com/Israel_E/Hamat_Gader.html. Accessed 20.4.2008.

Arctic Adventure (2008) *Alluitsup Paa – Summer*. On WWW at http://www.arctic-adventure.dk/destinations.php?id=3. Accessed 20.4.2008.

Arieff, A. and Burkhart, B. (2005) *Spa*. Los Angeles: Taschen America.

Arriaga, M.C.S., Cataldi, R. and Hodgson, S.F. (1999) Cosmogeny and uses of geothermal resources in Mesoamerica. In R. Cataldi, S.F. Hodgson and J. Lund (eds) *Stories from a Heated Earth* (pp. 499–519). Sacramento, CA: Geothermal Resources Council, International Geothermal Association.

Arvigo, R. and Epstein, N. (2003) *Spiritual Bathing: Healing Rituals and Traditions from Around the World*. Berkeley, CA: Celestial Arts.

Asensio, P. (2002) *Spa & Wellness Hotels*. New York: teNeues Publishing Group.

Ashkenazi, M. (1993) *Matsuri: Festivals of a Japanese Town*. Honolulu: University of Hawaii Press.

ASHRAE (1999a) *FIVAC Application Handbook, Chapter 48 – General Applications: Swimming Pools/Health Clubs* (pp. 48.19–48.21). Atlanta: ASHRAE.

ASHRAE (1999b) *FIVAC Application Handbook, Chapter 4 – Common Applications, Natatoriums* (pp. 4.5–4.7). Atlanta: ASHRAE.

Asia Spa Magazine (2005a) *September/October Issue*. Hong Kong: Adkom Asia Pacific.

Asia Spa Magazine (2005b) *November/December Issue*. Hong Kong: Adkom Asia Pacific.

Asian Info (2000) *The Literature of Japan*. On WWW at http://www.asianinfo.org/asianinfo/japan/pro-literature.htm. Accessed 10.12.2008.

Association Resource Centre (2006) *2006 Canadian Spa Sector Profile*. Toronto: Canadian Tourism Commission.

Australian Academy of Science (1994) *Environmental Science*. Canberra: Australian Academy of Science.

Austria Info (n.d.) *Water and Wellness*. On WWW at http://cms1.austria.info. Accessed 28.11.2005.

Awofeso, N. (2005) *Re-defining 'Health'*, Bulletin of the World Health Organization, 83, 802. On WWW at http://www.who.int/bulletin/bulletin_board/83/ustun11051/en/. Accessed 20.4.2008.

Bachvarov, M. (2004) *Spas in Central-Eastern Europe between Decline and Revitalization*. Poland: University of Lodz.

Baden Austria (n.d.) *The Roman Health Resort of "Aquae"*. On WWW at http://www.baden.at/pages/english/kurhaus_e1.shtml. Accessed 28.11.2005.

Baden Baden (n.d.) *Römische Badruinen, Museum antiker Badekultur -Geschichtliche Daten*. On WWW at http://www.badruinen.de/. Accessed 28.11.2005.

Baden Switzerland (n.d.) *Die Geschichte der Bäder zu Baden*. On WWW at www.thermalbaden.ch/die_geschichte_der_baeder_zu_baden.pdf. Accessed 28.11.2005.

Bakht, M.S. (2000) An overview of geothermal resources of Pakistan. In *Proceedings World Geothermal Congress 2000*, Kyushu, Tohoku, Japan, 28 May–10 June.

Balneario de Archena. (n.d.) *Termalium – History*. On WWW at http://www.balnearioarchena.com/english/index.html. Accessed 28.1.2006.

Banos (n.d.) *Ecuador in Pictures Baños, Ecuador –* Nuestra Señora del Agua Santa. On WWW at http://gosouthamerica.about.com/cs/ecuador/l/blpixBanos.htm. Accessed 18.6.2007.

Baptism Land (2000) *Jordan – Hot Springs*. On WWW at http://holysites.com/hotsprings_touristic.htm. Accessed 20.4.2008.

Barabanov, L.N. and Disler, V.N. (1968) Principal regularities of the formation of nitrogenous thermal waters in the U.S.S.R. and some other countries. In G. Kaèura (ed.) *International Geological Congress, Proceedings of Symposium II Genesis of Mineral and Thermal Water* (Report of the 23rd Session Czechoslovakia, 1968). Prague: Academia.

Bargar, M.L. and Muffler, L.J.P. (1975) Geologic map of the travertine deposits, Mammoth Hot Springs, Yellowstone National Park. Wyoming, *Geological Survey Miscellaneous Field Studies Map MF-659 1:48000 and 1:2400 Scale*. Washington DC: USGS.

Barnett, N.D., Kaplan, A.M., Hopkin, R.J., Saubolle, M.A. and Rudinsky, M.F. (1996) Primary amoebic meningoencephalitis with *Naegleria fowleri*: Clinical review. *Ped Neuro* 15, 230–234.

Barry, M. (2008) *ISPA 2006 Consumer Trends Report*. Washington State: The Hartman Group.

Bartram, J. and Rees, G. (eds) (1999) *Monitoring Bathing Waters: A Practical Guide to the Design and Implementation of Assessments and Monitoring Programs*. London: E & FN Spon.

Bastmeijer, K. and Roura, R. (2004) Regulating Antarctic tourism and the precautionary principle. *The American Journal of International Law* 98 (4), 763–781.

Bath and North East Somerset Council (2002) *The Hot Springs of Bath: Geology, Geochemistry, Geophysics*. Bath: Bath and North East Somerset Council.

Bathing and Spa Information (n.d.) *China*. On WWW at http://www.bathe.com.au/Pages/Info/info.html. Accessed 28.11.2008.

Benedetto, A.V. and Millikan, L.E. (1996) Mineral water and spas in the United States. *Clinics in Dermatology* 14 (6), 583–600.

Bennett, M., King, B. and Milner, L. (2004) The health resort in Australia: A positioning study. *Journal of Vacation Marketing* 10 (2), 122–137.

Ben Mohamed, M. (2003) Multiple integrated use of geothermal resources in the Kebili region, southern Tunisia. Presented to the *International Geothermal Conference*, Reykjavík, September.

Beppu International Tourist Office (2007) *The Use of Japanese Hot Springs by Prefecture*. Beppu: Beppu International Tourist Office, Summary Table.

Berger, C.R. and Dibattista, P. (1993) Communication and plan failure. *Communication Monographs* 60, 220–238.

Berry, G.W., Grim, P.J. and Ikelman, J.A. (1980) *Thermal Springs List for the United States*. Washington: U.S. Department of Commerce, National Oceanic and Atmospheric Administration – Environmental Data and Information Service.

Biddle, R. (2001) *Heat and Healing: The Hot Spring Culture of Japan*. On WWW at http://www.crossculturedtraveler.com/Archives/NOV2001/Hot_Spring_JP.htm.

Bio Analogics (2001) *Wellness Industry Top Trends for the New Millennium – Increasing Ned for Emphasis on Weight Management Programs*. On WWW at http://www.imakenews.com. Accessed 28.11.2008.

BioFach (2004) *Trendreport*. On WWW at http://www.powtech.de/main/Inhalt+ohne+Links.pdf Accessed 28.11.2008.

Bischoff, M. (2001) *Touring New Mexico Hot Springs, A Falcon Guide*. Guilford, CT: Globe Pequot Press.

Bird, J.W. (n.d.) *Cameroon is Africa in One Country*. On WWW at http://www.africa-ata.org/cameroon_diversity.htm. Accessed 28.11.2008.

Bitner, M.J. (1995) Building service relationships: It's all about promises. *Journal of the Academy of Marketing Science* 23 (Fall), 246–251.

Blomfield, C. (1884) *Lake Rotomahana, Painting by Charles Bromfield*. On WWW at http://www.teara.govt.nz/NewZealanders/MaoriNewZealanders/TeArawa/5/ENZ-Resources/Standard/1/en.

Blomfield, C. (1890) *Painting of the White Terraces, Near Rotorua, New Zealand*. On WWW at http://en.wikipedia.org/wiki/Image: White_Terraces,_Blomfield.jpg. Accessed 14.11.2008.

Blue Lagoon Iceland (2005) *About Us*. On WWW at http://www.bluelagoon.com/. Accessed 18.11.2006.

Blue Lagoon Iceland (2008) *About Us*. On WWW at http://www.bluelagoon.com/top_en/About_Blue_Lagoon/. Accessed 28.11.2008.

Blue World Travel (2006) *Hot Spring History*. On WWW at http://www.psoriasisfishcure.com/moreinfo.htm. Accessed 28.11.2008.

Bolivia in Pictures (n.d.) *Altiplano and the Salar de Uyuni*. On WWW at http://gosouthamerica.about.com/library/blBolpixSalar4.htm. Accessed 18.11.2008.

Boulangé, M. (1982) Thermal treatment: Current therapeutic status. *Phlébologie* 35 (2), 571–579.

Bowen, R. (1989) *Geothermal Resources*. New York: Elsevier.

Bowman, M. (1998) Belief, legend and perceptions of the sacred in contemporary bath. *Folklore* 109, 25–31.

Brazil Spas (n.d.) *Costão do Santinho Spa*. On WWW at http://gosouthamerica.about.com/cs/southamerica/a/hotsprings_2.htm. Accessed 18.11.2008.

Breckenridge, R.M. and Hinckley, B.S. (1978) Thermal springs of Wyoming. *Geological Survey of Wyoming Bulletin* 60, 104.

Brooke, B. (n.d.) *Taking the "Waters" in Mexico – An Exploration of Some of Mexico's Wonderful Spas*. On WWW at http://www.mexconnect.com/mex_/travel/bbrooke/bbspas.html

Brown, A. (2005) *Top Ten Spa Trends*. On WWW at http://spas.about.com/od/spareviews/a/topspatrends.htm. Accessed 13.2.2006.

Brown, A. (2006) *Types of Spas*. On WWW at http://spas.about.com. Accessed 13.2.2006.

Bryan, T.S. (1986) *The Geysers of Yellowstone*. Boulder, CO: Colorado Associated University Press.

Buckley, R. (2007) *Adventure Tourism*. London: CABI.

Bullard, L. (2004) *Healing Waters – Missouri's Historical Mineral Springs and Spas*. Columbia: University of Missouri Press.

Burachovic, S. (n.d.) *History of Karlovy Vary*. On WWW at http://karlovyvary.cz/static/history_2asp?LangId=2&Kol=1. Accessed 10.12.2008.

Buzzle.Com (2007) *Reverse Sushi: Let Doctor Fish Nibble Your Dead Skin Away*. On WWW at http://www.buzzle.com/articles/reverse-sushi-let-doctor-fish-nibble-your-dead-skin-away.html. Accessed 18.6.2008.

Cabanillas, R. (n.d.) *Balnearios de Galicia, Turgalicia, Santiago de Compostela*. On WWW at www.balneariosdegalicia.com. Accessed 18.6.2008.

Caldas Novas (n.d.(a)) *Information About the Hot Water of Caldas Novas*. On WWW at http://www.answers.com/topic/caldas-novas. Accessed 18.6.2008.

Caldas Novas (n.d.(b)) *The Largest Hydrothermal Place in the World – Tourism*. On WWW at http://www.geocities.com/TheTropics/5342/usframe.htm. Accessed 18.6.2008.

Calderón, G.R. (1999) Andean cultures and geothermal phenomena. In R. Cataldi, S.F. Hodgson and J.W. Lund (eds) *Stories from a Heated Earth* (pp. 555–569). Sacramento, CA: Geothermal Resources Council, International Geothermal Association.

Caldes de Malavella (n.d.) *Tourism*. On WWW at http://www.caldesdemalavella.cat/Turisme_eng.htm. Accessed 18.6.2008.

Caldes de Montbui (n.d.) *Caldes de Montbui – Online Document*. On WWW at http://en.wikipedia.org/wiki/Caldes_de_Montbui. Accessed 18.6.2008.

Canadian Rockies Hot Springs (2006) *Natural Wonders & Cultural Treasures, Hot Springs Comparison Chart*. On WWW at http://www.pc.gc.ca/regional/sourcesthermales-hotsprings/itm3-/natcul2_E.asp. Accessed 18.6.2008.

Canadian Spa Imports (n.d.) *Your Wholesale Supplier of Garra Rufa Doctor Fish*. On WWW at http://www.canadianspaimports.com/. Accessed 18.6.2008.

Canadian Tourist Commission (2008) *Tourism Snapshot*. On WWW at www.canada.travel. Accessed 18.6.2008.

Carasana Bäderbetriebe GmbH. (n.d.) *Thermal Spring Water*. On WWW at http://www.carasana. de/home/en/ri_angebot_thermalwasser.html. Accessed 18.6.2008.

Cataldi, R. and Burgassi, P.D. (1999) Flowering and decline of thermal bathing and other uses of natural heat in the Mediterranean area, from the birth of Rome to the end of the first Millennium. In R. Cataldi, S.F. Hodgson and J.W. Lund (eds) *Stories from a Heated Earth* (pp. 147–164). Sacramento, CA: Geothermal Resources Council, International Geothermal Association.

Cataldi, R., Hodgson, S.F. and Lund, J.W. (1999) *Stories from a Heated Earth – Our Geothermal Heritage*. Sacramento, CA: Geothermal Resources Council, International Geothermal Association.

Catania (n.d.) *Catania, wo die Erde atmet*. On WWW at http://www.tuifly.com/de/destinations/ catania.html. Accessed 18.6.2008.

Chandrasekharam, D. (1999) A prehistoric view of the hot springs of India. In R. Cataldi, S.F. Hodgson and J.W. Lund (eds) *Stories from a Heated Earth* (pp. 357–367). Sacramento, CA: Geothermal Resources Council, International Geothermal Association.

Chandrasekharam, D., Alam, M.A. and Minissale, A. (2005) Thermal discharges at Manikaran, Himachal Pradesh, India. In *Proceedings of the World Geothermal Congress*, Anatalya (pp. 1–4), 24–29 April.

Chapman, J. (2005) Suite Voyage. *Spa Asia Magazine*, November/December, 42.

Chaterji, G.C. and Guha, S.K. (1968) The problem of origin of high temperature springs in India. In *Proceedings of Symposium II – International Geological Congress, Genesis of Mineral and Thermal Waters* (Report of the 23rd Session). Prague, Czechoslovakia.

Chile (n.d.(a)) *Chile's Spas Attracting More Attention*. On WWW at http://gosouthamerica. about.com/b/a/257976.htm. Accessed 18.6.2008.

Chile (n.d.(b)) *Chillan, Concepcion and Los Angeles*. On WWW at http://gosouthamerica. about.com/od/chillan1/Chillan_Concepcion_Los_Angeles.htm. Accessed 18.6.2008.

China Travel and Experience (n.d.) *Huaqing Hot Springs*. On WWW at http://www.cntravel. biz/cityguides/xian/huaqing_springs/index.htm. Accessed 18.6.2008.

Chris73 (2004) *Nachikatsuura Onsen*. On WWW at http://commons.wikimedia.org/wiki/ Image: Onsen_in_Nachikatsuura_Japan.jpg. Accessed 18.6.2008.

CIA (2008) *World Factbook: Area and Population of Countries*. On WWW at https://www.cia. gov/library/publications/the-world-factbook/. Accessed 28.7.2008.

Ciater Hot Spring (n.d.) *Unique Heritage and Culture – Interesting Places*. On WWW at http:// www.indonesia-tourism.com/west-java/ciater-hot-spring.html. Accessed 18.6.2008.

Cieplice Śląskie-Zdrój (2007) *Health Spa*. On WWW at http://www.pl-info.net/poland/ health-spas/cieplice_slaskie-zdroj.html. Accessed 18.6.2008.

City of Kyustendil (n.d.) *Kyustendil History*. On WWW at http://www.visitbulgaria.net/ en/kyustendil/. Accessed 18.6.2008.

Clark, A.J. (2005) *Australia's Best Spas: The Ultimate Guide to Luxury and Relaxation*. Singapore: Periplus Editions (HK) Ltd.

Clark, S. (1999) *Japan, A View from the Bath*. Honolulu: University of Hawaii Press.

Clews, S.R. (ed.) (2000) *Roman Baths and Pump Room Conservation Statement*. Bath: Bath and North East Somerset Council.

Clugston, M.J. (2004) *The New Penguin Dictionary of Science*. London: Penguin Books.

Cohen, M. (2008) Spas, wellness and human evolution. In M. Cohen and G. Bodeker (eds) *Understanding the Global Spa Industry: Spa Management* (pp. 3–25). London: Butterworth & Heinemann.

Cohen, M. and G. Bodeker (2008) *Understanding the Global Spa Industry: Spa Management*. London: Butterworth & Heinemann.

Cohut, I. and Árpási, M. (1995) Ancient uses of geothermal waters in the precarpathian area of Romania and the Pannonian Basin of Hungary. In R. Cataldi, S.F. Hodgson and J.W. Lund (eds) *Stories from a Heated Earth* (pp. 239–251). Sacramento, CA: Geothermal Resources Council, International Geothermal Association.

Cooper, M. J. (2009) River Tourism in the South Asian Subcontinent. In B. Prideaux and M. Cooper (eds) *River Tourism* (pp. 23–40). New York: CAB International.

Cooper, M.J., Abubakar, B. and Erfurt, P. (2001) Eco-tourism development into the new millennium on Fraser Island: Tour operators perspectives. *Tourism* 49 (4), 359–367.

Cooper, M. and Erfurt, P. (2002) Eco-tourism accreditation: A planning tool for Asia–Pacific countries? In K-S. Chon, V.C.S. Cheung and K. Wong (eds) *Proceedings of the 5th Biennial Conference on Tourism in Asia* (pp. 115–125). Hong Kong, 23–25 May. University of Houston: Haworth Hospitality Press.

Cooper, M.J. and Erfurt, P. (2003) Lake management under conditions of heavy tourist pressure: The case of Fraser Island. *Ritsumeikan Journal of Asia Pacific Studies* 12, 61–74.

Cooper, M.J. and Flehr, M. (2006) Government intervention in tourism development: The case of Japan and South Australia. In D. Harrison (Guest ed.) *Tourism and Land Development: A Special Issue of Current Issues in Tourism* 9 (1), 69–85.

Cooper, M., Ogata, M. and Eades, J.S. (2008) Heritage tourism in Japan – A synthesis and comment. In B. Prideaux, D. Timothy and K. Chon (eds) *Culture and Heritage Tourism in the Asia Pacific* (pp. 107–117). London: Routledge.

Corbett, T. (2001) *The Making of American Resorts – Saratoga Springs, Ballston Spa, Lake George.* New York: Rutgers University Press.

Cordes, R. (2004) *Splashing in Spa.* On WWW at http://www.expatica.com/actual/article. asp?subchannel_id=51&story_id=8660. Accessed 26.1.2008.

Corsica (2003) *Thermal Baths – The Spas in Corsica.* On WWW at http://www.corsica.net/ corsica/uk/sejours/thermal/index.htm. Accessed 18.6.2008.

Courier Mail (2006) *Baby Boomers Enter Prime Time*, Opinion, 2 January. Brisbane: Queensland Newspapers Ltd.

Crompton, J.L. (1979) Motivations for pleasure vacation. *Annals of Tourism Research* 6 (4), 408–424.

Crossley, A. (2003) *Lifestyles Continue to Shape Global OTC Market.* On WWW at http://www. euromonitor.com/article.?id=2195. Accessed 26.1.2006.

Cruey, G. (n.d.) *Asia for Visitors – In the Yellow Mountains of Anhui Province: Huangshan Scenic Area.* On WWW at http://goasia.about.com/od/china/a/huangshan.htm. Accessed 18.6.2008.

Cunningham, N., Kagan, R.A. and Thornton, D. (2003) *Shades of Green: Business, Regulation, and Environment.* Stanford: Stanford University Press.

Current Archaeology in Turkey (2007) *Hierapolis (Denizli).* On WWW at http://cat.une.edu. au/page/hierapolis. Accessed 18.6.2008.

Czech Tourism (2008) *Domestic and Outgoing Tourism in the Czech Republic, 2007.* On WWW at http://www.czechtourism.cz/files/statistiky/aktualni_data/25_06_08_domaci_ vyjezd_cr_2007.pdf. Accessed 10.12.2008.

Dabrowska, K. (2004) *St Lucia: Waiting to Welcome Middle Easterners and Muslims.* On WWW at http://www.islamictourism.com/news_E.php?id=604&search=hot%20springs. Accessed 26.1.2006.

Danino, M. (1999) *The Indus–Sarasvati Civilization and its Bearing on the Aryan Question.* On WWW at http://micheldanino.voiceofdharma.com/indus.html#_ednref6. Accessed 18.6.2008.

Davison, P. (2003) *Volcano in Paradise – Death and Survival on the Caribbean Island of Montserrat.* London: Methuen Publishing Ltd.

Deception Island (n.d.) *Pendulum Cove.* On WWW at http://www.galenfrysinger.com/ deception_island_antarctica.htm. Accessed 26.1.2006.

de Garis, F. (1922) *The Hot Springs of Japan.* Tokyo: Japan Government Railways.

de la Barre, K., de la Barre, S. and Taggart, M. (2005) *A Feasibility Study for a Yukon Health and Wellness Tourism Industry.* Prepared for the North to Knowledge, Learning Travel Product Club and the Department of Tourism and Culture, Yukon Territorial Government, Whitehorse, Yukon (May).

Denizli (n.d.) *Pamukkale*. On WWW at http://www.adiyamanli.org/denizli.html. Accessed 22.1.2007.

Department of Tourism, Philippines (2007) *Puning Hot Springs*. On WWW at http://www.visitmyphilippines.com/index.php?title=Mt.PinatuboHotSprings&func=all&pid=1295 &tbl=0. Accessed 12.1.2008.

Department of Tourism, Philippines (2008) *Philippines Tourism Data*. On WWW at http://www.wowphilippines.com.ph/dot/statistics.asp. Accessed 10.12.2008.

Deutscher Heilbäderverband (1999) *Heilbäder und Kurorte in Zahlen*. On WWW at http://www.deutscher-heilbaederverband.de/body_kurinformationen5.html. Accessed 14.12.2005.

De Villiers, M. (2000) *Water – The Fate of our Most Precious Resource*. Boston, MA: Mariner Books, Houghton Mifflin Company.

Die Welt des Bades (n.d.) *Bad – Geschichte: Vom Marmorbad in den Holzzuber*. On WWW at http://www.dasbad.ch/pages/ueberuns/geschichte.asp?m=m100. Accessed 24.2.2008.

Discover Spas (2006) *Different Types of Spas*. On WWW at http://www.discoverspas.com. Accessed 24.2.2006.

Dōgo Onsen [n.d.(a)] *Japanese Lifestyle*. On WWW at http://www.japaneselifestyle.com.au/travel/dogo_onsen.html. Accessed 12.2.2007.

Dōgo Onsen [n.d.(b)] *History*. On WWW at http://en.wikipedia.org/wiki/Dogo_Onsen. Accessed 12.2.2007.

Dōgo Onsen [n.d.(c)] *Dōgo Hot Spring*. On WWW at http://www.jlpp.jp/english/list/works17/column.html. Accessed 12.2.2007.

Dōgo Onsen [n.d.(d)] *Matsuyama – Home of History and Literature*. On WWW at http://www.japannuclear.com/nihonsalon/articles/16-jDSBHkKPEq3HYB1gxKHx/view. Accessed 12.2.2007.

Dōgo Onsen [n.d.(e)] *Ehime – Dogo Onsen Hot Spring* – Online Document. On WWW at www.jnto.go.jp/eng//location/regional/ehime/dogoonsen.html. Accessed 12.2.2007.

Donovan, P. and Sammler, T. (1994) *Delighting Customers: How to build a Customer-Driven Organization*. New York: Chapman & Hall.

Dorsch, M.J., Grove, S.J. and Darden, W.R. (2000) Consumer intentions to use a service category. *Journal of Services Marketing* 14 (2), 92–117.

Douglas, N., Douglas, N. and Derrett, R. (2001) *Special Interest Tourism*. Sydney: John Wiley & Sons.

Dowling, R. and Newsome, D. (2006) *GeoTourism*. London: Elsevier.

Dukinfield Astley, H.J. (1910) A sacred spring and tree at Hammam R'Irha, Algeria. *Man* 10, 122–123.

Dunn, H.L. (1961) *High-Level Wellness*. Arlington, VA: Beatty Press.

DWV (Deutscher Wellness Verband) (2006) *Der unabhängige Ratgeber für Wellnessgenießer und Wellness-Anbieter*. On WWW at http://www.wellnessverband.de/medical/index.php. Accessed 30.1.2006.

DWV (Deutscher Wellness Verband) (2007) *Der unabhängige Ratgeber für Wellnessgenießer und Wellness-Anbieter*. On WWW at http://www.wellnessverband.de/. Accessed 12.2.2007.

Dwyer, L., Jago, L., Deery, M. and Friedline, L. (2007) Corporate responsibility as essential to sustainable tourism yield. *Tourism Review International* 11, 155–166.

Eades, J.S. (2010) Sun, surgery and cyberspace: The role of the Internet in the rise of medical tourism. In M.J. Cooper, W. Pease and R. Gujurajan (eds) *Biomedical Knowledge Management: Infrastructures and Processes for E-Health Systems*. Hershey: IGI Global (forthcoming).

Eaton, G.P., Christiansen, R.L., Iyer, H.M., Pitt, A.M., Mabey, D.R., Blank, H.R. Jr., Zietz, I. and Gettings, M.E. (1975) Magma beneath Yellowstone National Park. *Science* 188, 787–796.

Ecuador (n.d.) *Popular Tours in and around Quito*. On WWW at http://gosouthamerica.about.com/od/ecuquito/tp/PopularTours.–Mt.htm. Accessed 18.2.2007.

Edipsos Health Spas (n.d.) *Indications for Bathing in the Curative Hot Springs of Edipsos*. On WWW at http://www.capri-sa.gr/en/hot-springs.php. Accessed 12.2.2007.

Editorial Team (n.d.) *Wet World Pedas Hot Springs at Negri Sembilan*. On WWW at http://www.streetdirectory.com/travel_guide/malaysia/theme_parks/36/wet_world_pedas_hot_springs_at_negri_sembilan.php. Accessed 18.2.2007.

Ellis, S. (2008) Trends in the global Spa industry. In M. Cohen and G. Bodeker (eds) *Understanding the Global Spa Industry: Spa Management*. London: Butterworth & Heinemann, 66–84.

Emoto, M. (2005) *The True Power of Water – Healing and Discovering Ourselves*. New York: Atria Books.

Emoto, M. (2006) *The Secret Life of Water*. Oregon: Beyond Words Publishing.

Erfurt-Cooper, P.J. (2006) Hot springs – a natural resource as tourist attraction. Presented to the *Global Movements in the Asia Pacific RCAPS Conference*, Beppu, Japan, 17–18 November.

Erfurt-Cooper, P. (2008) Geotourism – Active geothermal and volcanic environments as tourist destinations. Presented to *The Inaugural Global Geotourism Conference*, Perth, Australia, 17–20 August.

Erfurt-Cooper, P., Cooper, M.J. and Prideaux, B. (2008) Volcanic environments as tourist destinations. Presented to *The Inaugural Global Geotourism Conference*, Perth, Australia, 17–20 August.

European Public Health Association (EUPHA) (2005) *Green Paper on How to Promote Healthy Diets and Physical Activity*. On WWW at http://eupha.org/html/2005graz/1-5.doc. Accessed 14.1.2005.

European Spa Industry (2006) *European Spas and Health Resorts*. On WWW at http://www.european-spas-health-ressorts.com/european-spa-industry/. Accessed 6.3.2006.

Eytons' Earth (2004) *Balneotherapy and Balneology, The Science and Art of Mineral Water Therapy. In Pursuit of Excellent Water*. On WWW at http://www.eytonsearth.org/balne-ology-balneotherapy.php#hot_spring. Accessed 12.2.2007.

Fabiani, D., Partsch, G., Casale, R. and Cerinic, M. (1996) Rheumatologic aspects of mineral water. *Clinics in Dermatology* 14, 571–575.

Fabulous Philippines (2008) *Asin Hot Springs – Baguio City*. On WWW at http://www.fabulousphilippines.com/asin-hot-springs.html. Accessed 12.7.2008.

Faiola, A. (2004) *Exposed, Japan's Hot Springs Come Clean*, Washington Post Foreign Service, Monday, 18 October, AO1.

Fekraoui, A. and Kedaid, F-Z. (2005) Geothermal resources and uses in Algeria: A country update report. *Proceedings of the World Geothermal Congress* (pp. 1–8). Anatalya, Turkey, 24–29 April.

Forum on Thermalism in Japan (2006) *Official Report on Hot Springs in the Islamic Republic of Iran*. Tehran and Tokyo: Forum on Thermalism in Japan and The Iran Culture Heritage and Tourism Organisation.

Foster, L.T. and Keller, C.P. (2008) *British Columbia Atlas of Wellness*. On WWW at http://www.geog.uvic.ca/wellness/, updated 28 June, 2008. Accessed 28.6.2008.

Fouke, B.W., Farmer, J.D., Des Marais, D.J., Pratt, L., Sturchio, N.C., Burns, P.C. and Discipulo, M.K. (2000) Depositional facies and aqueous–solid geochemistry of travertine-depositing hot springs (Angel Terrace, Mammoth Hot Springs, Yellowstone National Park, USA). *Journal of Sedimentary Research* 70 (3), 565–585.

Frazier, D. (2000) *Colorado's Hot Springs* (2nd edn). Boulder, CO: Pruett Publishing Company.

Frédéric, L. (2002) *Japan Encyclopaedia*. Cambridge, MA: Harvard University Press.

Freedman, D. and Waugh, M.A. (1996) The spa and sexually transmitted diseases. *Clinics in Dermatology* 14 (6), 577–582.

Freeston, D. and Lund. J.W. (2005) Miranda Hot Springs. *Geo Heat Bulletin* 19 (3), 35–36.

Freisleben-Teutscher, C.F. (2004) Kurärzte als Gesundheitsmanager – Die moderne Kurmedizin sollte mehr bieten als nur Standardprogramme. *Ärzte Woche*, 18. Jahrgang Nr. 14.

French Health Spas (n.d.) *About French Health Spas – Background*. On WWW at http://frenchhealthspas.com/html/background.html. Accessed 12.2.2007.

Fridleifsson, I.B. (1999) Historical aspects of geothermal utilization in Iceland. In R. Cataldi, S.F. Hodgson and J.W. Lund (eds) *Stories from a Heated Earth*. Sacramento, CA: Geothermal Resources Council, International Geothermal Association.

Fytikas, M., Leonidopoulou, G.M. and Cataldi, R. (1999) Geothermal energy in ancient Greece: From mythology to late antiquity (3rd century AD). In R. Cataldi, S.F. Hodgson and J.W. Lund (eds) *Stories from a Heated Earth* (pp. 69–102). Sacramento, CA: Geothermal Resources Council, International Geothermal Association.

Gamulin, S. (2001) The two millennia of Varazdinske Toplice (Varazdin's Spa). *Croatian Medical Journal* 42 (1), 1–3.

Garcia, C.R.A. (2007) *Escape to the Hot Springs*. On WWW at The Korea Times, Arts and Living, http://www.koreatimes.co.kr/www/news/art/2007/12/142_15863.html. Accessed 16.2.2008.

Garelli, S. (2002) *The World Competiveness Yearbook 2002*. Lausanne, Switzerland: International Institute for Management Development (IMD).

George, W.R. and Kelly, T. (1983) *Personal Selling of Services: Emerging Perspectives on Service Marketing*, Chicago: AMA.

Geothermal Energy Resources (n.d.) *Energy Sector of Mongolia – Energy Resources of Mongolia*. On WWW at http://www.investmongolia.com/forum/t4a.htm. Accessed 12.2.2007.

Ghersetich, I. and Lotti, T.M. (1996) Immunologic aspects: Immunology of mineral water spas. *Clinics in Dermatology* 14 (6), 563–566.

Gideon International Australia (2000a) *Exodus 19:10, 14 The Holy Bible, King James Version*. Sydney: Gideon International Australia.

Gideon International Australia (2000b) *Genesis 1:2 The Holy Bible, King James Version*. Sydney: Gideon International Australia.

Gideon International Australia (2000c) *John 5:2 – 4, 9:2 – 11 The Holy Bible, King James Version*. Sydney: Gideon International Australia.

Gideon International Australia (2000d) *Revelations 21:6 The Holy Bible, King James Version*. Sydney: Gideon International Australia.

Gingerich, B.S. (2004) Geothermal care and treatment: An Icelandic perspective. *Home Health Care Management Practice* 17 (1), 35–38.

Globe Health Tours News (2008) *Medical Leaves in US on Rise to Get Treatment Abroad*. On WWW at http://www.globehealthtours.com/medical_news/category/medical-tourism-statistics/page/2/. Accessed 10.12.2008.

Goeldner, C.R. and Ritchie, J.R.B. (2003) *Tourism – Principles, Practices, Philosophies* (9th edn). New York: John Wiley & Sons.

Goodrich, J.N. and Goodrich, G.E. (1987) Health-care tourism – An exploratory study. *Tourism Management* 8, 217–222.

Goodrich, J.N. (1994) Health tourism: A new positioning strategy for tourist destinations. In M. Uysal (ed.) *Global Tourism Behaviour* (pp. 227–238). New York: International Business Press.

Gray, M. (2003) *Sacred Waters – Ocean, Lake, River, and Spring*. On WWW at http://www.world-mysteries.com/gw_mgray3.htm#Ocean. Accessed 18.2.2005.

Greenland.com (n.d.) *South Greenland's Natural Pools – Uunartoq's Hot Springs*. On WWW at http://wwwgreenland.com/content/english/tourist/nature_climate/hot_springs. Accessed 12.2.2007.

Gregory, D. (1992) *Wales Before 1066: A Guide*. Cardiff: Gwasg Carreg Gwalch.

Größchen, H-W. (1998) *Heilbäder und Kurorte in Deutschland*. Berlin: Conradi-Bäderkunde-Lexikon.

Guinness World Records Limited (2006) *Guinness Book of Records*. London: Guinness World Records Limited.

Gujelashvili, V. (2007) *Warmth at Tbilisi's Heart*. On WWW at http://impressions-ba.com/features.php?id_feature=10347. Accessed 12.7.2007.

Haast, J. (1870) *Notes on the Thermal Springs, in the Hanmer Plains, Province of Nelson*. Nelson: Nelson Association for the Promotion of Science and Industry, Art. LIV.

Habermehl, R. and Pestov, I. (2002) Geothermal resources of the Great Artesian Basin, Australia. *GHC Quarterly Bulletin* 23 (2), 20–26.

Habu, J. (2004) *Ancient Jomon of Japan*. Cambridge: Cambridge University Press.

Hainan (n.d.(a)) *Guantang Thermal Springs*. On WWW at http://www.wanquanriver.org/en/tguantang.html. Accessed 12.2.2007.

Hainan (n.d.(b)) *Local Features: Hot Springs (Hainan)*. On WWW at http://english.ctrip.com/Desinations/DistrictHighlight.asp. Accessed 12.2.2007.

Haley, A.J., Snaith, T. and Miller, G. (2005) The social impacts of tourism a case study of Bath, UK. *Annals of Tourism Research* 32 (3), 647–668.

Hall, C.M. (2003) Spa and health tourism. In S. Hudson (ed.) *Sport and Adventure Tourism* (pp. 273–292). New York: Haworth Hospitality Press.

Hamat Gader (1999) *Baths of Medicinal Hot Springs*. On WWW at http://www.mfa.gov.il/MFA/History/Early%20History%20Archaeology/Hamat%20Gader%20-%20Baths%20of%20Medicinal%20Hot%20Springs. Accessed 12.2.2007.

Hamre, B. (n.d.) *Volcanoes, Miracles and Tourists – Baños*. On WWW at Ecuador, http://gosouthamerica.about.com/cs/southamerica/a/EcuBanos.htm. Accessed 12.2.2007.

Hank-Haase, G. and Illing, K. (2007) *Wirtschaftlichkeit und Rentabilität von Wellnessbereichen in Hotels*. Weisbaden: ghh consult GmbH.

Hank-Haase, G. (2006) *Hotellerie und Medical Spa Markt, Konzept und Wirtschaftlichkeit*. Wiesbaden: ghh consult GmbH.

Hanmer Springs Thermal Pools & Spa (2008) *Hanmer Springs Thermal Pools & Spa*. On WWW at http://hanmersprings.co.nz/. Accessed 14.11.2008.

Hanmer Springs Thermal Reserve (n.d.) *Most Common Questions – History of the Thermal Reserve*. Brochure for visitors of the Hanmer Springs Thermal Reserve.

Hann, S.-K. (1996) Mineral water and spas in Korea. *Clinics in Dermatology* 14 (6), 633–635.

Harahsheh, S.S. (2002) Curative tourism in Jordan and its potential development. Unpublished MA thesis, Bournemouth University.

Harris, R. (1999) *Lourdes: Body and Spirit in the Secular Age*, London: Penguin Books.

Harrison, D. (2007) Towards developing a framework for analysing tourism phenomena: A discussion. *Current Issues in Tourism* 30 (1), 61–86.

Havins, P.J.N. (1976) *The Spas of England*. London: Robert Hale & Company.

Health Spa Guru (2008) *Fish Spas and Fish Treatments – Weird or Wonderful?* On WWW at http://healthspaguru.com/Spa-Article.aspx?Article=e7b193db-c2c1-4545-90bf-0eaaa8e1fa76. Accessed 12.6.2008.

Health Tourism in Jordan (n.d.) *Therapeutic Tourism – Spas with Amazing Healing Properties*. Amman: Amman Islamic Tourism Co.

Helidon Mineral Spa Park (2005) *Taking the Waters at Helidon Spa*. On WWW at http://www.mineralspas.com.au/naturalsprings_mineralwater_hydrotherapy_spas_saunas.htm. Accessed 22.6.2006.

Helman, D. and De Chernatony, L. (1999) Exploring the development of lifestyle retail brands. *Service Industries Journal* 19 (2), 42–68.

Hilton Hotels Corporation (2007) *Hilton Hotels Corporation Partners with Leading Brands of LVMH, the World's Largest Luxury Group, and Spa Chakra to Offer Personalized Spa Services*. On WWW at http://phx.corporate-ir.net/phoenix.zhtml?c=88577&p=irol-newsArticleOther&ID=1014595&highlight=. Accessed 12.4.2008.

Himachal Pradesh (n.d.) *Hot Springs in Himachal Pradesh*. On WWW at http://www.himachalpradesh.us/webs/geography/hotsprings.htm. Accessed 12.6.2008.

History of Warmbaths (n.d.) *Bela Bela – The Golden Sunshine Town has an Interesting History*. On WWW at http://www.accommodation-warmbaths.co.za/history.htm. Accessed 12.6.2008.

Hjálmarsson, J.R. (1993) *History of Iceland – From the Settlement to the Present Day*. Reykjavík: Iceland Review/Edda Publishing.

Hodgson, S.F. (1999) Heat over time, geothermal stories from Mexico. In R. Cataldi, S.F. Hodgson and J.W. Lund (eds) *Stories from a Heated Earth* (pp. 535–554). Sacramento, CA: Geothermal Resources Council, International Geothermal Association.

Hodgson, S. F. (2004) A beautiful spa – Thermal waters at San Bartolo Agua Caliente, Mexico. *GHC Quarterly Bulletin* 25 (2), 3–5.

Högl, O. (1980) *Die Mineral- und Heilquellen der Schweiz*. Bern und Stuttgart: Verlag Paul Haupt.

Hot Springs Hotel (2008) *SavuSavu – Activities and Sightseeing*. On WWW at http://www.fiji-resorts.com.au/hot-springs-hotel.cfm. Accessed 12.6.2008.

Hotta, A. and Ishiguro, Y. (1986) *A Guide to Japanese Hot Springs*. Tokyo: Kodansha International.

Hróarsson, B. and Jónsson, S.J. (1992) *Geysers and Hot Springs in Iceland*. Reykjavik: Mál og Menning.

Huaqing (n.d.(a)) *Huaqing Hot Spring*. On WWW at http://www.chinahighlights.com/xian/attractions/huaqing-hot-spring.htm. Accessed 18.2.2008.

Huaqing (n.d.(b)) *Huaqing Hot Springs*. On WWW at http://www.travelblog.org/Asia/China/Shaanxi/blog-156873.html. Accessed 18.2.2008.

Huaqing (n.d.(c)) *Welcome to Huaqingchi*. On WWW at http://www.hqc.cn/english/index.asp. Accessed February 2008.

Hungarospa (n.d.) *Hungarospa Hajdúszoboszló Medicinal and Health Tourism*. On WWW at http://www.hajduszoboszlo.hu/digitalcity/startpages/hajduszoboszlo_en.jsp?dom=AAAACWTC&prt=AAAADZZF&fmn=AAAAZFPT. Accessed 18.2.2008.

Iceland Express Newsletter (2006) *27 February*. On WWW at http://www.icelandexpress.com/iceland/wellness/. Accessed 7.3.2008.

Icelandic Tourist Board (2008) *Foreign Visitor Arrivals in Iceland 1990–2007*. Reykjavik: Icelandic Tourist Board. Accessed 18.7.2008.

IndiaLine (2006) *Famous Hot Springs*. On WWW at http://www.indialine.com/travel/himachalpradesh/lakes-springs.html. Accessed 11.10.2006.

India Times (2004) *A State of Wellbeing*. On WWW at http://spirituality.india.com. Accessed 10.10.2005.

Intelligent Spas (2003) *Spa Consumer Survey Asia 2003*. Singapore: Intelligent Spas Pte Ltd.

Intelligent Spas (2004) *Spa Industry Survey New Zealand 2003*. Singapore: Intelligent Spas Pte Ltd.

Intelligent Spas (2005) *Spa Industry Survey Thailand*. Singapore: Intelligent Spas Pte Ltd.

Intelligent Spas (2005) *Key Differences between Female versus Male Spa Customers*. On WWW at http://www.intelligentspas.com/MediaReleases/Press%20Release_Spa_Consumer_Survey_Female_Male.asp. Accessed 10.10.2006.

Intelligent Spas (2007) *Spa Industry Survey Taiwan*. Singapore: Intelligent Spas Pte Ltd.

Intelligent Spas (2008a) *Using Spa Industry Benchmarks for Success*. Singapore: Intelligent Spas Pte Ltd.

Intelligent Spas (2008b) *Spa Industry Newsletter 23*. Singapore: Intelligent Spas Pte Ltd.

International Spa Association (n.d.) *10 Spa Domains*. On WWW at http://www.experienceispa.com/ISPA/Education/Resources/10+Spa+Domains.htm. Accessed 10.10.2006.

International Spa Association (2007) 2007 ISPA spa industry study. Presented at *the ISPA Conference & Expo*, Kissimmee, Florida, November 12–15. On WWW at http://www.experienceispa.com/ISPA/Media+Room/Press+Releases/Global+Spa+Research+Release.htm. Accessed 12.10.2008.

International Union of Tourist Organisations (IUTO) (1973) *Health Tourism*. Geneva: United Nations.

Islamic Tourism (2004) *Tanzania is the Ultimate Destination*. On WWW at http://www.islamictourism.com/news_E.php?id=180&search=hot%20springs. Accessed 8.7.2006.

Israel Tourism & Leisure Division (n.d.) *Tiberias Hot Springs*. On WWW at http://www.africa-israel.com/eng/inner.asp?id=9500&pid=6200. Accessed 10.10.2006.

Israel Foreign Ministry (n.d.) *Hamat Gader: Baths of Medicinal Hot Springs*. On WWW at http://www.jewishvirtuallibrary.org/jsource/Archaeology/Hamat.html. Accessed 10.10.2006.

Iwata, N. (2006) The human contexts of local community development through the concept of sustainable tourism. Unpublished PhD thesis, Beppu: Ritsumeikan Asia Pacific University.

Jackson, S. (2003) *Hot Springs of New Zealand*. Auckland: Reed.

Jaffé, F.C., Dvortjetski, E., Levitte, D., Massarwieh, R. and Swarieh, A. (1999) Geothermal energy utilization in the Jordan valley between Lake Kinneret and the Dead Sea: A view from antiquity. In R. Cataldi, S.F. Hodgson and J.W. Lund (eds) *Stories from a Heated Earth* (pp. 35–50). Sacramento, CA: Geothermal Resources Council, International Geothermal Association.

Japan Echo Inc (2005) *Healthy Holidays: Combining Leisure Travel with Medical Treatment (May 19)*. On WWW at http://web-japan.org/trends/business/bus050518.html. Accessed 10.10.2006.

Japan Industrial Standards Committee (2008) *JIS B 9940-9944, JIS K 0102*. Tokyo: Ministry of Economy, Trade and Industry.

Japan's Natural Hot Springs (n.d.) *Japanese Baths – Origins*. On WWW at http://www.about-vacations.com/asia/japan/japanese-hot-springs.php. Accessed 10.9.2007.

Japan Today (2008) *Hot Spring Disaster*. On WWW at http://www.japantoday.com/category/national/view/death-toll-in-quake-rises-to-9. Accessed 10.11.2008.

Jasen, P. (1995) *Wild Things: Nature, Culture and Tourism in Ontario 1790–1914*. Toronto: University of Toronto Press.

Jordan Touristic Sites (n.d.) *South of Amman.– Hammamat Ma'een*. On WWW at http://www.kinghussein.gov.jo/tourism6b.html. Accessed 10.10.2008.

Jorden, E. (1631) *A Discourse of Naturall Bathes and Minerall Waters*. London: Thomas Harper (Reproduced and published by Theatrum Orbis Terrarum Ltd, Amsterdam, 1971).

Kanokratana, P., Chanapan, S., Pootanakit, K. and Eurwilaichitr, L. (2004) Diversity and abundance of bacteria and archaea in the Bor Khlueng hot springs in Thailand. *Journal of Basic Microbiology* 44 (6), 430–444.

Katsambas, A. and Antoniou, C. (1996) Mineral water and spas in Greece. *Clinics in Dermatology* 14 (6), 615–618.

Keary, P. (1996) *The New Penguin Dictionary of Geology*. London: Penguin Books.

Kenoyer, J.M. (2005) *Mohenjo-Daro, An Ancient Indus Valley Metropolis*. On WWW at http://www.mohenjodaro.net/mohenjodaroessay.html. Accessed 10.10.2008.

Kepinska, B. (2002) Thermal springs and spas in Poland. *GHC Bulletin* 23 (1), 10–17.

Kimes, S.E. (1989) The basics of yield management. *Cornell Hotel and Restaurant Administration Quarterly* 30 (3), 15–19.

King, T. (1966) *Water: Miracle of Nature*. New York: Collier Books.

Kotler, P., Armstrong, G., Meggs, D., Bradbury, E. and Makens, J. (1999a) *Marketing: An Introduction*. Sydney: Prentice-Hall.

Kotler, P., Bowen, J. and Makens, J. (1999b) *Marketing for Hospitality and Tourism*, Englewood Cliffs, NJ: Prentice-Hall.

Kouba, V. (n.d.) *Karlovy Vary Architecture*. On WWW at http://www.karlovyvary.cz/static/historie_4.aspangId=2&Kol=1. Accessed 10.7.2006.

Kozak, M. (2002) Comparative analysis of tourist motivations by nationality and destinations. *Tourism Management* 23 (2), 221–232.

Kralis, B. (2004) *Lourdes, Catholic Online*. On WWW at http://www.catholic.org/featured/sheen.php?ID=1202. Accessed 10.10.2005.

Kruse, F.A. (1997) Characterization of active hot-springs environments using multispectral and hyperspectral remote sensing. Presented at the Twelfth International Conference and Workshops on Applied Geologic Remote Sensing, Denver, Colorado, 17–19 November.

Kudo, K. (1996) 3,000 kW Suginoi Hotel Geothermal Power Plant. *Geo-heat Center Quarterly Bulletin* 17 (2), 7–8.

Kuntscher, H. (1990) *Bergwerke, Höhlen, Heilquellen*. Tirol, Österreich: Süd Tirol Bildwanderbuch, Steiger Verlags-GmbH.

Kurillowicz, K. (1995) *The Canadian Rockies*. Vancouver: Irving Weisdorf & Co. Ltd.

Kurakowa, J. (2008) *Death toll from Japan earthquake rises to 10*. On WWW at http://news.yahoo.com/s/ap/20080616/ap_on_re_as/japan_earthquake. Accessed 10.11.2008.

Kyrgyzstan (n.d.) *Issyk-Ata Sanatorium*. On WWW at http://www.kyrgyztantravel.info/resorts/issyk-ata.htm. Accessed 10.10.2005.

LaForest, N. (2004) *A New Kind of Wellness? More Hungarians heading to Day Spas for Indulgence*. On WWW at http://www.budapestweek.com/nesites/trends/trends08.html. Accessed 10.10.2005.

Laguna Hotspring Resort Philippines (n.d.) *Hidden Valley Springs*. On WWW at http://www.laguna-hotspring.com/hidden-valley-springs/. Accessed 8.10.2006.

LaMoreaux, P.E. (2005) History and classification of springs. *Geological Society of America Abstracts with Programs 37* (7), 324.

Lang Research Inc (2002) *Travel Attitudes and Motivation Survey: Emergent Vacation Interests*. April, Ontario: Ministry of Tourism and Recreation & Lang Reseach Inc.

Larson, H. (2006) *Feeling The Heat – Hot Springs and Thermal Spas Make Tiberias a Hot Vacation Spot, The Jewish Week*. On WWW at http://www.thejewishweek.com/bottom/special-content.php3?artid=1310. Accessed 10.11.2006.

Laugar Spa (n.d.) *Five Star Health and Swimming Centre for the Whole family*. On WWW at http://www.randburg.com/is/laugarspa/. Accessed 10.10.2005.

Laushway, E. (1996) *Aix marks the Spot, Europe 3/1/96*. On WWW at http://findarticles.com/p/articles/mi_hb3134/is_199603/ai_n7798624. Accessed 10.10.2005.

Laws, E. (2004) *Improving Tourism and Hospitality Services*. Wallingford: CABI.

Laws, E. (2006) Considerations in improving services. In B. Prideaux, G. Moscardo and E. Laws (eds) *Managing Tourism and Hospitality Services* (pp. 225–236). Wallingford: CABI.

Leavy, H.R. and Bergel, R.R. (2003) *The Spa Encyclopedia: A Guide to Treatments & Their Benefits for Health & Healing*. New York: Thomson Delmar Learning.

Lee, Cheng-Fei. and King, B.E. (2008) Using the Delphi method to assess the potential of Taiwanese hot springs. *International Journal of Tourism Research 10* (4), 341–352.

Lee, G. (2004) *Spa & Wellness in Europa: Hotels, Anwendungen, Rezepte*. München, Germany: Christian Verlag.

Lee, Y. (2003) Application and evaluation of the Spa town life cycle model through a case study of bath spa, United Kingdom. *Journal of the Korean Geographical Society 38* (3), 413–425.

Ledo, E. (1996) Mineral water and Spas in Spain. *Clinics in Dermatology 14* (6), 641–646.

Leitner, G. (2001) *Argentina Travel Companion* (2nd edn). Edison, New Jersey: Hunter Publishing.

Lerner, C.B. (2001) The "River of Paradise" and the legend about the city of Tbilisi: A literary source of the legend. *Folklore 16*, 72–77.

Les Thermes Natioanaux d'Aix-les-Bains (n.d.) *Thermal Therapy: For Your Wellbeing between Lakes and Mountain*. On WWW at http://www.thermaix.com:82//BACKOFFICE/PUBLINOW/uploadDocuments/00007/Thermal%20therapy.pdf. Accessed 10.10.2005.

Life in the Fast Lane (2007) *Fish Spa Feasts on Your Flesh*. On WWW at http://www.lifeinthefastlane.ca/fish-spa-feasts-on-your-flesh/offbeat-news. Accessed 10.7.2008.

Limpopo Happenings (n.d.) *Information on Warmbaths (Warmbad) Bela-Bela Homepage*. On WWW at http://www.limpopohappenings.co.za/warmbadhomepage.htm. Accessed 10.12.2008.

Linhart, S. and Frühstuck, S. (eds) (1998) *The Culture of Japan as seen through its Leisure*. New York: SUNY.

Longsheng (n.d.) *China's National Forest Park – Longsheng Hot Springs National Forest Park*. On WWW at http://www.chinaplanner.com/forestparks/nationalparks/np_lhfp.htm. Accessed 10.10.2006.

Loutraki City Guide (n.d.) *2500 Years of History and Culture*. On WWW at http://www.city-of-loutraki.gr/history-culture/the-history-of-loutraki.htm. Accessed 10.7.2007.

Lund, J.W. (1993) Spas and balneology in the United States. *GHC Quarterly Bulletin*, March, 1–3.

Lund, J.W. (2000a) Geothermal spas in the Czech Republic and Slovakia. *GHC Quarterly Bulletin* 21 (3), 35–37.

Lund, J.W. (2000b) Balneological use of geothermal water in the USA. *GHC Quarterly Bulletin* 21 (3), 31–34.

Lund, J.W. (2000c) Les Thermes Aix-les-Bains. *GHC Quarterly Bulletin* 21 (3), 27–28.

Lund, J.W. (2000d) Design considerations for pools and spas (Natatoriums). *GHC Quarterly Bulletin* 21 (3), 6–8.

Lund, J.W. (2002) *Balneological Use of Geothermal Waters*. Oregon: Geo-Heat Center.

Lund, J.W. (2003) Hot spring resorts in the Canadian Rockies. *GHC Quarterly Bulletin* 24 (1), 17–21.

Lund, J.W. (2005) Basic principles of balneology and examples in the United States. In *Proceedings of the World Geothermal Congress 2005*, Antalya, Turkey, 24–29 April.

Lund, J.W. and Freeston, D.H. (2001) World-wide direct uses of geothermal energy 2000. *Geothermics* 30 (1), 29–68.

Lüscher, G. (1946) *Die Thermen von Baden und die Mineral und Heilquellen der Schweiz*. Aargau, Switzerland: Buchdruckerei Neue Aargauer Zeitung.

Luxury Spa Finder Magazine (2006) *The Renewal Issue*, January – February Issue. New York: Spa Finder Inc.

Mackaman, D.P. (2007) *Leisure Settings: Bourgois Culture, Medicine and the Spa in Modern France*. Chicago and London: The University of Chicago Press.

Madigan, M. and Martinko, J. (eds) (2005) *Brock Biology of Microorganisms* (11th edn). Englewood Cliffs, NJ: Prentice-Hall.

Maier, D. and Fiedler, H.G. (2004) *Der Grosse Thermenführer – Wellness und Badespaß in Österreich und den benachbarten Regionen*. Wien, Österreich: NP Buchverlag.

Maji Moto Camp (n.d.) *Maji Moto Camp*. On WWW at http://www.intotanzania.com/safari/tanzania/north/parks/manyara/04a-lodges/manyara-04–2-majimoto-11.htm. Accessed 10.10.2006.

March, R. and Woodside, A.G. (2005) *Tourism Behaviour: Travellers Decisions and Actions*. Wallingford: CABI.

Marktl, W. (2000) Wellness – Kur – Rehabilitation. Editorial. *Forschende Komplementärmedizin und Klassische Naturheilkunde* 7, 69–70.

Marini, L., Cioni, R. and Guidi, M. (1998) Water chemistry of San Marcos area, Guatemala. *Geothermics* 27 (3), 331–260.

Mattingly, S.R. and Griffith, E.S. (2008) *US Travel and Tourism Satellite Accounts for 2004–2007*. Washington: Bureau of Economic Analysis, June.

McClure, M. (2004) *The Wonder Country: Making New Zealand Tourism*. Auckland: Auckland University Press.

McCool, S. and Moisey, N.R. (eds) (2001) *Tourism, Recreation and Sustainability*. Wallingford: CABI.

McCurry, J. (2004) *Spa Resorts in Hot Water as Springs Run Dry*. Tokyo: The Guardian, Friday, 3 September, 5.

McDermott, M.J. (2004) *Wellness Trend Creates Opportunities in Health, Nutrition and Fitness Sectors*. On WWW at http://www.busop1.com/wellness.html. Accessed 14.11.2008.

McGeary, D., Plummer, C. and Carlson, D. (2001) *Physical Geology – Earth Revealed* (4th edn). New York: McGraw-Hill.

McNeil, K.R. and Ragins, E.J. (2005) Staying in the Spa marketing game: Trends, challenges, strategies and techniques. *Journal of Vacation Marketing* 11 (1), 31–39.

McWilliams, A. (2001) Corporate social responsibility: A theory of the firm perspective. *Academy of Management Review* 26 (1), 117–128.

Mellilo, L. (1995) Thermalism in the ancient world. *Medicina dei Secoli* 7 (3), 461–83.

Menadue, J.E. (1972) *The Mineral Springs Spa Waters of Australia – A Unique National Resource and A Challenge for Development*. Melbourne: Horticultural Press Pty, Ltd.

Merida, L. (1999) Curing blocks and drying fruit in Guatemala. *GHC Quarterly Bulletin* 20 (4), 19–22.

Merriam-Webster Medical Dictionary [n.d.(a)] *Health*. On WWW at http://dictionary.reference. com/browse/health. Accessed 4.3.2006.

Merriam-Webster Medical Dictionary [n.d.(b)] *Wellness*. On WWW at http://dictionary. reference.com/browse/wellness. Accessed 4.3.2006.

Michelin (2002) *Der Grüne Reiseführer: Portugal, Madeira, Azoren*. Karlsruhe, Germany: Michelin Reise-Verlag.

Mielke, R. (n.d.) *Aachen Impressionen – Badegeschichte*. On WWW at http://www.aachen.de/ DE/tourismus_stadtinfo/20_aachen_historie/index.html. Accessed 10.7.2007.

Miller, J.W. (2005) Wellness: The history and development of a concept. *Spectrum Freizei*, 2005/1, 84–102.

Mineral Waters of Hungary (n.d.) *Mineral Waters – A Hungarian Asset for Thousands of Years*. On WWW at http://www.asvanyvizek.hu/english/waters/. Accessed 10.10.2005.

Ministry of Economic Affairs and Transport, Hungary (2002) *The Széchenyi Plan*. On WWW at http://www.amcham.hu/BusinessHungary/16-08/articles/16-07_06.asp. Accessed 10.10.2005.

Ministry of the Environment, Japan (2003) *Preservation and Use of Hot Springs, Government of Japan*. On WWW at http://www.env.go.jp/policy/hakusyo_e/honbun.php3. Accessed 10.10.2005.

Ministry of the Environment, Japan (2006) *Ministry of the Environment, Japan*. On WWW at http://www.env.go.jp/en/nature/npr/fcpn/parts/10-2.pdf. Accessed 10.7.2007.

Ministry of Foreign Affairs of the Republic of Cuba (2005) *Tourism*. On WWW at http:// embacu.cubaminrex.cu/Default.aspx?tabid=2807. Accessed 10.10.2005.

Ministry of Public Health, Thailand (2008) *Thailand – The Wellness capital of Asia*. Bangkok: Ministry of Public Health and Tourism Authority of Thailand.

Ministry of Public Security, China (2007) *Major Statistics of China Tourism 2006*. Beijing: Ministry of Public Security.

Ministry of Road, Transport and Tourism Mongolia (2006) *Tourism Sector Profile*. On WWW at http://www.mongoliatourism.gov.mn/index.php?action=menudata&id=7. Accessed 10.7.2008.

Ministry of Water, Land and Air Protection, BC (2003) *Liard River Hot Springs Provincial Park Approved Master Plan*. Vancouver: BC Parks.

Mintzberg, H. and Walters, J.A. (1982) Tracking strategy in an entrepreneurial firm. *Academy of Management Journal* 25 (3), 465–499.

Mircea, E. (1995) *The Encyclopaedia of Religion 11*. McMillan Library Reference. New York: Simon & Schuster and Prentice-Hall International.

Mircea, E. (1995) *The Encyclopedia of Religion 13*. McMillan Library Reference. New York: Simon & Schuster and Prentice-Hall International.

Mitchell, S. (1994) *Pura Vida, the Waterfalls and Hot Springs of Costa Rica*. Birmingham, AL: Menasha Ridge Press.

Mongolia Investors Forum (2006) *The Energy Sector of Mongolia*. On WWW at http://www. investmongolia.com/forum/t4a.htm. Accessed 10.7.2007.

Mongolia Web News (2007a) *Sanatoriums and Health Resorts*. On WWW at http://www. mongolia-web.com/content/view/147539/. Accessed 10.7.2007.

Mongolia Web News (2007b) Mongolia Web News. On WWW at www.mongolia-web.com/ content/view/883/2/ Accessed 10.7.2007.

Monti, S. (n.d.) *Thermalism Between Past and Future*. Salerno: University of Salerno.

Moree History (1995) *Centenary of Moree Bore Baths*, Moree: Moree and District Historical Society, Yilaalu no 22.

Moree Plains Shire Council (2004) *Baths – Nature's Magic*. On WWW at http://www.mpsc. nsw.gov.au/content/view/100/74/. Accessed 8.7.2006.

Moscardo, G., Morrison, A.M., Pearce, P.L., Lang, C. and O'Leary, J.T. (1996) Understanding vacation destination choice through travel motivation and activities. *Journal of Vacation Marketing* 2 (2), 109–121.

Moscardo, G., Prideaux, B. and Laws, E. (2006) Researching and managing tourism and hospitality service: Challenges and conclusions, In B. Prideaux, G. Moscardo and E. Laws (eds) *Managing Tourism and Hospitality Services*. Wallingford: CABI.

Mosquera, M. (2003) *Will Retiring Boomers Bust Medicare Apps*? On WWW at http://www.gcn.com/22_departments/23916-1.html. Accessed 13.2.2006.

Mossman, M. (2007) *Relax, and Let the Nibbling Begin – Use of 'Doctor Fish' has Spread from a Turkish Resort to Asian and European Spas.* . On WWW at http://www.theglobeandmail.com/servlet/story/LAC.20070825.FISH25/TPStory/specialTravel. Accessed 10.7.2007.

Mueller, H. and Kaufmann, E.L. (n.d.) *Wellness Tourism: Market Analysis of a Special Health Tourism Segment and Implications for the Hotel Industry.* Research Institute for Leisure and Tourism. Berne: University of Berne.

Municipality of Loutraki (n.d.) *Loutraki – Hydrotherapy Spa Center.* On WWW at http://www.loutraki.gr/pages.asp?pageID=79&langID=2. Accessed 10.7.2007.

Myers, J.E., Sweeney, T.J. and Witmer, M. (2005) *A Holistic Model of Wellness.* On WWW at http://www.mindgarden.com/products/wells.htm. Accessed 10.7.2007.

Mývatn Nature Baths (2008) *Iceland's Newest Geothermal Spa.* On WWW at http://www.jardbodin.is/English/About_us/. Accessed 10.12.2008.

Nahrstedt, W. (2002) *Austria: Leadership in Wellness Tourism.* On WWW at http://internationalhotelbrokers.com. Accessed 14.11.2008.

Nahrstedt, W. (2004) Wellness: A new perspective for leisure centers, health tourism and spas in Europe on the global health market. In K. Weiermair and C. Mathies (eds) *The Tourism and Leisure Industry: Shaping the Future* (pp. 181–198). New York: Haworth Hospitality Press.

Namibia Tourism (n.d.(a)) *Discovering the Vicinity.* On WWW at http://www.namibiatourism.com.na/country_c_region.php. Accessed 10.7.2007.

Namibia Tourism (n.d.(b)). *The Fish River Canyon.* On WWW at http://www.travelafricamag.com/content/view/377/56/. Accessed 10.7.2007.

Needham, J. and Liu, G-D. (1962) Hygiene and preventive medicine in Ancient China. *Journal of History of Medicine and Allied Sciences* XVII, 429–478.

Nedelcu, F. (2008) *The Incredible Doctor Fish Spa, HotelClub Travel Blog.* On WWW at http://blog.hotelclub.com/the-incredible-doctor-fish-spa/. Accessed 10.10.2008.

Neisser, D. (2007) *The 'Top Ten' of Marketing Industry Trends for 2008.* New York: Renegade Marketing Agency.

Nguyen, T. (2006) *In Reykjavik, Dont Sweat It – Unless You Want to.* On WWW at http://www.washingtonpost.com. Accessed 10.7.2007.

Nickell, J. (2005) *Healing Waters – Investigative Files, Sceptical Briefs June 2005.* On WWW at http://www.csicop.org/sb/2005-09/i-files.html. Accessed 10.7.2007.

Nipponia. (2003) *Hot Springs in Japan: Facts and Figures.* On WWW at http://web-japan.org/nipponia/nipponia26/en/feature/feature12.html. Accessed 10.12.2008.

Nouira, H. (1975) Creation de l'Office du Thermalisme. *Journal Officiel de la Republique Tunisienne*, 30 June, 75: 535.

Nordic Adventure Travel (2008) *Mývatn Nature Baths.* On WWW at http://www.nat.is/travelguideeng/nature%20baths%20myvatn.htm. Accessed 10.12.2008.

Nubra Valley (n.d.) *Jammu & Kashmir – Paradise on Earth.* On WWW at http://www.traveliteindia.com/guide/state/jammu.asp. Accessed 10.7.2007.

Nüchtern, M. (2002) *Weil ich es mir wert bin oder die grosse Lust auf Wellness.* On WWW at http://www.ekiba.de/glaubeakt_386.htm. Accessed 10.7.2007.

O'Brien, J. (2006) *This Place called Lourdes.* On WWW at http://www/consecration.com/JFM06Feat5.html. Accessed 10.7.2007.

Oddy, J. (1999) *Sanatoriums: Collective Memory.* On WWW at http://findarticles.com/p/articles/mi_qn4158/is_19991106/ai_n14268660/print. Accessed 10.7.2007.

Office du Thermalisme (n.d.) *Thermalism in Tunisia* – Online Document. On WWW at http://www.thermalisme.nat.tn/publish/content/article.asp?ID=248. Accessed 10.7.2007

Office National du Tourisme (1921) *The Spas of France.* Paris: Ministère de Traveaux.

Okada, M. and Peterson, S.A. (2000) *Water Pollution Control Policy and Management: The Japanese Experience.* Tokyo: Gyosei.

Ólafsson, J.H. (1996) Therapeutic climatology, the Blue Lagoon in Iceland and Psoriasis. *Clinics in Dermatology* 14 (6), 647–651.

Olsen, J.K. (2002) *Introduction to Japanese Hot Springs*. On WWW at http://www2.gol.com/users/jolsen/onsen/intro.html. Accessed 11.7.2005.

Omulecki, A., Nowak, A. and Zalewska, A. (1996) Spa therapy in Poland. *Clinics in Dermatology* 14 (6), 679–683.

Oobuka Onsen, Akita (2005) *Oobuka Onsen*. On WWW at http://commons.wikimedia.org/wiki/Image: Oobuka_Onsen_Akita_02.jpg. Accessed 10.7.2007.

Osborne, B. (2006) Health and wellness tourism. Presented to the *World Travel Market*. Docklands, London, 6–9 November.

Ottaway, P. and Cyprien, M. (1987) *A Traveller's Guide to Roman Britain*. London: Routledge & Kegan Paul.

Oumeish, O.Y. (1996) Climatotherapy at the Dead Sea in Jordan. *Clinics in Dermatology* 14 (6), 653–658.

Oxford Analytica (2007) *Georgia – Russia Conflict Intensifies*. On WWW at http://www.forbes.com/business/2007/08/07/russia-georgia-conflict-cz_0808oxfordanalytica.htmlrea. Accessed 10.10.2007.

Oyu Monogatari (2004) *Hot Spring in Japan*. On WWW at http://www.east.co.jp/oyu/english/. Accessed 10.12.2008.

Özgüler, M.E. and Kasap, A. (1999) The geothermal history of Anatolia, Turkey. In R. Cataldi, S.F. Hodgson and J.W. Lund (eds) *Stories from a Heated Earth*. Sacramento, CA: Geothermal Resources Council, International Geothermal Association.

Pacific Asia Travel Association (2005) *PATA Travel Mart 2005*. Kuala Lumpur: PATA.

Pamukkale (n.d.) *A Natural Wonder in Turkey*. On WWW at http://www.bitez.net/turkey/pamukkale/. Accessed 14.11.2008.

Parasuraman, A., Zeithaml, V.A. and Berry, L.L. (1985) A conceptual model of service quality and its implications for further research. *Journal of Marketing* 49 (Fall), 41–50.

Parasuraman, A., Zeithaml, V.A. and Berry, L.L. (1994) Reassessment of expectations as a comparison standard in measuring service quality: Implications for further research. *Journal of Marketing* 58, 111–124.

Parish, L.C. and Lotti, T.M. (1996), Commentary. *Clinics in Dermatology* 14 (6), 457–458.

Parks Canada (2008) *Canadian Rockies Hot Springs – Visit the Park*. On WWW at http://www.pc.gc.ca/regional/sourcesthermales-hotsprings/index_e.asp. Accessed 10.12.2008.

Pearce, P.L. (1993) Fundamentals of tourist motivation. In D.W. Pearce and R.W. Butler (eds) *Tourism Research: Critiques and Challenges* (pp. 113–134). London: Routledge.

Pearce, P.L. and Benckendorff, P.J. (2006) Benchmarking, usable knowledge and tourist attractions. *Journal of Quality Assurance in Hospitality & Tourism* 7, 29–52.

Pearn, J.H. and Little, V. (1998) The taking of the waters: Health springs and Spa waters of high lithium content at Helidon, Queensland. In Collected Papers of *the Fifth Biennial Conference of the Australian Society of Medicine, Occasional Papers in Medical History*. Brisbane: Australian Society of Medicine.

Pegg, S. and Suh, J-H.K. (2006) Service recovery in tourism and leisure industries. In B. Prideaux, G. Moscardo and E. Laws (eds) *Managing Tourism and Hospitality Services* (pp. 26–37). Wallingford: CABI.

Peninsula Hot Springs (n.d.) *Peninsula Hot Springs: A Summary of Interesting Facts*. On WWW at http://www.peninsulahotsprings.com/downloads/about-us.pdf. Accessed 10.12.2008.

Peninsula Hot Springs (n.d.) *Welcome*. On WWW at http://www.peninsulahotsprings.com/welcome.htm. Accessed 10.12.2008.

Pentecost, A., Jones, B. and Renaut, R.W. (2003) What is a hot spring? *Canadian Journal of Earth Sciences* 40 (11), 1443–1446.

Peru Hot Springs (n.d.(a)) *Experiential Tourism – Hot springs*. On WWW at http://www.peru.info/e_ftointereseseng.asp?pdr=933&jrq=9.3&ic=2&ids=1855. Accessed 18.4.2008.

Peru Hot Springs (n.d.(b)) *Baños del Inca: Cajamarca, Peru*. On WWW at http://gosouth-america.about.com. Accessed 18.4.2008.

Peru Hot Springs (n.d.(c)) *Aguas Calientes (Machu Picchu Pueblo)*. On WWW at http://images.google.com/. Accessed 18.4.2008.

Peruvian Waters: Lakes and Lagoons in Peru (n.d.) *Peruvian Waters: Lakes and Lagoons in Peru*. On WWW at http://www.perutravels.net/peru-travel-guide/nature-water-lakes-lagoons.htm. Accessed 18.4.2008.

Pesce, A. (2002) Thermal Spas: An economic development alternative along both sides of the Uruguay River. *GHC Quarterly Bulletin* 23 (3), 22–28.

Pescovitz, D. (2008) *Fish pedicure*. On WWW at http://www.boingboing.net/2008/07/22/fish-pedicure.html. Accessed 18.10.2008.

Pfeiff, M. (2000) *Geothermal Activity, Maori Culture Heat Up North Island of New Zealand*. San Francisco Examiner Special, Sunday, January 2, T1.

Pilzer, P.Z. (2002) *The Wellness Revolution – How to Make a Fortune in the Next Trillion Dollar Industry*. New Jersey: John Wiley & Sons.

Plutschow, H. (1996) *Matsuri: The Festivals of Japan*. Richmond: Japan Library.

Politikerscreen.de (2002) *Sachstandsbericht zur Bewertung von Kur und Rehabilitation unter Berücksichtigung der politischen Situation*. Munich: European Health Centre for Natural Healing Therapies.

Polynesian Spa (n.d.) *Polynesian Spa*. On WWW at http://www.travelplanner.co.nz/referral.cfm?site=http://www.polynesianspa.co.nz. Accessed 18.4.2008.

Prazak, L. (n.d.) *Peru – Country of Thermal Springs*. Polynesian Spa http://gosouthamerica.about.com/gi/dynamic/offsite.htm?zi=1/XJ&sdn=gosouthamerica&zu=http%3A%2F%2Fartourperu.com%2FTuenther.htm. Accessed 18.4.2008.

Provence Beyond (n.d.) *Gréoux-les-Bains – Towns and Villages*. On WWW at http://www.beyond.fr/villages/greouxbains.html#thermalbaths. Accessed 18.7.2005.

QE Health (n.d.) *QE Health Programs, Rotorua– New Zealand*. On WWW at http://www.qehealth.co.nz. Accessed 20.4.2007.

QE Health (n.d.) *Rachel Spring, Rotorua – New Zealand*. On WWW at http://www.qehealth.co.nz. Accessed 20.4.2007.

Qionghai Tourist Guide (2006) *Guantang Thermal Spring*. On WWW at http://www.wanquanriver.org/en/tguantang.html. Accessed 20.4.2007.

Rafferty, K. (1998) Aquaculture. In P.J. Lienau, J.W. Lund, K. Rafferty and G. Culver (eds) *Geothermal Direct-Use Engineering and Design Guidebook* (Chapter 15, pp. 327–332). Klamath Falls, OR: Geo-Heat Center, Oregon Institute of Technology.

Raksaskulwong, M. (2000) Current issues of the hot spring distribution map in Thailand. In *Proceedings World Geothermal Congress*, Kyushu – Tohoku, Japan, 28 May–10 June.

Rando, E. (2003) *Ischia, Island of the Soul*. Ischia: Imagaenaria Edizioni Ischia.

Reference.com (n.d.) *Wellness*. On WWW at http://www.reference.com/search?q=wellness. Accessed 10.12.2008.

Regenttour (n.d.) *North Hot Springs Park and South Hot Springs Park*. On WWW at http://www.regenttour.com/chinaplanner/ckg/cq-sights-other.htm#. Accessed 20.4.2007.

Register, J. (2008a) *Spa Evolution: A Brief History of Spas*. On WWW at http://spas.about.com/cs/spaarticles/l/aa101902.htm. Accessed 10.12.2008.

Register, J. (2008b) *Spa Places in the News*. On WWW at http://wwwdiscoverspas.com/news/newsplace349.shtml. Accessed 10.12.2008.

Reeves, R. (1961) *Reality in Advertising*. New York: Alfred A. Knopf.

Renaut, R.W. (2004) Mineral precipitation at thermal springs in the Kenya Rift Valley. *Geological Society of America Abstracts with Programs* 36 (5), 471.

Renaut, R.W. and Jones, B. (2003) Sedimentology of hot spring systems. *Canadian Journal of Earth Sciences* 40, 1439–1442.

Research and Markets (2007) *The European Spa Market 2007* (Diagonal Reports), June.

Rhinehart, J.S. (1980) *Geysers and Geothermal Energy*. New York: Springer-Verlag.

Rockel, I. (1986) *Taking the Waters: Early Spas in New Zealand*. Wellington: Government Printing Office.

Rodrigues, A.G.B. (n.d.) *The Largest Hydrothermal Place in the World* Needham, J. and Liu, G-D. (1962) Tourism. On WWW at http://www.geocities.com/TheTropics/5342/usframe.htm. Accessed 10.12.2008.

Ros, M. (2006) *Renaissance – The Elizabethan World.* On WWW at http://elizabethan.org/. Accessed 10.7.2007.

Rosenberg, M. (2007) *Ring of Fire – Home to Earthquakes and Volcanoes of the Earth.* On WWW at http://geography.about.com/cs/earthquakes/a/ringoffire.htm. Accessed 12.12.2007.

Ross, K. (2001) *Health Tourism: An Overview (HSMAI Marketing Review), Hospitality Net.* On WWW at http://www.hospitalitynet.org. Accessed 10.12.2008.

Rotorua Museum of Art and History (2008) *Taking the Cure.* On WWW at http://www.rotoruamuseum.co.nz/StoryTakingTheCure5.asp. Accessed 10.12.2008.

Routh, H.B. and Bhowmik, K.R. (1996) Basic tenets of mineral water, a glossary of concepts relating to balneology, mineral water, and the spa. *Clinics in Dermatology* 14 (6), 551–554.

Royal Spas of Europe (2001a) *Abano.* On WWW at http://www.teletour.de/royal-spas/abano.html. Accessed 23.2.2006.

Royal Spas of Europe (2001b) *Archena.* On WWW at http://www.teletour.de/royal-spas/archena.html. Accessed 23.2.2006.

Royal Spas of Europe (2001c) *Budapest.* On WWW at http://www.teletour.de/royal-spas/budapest.html. Accessed 23.2.2006.

Royal Spas of Europe (2001d) *Naantali.* On WWW at http://www.teletour.de/royal-spas/naantali.html. Accessed 23.2.2006.

Rumpf, M. and Sollner, G. (2006) *Bädertempel & Kuroasen – Die 75 schönsten Termal- und Kurbäder mit Flair und Tradition in Mittel- und Osteuropa.* München, Germany: Merian-Guide, Travel House Media.

Ryrie, C. (1999) *The Healing Energies of Water.* Boston–Tokyo: Journey Editions.

Sacred Destinations (2007) *Hierapolis (Pamukkale) History.* On WWW at http://www.sacred-destinations.com/turkey/hierapolis-pamukkale.htm. Accessed 3.2.2008.

Sagawa, S. and Segal, E. (2001) *Common Interest Common Good: Creating Value Through Business and Social Sector Partnerships.* Boston: Harvard Business School Press.

Sainsbury, B. (2006) *Cuba.* London: Lonely Planet.

Salgado-Pareja, J.S. (1988) Hydrothermal activity in Mexico – Its utilization for heat generation and balneology. *GHC Quarterly Bulletin* 11 (2), 4–7.

Salloum, H. (n.d.) *The Aura of Carthage and Hannibal Still Live On.* On WWW at http://www.airhighways.com/best_tunisia.htm. Accessed 23.2.2006.

Salto Uruguay (n.d.) *Termas del Daymán.* On WWW at http://www.termasdayman.com/. Accessed 23.2.2006.

Sanjuan, B., Millot, R., Brach, M., Foucher, J.C., Roig, J.Y. and Baltassat, J.M. (2005) Geothermal exploration in the Mount Pelee Volcano-Morne Rouge and Diamant areas (Martinique, West French Indies): Geochemical data. In *Proceedings of the World Geothermal Congress 2005,* Antalya, Turkey, 24–29 April.

Sanner, B. (2000) *Baden Baden A Famous Thermal Spa with a Long History* (pp. 16–22). Klamath Falls, OR: GHC Bulletin, September.

Santa Catarina Brazil (n.d.) *Thermal Mineral Resorts.* On WWW at http://www.santacatarinaturismo.com.br/inter ~ 48.htm. Accessed 3.2.2008.

Santos, R.L. (n.d.) *Azores Islands – Discovery of the Azores.* On WWW at http://library.csustan.edu/bsantos/azores.html. Accessed 14.11.2008.

Sanctuario School of Spa, Philippines (n.d.) *Sanctuario School of Spa, Philippines.* On WWW at http://www.sanctuario.com.ph/default2.asp. Accessed 23.2.2006.

Saracci, R. (1997) The World Health Organization needs to reconsider its definition of health. *British Medical Journal* 314, 1409–1410.

Saraya Holdings (2008) *Saraya Islands.* On WWW at http://www.dubaifaqs.com/saraya-island.php. Accessed 3.12.2008.

Savusavu Tourism Association (n.d.) *About Savusavu.* On WWW at http://www.fiji-savusavu.com/about.html. Accessed 23.2.2006.

Schafer, E.H. (1956) The development of bathing customs in Ancient and Medieval China and the history of the Floriate Clear Palace. *Journal of the American Oriental Society* 76 (2), 57–82.

Scheer, R. (n.d.) *Holy Wells and Healing Springs*. On WWW at http://www.aquarius-atlanta,com/narticles/travel.html. Accessed 23.2.2006.

Schobersberger, W., Greie, S. and Humpeler, E. (2004) Alpine health tourism: Future prospects from a medical perspective. In K. Weiermair and C. Mathies (eds) *The Tourism and Leisure Industry: Shaping the Future* (pp. 199–208). New York: Haworth Hospitality Press.

SGVSB (Schweizerischer Grosshandesverband der Sanitären Branche) (n.d.) *Die Welt des Bades, Badgeschichte – auf der Suche nach Regeneration*. On WWW at www.sgvsb.ch/pages/ueberuns/geschichte.asp?m=m100. Accessed 23.2.2006.

Scully, F.J. (1966) *Hot Springs, Arkansas, and Hot Springs National Park*. Little Rock, AR: Pioneer Press.

Sekioka, M. and Yoshii, M. (2000) Country update: Report of geothermal direct uses in Japan. In *Proceedings of the World Geothermal Congress 2000* (pp. 433–437). Kyushu-Tohoku, 28 May–10 June.

Shaanxi Huaqingchi Tourism (n.d.) *Imperial Pool Site of Tang Dynasty*. On WWW at Shaanxi Huaqingchi Tourism Limited Corporation, http://www.hqc.cn/english/gar6.asp. Accessed 3.7.2006.

Shiva, V. (2002) *Water Wars: Privatisation, Pollution, and Profit*. Cambridge, MA: South End Press.

Šilar, J. (1968) On the origin of hot springs in Yunnan (China). In *Proceedings of Symposium II – International Geological Congress, Genesis of Mineral and Thermal Waters* (Report of the 23rd Session). Prague, Czechoslovakia.

Siloam. (n.d.) *The Lower Pool*. On WWW at www.answers.com/topic/pool-of-siloam. Accessed 23.2.2006.

Silverkris (2005) *Ananda Spa India, The Palace Estate*. On WWW at http://www.anandaspa.com. Accessed 23.2.2006.

Simkins, K.L. (1986) Physical therapy and Spa treatment. *Medical Anthropology Quarterly* 17 (5), 146–147.

Simons, P. (n.d.) *The Good Life: Health Tourism and the British Spas*. Bath: British Spas Federation. Accessed 3.7.2006.

Singapore Airlines (n.d.) *Singapore Airlines*. On WWW at www.singaporeair.com/saa/en_UK/content/promo/ssh/hotels/SG/index.jsp. Accessed 15.8.2008.

Singer, J.L. (2005). On WWW at http://www.spatrade.com/knowledge/idx/0/167/article/. Accessed 23.2.2006.

Six Senses Resorts and Spas (2007) *Green Globe Establishes International Benchmarking for Spa Operations Using Six Senses as Model*. On WWW at http://www.sixsenses.com/Environment/Green-Globe-establishes.php. Accessed 3.2.2008.

Slovenija (2006) *Slovenian Spas Community – With Nature to Health*. On WWW at http://www.terme-giz.si/en/informacija.asp?id_meta_type=1&view=Splosno. Accessed 23.9.2006.

Smith, C. and Jenner, P. (2000) Health tourism in Europe. *Travel and Tourism Analyst* 1, 41–59.

Smith, M. and Kelly, C. (2006) Wellness tourism. *Tourism Recreation Research* 31 (1), 1–4.

Smith, M. and Puczko, L. (2008) *Health and Wellness Tourism*. Oxford: Butterworth-Heinemann.

Snorralaug Hot Spring (2008) *Snorralaug Hot Spring*. On WWW at http://commons.wikimedia.org/wiki/Image: Snorralaug 10.jpg. Accessed 18.9.2006.

Sochi Geschichte (n.d.) *Sochi Geschichte*. On WWW at http://www.sochi.de/Sochi_Geschichte.html. Accessed 23.2.2006.

Song, H. and Witt, S.F. (2000) *Tourism Demand Modelling and Forecasting: Modern Econometric Approaches*. Oxford: Pergamon.

South Greenland's Natural Pools – Uunartoq's Hot Springs (n.d.) On WWW at http://wwwgreenland.com/content/english/tourist/nature_climate/hot_springs. Accessed 23.2.2006.

Spa and Wellness in Bulgaria (n.d.). On WWW at http://www.visitbulgaria.net/en/spa_wellness/. Accessed 23.2.2006.

Spa Asia Magazine (2005) *September/October Issue*. Singapore: Wellness Media Pte Ltd.

Spa Asia Magazine (2005) *November/December Issue*. Singapore: Wellness Media Pte Ltd.

Spafinder.com (n.d.) *Spa Glossary*. On WWW at http://www.spafinder.com/spalifestyle/spa101/glossary.jsp. Accessed 3.8.2008.

Spafinder.com (2006) *The Spa Finder Magazine, July–August*. On WWW at http://www.spafinder.com/archive/issue.jsp?id=26. Accessed 3.12.2006.

Spa Knowledge (2008) *The Top 10 Marketing Trends of 2008*. On WWW at http://www.spatrade.com/knowledge/idx/84/331/article/. Accessed 3.2.2008.

Spa Life Online Magazine (2006) *The Ultimate Lifestyle – Vitality, Wellness, Bliss* (Summer Edition). Sydney: Edge Publishing Group.

Spa Life Online Magazine (n.d.) *The History of Spas*. On WWW at http://www.spalife.co.kr/academy/aca_01.html. Accessed 11.7.2006.

Spa Temptations in Bulgaria (n.d.). On WWW at http://www.visitbulgaria.net/en/pages/spa_and_wellness.html. Accessed 23.2.2006.

Spa Trade [n.d.(a)]. On WWW at http://www.spatrade.com/knowledge/idx/82/270/article/. Accessed 13.2.2007.

Spa Trade [n.d.(b)]. On WWW at http://www.spatrade.com/knowledge/idx/84/331/article/. Accessed 13.2.2007.

Spas Canada (2008) *Kurotel Longevity Center and Spa*. On WWW at http://www.spascanada.com/news_details.php?nid=24. Accessed 18.8.2007.

Stafford, D.M. (1986) *The Founding Years in Rotorua: A History of Events to 1900*. Rotorua: Ray Richards.

Stafford, D.M. (1988) *The New Century in Rotorua*. Rotorua: Ray Richards.

St. Lucia (2007) *Bringing History to Life*. On WWW at http://www.slucia.com/visions/2005/baths.html. Accessed 13.2.2007.

Stanton, L. (2008) Research: World service. *Spa Business* 4, 40–43.

Stanwell Smith, R. (2002) *World Water Day Water for Positive Health: Springs and Spas*. On WWW at http://www.worldwaterday.org/wwday/2001/thematic/poshealth.html. Accessed May 2005.

Steiner, C.J. and Reisinger, Y. (2006) Ringing the fourfold: A philosophical framework for thinking about wellness tourism. *Tourism Recreation Research* 31 (1), 5–14.

Suanbo Hot Springs (n.d.) *Suanbo Hot Springs*. On WWW at http://www.lifeinkorea.com/Travel2/nchungchong/385. Accessed 13.2.2007.

Sunway (n.d.) *Lost World of Tambun*. On WWW at http://www.sunway.com.my/lostworld-oftambun/. Accessed 13.2.2007.

Svalova, V. (2000) The history of geothermal resource use in Russia and the former USSR. In *Proceedings of the World Geothermal Congress 2000* (pp. 713–718). Kyushu-Tohoku, Japan: International Geothermal Association.

Svart, G. (2006) *Massage Messages – Wet Etiquette can Raise a Sweat, The Age, 1 January*. On WWW at http://www.theage.com.au/news/victoria/massage-messages/2005/12/31.

Swanson, P.L. (2001) Thoughts on the translation of Buddhist texts into English. *Journal of Indian and Buddhist Studies* 50 (1), 518–525.

Swarbrick, N. (2006) *Thermal Pools and Spas*. Wellington: Te Ara – Encyclopedia of New Zealand.

Tabacchi, M. (2003) *The Spa Industry & Consumer Study*. On WWW at http://industry.leading-spasofcanada.com/index.php?option=com_content&task=view&id=29&Itemid=64. Accessed 3.5.2005.

TAG (2006) Soaking It Up. *The Geological Society of Australia Newsletter*, 140, September, 21–25.

Taipei Journal (2002) *Taiwan Headlines – Natural Spring Resorts Enjoy New Popularity*, 21 May. Taipei: Taiwan Journal.

Taipei Times (2004) *News 13 October.* On WWW at http://www.taipeitimes.com/News/taiwan/ archives/2004/10/13/2003206666/print. 13. Accessed 5.1.2005.

Taiwan Government Information Office (n.d.(a)) *Hot Springs.* On WWW at http://202.39.225.132/jsp/Eng/html/travel_tour/index.jsp. Accessed 3.2.2008.

Taiwan Government Information Office (n.d.(b)) *Yangmingshan National Park – A Breath of Mountain Air.* On WWW at http://www.gio.gov.tw/taiwan-website/gogo/goen_32.htm. Accessed 3.2.2008.

Taiwan Government Information Office (n.d.(c)) *Wulai – Echoes of the Atayal.* On WWW at http://www.gio.gov.tw/taiwan-website/gogo/goen_34.htm. Accessed 3.2.2008.

Taiwan News (2007) Wunshan Hot Spring Given Level-A Danger Rating in Geological Safety Assessment. *Taiwan News,* 27 August. Accessed 3.2.2008.

Taiwan Water Resources Agency, Ministry of Economic Affairs, Taiwan (2008a) *Hot Spring Act 2003.* On WWW at http://eng.wra.gov.tw/ct.asp?xItem=25880&ctNode=5523&comefrom=lp. Accessed 3.2.2008.

Taiwan Water Resources Agency, Ministry of Economic Affairs, Taiwan (2008b) *Water management in Taiwan.* On WWW at http://eng.wra.gov.tw/ct.asp?xItem=25880&ctNode=5523&comefrom=lp. Accessed 3.2.2008.

Takahashi, P.K. and Woodruff, J.L. (1990) The development of alternative energy systems for island communities. In W. Weller, P.G. d'Ayala and P. Hein (eds) *Sustainable Environmental Management of Small Islands,* Man and the Biosphere Series 5. New York: Informa Health Care.

Takamura, H. (2004) The techniques and tools of the Kuzusabori well-boring method. *World Environmental Science* 6, 37–49.

Talmadge, E. (2006) *Getting Wet – Adventures in the Japanese Bath.* Tokyo: Kodansha International.

Tangshan (n.d.) *Tangshan Hot Springs.* On WWW at http://www.shanghai.ws/TIClook1135.html. Accessed 3.2.2008.

Tanko, K. (1999) *Philippines Haven Intrigues – and Disappoints: Island of Legendary Charms, International Herald Tribune.* On WWW at http://www.iht.com/articles/1999/10/15/trphil.2.t.php. Accessed 8.5.2005.

Tatralandia Aquapark (2006) *Aquapark Tatralandia.* On WWW at http://www.tatralandia.sk/old/accommodition-aquapark-liptov-jasna-pension-apartament-hotel-skiing.php?tatralandia-aquapark-accommodition-liptov-tatry. Accessed 3.11.2006.

Tattapani (n.d.) *Hot Water Spring.* On WWW at http://www.indiasite.com/himachalpradesh/shimla/tattapani.html. Accessed 3.2.2008.

Tattapani Travel Information (n.d.) On WWW at http://travels.talash.com/tattapani-travel/index.html.

Te Ara Encyclopaedia of New Zealand (2005) *Thermal Pools and Spas: Corroded Pipes – Rotorua.* On WWW at http://www.teara.govt.nz/EarthSeaAndSky/HotSpringsAndGeothermal Energy/ThermalPoolsAndSpas/4/ENZ-Resources/Standard/2/en. Accessed 3.2.2008.

Termatalia (2006) *The Melting between Tradition and Modernity, the Aim of the III Thermal Cities Meeting.* On WWW at http://www.termatalia.com/index.php?pagina=6&f=1&id=20. Accessed 13.2.2007.

Termatalia (2007) *Spa Offer in Castilla-La-Mancha, a Roman and Arab Heritage.* On WWW at http://www.termatalia.com/index.php?pagina=9&f=1&id=63. Accessed 8.12.2007.

Termasworld (n.d.) *Excavations in the Baths of the Inca.* On WWW at http://www.termasworld.com/ing_actualidad48.asp. Accessed 3.2.2008.

Thai Airways (2008) On WWW at http://www.thaiair.com/Royal_Orchid_Holidays/Special_Interest_Holidays/Spa_Wellness/default.htm. Accessed 8.8.2008.

Thailand Travel Information (2008) *Natural Hot Springs and Raksawarin Park Arboretum in Ranong.* On WWW at http://www.discoverythailand.com/Ranong_Natural_Hot_Springs_and_Raksawarin_Park_Arboretum.asp. Accessed 8.8.2008.

The Age (2005) *Some like it Boiling – Hungarians are Obsessed with Bathhouses.* On WWW at http://www.theage.com.au/news/europe/some-like-it-boiling/2005/02/11. Accessed 19.8.2006.

The Kojiki (n.d.) *Records of Ancient Matters* (B. Hall Chamberlain, transl.) (2nd edn) 1982, with annotations by the late W.G. Aston, Sometime Japanese Secretary to the British Legation, Tokyo. Tokyo: Tuttle Publishing.

Thermae Bath Spa (n.d.) *The Healing Springs*. On WWW at http://www.thermaebathspa.com/visitorcentre/hot_springs/medical/index.html. Accessed 8.8.2008.

Thermalbaden (n.d.) *Im Mineralreichsten Thermalwasser der Schweiz*. On WWW at http://www.thermalbaden.ch/. Accessed 8.8.2008.

Thermal Baths (n.d.) *City of Therapeutic Waters*. On WWW at http://www.budapesthotels.com/touristguide/ThermalBaths.asp. Accessed 8.8.2008.

Thermal Chile (2000) *Chile Hot Springs Guide*. On WWW at http://www.gochile.cl/eng/Guide/ChileTermas/Chile-Termas-Articulos.asp. Accessed 3.5.2005.

Thermalism Office Tunisia (n.d.) *Man and Water – What is the Role of Water in the Body?*. On WWW at http://www.thermalisme.nat.tn. Accessed 8.8.2008.

The Spa Association (2005) *Basic Types of Spas*. On WWW at http://www.thespaassociation.com/content/index.php?spage=38. Accessed 3.8.2006.

Tiberias (2007) *Virtual Israel Experience*. On WWW at http://www.jewishvirtuallibrary.org/jsource/vie/Tiberias.html. Accessed 8.8.2008.

Tilton, E.M. (1981) Mineral and thermal spas in France. *The French Review* 54 (4), 566–572.

Tole, M.P. (2002) The potential of geothermal systems in Kenya for balneological use. *Environmental Geochemistry and Health* 24 (2), 103–110.

Tourism Industry Association of Canada (TIAC). (n.d.) *Glossary – General Terms – Tourism*. On WWW at http://www.tiac-aitc.ca/english/glossary.asp. Accessed 8.8.2008.

Tourism Industry Association New Zealand Inc (2008). On WWW at www.tourismawards.co.nz/Award-Winners/Past-Tourism-Awards-Winners.asp. Accessed 18.11.2008.

Turismo Chile (2007) *Chile*. On WWW at www.visit-chile.org. Accessed 8.12.2008.

Tourism Queensland (2002) *Health and Spa Tourism*. Brisbane: QTTC.

Tourism Review.com (2008) Spa and medical: Medical tourism and the side effects. *Tourism Review* February, 25,35.

Tourism Review.com (2008) Russian Spas in great demand. *Tourism Review* 18 August.

Tourism Statistics Bulletins (2006) *Number of Arriving and Departing Visitors, October 2006*. On WWW at http://www.die.gov.tr/english/SONIST/TURIZM/turizm.html. Accessed 5.5.2007.

Travel Guide (2008) *Spas and Wellbeing in Thailand*. On WWW at http://www.discoverythailand.com/spa.asp. Accessed 8.8.2008.

TreatmentAbroad.net (2006) On WWW at http://www.treatmentabroad.net/medical-tourism/news/october-2007/britons-going-on-a-nip-and-tuck-holiday-239/). Accessed 3.7.2006.

Tremplin (n.d.) *The National Report of Germany Tourism Sector*. On WWW at http://www.gla.ac.uk/tremplin/DETourism_en.pdf. Accessed 10.8.2006.

Travel China Guide (2008) *Huaqing Hot Springs*. On WWW at http://www.travelchinaguide.com/attraction/shaanxi/xian/huaqing.htm. Accessed 10.8.2008.

Tsankov, N.K. and Kamarashev, J.A. (1996) Spa therapy in Bulgaria. *Clinical Dermatology* 14 (6), 675–678.

Tsenkher Hot Springs (n.d.) *Tsenkher Hot Spring & Community Based Rehabilitation of Greenhouses, Spring Head and its Zone (MON/05/04)*. On WWW at http://sgp.undp.org/web/projects/8349/tsenkher_hot_spring_community_based_rehabilitation_of_green_houses_spring_head_and_its_zone.html. Accessed 8.8.2008.

Turkish Odyssey (2004) *Places of Interest, Pamukkale (Hierapolis)*. On WWW at http://www.turkishodyssey.com. Accessed 5.5.2005.

TurkStat (2008) Tourism Statistics – Results of 2000–2007 Period. On WWW at http://www.turkstat.gov.tr/PreTablo.do?tb_id=51&ust_id=14. Accessed 18.8.2008.

Turner, G. (1985) Geothermal exploitation and the decline of the Rotorua geothermal field. *Geophysical Research Letters* 12 (1), 21–24.

Tversky, A., Sattah, S. and Slovic, P. (1988) Contingent weighting in judgment and choice. *Psychological Review* 95, 371–384.

UNESCO (2008) *Hierapolis – Pamukkale*. On WWW at http://whc.unesco.org/en/list/485. Accessed 18.8.2008.

United Nations World Tourism Organization (2008) *World Tourism Barometer 2008*, Madrid: UNWTO.

Urry, J. (1990) *The Tourist Gaze: Leisure and Travel in Contemporary Society*. London: Sage.

US Department of Commerce (2008) *2007 International Arrivals to the United States*. On WWW at http://www.tinet.ita.doc.gov/view/m-2007-I-001/index.html. Accessed 20.8.2008.

Uunartoq (n.d.). On WWW at http://en.wikipedia.org/wiki/Uunartoq. Accessed 5.5.2005.

Valenza, J.M. (2000) *Taking the Waters in Texas – Springs, Spas and Fountains of Youth*. Houston, TX: University of Texas Press.

Vanderbilt, S. (2002) Medical Spas: A journey full-circle. *Massage & Bodywork Magazine*, August/September.

Vassileva, S. (1996) Mineral water and spas in Bulgaria. *Clinics in Dermatology* 14 (6), 601–605.

Verdel, H. and Pittler, A.P. (2003) *Kurbäder, Europa Erlesen*. Klagenfurt, Österreich: Wieser Verlag.

Virtual Malaysia (n.d.) *Hot Springs – Air Hangat Village Kedah*. http://wwwvirtualmalaysia.com/destination/hot%20springs-cat.html. Accessed 18.8.2006.

VisitNepal (2007) *Nepal's Hot Water Springs*. On WWW at http://www.visitnepal.com/nepal_information/hot_springs.php. Accessed 8.5.2008.

Von Furstenberg, D. (1993) *The Bath*. New York: Random House.

Walker, L. and Page, S.J. (2003) Risks, rights and responsibilities in tourist well-being: Who should manage visitor well-being at the destination? In J. Wilks and S. Page (eds) *Managing Tourist Health and Safety in the New Millennium* (pp. 215–236). London: Pergamon.

Waring, G.A. (1965) Thermal springs of the United States and other countries of the world – A summary. US Geological Survey Professional Paper 492, Washington: USGS.

Warmbaths (n.d.) *Warmbad (Warmbaths) South Africa*s. On WWW at http://www.africa4u.co.za/NorthernProvince/WarmBaths.htm; http://www. go2africa.com/south-africa/waterberg/warmbaths/; http://www.limpopohappenings.co.za/warmbadhomepage.htm. Accessed 8.8.2008.

Wave, B. (1999) *Our Good Doctor – Fish*. On WWW at http://www.bigwave.ca/ ~ doug_lewis/book/chap11.htm. Accessed 3.9.2005.

Weaver, D. and Lawton, L. (2002) *Tourism Management* (2nd edn). Sydney: John Wiley & Sons.

Webb, C. (2005) *Brothers Keep Their Dream Afloat*. On WWW at http://www.theage.com.au/articles/2005/06/23/1119321850056.html. Accessed 3.9.2005.

Weiser, J. and Zadak, S. (2000) *Conversations with Disbelievers, Persuading Companies to Address Social Challenges*. New York: Ford Foundation.

Weisz, G. (2001) Spas, mineral waters, and hydrological science in twentieth-century France. *Isis* 92 (3), 451–483.

Werther, W.B. Jr. and Chandler, D. (2005) Strategic corporate social responsibility as global brand insurance. *Business Horizons* 48, 317–324.

Westgate, C.E. (1996) Spiritual wellness and depression. *Journal of Counselling and Development* 75, 26–35.

White, D.E. (1955) Thermal springs and epithermal ore deposits. *Economic Geology, Fiftieth Anniversary Volume* 99–154.

White, D.E. (1981) Active geothermal systems and hydrothermal ore deposits. *Economic Geology, 75th Anniversary Volume*, 392–423.

White, D.E., Hutchinson, R.A. and Keith, T.E.C. (1988) The geology and remarkable thermal activity of Norris Geyser Basin, Yellowstone National Park, Wyoming. US Geological Survey Professional Paper 1456. Washington: USGS.

White, G. (2000) Bath: A world heritage site – The Bath Spa project. *GHC Bulletin* 21 (3), 12–15.

Whittow, J. (1984) *The Penguin Dictionary of Physical Geography*. London: Penguin Books.

Wightman, D. and Wall, G. (1985) The spa experience at radium hot springs. *Annals of Tourism Research* 12 (3), 393–416.

Wikipedia (2008) *Iwate-Miyagi Nairiku Earthquake*. On WWW at http://en.wikipedia.org/wiki/2008_Iwate-Miyagi_Nairiku_earthquake. Accessed 14.9.2008.

Wikitravel (2008) *Hot Springs*. On WWW at http://wikitravel.org/en/Hot_springs. Accessed 3.9.2008.

Wilkie, W. (1986) *Consumer Behaviour*. New York: John Wiley.

Williams, G. (n.d.) On WWW at http://www.welldressing.com. Accessed 3.9.2005.

Williams, P., Gill, A. and Ponsford, I. (2007) Corporate social responsibility at tourism destinations: Toward a social license to operate. *Tourism Review International* 11, 133–144.

Williams, P.W. (1996) Health spa travel markets: Mexican long-haul pleasure travelers. *Journal of Vacation Marketing* 3 (1), 10–31.

Witcher, J.C. (2002a) Ojo Caliente – America's Oldest spa? *GHC Quarterly Bulletin* 22 (4), 47.

Witcher, J.C. (2002b) Faywood hot springs. *GHC Quarterly Bulletin* 22 (4), 46.

Wolf, R. (1996) Mineral waters and spas in Israel. *Clinics in Dermatology* 14 (6), 619–626.

Witt, S. F. and Moutinho, L. (1995) *Tourism Marketing and Management Handbook*. London: Prentice Hall.

Woodruff, J.L. (1987) *Geothermal Spas in Hawaii: A New Tourist Industry?* (A Preliminary Report). University of Hawaii, Honolulu: Hawaii Natural Energy Institute.

Woodruff, J.L. and Takahashi, P.K. (1993) A new business opportunity in Hawaii. *Geo-Heat Utilization Center Quarterly Bulletin* 14 (4).

Woodsworth, G. (1997) *Hot Springs of Western Canada*. West Vancouver: Gordon Soles Book Publishers Ltd.

World Bank (2007) *World Development Indicators Database*, April. Washington: World Bank.

World Health Organization (1999) *Annapolis Protocol, Health based monitoring of Recreational Waters: The Feasibility of a New Approach*. Geneva: WHO/SDE/WSH99.1.

World Health Organization (2000) *The World Health Report 2000 – Health Systems: Improving Performance*. Geneva: WHO.

World Health Organization (2003) *Guidelines for Safe Recreational Water Environments Volume 1: Coastal and Fresh Waters*. Geneva: WHO.

World Health Organization (2006) *Constitution of the World Health Organization, Basic Documents* (45th edn), Supplement, October. On WWW at http://www.who.int/governance/eb/constitution/en/index.html. Accessed 8.9.2008.

World Travel and Tourism Council (2002) *Corporate Social Leadership in Travel and Tourism*. London: WTTC.

WOW Philippines (n.d.) *Laguna – Resort Province of the Philippines*. On WWW at http://www.tourism.gov.ph/explore_phil/place_details.asp?content=description&province=18. Accessed 14.11.2008.

Yaeger, M. and Lepkowski, M. (n.d.) *Volcanoes and Hot Springs of Banos - Ecuador*. On WWW at http://gosouthamerica.about.com/gi/dynamic/offsite.htm?zi=1/XJ&sdn=gosoutham erica&zu=http%3A%2F%2Fwww.travelsinparadise.com%2Fecuador%2Fbanos_1.html. Accessed 3.9.2005.

Yeatts, D.S. (2006) *Characteristics of Thermal Springs and the Shallow Ground-Water System at Hot Springs National Park, Arkansas* (Scientific Investigations Report 20065001). Prepared in cooperation with the National Park Service. Reston, VA: US Geological Survey.

Yellowstone National Park (2006) *Mammoth Terraces and How They Work*. On WWW at National Park Services, http://www.nps.gov/yell/naturescience/mamterr.htm. Accessed 17.10.2006.

Yemeni Times (2004) *Therapeutic tourism in Yemen, 9 May*. On WWW at http://www.islamic-tourism.com/news_E.php?id=476&search=hot%20springs. Accessed 3.5.2005.

Yemen (n.d.) *Ibb: A Tour Through Beautiful Nature*. On WWW at http://www.islamictourism.com/news_E.php?id=852&search=hot%20springs. Accessed 5.5.2005.

Yesawich, Pepperdine and Brown (1999) *The American Spa-Goer: Market Habits, Preferences and Intentions*. On WWW at http://www.ypartnership.com/#about/insights/publications. Accessed 8.9.2005.

Young, E. (1909) *Corsica*. London: A. and C. Black.

Young, H. (1998) In hot water. *New Zealand Geographic* 40, October–December, 52–74.

Young, R.F. (1995) The advertising of consumer services and the hierarchy of effects. In R. Zemke (ed.) *Service Recovery: Fixing Broken Customers*. Portland: Productivity Press.

Yum, B.W. (1999) Historical review of hot spring waters in the Republic of Korea. In R. Cataldi, S.F. Hodgson and J.W. Lund (eds) *Stories from a Heated Earth* (pp. 379–392). Sacramento, CA: Geothermal Resources Council, International Geothermal Association.

Yusa, Y. and Ohsawa, S. (2000) Age of the Beppu hydrothermal system, Japan. In *Proceedings of the World Geothermal Congress 2000* (pp. 3005–3008). Kyushu-Tohoku, Japan, 28 May–10 June.

Zaigham, N.A. (2005) Geothermal energy resources of Pakistan. In *Proceedings of the World Geothermal Congress*, Antalya. 24–29 April.

Zapletnyuk, K. (2006) Ostrava Spa looks to Russia for new clients. *The Prague Post*, 17 May.

Zhuhai Daily (2005) Tourism vibrant in 2004. *Zhuhai Daily*, 20 February.

Zhuhai Hot Springs (2003) *Touring Around*. On WWW at http://www.visitzhuhai.com/english/touringaround/. Accessed 16.3.2006.

Zieroth, D. (1978) *Nipika – A Story of Radium Springs*. Quebec: Supply and Services Canada.

Zeithaml, V.A. (1981) How consumer evaluation processes differ between goods and services. In J.H. Donnelly and W.R. George (eds) *Marketing of Services* (pp. 186–190). Chicago: American Marketing Association.

Zeithaml, V.A. and Bitner, M.J. (2000) *Services Marketing* (2nd edn). New York: McGraw-Hill.

Zúñiga, A., Su, M. and Sánchez, M. (2003) Thermal manifestations in Nicaragua. *GHC Quarterly Bulletin* 24 (3), 23–25.

Zúñiga, P.A. (2006) *The Dead Sea – 50th Anniversary and Opening of the Tourism of Health and Leisure*. On WWW at http://termasworld.com/content/view/188/43/. Accessed 18.11.2006.

Additional websites accessed

http://www.aaa.com/. Accessed 20.3.2008.

http://wwwdanubiushotels.com. Accessed 20.3.2008.

http://www.die.gov.tr/english/SONIST/sonist.html. Accessed 20.7.2008.

http://www.discoverspas.com/news/newsplaces349.shtml. Accessed 20.3.2008.

http://www.discoverythailand.com/Ranong_Natural_Hot_Springs_and_Raksawarin_Park_Arboretum.asp. Accessed 3.9.2008.

http://www.discoverythailand.com/spa.asp. Accessed 3.9.2008.

http://geoheat.oit.edu/bulletin/bull17-2/art13.htm. Accessed 11.5.2004.

http://www.germany-extranet.net/pages/ 1777_12422_ENG HTML.htm. Accessed 20.3.2008.

http://www.hajduszoboszlo.hu. Accessed 20.3.2008.

http://www.heritageaustralia.com.au. Accessed 20.3.2008.

http://www.jlpp.jp. Accessed 20.3.2008.

http://www.japaneselifestyle.com.au. Accessed 20.3.2008.

http://www.karlovyvary.cz. Accessed 20.3.2008.

http://www.mongoliatourism.gov.mn/index.php?action=menudata&id=7. Accessed 20.7.2008.

http://www.moohin.com/eng/thailand-MEDICAL-SERVICES.shtml. Accessed 20.3.2008.

http://www.namibiatourism.com.na/trade_cat_main.php?main_cat_id=35. Accessed 20.7.2008.

http://www.newzealand.com/travel/destinations/regions/waikato/waikato-towns.cfm/nodeid/237.html. Accessed 27.7.2008.

http://www.peninsulahotsprings.com/downloads/about-us.pdf. Accessed 20.10.2007.

http://www.psoriasisfishcure.com. Accessed 20.3.2008.

http://www.randburg.com/is/laugarspa/. Accessed 4.9.2008.

http://www.sgvsb.ch/pages/ueberuns/geschichte.asp?m=m100. Accessed 20.3.2008.

http://www.showcaves.com/english/explain/Speleothem/RimstonePool.html. Accessed 14.11.2008.

http://www.singaporeair.com/saa/en_UK/content/promo/ssh/hotels/SG/index.jsp. Accessed 20.3.2008.

http://www.spatrade.com/knowledge/idx/84/331/article/. Accessed 20.3.2008.

http:// www.thermaebathspa.com. Accessed 20.3.2008.

http://www.tourismawards.co.nz/Award-Winners/Past-Tourism-Awards-Winners.asp. Accessed 20.3.2008.

http://www.traveliteindia.com/medical.asp#2. Accessed 20.3.2008.

http://www.treatmentabroad.net/medical-tourism/news/october-2007/britons-going-on-a-nip-and-tuck-holiday-239/. Accessed 20.3.2008.

http://www.tuscany-charming.it. Accessed 20.3.2008.

http://www.visitzhuhai.com/english/touringaround/. Accessed 3.9.2008.

http://www.wanquanriver.org/en/tguantang.html. Accessed 3.9.2008.

http://en.wikipedia.org/wiki/Medical_tourism. Accessed 3.9.2008.

Index